Contacts Desired

CONTACTS
DESIRED ✛

*Gay and Lesbian Communications and
Community, 1940s–1970s*

Martin Meeker

The University of Chicago Press • *Chicago and London*

MARTIN MEEKER is a historian at the Regional Oral History Office, the Bancroft Library, University of California, Berkeley.

The University of Chicago Press, Chicago 60637
The University of Chicago Press, Ltd., London
© 2006 by The University of Chicago
All rights reserved. Published 2006
Printed in the United States of America

15 14 13 12 11 10 09 08 07 06   1 2 3 4 5
ISBN: 0-226-51734-9 (cloth)
ISBN: 0-226-51735-7 (paper)

Library of Congress Cataloging-in-Publication Data

Meeker, Martin
   Contacts desired : gay and lesbian communications and community,
1940s–1970s / Martin Meeker.
      p.   cm.
   Includes index.
   ISBN 0-226-51734-9 (cloth : alk. paper)
   1. Gays—History—20th century. 2. Gay culture—History—20th century.
3. Gay communities—History—20th century. 4. Gays—Social networks—
History—20th century. 5. Gay liberation movement—History—20th century.
I. Title.
   HQ76.25.M44 2006
   306.76′6′0904—dc22
                                                            2005021934

This book is dedicated to the memory of Willie Walker (1949–2004), archivist, rabble-rouser, mentor, and friend, and to the founders, volunteers, and staff of the Gay, Lesbian, Bisexual, Transgender Historical Society in San Francisco.

CONTENTS

ACKNOWLEDGMENTS

Acknowledgements take on a special importance when placed at the beginning of a book about the relationship between communications and community. Not only did the countless exchanges with advisors, students, friends, and oral history narrators make the process of writing a book feasible, but the sum total of those conversations played an important role in helping me formulate the overall thesis of this book on the creation of new social networks. After all, I could not have written about the struggle to connect with and to build community without recognizing all that I have gained through contacts and conversations with all of the people mentioned below.

This book began as a dissertation in the History Department at the University of Southern California (USC). Phil Ethington showed interest in my work from the first moment I shared my ideas with him. As the chair of my dissertation committee he never ceased providing intellectual inspiration and camaraderie and even now, five years after graduation, he continues as a mentor. Thank you. During my time at USC, I was fortunate to have a number of excellent scholars and teachers serve on committees for my exams and my dissertation. For their insights and guidance, I want to thank Lois Banner, Philippa Levine, Richard Meyer, David Román, Steve Ross, and Vanessa Schwartz.

Next to my grad school mentors stands another group of individuals, both scholars and friends, who helped guide me with considerable grace, skill, and tolerance through the many years working on the dissertation and then the book manuscript. This "kitchen cabinet" of advisors and partners-in-crime saw that I got the work done while never forgetting the joy that research and writing can be. Importantly, a few friends and mentors took on the task of reading the book manuscript (at various stages of completion) in its entirety and, subsequently, offered many useful suggestions for revisions along with words of encouragement. For their time spent and for the incisive critiques they offered, I want to thank Nan Alamilla Boyd, George Chauncey, Gerard Koskovich, and Craig Loftin. Thanks also to Marc Stein for reading and providing substantial and useful comments on an early version of what became chapter 1. Aside from its fantastic, one-of-a-kind archival collections, the Gay, Lesbian, Bisexual, Transgender Historical Society is notable for fostering informal networks of scholars. While researching, volunteering, or merely lounging at the archives, I have benefited from conversations with Chris Agee, Daniel Bao, Loren Basham, Cathy Cade, Ms. Bob Davis, John Fagundes, Paul Gabriel, Marcia Gallo, Terence Kissack, Peter Lundberg, Ruth Mahaney, Don Romesburg, Gayle Rubin, Susan Stryker, the late Willie Walker, and many others. Jennifer Joyce, David Hall, Ray Brizendine, Aric Lasher, Tom Zakim, Liberty Bradford Conboy, Dave Neubecker, Joe Boone, Barbara Berglund, Mike Blubaugh, James Mallery, Paul Herman, Philip Fucella, Mike Voran, John Lake, Chris Lalli, Chris Nealon, Glen Robinson, Michael Ehrenberg, Steven Pollack, Ian Cartan, Kurt Culver, Mike Tossey, Mark Grantham, Joe Kowalski, Scot Righter, Bert Green, James Ormsby, Chris Comis, Cristina Grasso, Bennett Smith, Lisa Joy Rosener, the late Carol Shellhorn, Tim Massey, and Beth Castle all listened generously while I talked incessantly about "the project." They gave even more as they shared ideas and asked probing questions. Paul Robinson helped me articulate my thesis at a critical point between researching and writing the dissertation.

Elizabeth Lapovsky Kennedy and Richard Meyer each served as press readers for the book manuscript. I want to thank both Kennedy and Meyer for offering substantial, challenging, and thorough reviews. I further want to thank them for making their identities known to me so that I could benefit from a continued dialogue about the many issues they raised. Although I suspect that both Kennedy and Meyer would seek further revisions, I hope that the positive impact of their critiques upon the manuscript also is clearly evident.

Douglas Mitchell, executive editor at the University of Chicago Press, has been a stalwart supporter of this project from its inception. Not only has he done a fantastic job shepherding this project along at various stages, but he demonstrated great flexibility and provided sage advice as the book morphed into something quite different than what I originally proposed. For those reasons—and, of course, for the memorable meals—I owe him a debt of gratitude. I also wish to thank Tim McGovern, Peter Cavagnaro, and Maia Rigas of the press for making the production process a smooth one.

Several teachers, both at USC and at San Francisco State University, have had a profound influence upon me in the classroom and out. These teachers include Elinor Accampo, Alice Echols, Bill Issel, Barbara Loomis, the late Mauricio Mazon, Frank Mitchell, Julyana Peard, Sally Scully, and Nancy Unger. Joe Styles, the graduate coordinator at USC, taught me how to navigate that university's bureaucracy in addition to offering wry yet appreciated commentary on the whole process.

Although they did not teach me in any classroom, I learned a great deal from every person I had the opportunity to interview while researching for the book. All my oral history narrators deserve thanks for contributing to the process, but I especially want to thank Bruce Baird, David Barnard, Mike Caffee, the late Hal Call, Gina Covina, Gerson Goodkind, Laurel Holliday, Larry Howell, the late Don Lucas, Phyllis Lyon, Del Martin, Marijane Meaker, Carol Seajay, Bill Tellman, Walter Wedigo Watson, and Perry Wood. I also want to thank the late Rod Geddes, a volunteer extraordinaire with the GLBT Historical Society, who transcribed many hours of my oral histories. And, I need to acknowledge the Society's Oral History Project, which provided a nurturing atmosphere to grow my project long before it was a book.

Archivists Willie Walker, Kim Klausner, and Paula Jabloner (along with a host of volunteers) at the GLBT Historical Society allowed me easy and unfettered access to that immensely important archive. Walker made the process of researching much less lonely if a little more surreal and perverse. I miss him immensely. Bill Hooper, the archivist at Time-Life, Inc., was incredibly helpful, providing me with much useful information and donating his valuable time. Also helpful were Susan Goldstein and her staff at the San Francisco History Center of the San Francisco Main Public Library; Stuart Timmons at the ONE Institute archive in Los Angeles; and the staff at the San Francisco Performing Arts Library and Museum. Much gratitude goes to Gerson Goodkind and Stephen Frisch for allowing me to publish their photographs here; also, sincere thanks to Larry and Judy Couzens and the powers that be at Time-Life for taking account of the limited resources of a university press (and its author) while putting together a licensing agreement.

Over the past several years I have had the opportunity to work with several bright and motivated students while teaching at UC Berkeley and

SFSU. I thank the students in my courses for asking stimulating questions and forcing me to become a better communicator. I also wish to thank members of the Department of History at SFSU, especially Bill Bonds, Richard Hoffman, and Barbara Loomis, for their congeniality while I was teaching there.

While completing the book manuscript, I was fortunate to find an academic home at the Regional Oral History Office (ROHO) in the Bancroft Library at University of California, Berkeley. ROHO's director, Richard Cándida Smith, has been an important mentor ever since he responded favorably to an e-mail I sent in 2002 asking to arrange an informal affiliation with the office. Since the arrangement has become decidedly more formal, I have had the good opportunity to work with many accomplished scholars and interviewers at ROHO, most especially Lea Barker, Beth Castle, Esther Ehrlich, Vic Geraci, Laura McCreery, Shannon Page, Linda Norton, Lisa Rubens, Sally Hughes, David Washburn, and Nadine Wilmot.

I was fortunate to receive funding from a number of sources that enabled me to devote many of my waking hours (and a few unwaking hours) to research and writing. Just when I was about to give up hope of ever completing this book manuscript, the Sexuality Research Fellowship Program of the Social Science Research Council awarded me a fellowship funded by the Ford Foundation. Along with introducing me to the vibrant, interdisciplinary cohort of sexuality researchers convened by the program, the fellowship provided me with twelve months (2003–2004) to complete the research and writing for the book. Without the gift of those twelve months, you would not be holding this book today. Thanks especially to Diane Di Mauro, director, and Lissa Gundlach, program assistant, of the Sexual Research Fellowship Program. The Haynes Foundation Dissertation Fellowship and the College Dissertation Fellowship, both at USC, each funded a year of research and writing early on in the project. USC's Center for Feminist Research and History Department also provided generous grants to help me finish the dissertation.

A few people have been close to me from the beginning through the end of this project and they all have my gratitude. I want to thank my mother, Carol, for believing in me as I struggled to complete a project that exacted personal and professional consequences (but also provided its rewards). My sisters Jennifer Joyce and Judy Palmieri have also been supportive beyond belief. I cherish them immensely for that. And I want to acknowledge the support and kindness of Carole and John Lietzke as they have welcomed me as a member of their family.

I met my partner Scott Lietzke just I was in the final difficult months of graduate school. Having survived that test of will, stamina, and understanding so early in a relationship, it was clear to me that Scott was a keeper. That he has been unswervingly by my side as I have struggled through the equally difficult process of completing the book while constantly searching for an academic home in which to work has only confirmed my earlier conclusions. From Scott I have learned the meaning of sacrifice; the rewards of commitment; and the joy of companionship. Thank-you, Scott, for everything.

Finally, I want to thank the founders, volunteers, and staff of the GLBT Historical Society, to whom this book is dedicated. The volunteers and the staff are a goldmine much like the holdings of the archive itself. They are simply irreplaceable. This book could not have been completed without all that resides in and dedicates itself to the third floor of 657 Mission Street in San Francisco.

The most important sources in this book are the voices of people who struggled to connect with information and desired to contact people they imagined to be like themselves. The voices quoted in the following pages primarily come from two sources: correspondence and oral history interviews. The correspondence is mostly drawn from the collections of two homophile organizations, the Mattachine Society and the Daughters of Bilitis. Because of donor stipulations and archival policy, I have changed the names of the correspondents when I refer to them in the main text and in the notes of this book except for individuals (e.g., Del Martin or Hal Call) already publicly identified. All oral history narrators except one allowed me to use their real name. I do not quote from every interview I conducted in the course of researching this book, so I have provided a complete list of interviews that contributed to this book below.

Oral history interviews (all interviews conducted by the author in San Francisco unless otherwise noted)

Baird, Bruce, 12 August 2003
Barnard, David, 8 September 1999
Blackmore, Linda, 4 March 1997
Britt, Harry, 2 October 1998

Buttwinick, Larry, 25 February 2004, 1 March 2004, Hayward, CA

Caffee, Mike, 26 July 1999

Call, Harold (Hal), interviewed by Christopher Palumbo, 29 April 1998

Call, Harold (Hal), 13 October 1998, 13 May 1999

Choisser, Bill, 5 March 1997

Covina, Gina, 21 September 2003 in Laytonville, CA

Evans, Clyde, interviewed by Phil Miller, 21 December 1997–21 February 1998

Fort, Dr. Joel, interviewed by Paul Gabriel, 30 July 1997

Garnett, Jack, interviewed by Jim Duggins, 7 August 1994

Gatta, Gina, 18 July 2001

Gerharter, Rick, 15 April 1998

Goodkind, Gerson, 6 September 2003 in Oakland, CA

Guidos, Lori, 2 February 1997

Graves, Robert, by telephone, 14 September 1999 (not recorded)

Hicks, Jim, 26 February 1997

Holliday, Laurel (Galana), by telephone, 28 April 2004

Howell, Larry, 17 December 1998, 10 January 1999

Karlinsky, Simon, 16 July 1994, 6 August 1994

Lambert, Kenneth (pseudonym), 22 February 1997

Lichtenberg, Paula, 16 May 1998

Lucas, Donald, interviewed by Paul Gabriel, 1996-1999

Lucas, Donald, 11 September 1999

Lyon, Phyllis and Del Martin, 23 August 2000

Meaker, Marijane, by telephone, 10 May 2004

Plath, Bill, interviewed by Paul Gabriel, 18 April 1997

Ramirez, Tom, 22 April 1998

Red, Ida VSW, 6 March 1997

Reque, Bill, 8 September 1999

Ross, Bob, 9 January 2002

Seajay, Carol, 28 March 1998, 9 April 1998

Shapiro, Leonard, 9 March 1997

Tellman, Bill, 18 May 1999, 8 June 1999

Tooker, Richard, 8 August 1995

Turner, Philip, 16 April 1998, 6 May 1998

Van Egri, Edward, 28 April 1998

Watson, Wedigo Walter, 17 May 1998

Wood, Perry, 2 April 1998, 13 August 1999

The Sexual Communication Network as an Agent of Change

The emergence of gay male and lesbian communities in twentieth-century United States was in very large part the result of massive changes in the way that individuals could connect to knowledge about homosexuality. As homosexuals have struggled to claim an identity, build communities, map out their world, and secure equality, they have had to overcome many hurdles including but not limited to the actions of police, the diagnoses of psychologists, the sermons of ministers, the sentences of judges, the stamp of censors, and the surveillance of parents. But perhaps the most stubborn problem faced by homosexuals over the course of the twentieth century has been one of communication. Before people who erotically and emotionally preferred the same sex could organize to confront and challenge their antagonists, they have had to coalesce around an identity and gather themselves into collectivities, into communities, into specific places, and around certain ideas. The projects of articulating identities and building communities, however, are not ones that many homosexuals chose with purpose or foresight. Indeed, the entire process was fraught because for the boys, girls, men, and women who desired contacts there was neither innate knowledge nor a handbook given to them that shared the steps that must taken to achieve an identity and find a community. Yet, a connection had to be made, and throughout the twentieth century an apparently increasing number of individuals possessed a burning desire to connect.[1] This desire to connect and in effect reproduce homosexuality is a central yet woefully neglected current in the century's long history of homosexuality.[2] But while the desire to connect has been a relative constant, found in the diaries of American colonials, in the letters of twentieth-century bohemians, and in the oral histories of contemporary queer activists, the desire and the ways in which it has been expressed have a long and complex history.

Contacts Desired traces this history of connecting to the gay male and lesbian world through an exploration of a series of innovations that helped to transform the structure of homosexual communication networks from the 1940s into the 1970s. Furthermore, *Contacts Desired* seeks to recover communications as a central, perhaps the central, thread that makes queer history a recognizable and unified phenomenon. Communication networks, as I will show, not only were at the heart of the homophile movement of the 1950s and 1960s but were also a major preoccupation of lesbian authors in the 1950s, gay liberationists and lesbian feminists in the 1970s, and gay men and lesbians who simply wanted to locate bars throughout the period covered in this book. While the politics of reform and revolution were undeniable forces in queer social movements since World War Two, the problem of communication was informed by and influenced political debates, cultural innovations, and individual experience.

Before an individual might "come out" into the gay world or "come out" to the larger public as a homosexual, in most instances he or she would first become "connected to" the knowledge that same-sex attraction meant something, that it had social ramifications, and that it had a name.[3] Moreover, being connected to the knowledge often meant learning simultaneously that one was not alone *and* that one was alone. In other words, one might learn that he or she is part of a larger group but only gain that knowledge while isolated from that larger group. Thus, ironically, with the gaining of a sense of group identity oftentimes came the feeling of isolation from that group. In attempting to ameliorate this sense of isolation, homosexuals have reached out to the world beyond their immediate surroundings. In so doing, they pursued contacts and sought information; moreover, they were receptive to the information that appeared and those contacts who presented themselves. In seeking out information and contacts, these individuals reached out into a vast variety of established networks of communication, but they also helped expand and transform those networks and, as I will show, even created entirely new ones. Seeking and pursuing meant that individuals may have visited doctors, read psychology journals, or browsed the shelves at the local library in order to learn more about their sexual desires; they may have picked up a newspaper or walked the streets looking for something or someone that was different, that was a little queer; they may have asked around and scoured catalogs for books and magazines published on the fringes of society and legality that promised stories about "twilight men" and "odd girls"; they may have moved to a city or a particular neighborhood that was rumored to harbor certain kinds of people; or they may have mimeographed their own circulars, written their own newsletters, or formed their own organizations hoping that others would heed the call and join them. While individual desire and the laws and social mores that alternately curtail and nurture those drives are the forces that determine what can be communicated and how, the changing scale and content of these myriad manifestations of homosexual communication networks shape this history of gay male and lesbian identity, community, geography, and politics.

Contacts Desired provides an account of the transformation of the networks through which individuals connected to knowledge about homosexuality and connected to the people, places, and institutions of the gay male and lesbian worlds. Between the 1930s and the 1970s at least three major innovations took place, each of which transformed the content, form, and scale of homosexual communication networks, and these transformations influenced every conceivable facet of what today is understood to be gay male and lesbian life. The dominant modes of communication, of connecting to knowledge, people, and places before the 1950s are discussed briefly later in this introductory chapter. The three main sections of this book examine in detail the transformations. Part 1 explores the interventions of 1950s homosexual activists and their drive to create candid, stable, and authoritative networks. Part 2 examines the process by which the mainstream mass media "discovered" homosexuality in the late 1950s and early 1960s, which helped to usher in a new era of mass-mediated networks. Part 3 details the development of a do-it-yourself commercial and activist ethic among gay men and lesbians and the consequent building of a complex and extensive subcultural network in the late 1960s and early 1970s.

Along with providing an overview of the transformations in communication networks, this book paints a portrait of the world in which colorful personalities struggled to build connections among homosexuals. As part of that struggle, the men and women, both homosexual and heterosexual, fought over how those connections could and should be made; they grappled with obscenity laws and publishers and distributors who ran the gamut from censorious to sensationalist; they established trailblazing organizations that would accomplish a great deal in often uncertain milieus; they renegotiated the line between verbal disclosures and physical behavior appropriate in public space vis-à-vis private space; they traveled the country seeking to make friendships and forge alliances with people who they did not know and could only presume would be interested in pursuing connections among queers. This book, further, uncovers a series of pitched battles, subtle conflicts, and remarkable collaborations among journalists, homophile activists, psychologists, publishers, authors, photographers, reformers, police, travel writers, and hundreds of other participants (some homosexual, some not). As these groups and individuals struggled to silence or publicize, eradicate or advocate homosexuals and their communities, increasingly candid and widely distributed information about homosexuality appeared in the nation's newspapers, magazines, and books, and on its radio waves and television screens. Throughout the period covered by this study, increasing numbers of individuals in ever more far-flung and formerly isolated places read those stories, heard those words, saw those images, and concluded that they too were homosexual, thus providing the context for a multitude of individuals to begin imagining themselves as being homosexual and as identifying with that subculture in many cases before the physical experience of visiting a gay bar or having a homosexual encounter.[4]

Contacts Desired tells the story how and why the homosexual world emerged with its own unique geography, which by the early 1970s had its own national meccas, regional capitals, small-town outposts, and danger zones. This book also demonstrates how this geography differed considerably by gender; how it had boundaries that could be clearly mapped and often imaginatively so; and how it possessed a terrain that became well known not only to homosexuals but to heterosexuals as well. It further examines geography making in general but also offers a new perspective on why the lesbian bar became so closely identified with Greenwich Village and why a place like San Francisco became a "gay mecca" while other cities of similar character and size did not gain such a widely held reputation.

Finally, it bridges a number divides that have characterized not only gay male and lesbian history but the social history of community formation as well. The historical and sociological literature on queer communities has focused on "community" as it exists in measurable space. That is, scholarship has followed within the traditional social historical and urban sociological vein of examining patterns of politics, community, and culture as they emerge and evolve on the streets and in the neighborhoods of the city itself. This book, however, takes places as its prime category of analysis—like Greenwich Village, San Francisco, and the nation—that are given meaning by its residents but also ones that are the creation of representation and fantasy. Hence, I examine regions, cities, towns, and sites as they were known by people before they ever even visited those places. Moving beyond the urban isolationist mode of community studies, *Contacts Desired* demonstrates how community development is not simply a historical process that unfolds in a single city but is instead a much more complex phenomenon that includes local, regional, national, and global dimensions.

In one of the most influential books on the history of sexuality, *Gay New York*, George Chauncey argues that gay male lives before the 1940s in the United States were not ruled by the tyranny of isolation, invisibility, and internalized homophobia as had been widely presumed.[5] Although Chauncey does not explicitly emphasize the point, his hypothesis is contingent upon the spread of information: the male homosexuals in *Gay New York* were able to overcome and even contest social forces that prevented them from articulating an identity and building a community to support it, partly because they already were participants in the communication network of gay New York. While I firmly agree with Chauncey's challenge to the damaging myths of gay history, I'm afraid that these myths are in danger of being replaced with the equally problematic myths of homosexual visibility and connectivity. In reality, both invisibility and isolation are in flux; they are states that constantly have to be achieved and maintained or avoided and dismantled. For that matter never can there be a complete invisibility or visibility, a complete isolation or connectivity. Indeed, these are processes rather than stable states of being. I have found that the oppositions of visibility / invisibility and isolation / connection have been of great concern to homosexuals throughout the twentieth century. I also have found that homosexuals have not engaged in a wholesale rejection of invisibility and isolation in favor of visibility and connection; rather, they have negotiated between the two for a variety of reasons. This is not to imply that a change of attitudes toward visibility / invisibility and isolation / connection has not occurred. To make such a claim would be to ignore the very different kinds of invisibility and isolation and how those "kinds" have themselves changed over time. This book seeks to unravel the complexities and explain the changes.

Coming Out and Connecting

In one of the most repeated and recognizable tales in the history of homosexuality in the twentieth century we can see the themes of isolation and invisibility manifest in clear relief. The story is the coming-of-age tale of the man regarded by many as the founder of the modern gay rights movement, Harry Hay.[6] The story, which he loved to tell, goes something like this: at fourteen, Hay had exaggerated his age and landed himself a job on a steamship heading south from San Francisco Bay to Los Angeles. Late one evening while in port, when the rest of the crew was being entertained at a brothel, Harry found himself in the company of a handsome young man named Matt who also had avoided the nighttime diversions. A knowing connection was made as the men gazed in each other's eyes, and they agreed to explore a remote beach during the next port of call. While strolling on the beach, "Harry was swept up by bracing physical sensations," Hay's biographer Stuart Timmons tells. "His mouth was dry, his flesh tingled, Matt's hand dangled next to his. When he clasped it, he momentarily feared that the sailor would respond violently. Instead, Matt pulled him close and kissed him."[7] Within a moment the two headed for a grove of trees, and soon Hay was having his first adult sexual experience. In the afterglow of their encounter, Matt shared with the young and inexperienced Hay the idea that men like them were members of a "silent brotherhood" that existed throughout history and spanned the globe; that at times he will feel isolated, but even in "that frightening and alien place" he will look across a street or a square and "see a pair of eyes open and glow at you . . . at that moment, in the lock of two pairs of eyes, you are *home* and you are *safe!*"[8]

The reason Hay undoubtedly relished telling this tale and the reason why so many have enjoyed hearing it is that even more than the contemporary coming out story it is the quintessential saga of homosexuality. The experience of this process is shared not by all but by an untold number of women and men who come to identify themselves as homosexual. Even more than coming out (the moment of revealing one's homosexuality to friends, family, and the world at large), connecting (the moment of emerging from the isolation and invisibility into which most who would later identify as gay or lesbian are born) is the point at which someone becomes homosexual—or, rather, gay male or lesbian.

Yet, even while many homosexuals would likely identify with Hay's tale and be able to offer similar examples for their own lives, his story in today's context strikes me as both quaint and incomplete: quaint because his tale emphasizes a mystical bond among gay men while ignoring the influence of outside, institutional forces that bring them together; incomplete because rarely does meeting and engaging in sexual relations with a single person entail an entrée into a community, a world—other steps too must be taken, other connections must be made. Hay, as he tells it, has merely connected with a single person who suggested a larger world existed but could offer no concrete proof and did not introduce him to any other members of that world. Moreover, while Matt informed Hay that he was a member of a "secret brotherhood," Hay makes no indication that he provided him with the name of that brotherhood. Therefore, while the special time spent with Matt was an important episode in Hay's journey toward a homosexual identity, it was merely one step taken on a much longer path.

While Hay's favorite tale does not encompass the different stages of connecting to homosexuality, his biography does. Years before meeting Matt, Hay reports that while in grade school and feeling alienated from the company of his peers, he found refuge in books and even professes to have read through his school's library from beginning to end. Along the way he claimed to have come across Edward Carpenter's *The Intermediate Sex* (1908). *The Intermediate Sex* was one of the first books available to a wide readership that treated homosexuality not primarily as a medical or moral problem but as a condition of humanity. Hay's biographer asserts that "this book brought an 'earthshaking revelation' and lasting change to Hay's life" because it included the word "homosexual," a word with which Hay claimed to have identified intuitively.[9] So, if we are to believe Hay's memories, he actually came to a state of knowing long before his fortuitous encounter with Matt in a way that was much less mystical and much more tied to the emerging print culture of homosexuality and the circulation of knowledge within established social institutions such as the modern public or school library.

Hay's reading, however, represents an act of gaining information but it would not necessarily bring him into contact with other homosexuals. Perhaps reading *The Intermediate Sex* prepared him for his encounter with Matt, but that liaison only hinted at a larger, connected world. Again, Hay's biography reveals the process by which he moved from mere knowing and from a solitary acquaintance to a connection with a much larger culture, what Chauncey has termed the "gay world." Indeed, Hay recalls that in the years after meeting Matt his encounters with the "silent brotherhood" were fleeting and anonymous, making him feel isolated rather than connected. Seeking to make a more lasting connection, Hay ventured into downtown Los Angeles's Pershing Square, a place about which it was rumored that men could meet similarly inclined men. Armed with little more than suspicion, intuition, and desire, Hay managed to make contact in the park's toilets with a man who was in his mid-thirties and had many years of experience living in the gay world. Although Hay remembers that this man taught him a good deal about sex, perhaps more important was that this man "brought Harry out to many arcane elements of gay culture, relaying bits of information the youngster absorbed like a sponge."[10] The information included the location of specific sites where assignations might be made and the euphemistic language that gay men used to communicate with one another while keeping their words hidden from a judgmental public; through this man Hay also was introduced to a wider circle of "sophisticated" and "temperamental" men. By the time he headed off for college in the early 1930s, he had learned about and connected to the gay world. As his future experience would demonstrate, the act of connecting was not something that could be completed; it was a lifelong process. But Hay would carry with him throughout his life the knowledge he learned about the process of making contacts.

Although Harry Hay's story as told by his biographer includes a variety of means through which a young man might connect to knowledge and connect with people that will be familiar to gay men and lesbians who connected to gay male and lesbian worlds in subsequent decades, I think that his story is a product of its time and also perhaps evidence of a very unique, far from average personality. Unlike subsequent generations, Hay was never presented with knowledge or connections: he sought them out—whether by scouring the library or by actively seeking out contacts that might provide him with additional contacts. For people in Hay's era who were not as inquisitive or as fortunate, the chances of happening upon knowledge, lucking into a relationship, or falling into a circle of friends were probably rare. The distribution of information about homosexuality was simply not very widespread or democratic during the period in which Hay came to knowledge—and the number of school libraries with *The Intermediate Sex* available to students undoubtedly would have been few. Moreover, as we shall see, the information that did exist more often than not was tainted with negative judgment and condemnation, or it was coded in a language that was known only to the already initiated. And while Hay recalls reading a famous book on homosexuality, he did not mention magazines, newspaper articles, radio shows, or organizational newsletters (not to mention later innovations like television and the Internet) that provided him with information and connections. Discussions of homosexuality in those venues were anything but regular, candid, and informative during the period. Previous studies have shown that many men and women who engaged in homosexual behavior during Hay's era relied primarily upon subcultural communication networks (sometimes tight-knit but often fleeting) for their information.[11] Thus, one could surmise that information about sexuality that traveled through well-established communication networks was only marginally influential until well after Hay came to knowledge and to connection with the nascent gay world.

Contacts Desired examines sexual communication networks as historical, changing entities that have gone through a radical transformation over the course of the twentieth century. This book charts that transformation as the passage from an era in which connecting was dominated by networks that generally were hidden, coded, unstable, and small-scale to another era when regular and important innovations in networks introduced new means through which connections happened, to an era in which the new networks were public, candid, stable, and large-scale. As we shall see, though, this apparent narrative of ever-expanding sexual communications should not be taken as an unqualified story of progress. Indeed, "progress" would be the wrong word to describe a process that does not necessarily result in a better world and a more fulfilling way of life for the people involved. Along the way to increasing visibility and integration into the mainstream a good deal was lost; along the way new divisions appeared among homosexuals; along the way communications became commercialized and subject to the demands of mass culture; and along the way the medium of communication became part of mass culture, as did homosexual identity itself. Neither does "progress" aptly describe the process by which these networks transform; the newly dominant modes of communication were more candid and more regularly mediated by institutions, but that does not mean that more traditional forms of communicating ceased to persist. Rather, as this book will demonstrate especially in part 3, the use of codes, face-to-face exchange, and the refusal to communicate through the mainstream mass media flourished in the years after which such modes would have become anachronistic in a narrative of progress. Still, it would be naïve to say that those more traditional modes of communication were unchanged by the innovations. Instead, those modes also underwent important transformations, responding to and accommodating the new contexts.

This is not merely a history of how a series of communications shifts influenced an already stable social group. Instead, it is a historical account of how changing networks of communication helped to bring that social group into being, how the narrative of a communications shift is tantamount to the history of a homosexual identity forming into a collective sense of itself so that it could see itself as a whole and seek to know itself and its constituent parts, its diversity, and its contradictions. Few arenas of American life, let alone homosexual life, remain untouched by the transformation of sexual communication networks through the twentieth century. In this book, I have provided an integrated account of at least four arenas in which sexual communication networks have exerted profound influence: identity formation, community building, geography making, and social movement organizing.

Identity Formation

Innovations in the expanding media in which information about homosexuality is communicated influence the process of gay male and lesbian identity formation in any number of ways.[12] The contexts in which individuals identify as homosexual change according to the transformation of networks carrying information about that identity. The three innovations that I detail in this book if nothing else brought people into contact with ideas and other people that otherwise might have been inaccessible to them in another time and place. Historians have rightly pointed out that the acquisition of sexual identity is not necessarily a top-down matter. Chauncey demonstrated that before the 1930s many who asserted a queer identity and who gathered into groups around that identity claimed to be unaware of the scientific discourse on sexuality that was then circulating; the men he studied were found to be unacquainted with the terms the sexologists used to describe them and, instead, they favored their own terms, terms that rarely if ever made their way into professional journals.[13] In other cases, scholars like Jennifer Terry, Henry Minton, and Lois Banner have found that individuals, often of the white middle class, have articulated their identities in close relation to sexological thought and scientific categories.[14] Whether or not an individual interacts with an elite discourse in the shaping of her or his sexual identity is not exactly beside the point, but it fails to account for the similar processes through which individuals from a variety of backgrounds acquired sexual identities in the past. What was shared by the working-class men studied by Chauncey and the educated women studied by Banner was that each articulated their sexuality through an interactive process: it was neither given to them from on high nor did it percolate up from below. The interaction could have occurred in a variety of settings. For the working-class men it might have happened at a worksite or inside a saloon where a mixture of words and behaviors resulted in a group understanding. For the educated women it might have happened while alone reading a dense journal article and simultaneously reflecting upon one's sexual and emotional life history. That the acquisition of identity is interactive also means that it is communicative, that the stuff of everyday life is transmitted across space: from one person to another, from an author to a reader, a reader to a publisher, a publisher to a teacher, a teacher to a pupil, a student to an administrator, an administrator to a doctor, a doctor to a patient, a patient to a psychologist, and so on. By examining what happens when information about sexuality begins to travel through altered or newly constructed networks, this book demonstrates that changes in those communication networks influence the very processes by which individuals encounter ideas about identity and then articulate their own.

Community Building

Identity formation and community building are related processes, especially in the context of gay male and lesbian history. Because many who identify as homosexual recount the process by which they came to that identity as one that involved feeling, longing, sensing, and thinking and not necessarily firsthand experience and experiential knowledge of a particular place or group of people, the desire to contact others like themselves is a logical next step.[15] This might entail visiting a local gay bar; it might send one packing to move to a distant city. The ability of an individual to move from identification to association is contingent upon the place of that individual in communication networks, with "place" meaning either proximity to information or situatedness within a social identity such as one's race, class, or gender. Scholars from a variety of disciplines— from physics to sociology—have shown that social networks are rarely arranged randomly, that the points in the network (whether they are individuals or bits of information) gravitate to and push away from one another to create a complex series of relationships.[16] I propose that in the case of gay male and lesbian worlds the number and type of links changed vastly between the 1940s and 1970s, thus altering the structure of the network as a whole.

Sociologists, particularly those studying networks, have shown that preexisting networks influence newly forming ones. Such was the case of emerging homosexual networks, which were built upon a dense and interlocking grid of already established social networks of gender, race, and class. Thus, the ground upon which homosexual communication networks was built already had an established history of patterns of racism, sexism, and economic inequality that would, in turn, play a role in structuring new networks.[17] While the primary focus of this book is on the development of new sexual communication networks, it takes account of the continuing influence of gender and sexism as a central organizing principle differentiating gay male from lesbian networks (and vice versa). Moreover, while a thorough examination of the variables of race and class is too large to be contained within the scope of this book, *Contacts Desired* considers and explores in a speculative fashion the moments at which race and class enter into and sometimes help structure sexual communication networks.[18] Although I will not replicate the complex statistical mathematics of network analysis in this book, I will borrow portions of its terminology in order to describe the phenomena and transformations of homosexual communication networks more precisely. In this book, I am interested in how the links between individuals and groups and between different clusters of already interlinked individuals change over time, why those changes happen, and how those changes influence the lives of people inside the network as well as outside of it.

Geography Making

As networks shift and the ties binding people to one another and groups to other groups change, individuals' perspectives of the worlds they inhabit transform. Changing experiences of place and the imaginations of place are two of the ways in which this book charts the influential transformation of communication networks. As more and different kinds of links are drawn between individuals and between groups, the imagined geography of the surrounding world morphs. *Contacts Desired* follows the paths of dozens of individuals who, between the 1940s and the early 1970s, made those connections that became the links in a larger network. In making those connections, these individuals helped to transform the geography of the gay world and to make better known that geography. They did this by sharing information about various places: bars not to miss as well as those that had been raided and closed; neighborhoods that might prove 'interesting' and cities that one would want to avoid; institutions that were helpful and those that were misleading.

After many years in which such information circulated to a widening circle of interested folk, patterns started to emerge and people began to gain a sense of what the world looked like beyond their own immediate experience; if they wished, they could create mental maps of the homosexual world. Indeed, some went beyond creating mental maps and became amateur cartographers by the early 1960s, drawing maps that pinpointed the locations of queer sites within particular cities or, later, queer cities within the nation as a whole.[19] Because of the changes in the networks connecting these people, the mental and the drawn maps transformed as well. By the early 1970s there existed a highly complex yet widely known homosexual geography of the United States that had points for national meccas, regional capitals, and small-town outposts and lines drawn around gay enclaves, other safe zones, and dangerous places. But this geography also replicated many of the salient social differences within the overall gay world as gender, class, and racial/ethnic identities influenced the occupation as well as idealization of space. Again, while this book focuses on the intersections of sexuality and gender, it grapples with race and class at key moments of linked constructions.[20]

Social Movement Organizing

The agendas of gay male and lesbian political organizations and movements have been as varied as the organizations themselves, from liberal Daughters of Bilitis in the 1960s to the revolutionary Gay Liberation Front in the early 1970s to the avowedly conservative Log Cabin Club in the 1990s. Gay male and lesbian social and political movements in the 1950s and 1960s also adhered to widely divergent ideologies, employed a variety of tactics, and even articulated goals that were not always in line with one another. What united the emergent gay and lesbian organizations of the 1950s, 1960s, and 1970s—and the political movement they composed— was that the leaders and the organizations they built developed a politics of communication. Those who became leaders of this movement claimed that the second-class status of homosexuals in the United States was largely due to a few interlocking factors, which included the misinformation (or lack of information) about homosexuals that circulated through the media, the poorly informed or uninformed notions about homosexuals held by experts and professionals (like the police, psychiatrists, and the clergy), and, perhaps most important, the difficulty homosexuals experienced when trying to connect with one another and the sense of isolation that resulted. Taken together, these issues placed the politics of communication squarely at the center of the emerging movement for homosexual civil rights—and this politics remained an organizing principle well into the 1970s when it reached its most forceful articulation in the context of lesbian feminism. *Contacts Desired* traces the impact of activists on sexual communication networks as well as how new innovations in sexual communications influenced the work and ideologies of the activists.

The Sexual Communication Network and Historical Change

My use of "communication networks" as an analytic tool, although somewhat new within the context of the history of homosexuality, is far from a new conceptual historiographical approach. Perhaps the most prominent and, arguably, successful proponent of this analytical and methodological approach to the study of history has been historian of France Robert Darnton. Darnton developed his idea of "communication networks" not as a theory but as an analytic tool to help him answer the admittedly large question (in the context of the French Revolution), "Do books cause revolutions?"[21] He claimed that previous attempts to address this question have faltered because they have focused either on the question of diffusion (how widely and how quickly do ideas spread?) or the analysis of discourse (how do texts produce cultural meaning?). Valuing contributions in both approaches, Darnton proposed to combine the two intellectual strains of thought, diffusion and discourse, through a study of the "communication networks of everyday life." Although there are important differences between the strains, I think it worth pointing out that the diffusion/discourse divide is in many ways parallel to the divide between communication "medium" and media "content" as theorized by Marshall McLuhan beginning in the 1960s.[22] Seeking to build a more complex analytical model, Darnton argued that the "production, distribution, and (to a certain extent) consumption [of books] can be studied systematically." He added, "One can think of the system as a communications circuit, which runs from author to reader—and ultimately back to the author again, because authors respond to readers, reviewers, and other sources of information and inspiration in the surrounding society."[23] Darnton calls this circuit a "communication network." He suggests that this analytical model improves upon diffusion/medium or discourse/content models for two reasons: it allows for meaning creation in a circular rather than top-down motion, therefore sidestepping the cause-effect tautology in favor of a more organic and systemic approach; and, it accounts for the influence of publishers, distributors, politicians, gossips, and censors alongside authors and readers, the usual focus of cultural history.

Certainly other scholars of American cultural history have explored the process, but few have chosen to use "communication networks" as an analytic tool. Instead, scholars have generally favored using the idea of the "public sphere" as expounded by Jürgen Habermas in *The Structural Transformation of the Public Sphere* (1962) or Stuart Hall's work on cultural production and reception as articulated in his article, "Encoding/Decoding" along with other sources.[24] While the concept of the public sphere and Hall's cultural approach inform *Contacts Desired*, I decided early to take on Darnton's "communication networks" as the prime analytic tool that would help me structure my narrative. The reasons Darnton's particular articulation of a "communications network" model sounded much more useful to me as a model to explain social change and the relationship of self to society is because it provided not an overarching predictive theory of how identities emerge and social change erupts, but rather a much more practical model for studying such changes and gaining understanding of the dynamics internal to the process of change. This provides a means to measure and evaluate the relative influence of cultural documents, for instance, both through diffusion and discourse, both in the extent and nature of distribution as well as in what it had to say to about homosexuality.

Change in communication networks is measured both with regard to the size, variety, and social impact of the networks and to the content of the information transmitted. This book provides a close reading of how people communicate, how information diffusion occurs in modern society, and how such communication brings about important social changes. Through an examination of communication networks transforming over a period of time, I demonstrate how communication networks serve as engines of social change and cultural invention. To paraphrase Elizabeth Eisenstein, a historian of the printing press, this history examines the sexual communication network as an agent of change.[25] Yet, I take heed of some of Eisenstein's detractors, who criticize her attribution of agency to an inanimate object, the printing press.[26] While the printing press was certainly invented by as well as operated with human hands, the concept of communication networks contains within it not only the physical machinations of people but also their drives, ideas, passions, ambitions, and mistakes; the sexual communication network has agency only because it is made up of the people who participate in it.

In order to best demonstrate the influence that the transformation of sexual communication networks has upon society, I have chosen to devote much of my analysis to one place: San Francisco. San Francisco can hardly be said to occupy a typical place in gay male and lesbian history. Indeed, by the early 1970s San Francisco had come to serve as a well-understood and widely used euphemism for homosexuality—one merely need to adopt the vocal mannerisms of an effeminate gay man and say "San Francisco" and the listener would likely also hear "homosexual." Yet, in mapping the place of San Francisco in communication networks and in charting the role of its residents in effecting change in those networks, my purpose is not to reify the importance of one single place and marginalize others. Further, I do not intend to claim that San Francisco became known as a gay mecca precisely at one time or another or that its ostensible renown as a licentious town inevitably translated into a latter reputation as a gay mecca or as a city that embraced tolerance and left-leaning politics. Indeed, depending upon where one lived, who one's friends were, where one traveled, what newspapers one read, and what class, race, and gender one identified with, one may or may not have thought San Francisco a morally wide-open town or gay mecca at any point in the twentieth century.[27]

For example, a few people in the 1920s might have considered San Francisco to be both a wide-open and a gay mecca, while to countless others during that period the city's name may have carried very little cultural currency at all, let alone a sexual one. The same could be said of San Francisco in subsequent decades, even, perhaps, into the late 1970s, the point at which the city could be said to symbolize homosexuality on a vast scale. Still, something very interesting happened between the 1940s and the 1970s that brought San Francisco close to the center of an expanding network of homosexual communications that encompassed both gay men and lesbians. And, as I argue throughout this book, the drawing of the national gay geography with San Francisco as a, or even, *the* capital is not something that was predetermined by San Francisco's history as an instant city or even its reputation as a frontier town wide open to vice. Rather, it was something that happened because of changing networks of communication, networks that placed San Francisco near the center of a new—new at least to a wider circle of people—sexual geography of the United States. And further, the networks changed not because of a free-floating and unchanging cultural reputation but because of the verifiable actions of countless activists, authors, readers, publishers, journalists, photographers, lawyers, bartenders, doctors, psychologists, and thousands of others. This book does contend, however, that San Francisco as a symbol and San Francisco as a city home to hundreds of thousands of permanent and temporary inhabitants provided a unique stage upon which people could build new links in the networks and could influence the wider cultural understandings of homosexuality across the United States and around the world.

The Gay Detective: Sexual Communications Prior to the 1950s

> Conversation between the smirking, willowy, handsome bartender and the lone male customer was desultory.
>
> "I've always heard that Bay City was really gay," the man offered rather pointedly.
>
> As if he'd used a password, which in a sense he had, the bartender became at once effusively chummy.
>
> "Well, my dear, it all depends on what you are looking for."
>
> He leered toward the blonde [woman] along the counter with a questioning lift of an eyebrow.

"Oh, heavens, no, not that," said the customer.

Both laughed shrilly in their quickly found intimacy.

"But where, I ask you, can one get a man?"

The nymph behind the bar pouted prettily. "Oh, the things you say, Nellie!" Then leaning forward confidentially, he rambled on effusively, illustrating each point with fluttering gestures of his hands and slim hips. "Of course, you can cruise the main drag—that's Market. You might pick up a service man . . . Well, there's the Square. Always a lot of hustlers around there . . . but so shopworn, I always say . . . being pawned over on the bargain counter . . . And there's the Baths, too. They're really best in the long run. Costs you a few bucks my dear. But goodness! There are always two or three dozen there, and you can simply take your pick. It's the best go in Bay City, I'm sure."

"Lou Rand," *The Gay Detective*[28]

In 1961, Lou Rand published what may have been the first gay detective novel, which was told as the story of a young detective's first case in a new town. The mystery, however, is not so much a whodunnit. Sure, there are murders at the beginning of the book, and the reader follows along to discover who committed them and for what reason, but there is also another story told between the cheap paperback covers. It is a story of a young gay man, newly arrived in "Bay City"—quickly identifiable as San Francisco—and his search for entry into the somewhat hidden gay world of the early 1950s. His act of sleuthing is made treacherous by violent and unpredictable police, corrupt politicians, and "rough trade"— presumably straight young men who solicit the affections of gay men and then make them pay with their wallets if not their lives. The subterranean narrative of the book follows the protagonist from complete ignorance about the locations and people of the city's clandestine gay world to his complete and total mastery of the world, both its most visible displays designed for consumption by the tourist and the most illegal and covert manifestations. In addition to being a conventional whodunnit, *The Gay Detective*, then, is also a "howdunnit." That is, it is a tale of how might one find a drag show, an after-hours gay bar, a bathhouse, or simply others who claimed membership in that secret club of gay identity.

American tourists in Paris in the age of Thomas Jefferson frequently chose to hire a *valet de place*, or a local guide, to show them sides of the city off the beaten path or deliberately hidden from the prying eyes of the government, the middle class, and the press.[29] Francis Morley, the gay detective of Rand's book, acts as a *valet de place* for readers as he guides them through the city, all the while unveiling the elicit entertainments and the extralegal institutions of the often impenetrable gay world.[30] As Morley descends into that world, the reader becomes privy not only to information but also to a mode of communication. Morley demonstrates how information about the locations of homosexuality is communicated and guarded in face-to-face though often coded contexts. *The Gay Detective* is more than just a piece of hard-boiled, if a bit fruity, fiction; it provides a key to the methods of communication in the gay world prior to the 1960s. Morely's descent into Bay City's queer underworld, guided by signs, symbols, and information passed surreptitiously, is simultaneously a journey to the heart of an identity and the community that is its home. Morley, moreover, emphasizes the primacy of communication in the formation of a gay identity by demonstrating that a flight of imagination instigated by chance revelations is among the most fundamental journeys made by a gay man or a lesbian: from ignorance compromised only by intuition to an increased level of awareness and knowledge fueled by assembled bits of information that reveal often more than was intended. In the novel and in the imagination of the reader, the gay detective eventually comes to a knowing identification with a real community that has its own distinctive institutions.

The central story of *The Gay Detective*, then, reflects a key narrative in the lives of several generations of gay men and lesbians: the process of finding a place where one is comfortable and with people with whom one feels affinity. It is about using the sources at one's disposal and, in some cases, creating those sources with little more to draw upon than one's libido and willingness to take risks. Whether the connections were fleeting, committed, intimate, institutionalized, and/or mediated, an almost infinite variety of communication pathways linked those seeking information and contacts with the extant information and with others seeking contacts.

Yet, like the guarded conversation between the bartender and bar patron in *The Gay Detective*, such early communication pathways were limited both by scale and by what could be said candidly. *Contacts Desired* picks up where *The Gay Detective* leaves off and traces this history from the beginning of the 1950s, a time when new organizations broke barriers in sexual communications, and continues through the early 1970s, when homosexual communications developed into a mass culture, albeit a partially segmented one. Yet, as *The Gay Detective* suggests, the search for sexual identity and sexual community among homosexuals precedes the 1950s by many years. In the following paragraphs, then, the stage is set for the chapters that follow, to show not only how the innovations in communication networks spurred widely felt changes but also what elements of the networks remained the same over the years and what patterns of queer communications persisted throughout the twentieth century.

Limited by the vigilant landlord, the reticent publisher, the zealous censor, and the inquisitive parent, the unpredictable and turbulent flow of information about sexuality before the 1950s proved a serious impediment to those who were seeking such information as well as to those who wished to share it. Although laws prohibiting obscenity, which included writings about and images of homosexuality, had been passed in the colonial era to curtail unbridled communication, the history of modern obscenity laws is usually traced to Anthony Comstock. By the early 1870s, Comstock was a leader within the YMCA as well as the guiding force behind the movement to ban the sale of erotica, particularly sexually explicit books.[31] Building upon the success of earlier antiobscenity statutes, Comstock, with the support of the YMCA, brought the battle to the federal level and helped win the passage of the 1873 bill that called for the "Suppression of Trade in, and Circulation of, Obscene Literature and Articles of Immoral Use" through the mail. This bill, which is referred to as the Comstock Act, provided the postmaster general with additional powers to investigate and seize obscene materials when sent through the mail. Until the 1957 U.S. Supreme Court decision *Roth v. United States,* which narrowed the definition of obscenity, judges and juries worked with an extremely ambiguous definition of obscenity, what was known as the Hicklin Test.[32] The Hicklin Test allowed the label of "obscene" to be applied to anything—literature, art, scholarship—that could be said to corrupt the minds or morals of the most susceptible members of a community, usually meaning children. Such a broad definition gave law enforcement officials great freedom in determining what and who would be subject to regulation, arrest, and punishment. While the Comstock Act sent hundreds of people to prison and left many more with stains on their records, it undoubtedly succeeded in catching only a very miniscule portion of people whose personal correspondence contained obscene passages as well as publishers who printed sexually explicit materials for a reading public. Even with a law as stringent and as widely and popularly enforced as the Comstock Act, it is likely that it functioned as a loosely woven net, with more space for obscenities to flow through than to get snagged within.[33]

Communication about homosexuality, however, was not only prohibited in letters, magazines, and other materials sent through the U.S. Postal Service. It was prohibited and policed in unpredictable and highly idiosyncratic ways around the country with states, counties, and municipalities writing their own legislation on the subject. Between 1900 and 1950, books and other printed material that might be sent through the mail and subjected to the federal Comstock Act also would have faced the actions of officials compelled by community pressure and local standards, which may have been more or less stringent than those employed by the U.S. Postal Service. It is this kind of varying and somewhat unpredictable perspective on the perceived threat of sexually oriented materials that gave the phrase "Banned in Boston" its cultural currency. Officials in Boston gained a reputation in the 1920s for being more vigilant in their fight on obscenity than officials in other localities around the country.[34] While the varying nature of obscenity regulation meant publishing sexually explicit materials was possible in some places while it was strongly prohibited in others, its unpredictability also meant that authors, publishers, and readers rarely could be sure on what side of the law they stood. The fact that different local and national laws and standards were applied to different media, like radio, stage, film, fine art, and so on, further exacerbated the state of uncertainty many producers as well as consumers of erotic material felt especially in the era before the *Roth* decision.[35]

When it came to print, the jobs of local and state censors were made easier by the fact that many publishers engaged in a good deal of self-censorship. In the era before the paperback revolution of the 1940s and 1950s, most books were published by quality publishing houses. To editors in those firms, the simple discussion of homosexuality or the inclusion of a homosexual character was enough to place a manuscript beyond the pale of good writing, unpublishable, and thus never were subjected to the censors.[36] Moreover, acts of censorship and self-censorship were not limited to printed materials; the visual arts of painting and film were subjected to regulation as well. In one of the most famous instances, a retired Navy admiral in 1934 insisted that the Corcoran Gallery in Washington, D.C., remove Paul Cadmus's painting *The Fleet's In!* from public view because of its alleged immoral content.[37] And four years earlier, the Motion Picture Producers and Distributors Association worked in conjunction with former postmaster general Will Hays to institute a regime of self-censorship called the Production Code, which included prohibitions on the representation or inference of "sexual perversions" among other perceived ills like drug use or interracial intimacies.[38]

The circulation of information, however, does not only happen through media like books or letters mailed through the postal system, films exhibited in a theater, or paintings hung in a gallery. The circulation of information happens in the immediate surroundings of everyday life: on the street, in the church, in the classroom, at the kitchen table, in the lunchroom, on the couch, and under the sheets. Even in these settings a pattern of self-imposed as well as outwardly mandated censorship impeded the free flow of information about sexuality. Although no one has yet completed a serious historical account of the discussion of sex in domestic settings, legions of oral history narrators have offered a great deal of anecdotal evidence that sex was not discussed in many homes. In fact, one of the reasons for the successful institution of a program of sex education in public schools in the 1910s was the reluctance of parents to speak about a subject upon which young people obviously needed some instruction, especially as it related to venereal disease. However, as scholars like Jeffrey Moran and Julian Carter make clear, while sex educators generally were eager to disseminate knowledge about sex, they also were near-unanimous in their hope that such instruction would curtail or, better, prevent premarital sexual activity.[39] As Carter argues, "The chief message of almost all twentieth-century sex education amounts to 'Just Say No.'"[40] In addition to discouraging sexual behavior, sex educators left a good deal out of their program of sex education: namely, sexuality. In general terms, sex education focused on the biological and physiological aspects of human sexual function (including, especially, sexually transmitted diseases) but very rarely addressed the social organization of sex such as concepts and identities like heterosexuality, homosexuality, and bisexuality; furthermore, completely beyond the pale of sex education was instruction about sociological formations like sexual sites and sexual communities. While a young person may have been introduced to a description of homosexual behavior in sex education, she would have to use her imagination to construct it as an identity and then would have to engage in a serious investigation to find people who might think about themselves in that manner.

Still, despite the tireless efforts of a whole population of ministers, police officers, psychologists, parents, publishers, authors, and judges who might each be called censors in their own right, those who wished to communicate about homosexuality or with homosexuals found holes in the nets of censorship, and they developed strategies for communicating in ways that avoided the attention of censors or even subverted their actions to enable new modes of communication. Art historian Richard Meyer astutely argues that censorship never prevented homosexuals from representing their lives in the arts—and from communicating with their brethren in general. Rather, homosexuals before the 1950s developed what Meyer calls an "outlaw" sensibility.[41] In the instances Meyer details, artists ranging from Cadmus to Andy Warhol had attracted the attention of censors and saw some of their work driven from the public sphere. But Meyer argues that neither artist capitulated to the demand that they remove homoeroticism from their palate and, instead, each responded by skirting or subverting the censors through imaginative productions that communicated a queer sensibility but in a way largely invisible to the larger, presumably heterosexual public. While skilled gay artists may have been particularly astute in making outlaw representations, they were by no means alone among homosexuals in their desire and ability to communicate with others like themselves.

Venues through which outlaw information flowed before the 1950s included a few do-it-yourself circulars that were born of the secretarial pools in various World War II–era military departments. One of these mimeographed circulars was called *Shawger's Illiterary Digest*.[42] Introduced in April 1943, the *Illiterary Digest* was originally "just a sheet of carbon between two V-Mails [Victory Mail letters] to kill two Australian-anchored GIs with one tome!" The circular, which eventually reached well beyond three dispersed friends, grew out of the desire of one man to keep in touch with friends overseas in the service and to help them stay informed about all the goings-on with their friends and acquaintances at home and abroad during the war; thus, it was "exclusively concocted for our boy and gal pals in the service!"[43] Quite different from many of the gay gossip or bar rags available today, the *Illiterary Digest* was presumably distributed only to individuals personally known to the author, making it a private or quasi-private medium of communication. Moreover, it is different because nowhere in the newsletter is there ever any explicit reference to homosexuality. Instead, what George Chauncey calls the "camp culture" of pre-1950s America determined the language that would be used. Chauncey argues that "gay men developed a variety of . . . cultural strategies that helped them manage a double life and resist the dominant culture's contempt. While offering them practical assistance in dealing with a hostile world, such strategies also affirmed their cultural distinctiveness and solidarity" and helped them build and maintain social networks they fought sustained battles to create.[44]

Although the full identities of the subjects of the gossip contained in the *Illiterary Digest* are lost to history, their assumed names tell a great deal about the publication itself. The names mentioned in the newsletter are one of two types: men's names perhaps undisguised (Peter Foster or Bruce Raeburn) or camp names like "Bessie Backstage," "Beatrice Salestax," "Nadia Nausea," or "Minnie Manhattan." This provided for an amusing read but also allowed the author to tell ribald tales about gay men involved in particularly queer, sometimes sexual, activities without specifically identifying them publicly or revealing them as gay. The reversal of gendered names and pronouns obscured the sex of the individuals involved and produced the appearance of heterosexual relations between the named men and the sham women mentioned in the publication.[45]

For example, in the March 1945 issue, readers enjoyed a fable that provides a glimpse of the wartime gay world in the camp of the *Illiterary Digest*. "Queenie Cochran" recounts her recent trip to Florida and her return to New York:

> The best part of going to Florida this year was returning to dear ole Manhattan! I wouldn't have gone but RUSS WEST'S pet flamingo at Fort Lauderdale contracted a STIFF neck and it wouldn't let anybody but me apply the Vick's Vapo Rub! So Doctress Cochran "Champion'd" down and "Silver Meteor'd" back and she didn't deprive the Armed Forces of any SEATS; she sat on the lap of the Army going and the Navy coming, and in Philadelphia she changed to a Marine![46]

Although we do not know who Russ West or "Queenie Cochran" was, a portion of the story remains susceptible to translation: apparently a man nicknamed "Queenie" had taken a trip to Florida, traveling on the "Champion" train line where "she" met an Army man on the way south, perhaps had an affair with Russ West, and then traveled on the "Silver Meteor" line on the way back to New York, where "she" spent some time with a sailor and a marine. These coded tales of sexual exploits and travels in the gay world across the United States—and around the world—provided readers with a sense of how large their world actually was and suggested that indeed they were everywhere, though no where in particular.[47] The *Illiterary Digest* likely grew out of one gay man's fear that his network of gay friends was dissolving as his friends went off to war; the circular, which was apparently distributed to a small number of people to points around the globe and maybe even at government expense in a wartime office pool, sought to maintain and grow the very important friendship network that a group of gay men struggled to build prior to being in the service and to which they hoped to return after victory.

Another example demonstrates how personal and informal sexual communication networks were created in the public sphere and thus were more widely accessible. Yet, these networks persisted only because the use of the outlaw sensibility cloaked them from those who would sanction homosexual expression. The *Hobby Directory*, a publication begun in 1946 that lasted into the 1950s, was published with the expressed purpose of providing "men and boys" a forum to contact each other to correspond about their "hobbies" and to form a shared bond.[48] At first glance, the

Hobby Directory appears innocuous enough: it was widely distributed at hobby stores throughout the country and advertised in magazines such as *Popular Science,* and it contained advertisements from people interested in pursuits such as Dixieland jazz, radios, photography, stamps, and model trains. This one from the June 1948 issue was typical:

> Southern Calif. Age 66, widower. 2 yrs. coll. Has built a few ship models and models of old muzzle-loading artillery, catapults, and ballistas; also model of English Castle. Wishes to contact other model builders.[49]

Such entries have remained standard fare for hobby correspondence societies to the present day. However, it turns out the sixty-six-year-old widower from Southern California was *not* a typical *Hobby Directory* member looking for contacts. Instead, the pages of the *Hobby Directory* were filled with entries like the one from a thirty-three-year-old single man from California whose hobbies were "physical culture, wrestling, outdoor life; music, particularly vocal; the theatre, arts and crafts; reading and gardening. Visits N.Y.C., Chicago, Milwaukee, and Los Angeles. C.D.: those who combine physical and cultural ideals with high standards of friendship."[50] Another advertisement read: "Age 57. Single. Coll. educ. Writer. Interests: Camping, nature study, cave exploring; short story writing; collecting of foreign paper money. Especially likes friends among cowboys, sheepherders, miners, lumberjacks, ranch hands, sailors, and 'guys who wear levis, cords, leather jackets with pep in their step and a sparkle in their eyes.'"[51] Or, in the June 1950 issue, a thirty-seven-year-old, single New Yorker placed this ad: "Hairdresser. Interests: opera, semi-classical music, the theatre (drama), good musicals, and the ballet. 2½ yrs. in the Navy. Visits N.J., Penna., and Conn. C.D.: those with similar interests his age or younger" (fig. 1).[52] The "C.D." in these ads stood for "Contacts Desired," which not only provides the title of this book, it also brought the language of desire, though buried in an initialism, into the pages of *The Hobby Directory.*[53] Reading and analyzing brief biographies now a half-century old is a treacherous project. Descriptions that appear "queer" to the eye today may have been "normal" in 1948. Certainly a fondness for the theater, gardening, or the ballet would not have necessarily marked a man as gay as much fifty years ago as it arguably does today. Yet, if one looks more closely at the personals, adds up the sum of the numerous biographies, and considers the source of the document (a gay man's life papers), a much clearer—and queerer—picture of the publication emerges.

Occupations and the other stated interests of the *Hobby Directory* members provide perhaps the most obvious statements about their different,

No. 620. John M. Larrabee, 402½ W. 33rd St., Los Angeles 7, Calif. Tel.: RI. 7-4071. Age 35. Railroad Clerk. Coll. ed. Interested in the drama, ballet, music, photography, physical culture, swimming, stamps, jewelry, souvenirs, and all things French such as cinema, paintings, literature, recordings, foreign foods and restaurants. Expects to visit France and N. Africa for a considerable time. Corr. also in French. Occasionally visits Chi., N. Y. C., Minneapolis, El Paso, Dallas, So. Cal. Three and one-fourth yrs., U. S. N. R.; 3 yrs., Casa Blanca. C. D.: Members of these interests, age 20 to 40.

No. 628. Paul R. Elick, Livingston, Calif. Age 35. Single. Postal Clerk. Interests: Travel and letter writing. Has made many friends by correspondence. Visits Ore. and Wash. Four yrs. in Navy. C. D.: Any members, especially in Pacific coast states.

No. 643. Erwin W. Carls, 1985 E. Phillips Blvd., Pomona, Calif. Age 40. Two yrs. U. of Idaho. Has collection of 4,000 different species of woods from all over the world, mineral collection of 400 types, herbarium of 500 specimens, and collections of shell, coral, sponges, seeds, wooden bowls and vases, kinds of sawdust and bark, plants and tree pods and cones, fossils, insects, starfish and marine novelties. Carves miniature animals in wood. C. D.: Those interested in exchanging such specimens as above.

1330 w Penn., SD-3

No. 646. Robert H. Scherer, 4729 Palm St., La Mesa, Calif. Age 24. College Student. U. S. Navy—5½ yrs. Originally from Rochester, N. Y. Interests: Stenotypy, court-reporting, classical and popular music, physical culture, hiking, tennis, swimming, camping and corresponding. Also collecting piggy banks and pennies. "Likes a faithful correspondent." C. D.: College students, ex-Navy men, high school teachers, and members his age and interests.

No. 751. Bois Burke, 2428 Channing Way, Berkeley 4. Age 41. Coll. grad. Office Clerk. Interests: Human interest stories, internationalism, politics and people. Hobbies: Correspondence, chess, giving intelligence, vocational and personality tests. Traveled in Europe. C. D.: Single members who are lonely.

No. 775. Fleming Hastings, 687 Shatto Pl., Apt. 102, Los Angeles 5, Calif. Tel.: Fitzroy 5047. Age 34. Single. Florist. Interests: The arts and outdoor sports. Likes to correspond with interesting members who enjoy discussing mutual likes and dislikes. Travels about widely over U. S. and Canada.

COLORADO

No. 219. Lewis A. Moore, Box 18, Rye Star Route, Pueblo, Colo. Age 50. Single. Bus. educ. Interests: Art photography, the great outdoors, camping, sunbathing. World War I. Visits West Coast, N. Y. C. and Boston. Seeks correspondence with other outdoor enthusiasts.

No. 400.* No. Central Colo. Age 54. Single. Hospital Manager. Interested in friendly, congenial correspondence.

1 Distributed through its private mailing list but also in hobby stores and through magazines like *Popular Mechanics,* the *Hobby Directory* achieved a wide readership. Not only did it appeal to those interested in stamp collecting and model trains, but also to men who professed a passion for modern dance, opera, floristry, and physique photography. Image courtesy of the GLBT Historical Society, San Francisco, CA.

queer preferences, making it easier for them to slyly self-identify as homosexual and assume other gays would catch on; careful readers of the *Hobby Directory* would encounter more than an average number of "male nurses," "interior decorators," "hairdressers," "actors," "florists," and so on.[54] All these professions implied some degree of gender inversion if males participated, thus highlighting the likelihood that those employed in such work might be homosexual. Moreover, in the contemporary world where "physical culture" and "outdoor life" would likely refer to leisure pursuits of readers of *Outdoor* magazine and customers of REI, a half century ago such a pairing more likely referred to one's aesthetic and erotic attraction to the well-toned male physique.[55]

In June 1950, a young Los Angeles resident placed an advertisement stating that he "collects and exchanges photos of physical activities. C.D.: other such collectors, weight-lifters, and athletic models."[56] In this era when the Comstock Act prohibiting the distribution of "obscene material" through the mail resulted in countless arrests and confiscations yearly and when the state's various antiobscenity laws outlawed the production, distribution, and possession of pornography, those who wished to obtain visual erotica had to communicate in a coded language. In this language, photos of nude or seminude men were called "athletic model photos" or "physique photos" and men would be interested—putatively, at least—in such pictures not for their potential to arouse but because physical culture or bodybuilding were among their hobbies.

Not all attempts at queer communication within the public sphere, however, were compelled to resort to vagaries of outlaw representation. Likely the most important novel in the history of lesbian literature was published well before the definition of obscenity began to shrink and censorship laws began to fall in the 1950s. British novelist Radclyffe Hall's *The Well of Loneliness* became a literary sensation following its publication then official censorship in the United Kingdom in 1928, its publication across the Atlantic at the end of the year, and its sensational obscenity trial the following year.[57] In April 1929, *The Well of Loneliness* was cleared of charges of obscenity by a New York court, but it retained its taint of disreputability, which is the one of the reasons that it gained a substantial readership in the ensuing years and decades. Previous media events like the well-publicized murder trial of Alice Mitchell in the early 1890s—skillfully detailed by historian Lisa Duggan in her book *Sapphic Slashers*—provided opportunities for the public to identify and categorize female social and sexual deviance well before Radclyffe Hall appeared on the scene.[58] But the publication of *The Well of Loneliness,* according to Laura Doan, became a key moment in "the shift from cultural indeterminancy to acknowledgement," or the moment at which a variety forces coalesce to both define and publicize a way of being, in this case modern lesbianism. Similarly, literary scholar Rebecca O'Rourke writes, "One of the most significant contributions *The Well of Loneliness* made was to render lesbianism visible."[59]

Over the course of the 1930s well over a hundred thousand copies of the novel made their way into the hands of U.S. readers. Although the novel was directed at heterosexual readers as a plea for tolerance, the populations most influenced by the book undoubtedly were women who either already had identified as lesbian and, even more, women and girls who began to imagine themselves as lesbian in relation to the feelings of desire elicited by the novel. A survey of one hundred lesbian readers conducted by the New York Lesbian Herstory Archives in 1986, as discussed by Rebecca O'Rourke, revealed the massive influence *The Well of Loneliness* had upon those surveyed.[60] While the readers each remembered their own reactions to the novel, a common response was expressed by one woman who first read it in 1946. "The most important things were," she recalled, "1) simply that the book existed and 2) it suggested to me that somewhere I might find a community, if only a small and beleaguered one—someday."[61] While on their way to claiming a lesbian identity, women in the United States have taken as divergent paths as their gay male counterparts; they have read and gleaned information and ideas from popular culture and sexological studies, from the words of their parents and those spoken by strangers on the street. Yet, as cultural historians like Janice Radway and Tania Modleski have so clearly demonstrated, women, particularly middle-class white women, in general have developed a much more intimate relationship with the novel than their male contemporaries.[62] The reasons for this are many, but the reliance upon novels for relief and companionship seems especially strong among lesbians, as evidenced by the special relationship many had with *The Well of Loneliness* and with the many lesbian-themed paperbacks published in the 1950s and 1960s. The process of rethinking the self in relation to a book had its limitations, though. Like types of outlaw communication favored by gay men, a relatively candid novel like *The Well of Loneliness* was of limited use to women who wanted to do more than imagine themselves as a certain kind of person who joined a particular crowd and spent time in unique places; in other words, the novel might be a good source to begin imagining, but it was less efficient in helping lesbians to connect with other lesbians or to specific places where they congregated.[63]

Again, though information about homosexuality might seep into public discourse or cloak itself to achieve distribution through means other than print and visual culture, information also made its way through the institutions of everyday life. Although not necessarily taking communication as a central focus of their studies, many historians of the queer past have detailed examples of how such acts of communication take place in a variety of settings. For instance, John Howard, in his important book *Men Like That,* shows how queer (if not precisely homosexual) kinds of identities appeared among men in rural areas and in the South—and in institutions not normally considered conducive to homoerotic connections, like the church. Providing a fascinating glimpse into the queer social world made possible by the church in both black and white communities, Howard notes that sex-segregated social events might lead to homoeroticism and that traditions like the all-male drag "wedding" might have produced "complicated thoughts and feelings" about gender and sexuality among the congregation. Howard goes further and argues that the church buildings, which were often open to the public but empty on most weekdays, were discovered by some men as "propitious sites for queer sex."[64] And in *Boots of Leather, Slippers of Gold*, Elizabeth Kennedy and Madeline Davis allowed their oral history narrators to explain how butch-fem lesbian identities grew out of the immediate needs and experiences, through patterns of everyday resistance, among the bar-going population. One of these immediate needs was to ease the sense of isolation felt by lesbians and to enable the possibility of making contact. Kennedy and Davis demonstrate that the corporeal visibility of the butch lesbian on the city street played a key role in making lesbianism publicly visible and in giving lesbians a sense that they were not isolated. Butch-fem roles "were the organizing principle for this community's relations with the outside world. The presence of the butch with her distinctive dress and mannerism, or of the butch-fem couple—two women in a clearly gendered relationship—announced lesbians to one another and to the public."[65] In both of these examples—of queer contacts made in the church and on the street—it is evident that connections could be made well outside of and prior to the larger, institutional innovations detailed in the following chapters. The differences between the smaller-scale, everyday connections and those that were mediated through organizations, the media, and other institutions reflect the difference between nascent and well-developed identities, fledging and mature communities, situational and highly articulate politics, and local and mass culture.

What is shared in each of the situations discussed in the preceding pages is a configuration in which factors both impeding and encouraging communication influence the ways in which identities are formed, communities are built, geographies are made, and, eventually social and political movements are organized. These examples are purposefully diverse and intentionally dissimilar. Some of the examples hint at the process of connecting to knowledge about homosexuality by individuals who had never considered their sexual behavior in the light of social categories; other instances refer to the experiences of individuals who already had come in contact with the gay world but continued to seek more information and additional contacts. The sum of these examples reveals a world in which the process of connecting to homosexual communication networks was possible but it was also a process that was fraught with a number of significant pitfalls, exclusions, and invisibilities—all of which were in some way or another overcome and mitigated as new communicative innovations appeared in subsequent decades. Yet, in the process, the place of subverting or skirting around norms and restrictions moves from the center of the gay experience to the periphery. While queers continued to deploy creative communications throughout the period covered by this book, the practice became a baroque element of queerness—merely an element of play—and, by the early 1970s, even was rejected by many gay men and lesbians as contrary to homosexual progress and self-respect.

As the 1950s opened and as social institutions and the mainstream public in general began to examine and talk about homosexuality more openly and frequently, sexual communication networks grew stronger, more expansive, more permanent, and more candid; they also became more commercial, more mainstream, and less distinctive to the people who participated in them. As a result, the relatively few and largely haphazard connections that resulted from the spread of information by word of mouth, through chance encounters, and through mediated yet outlaw communications started to increase correspondingly. The increase was slow and compromised by all the factors that kept homosexuals silent about their sexual identity during this period. However, by the middle 1950s, a small number of people began organizing and speaking very loudly about their homosexuality and about the injustices faced by homosexuals. These groups, the members of which called themselves homophiles, toiled for several years and against great odds before their message started to be heard. *Contacts Desired* begins with the emergence of the homophile movement and focuses on its leaders' goals, which included nothing less than intervening in and transforming the structure of sexual communication networks in the United States and beyond.

PART 1

✦～✦

Homosexuals Today—The 1950s

Introduction

Homosexuals Today—1956 is not only an exceedingly rare book, having been forgotten and out of print for decades, it presents the few who come across it today with a mystery demanding to be explained: how was it that in the middle of the 1950s, a decade commonly thought to be marked by fierce episodes of discrimination against and intense isolation of homosexuals, could a book have been published that took stock of the accomplishments of an international social movement on behalf of equality for gay men and lesbians?

The simple answer is that by 1956 there did in fact exist such a movement—called the Homophile Movement—of mutually independent but affiliated organizations not only in several states of the union but in many countries of Western Europe as well. The more complex answer, however, must take into account not only the fact that such organizations did exist but that they existed in large part because of a deep commitment to a shared goal: to bring an end to the isolation many who would come to identify as homosexual felt as they came of age in a social setting that not only pathologized their sexuality but because of a variety of legal and extralegal measures prevented them from gathering with others like themselves. Marvin Cutler, editor of *Homosexuals Today*, hinted at the larger project of this movement when he wrote, "Homosexuals today . . . are protesting against both ignorant condemnation and brutal suppression" with the goal of creating "a whole new pattern of social relationships."[1]

The book itself was a compendium of essays and listings—a handbook that mixed organizational histories, philosophies, and project descriptions. The book included, among other things, a short history of the homophile press by Don Slater, the editor of *ONE* magazine; a speech by Harry Hay about the origins of the movement; an account of a performance of American playwright James Barr's play *Game of Fools* staged by members of a homophile organization in Switzerland; and a brief introduction to the country's first lesbian organization. Most of the essays in the collection originated as papers read at the 1956 Midwinter Institute—the fourth annual meeting of the Los Angeles–based homophile organization One, Inc. Although conferences of homophile activists had been held in the past—including the International Congress of Sexual Equality in Amsterdam beginning in 1951—the Midwinter Institute was unique because it was the first large gathering of members from different organizations within the United States. Moreover, in the spirit of, according to Culter, creating "a whole new pattern of social relationships," the assembled activists agreed to produce a resource book that might help introduce ever more individuals into their world. In attendance were representatives of One, Inc., and the National Association for Sexual Research, both located in Los Angeles; the Mattachine Society and the Daughters of Bilitis, both of San Francisco; and unaffiliated individuals from around the country. Although these organizations—and the personalities that drove them— proved to be quite independent and at times acrimonious over the following decade, the conference itself (and the resulting book) was marked by a sense of common purpose and by an incipient knowledge that the activists gathered, simply by meeting, were in fact accomplishing one of the main goals of their movement: building networks among people and organizations that had previously been isolated—or, at least, unreliably connected.

The American homophile movement emerged in the early 1950s in California.[2] Within a few years of its founding, the leaders of the movement decided the most important contribution they could make to improving the situation of gay men and lesbians in the United States was to build new communication networks as well as reinforce the more precarious and small-scale networks that already existed. The three the most important groups that were founded in the early 1950s and persisted at least until the late 1960s were the gay male–oriented Mattachine Society, the lesbian-oriented Daughters of Bilitis, and the somewhat mixed-sex One, Inc. The organizations sought to build bridges among homosexuals in geographically disparate areas; between homosexuals and heterosexuals both distant and near; and between homosexuals and serious researchers who attempted to engage in objective studies of homosexuality and to foster permanent and varied knowledge networks across the nation. The creation of new sexual communication networks and the work of nurturing them to maturity have provided the organizations with their most lasting legacy.

Described by some historians as unwisely wed to a stifling strategy of progress through respectability, homophile activists, I argue, knowingly used respectability as a mask to hide a much more daring and creative approach.[3] Moreover, historians have repeatedly used the term "assimilationist" to describe homophile activists and thus critique them as insufficiently proud of their sexuality and all too willing to conform to the dominant ethos. However, this book argues that such critiques rest on an incomplete understanding of homophile activism and assimilation. The concept of assimilation, developed by scholars early in the twentieth century to describe what they considered to be the virtual surrender of unique cultural characteristics among immigrants as they became American, has long since been abandoned by historians of ethnicity in favor of concepts that reveal how dominant cultures are influenced often as much as minority ones. Aside from being an outdated sociological concept, assimilation in its precise formulation is the wrong term to describe the motivations and goals of the homophiles who, like immigrant ethnic groups, sought to change American culture as much as they expected that that culture would change them.[4] Finally, this book argues that previous scholars have attempted to place homophile activists within a post–gay liberationist/lesbian-feminist model—or, more generally, a post-1960s social movement model—of political activism. This book shows that homophile activists developed a grounded understanding of the source of the problems they experienced and a theory of how and why society discriminated against them and subsequently developed an activist agenda to address those issues directly. The fact that the approaches they developed did not look like the activist strategies that became popular later in the 1960s does not mean that the homophiles were apologetic or without vision. Rather, they were practical and committed to organizing where it would be most immediately effective and useful.

Early on, the homophile organizations realized that many heterosexuals—both the general public and the experts and opinion makers—were not going to allow a free-flowing and objective discourse on homosexuality to replace the tradition of selective silence and vocal condemnation surrounding the subject. Furthermore, the greatest tool of communication, the

mass media in its various manifestations, was by turns mute about or nois-
ily hostile to homosexuals. It is no surprise then that one of the first and
most labor-intensive undertakings of the homophile groups was to publish their own newsletters and journals directed toward both heterosexuals and homosexuals. Though having only limited reach, *ONE*, put out by
One, Inc.; the Mattachine Society's *Mattachine Review*; and the Daughters of
Bilitis's *Ladder*—founded in 1953, 1955, and 1956, respectively—became
conduits of communication between the homophile organizations and their
members as well as a means of outreach to those who had never heard of
such organizations. In addition to being distributed to members, the magazines were sold on newsstands around the country, were passed around
among friends, and were available for subscription through the mail.[5]

Publishing their own newsletters and magazines, though, was only
one path of building communication networks, and the groups' leaders
recognized that several factors would limit the distribution of such periodicals. And despite the virtual absence of representations of homosexuality in the mass media in the early 1950s that homophiles considered to be
objective, many in the homophile movement, determined to reach an ever
wider audience, sought attention through radio talk shows, television
news hours, mainstream magazines, and even the scores of sensationalist
tabloid magazines and pulp exposes sold at corner drugstores and bus de-
pots across the country. The activists of the homophile movement claimed
that there was a deliberate "conspiracy of silence" about the topic of homosexuality in all areas of the mass media, particularly in the more respectable venues like television news and the *New York Times*. The homophile movement struggled to break the selective silence by insisting that
the mass media begin talking about homosexuality, thereby hoping to initiate a national discussion on a topic that remained in many ways sub-
merged except when viewed as a grave social "problem."

The homophiles knew, however, that the silence was never complete
and that reporting about homosexuality constantly seeped into newspapers and magazines. The type of attention paid to homosexuality was
limited mostly to accounts of bar raids; arrests for "immoral conduct,"
murder and mayhem; or in some cases, innuendoes used to malign an individual with the taint of perversion.[6] The representation of homosexuals
was limited to portrayals of standard types: the violent dyke; the degraded
fairy; the mannish lesbian; the foppish, effete male decadent; or the relatively new Cold War invention of the homosexual security risk.[7] Homosexuals generally were portrayed either as a pitiable, dirty, and pathological underclass or as emotionally and psychologically corrupt ultra-rich.
Missing was what these activists thought was any representation that

hinted at normality—the mundane, the average, the middle class, or the patriotic.

Homosexuals in and out of the homophile movement realized that the mass media presented homosexuals as people entirely foreign to their own everyday experiences as they went to the bars, worked in businesses, held house parties, and formed lasting relationships. The homophile movement further understood that its task required action much more complex than simply raising the curtain of invisibility; it demanded a revolution in the manner in which homosexuality was represented and, hence, introduced into America's dominant public sphere. Many of the leaders thought that by building their own institutions that could speak with authority, the media would be forced not only to listen and discuss homosexuality but also to allow the organizations to represent homosexuality on their own terms and in their own language. In its struggle to build communication networks around sexual identity, the homophile movement hoped its voice in the mass media would introduce a new, surer path for the spread of accurate and unbiased information. With paved pathways of communication, the activists thought, homosexuals would be able to contact each other without going through the unknown and at times dangerous channels pursued by those in preceding decades and detailed in the introduction. Seeking to create more permanent, more direct, and safer sexual communication networks, the homophile movement nurtured and expanded the homosexual world and helped to end the isolation and invisibility suffered by so many. Yet, as would become clear, the agenda of building stable, authoritative, candid, and public networks ran counter to much of what had been definitive of queer culture in the preceding decades. By creating such networks and inviting homosexuals or the curious to participate, they also were unwittingly asking them to change their way of being queer, which was a change that would entail both loss and gain. As a result, more than a few gay men and lesbians came to question the viability as well as desirability of a project that sought to normalize homosexuality by making it respectable, that sought to remove it from isolation by making it public, and by making the network easily accessible and intelligible instead of hidden and arcane. Thus, as *Homosexuals Today* had predicted, homosexuals as well as heterosexuals were forced to contend with "a whole new pattern of social relationships" by the end of the 1950s.

CHAPTER 1

Establishing a Homosexual Headquarters

In 1951 in the hilly Silverlake district of Los Angeles—then known to locals as the "Swish Alps"—the Mattachine Foundation was established with the intention of fostering a sense of self-esteem, equal rights, and group consciousness among gay men and women.[1] The name was arrived at following a conversation in which founding member Harry Hay surmised that the "Mattachines," mediaeval traveling performers who satirized the ruling order from behind the safety of masks, might have been homosexual. The early leadership of the foundation structured the organization according to the example provided by the cell structure of the Communist Party; according to historian John D'Emilio, this meant that "secrecy, hierarchical structures, and centralized leadership predominated" in the organization.[2] The seven founding members were to occupy an anonymous and secret "fifth order" from which they would provide leadership to the subordinate lower orders, including discussion groups. Consequently, the leadership of the organization was unknown to its base rank-and-file participants.[3]

Rather than dictated by fiat, the policy of secrecy was based on perceived need. Hay and the others agreed upon a secretive structure because, like the Communist Party, the Mattachine founders were proposing some very bold ideas, ideas that if exposed to a wider public almost certainly would have attracted the unwanted attention of media and law enforcement.[4] The program of the Mattachine Foundation was quite varied during its brief existence, but it hinged upon a few key ideas, including that homosexuals were a separate people and should form communities and organize for equal rights along the same lines pursued by ethnic and racial groups. At the heart of their agenda, however, was the simple notion that before accomplishing such goals, they must first help isolated homosexuals connect to the larger gay world. This sentiment was reflected in the pledge written by Hay and to be recited by new recruits to the group: "We are sworn that no boy or girl, approaching the maelstrom of deviation, need make that crossing alone, afraid and in the dark, ever again."[5] The Mattachine Foundation, then, set out to solve the pressing problem of isolation and thus enable the creation of a connected group of people who might one day mature into a social movement.

The emphasis of the Mattachine Foundation, however, on secrecy in the very structure of the organization rendered the entire project problematic. As members of the early discussion groups were speaking in some cases for the first time about their lives as self-acknowledged homosexuals, the discussions themselves were taking place in an environment defined by secrecy, anonymity, and consequently, the threat of exposure. Not only was the organization's leadership unknown to the number of individuals participating in discussion groups (Were they movie stars? Were they Communists? Was it the FBI?), but even while sitting face-to-face and talking about very personal problems, many participants used pseudonyms or engaged in other practices to hide their identity from others in the group.[6] If asked, those attending the meetings would have been hard pressed to identify the links in their network; they would have had little idea who was involved and how many. It was a network empowered by its apparent security because of its secrecy, but it was enfeebled as well by its reliance upon the faith of its members and the strength of the few links holding the group together. For those who mustered enough nerve to attend meetings, there was a real degree of uncertainty whether the gathering in a private household might be raided by the police—an action that law enforcement officers actually carried out on at least one occasion acting on the rationale that such gatherings were illegal, much as was the public congregation of homosexuals in drinking establishments.[7]

The concerns of the rank-and-file participants became even more pronounced when a Los Angeles newspaper pointed out that the leadership of the organization was difficult to locate and that the treasurer was nowhere to be found.[8] The newspaper article not only raised fears of financial abuses but also introduced the specter of political subversion with the suggestion the group could grow to become a powerful voting bloc and then "a well-trained subversive could move in and forge that power into a dangerous political weapon." Not surprisingly, this made many participants nervous and fearful of the possible public exposure of their sexuality, not to mention the possible taint of subversion, an additional difficulty many participants did not want to take on.

About a year after its founding, many of those who attended Mattachine Foundation discussion groups came to the conclusion that secrecy might be as much a liability as an asset, that continued secrecy within their organization perpetuated rather than alleviated their own invisibility and isolation. Fueled by fears about financial improprieties and anti-Communist hysteria as well as by a critique of the secretive and nondemocratic structure of the organization, participants demanded accountability. The leadership consented by calling two general conventions, in April and May 1953. After fears were given voice at the conventions, new leaders emerged and the founding members, chastened by accusations of political subversion, agreed to disband, handing the membership lists over to the new leaders. Despite its raucous and ignoble birth, within a few months the new Mattachine Society took up where its predecessor had left off. The central activity of the reorganized group would be to create a visible presence of homosexuals through an organization whose leadership would be known publicly, easily accessible, and accountable for their actions.

Building the Bridge of Communication: The *Mattachine Review*

Insurgent groups often write their history to justify their actions. With the founding leadership and the foundation itself gone, the newly elected leadership of the society set out to create its own mandate—one in part formed in reaction to what they determined to be the shortcomings of the founders. Issued by the "publications committee" of the reorganized Mattachine Society in 1953, the "Brief History of the Mattachine Movement" declared: "As the Mattachine movement grew, it became apparent that a secret and nondemocratic society was proving too great a hindrance to accurate and adequate communication between the lowest 'order' and the fountainhead of command."[9] Noting that "it was the task of the lowest 'order' to organize and sponsor the discussion groups [and that they also] furnished the labor for the mailing committee and . . . gathered and forwarded to the Foundation the donations collected in the discussion groups," the document argued that "a new democratic and nonsecret society was very much needed."[10] Communication among homosexuals and between homosexuals and the larger society was paramount to the society's self-conception.

In the months immediately following the dissolution of the foundation and the ascendancy of the society, the newly elected officers attempted to wrangle the organization into shape. Meeting monthly prior to the next scheduled convention in November 1953, the leadership evolved and created several area councils and many chapters within the different councils. The area councils nurtured leadership in locations other than Los Angeles, especially in the San Francisco Bay Area, which became the second-largest council after Los Angeles. Even in Los Angeles, the home of the coordinating council, major changes were underway. Ken Burns, the first chair of the Mattachine Society Board of Directors, looked back on the previous year in May 1954, recalling "a series of resignations that have immeasurably hampered the functions of the Council and Board."[11] The few resignations not precipitated by conflicts of personality were attributable to the endemic lack of expertise among volunteers or their unwillingness to publicly identify with the society, which was attempting to pursue a very public profile. If those stresses were not enough, news that Federal Bureau of Investigation officers had questioned the society's legal counsel about the organization sent many early members running for cover.[12] Ultimately, with the rise of leadership in the area councils and a great deal of turbulence on the Los Angeles–dominated board of directors, the society witnessed the emergence of a strong northern California contingent in its leadership. The kind of leadership that appeared in San Francisco accounts for the eventual dominance of the northern wing in the society. Already playing a role in Mattachine politics when the foundation disbanded and the society organized, Harold "Hal" Call became increasingly involved with the organization as the summer passed and the November 1953 convention neared.

Born in Missouri in 1917, Hal Call remembered his two earliest passions as being his sexual desire for other boys and his pursuit of the printer's craft.[13] After earning a bachelor of arts degree in journalism at the University of Missouri, Call worked at several newspapers in that state before purchasing a daily paper in Colorado in 1948, which he ran as publisher until 1950. Returning to Missouri in 1950, Call joined the advertising department of the *Kansas City Star* and soon after was sent to Chicago to manage their accounts. As they would at many points later in his life, Call's two passions—for men and for publishing—converged, initially exacting rather dire consequences. While working for the *Star* in Chicago in 1952, Call was arrested for public indecency and promptly fired from his job. Remembering the beauty of San Francisco from his days serving in World War II—and emphatically, he remembers, not "because it was some kind of gay mecca"—Call left his home state and went out west to start his life anew.[14] Call arrived in San Francisco in the fall of 1952 and soon found a job as a copywriter for an insurance company.

In February 1953, however, Call made a discovery that would change his life. Participating in the face-to-face and word-of-mouth networks available to homosexuals at the time, Call learned of the Mattachine Foundation. "We heard about it from other gays," Call remembered. "We heard about it from gay students and through the gay bars and so on that were existing in San Francisco and in the Bay Area at the time."[15] Claiming that there "was no formal organization" at the time, the Mattachine Foundation he first encountered was an informal discussion group where "people came . . . and talked. [I] knew some gay students and they knew other gay students and they'd get together, fifteen or twenty of them maybe, in a dormitory room or some housing facility and just talk about their homosexual orientation."[16]

Within a few months of first learning of the Mattachine Foundation, Call began to discover some shortcomings of the organization. It was in this context that his homosexuality and his vocation as a journalist again converged. Years later he recalled, "[As] a journalist and a public relations man . . . I felt that education and getting the word out was the best thing we could do, so the whole society could ultimately say, 'Homosexuals are human beings in our midst.'"[17] Linking publicity with the fate of homosexuals, Call possessed a grand vision, but one that put him at odds with the leadership of the foundation era. Call attended both the April and May 1953, Mattachine constitutional conventions, and he sided with rank-and-file members who were demanding a more democratic organization—as well as demanding that the group distance itself from any suspicion of Communism that might threaten the legitimacy of their cause.[18] So, when the foundation folded in May 1953, Call was among the leaders who provided direction within the revamped organization.

Not surprisingly, during the summer months of 1953, as the society was coming into its own, Call brought together his two passions to help form a chapter to focus specifically on publications. As leader of the publications chapter, Call clearly positioned himself to take an active role in the leadership so he could push the organization toward a greater public role. By August 1953, the publications chapter issued a newsletter. And by the end of the summer, it had drafted a document detailing the aims and principles of the society that emphasized, first and foremost, education of the general public and of homosexuals "to correct . . . bigotries and prejudices resulting from lack of accurate information regarding sex variants"—a strategy that would give a central role to publications and public relations.[19] At the November convention, Call was elected to the vacant post of chair of the publications committee, further signaling the gradual migration of power from Los Angeles to San Francisco as well as setting the tone for the society's future activities.

Attending his first Mattachine Society convention in November 1953 was a twenty-seven year-old insurance company employee named Don Lucas. Lucas was born in rural Colorado in 1926.[20] His father abandoned the family when Lucas was an infant, leaving his mother to fend for him and his brother, who was disabled by cerebral palsy. For a time, Lucas even made his room in an abandoned railroad boxcar. He did experience occasional breaks in this hardscrabble upbringing, as he remembered traveling to Denver with his mother when he was a boy and being amazed at the magic that city life seemed to offer at every corner, whether it was electric streetcars or elevators. Part of the magic was the grandeur and beauty of such thrilling places, a sense that was especially heightened after he visited San Francisco in 1943. Recalling the visit, Lucas said, "It was just beautiful . . . at Powell and Market, this great big sign for Camel Cigarettes with the smoke billowing out of the billboard . . . these things were so incredible to me."[21] Perhaps it was the stark contrast between his spare domestic life and the wizardry he witnessed in the cities that piqued his interest in the performance of illusion. Community historian Paul Gabriel pointed out that performing the "illusion of conformity" was the defining dynamic of Lucas's life.[22] So, while he was attending junior college in Pueblo, Colorado, learning to become an accountant, he also was studying to become a magician. After living in Tacoma, Washington, where he was first introduced to the "gay world," Lucas moved to San Francisco in 1949. Within a few years, Lucas, like Call, learned of the Mattachine Society by word of mouth. He was immediately attracted to an organization where he could both meet other homosexuals in a safe environment outside the bars and assist other homosexuals with the problems they encountered living in a homophobic society. Combining his interests like Hal Call, Lucas brought his desire to care for people in difficult situations with his interest in illusion to the Mattachine Society. While working in the organization in the 1950s and 1960s he helped to develop the organization's program of presenting images of respectable homosexuals to the American public while behind the scenes providing specialized services for homosexuals, many of whom participated in what authorities at the time called deviant behavior.

Even as energetic, capable young volunteers like Call and Lucas were climbing on board, the society seemed to be in a steep nosedive. Throughout 1953 and into 1954, as the foundation transitioned to the society, membership in the organization declined, and many leaders bolted. Reflecting on the situation, the vice-chair of the San Francisco Area Council noted in

February 1954, "The greatest single thing that has abetted the dereliction to duty of so many members and the lethargy extant throughout the entire Society has been the breakdown of communications between members of the Coordinating Council, Area Council and Chapters." Like homosexuals not associated with organizations, those in the Mattachine Society encountered difficulties as they strove to establish an organizational network. However, the Mattachine Society's difficulties might also be attributable to the fact that their network (on the surface at least) would be built upon social work and an untested political agenda rather than the more common homosexual networks associated with leisure and sexual behavior. Seeking a solution to the organization's problems, the leader suggested, "that a Society Journal issued once monthly to all members of the Organization would do much to assist in this feeling of belonging and establish definite communicative contact."[23]

In his address to the 1954 society convention, chair Ken Burns concurred that communication within the organization must be improved for its survival. He also noted, "We have all realized the value, from an educational and public relations standpoint, of publicity."[24] Yet, up to that point, the society had only published intraorganization materials such as the chapter newsletters. Call knew that publishing newsletters for the benefit of their membership and working with journalists deaf to the struggles of homosexuals were inadequate to the job. Call later noted:

> We as homosexual individuals . . . never had the clout . . . we needed to . . . make the information service in our culture aware of us and the seriousness of what we were faced with. . . . So I knew that . . . as a homosexual person I couldn't go to one of the four daily newspapers in San Francisco and state the situation and what we were trying to do and have them write a sensible article about it. No, it was going to be turned out, if anything, as a sensationalized sexual and sexually emphasized kind of thing that pointed us out as deviants . . . and breakers of the law.[25]

Not only were homosexuals denied objective representation in the mass media, they lacked a reliable means to communicate with each other. Although some gay men and lesbians were remarkably adept at building and maintaining relationships across great distances and in sharing treasured and perhaps illegal information, the obstacles of distance and scale remained. Consequently, in the early 1950s the lines of communication employed by homosexuals often were hidden, subtle, and quite temporary. Call and the publications committee hoped that publishing a magazine would begin to change all that.[26] "We had to have a public relations voice," Call remembered, "We had to have the *Mattachine Review*."[27]

Having already praised Call's publications chapter for producing "publications which have proved of such excellent quality and value to the Society, its members and those interested persons outside of the Society," Burns made it clear that the northern branch of the society would take the lead in this department.[28] At the annual convention in May 1954, the membership approved a motion that the board of directors "authorize the publication of a Mattachine Magazine."[29] Publicity—including both publications and public relations—was fast becoming the society's key activity. So, as Call continued as chair of the publications committee and headed the publications chapter, San Francisco began to move to the fore, becoming the hub and workhorse of the organization. The society's leadership signaled that it was pursuing the goal of building nationwide sexual communication networks.[30]

For a struggling organization to create a magazine from scratch not only required a great deal of ambition but also an immense amount of work. "Time passed, and with it planning continued," Call reported. "Leads to interesting material were explored. Prospective lists of potential subscribers were compiled" and "production problems were being tackled, too."[31] The major "production problem" was how the society would create, compose, publish, publicize, and distribute a magazine on a shoestring budget. Call and six other members in San Francisco, including Don Lucas, came up with the solution of purchasing a press and setting up a printing firm, which they did in October 1954. The seven members dwindled to four and latter shrank to two, but the venture—named Pan-Graphic Press—was off the ground.[32] Located on the same floor of the building at 693 Mission Street as the San Francisco Mattachine offices, Pan-Graphic printed the vast majority of the society's published material; but it was distinct in that it was not owned by the society. Instead, the company was held independently by Call and Lucas.[33]

The first item Pan-Graphic Press printed in anticipation of the forthcoming magazine was called *Mattachine Review Extra.* In December 1954, a run of 2,500 copies of the teaser issue was printed and copies were "distributed to addresses in every state and 15 foreign countries" with the goal of generating excitement as well as subscriptions.[34] The fact that the first printing totaled 2,500 copies suggests that a rather sizable homosexual network already existed, that there already were thousands of homosexuals connected to a hub and that within a few links they could be connected to one another. So, rather than building a network from the ground up with this publication, the Mattachine Society sought to modify and expand the extant network in numerous ways, perhaps the most notable being to establish institutional permanence.

The publications chapter, however, was not overwhelmed with replies from this first mailing. Explanations for this are many, but one of the most likely reasons is that the individuals who first received the mailing were those already somehow participating in sexual communication networks (many likely already subscribed to *ONE* or to the European homophile press); they were the individuals who did not necessarily require the lifeline of information that would enable them to make sense of their affections and attractions and that would help them articulate a response to societal prejudices. In other words, those individuals on the Mattachine Society's mailing list in late 1954 already were caught up in the web of information distributed about homosexuality. Moreover, it is likely that prior to gaining access to the more formal networks through which published information was distributed, these individuals had participated in the more informal gay worlds centered around bars, bathhouses, and house parties and those networks provided what in reality most gay men were seeking, camaraderie and sex. For the Mattachine Society to elicit greater interest, they would have to reach those individuals who initially were beyond reach.

The *Mattachine Review* first appeared on 2 February 1955 and immediately became the chief method by which the Mattachine Society communicated with its members, with homosexuals around the country, and with the larger American public sphere. Various chapters had been producing newsletters since the summer of 1953 with the intention of informing members about the goings-on of the society. The *Mattachine Review*, on the other hand, was published with a much wider audience in mind; in fact, according to Call, all American adults would have benefited from reading the *Mattachine Review*. The initial impact of the magazine is difficult to measure. Call suggested that the task they set forth of influencing societal opinions was difficult because "our lives are 'plastered' with newspapers, magazines and books at every turn," because it was difficult to get one's voice heard in an information-saturated culture. Yet, despite such challenges, Call persisted because of his opinion that the long-term "prestige of the organization, as well as the measure of the Society's value as a public service group, may well stand or fall on what is included in each issue of the Review."[35]

Throughout the twelve years that the *Mattachine Review* was publishing, the society's leaders constantly encountered difficulties as they struggled to produce the magazine, distribute it to readers, and increase the size and scope of the communication network they were building through the magazine. The problems were evident early on, including the most basic: money. Under the headline "Income Must Be Increased," the publications chairman reported in 1955, "The financial situation . . . is serious, indeed."[36] Those working on the *Mattachine Review* hoped that not only would subscriptions and newsstand sales increase but that donors would come forward and help subsidize the magazine. Aside from attracting the grace of a financial angel, increasing the distribution of the magazine was the primary concern of the publishers. Not only would more sales generate revenue, but increased distribution would help accomplish the ultimate goal of building robust communication networks. In a letter to all members of the society before the first issue appeared, Burns stated, "Our goal . . . is to enlist every member's support in the Mattachine magazine. If this project is to succeed, all of us must not only subscribe . . . but we must get our friends to subscribe."[37] Similarly, one of the publication chapter members, Chal Cochran, wrote, "The subscribers by and large will be in our own group throughout the country."[38] Although a large membership and subscriber base was a goal, leaders soon discovered that most individuals participated only for a few months or years and then moved on, treating the organization as a source of information and an entrée into the larger gay world rather than as a base model for creating a new gay world.

The organization and the magazine, then, was serving the larger goal of helping to build large and stable communication networks, but it experienced difficulty with the more immediate aim of keeping the organization afloat and the magazine in print. Given this situation, the membership of the organization would remain a fraction of the several million homosexuals the literature suggested it represented. Moreover, the active membership and the number of subscribers to the magazine also would be a fraction of the number of people who knew of the organization and had benefited from its services or the information provided in its magazine.[39] So, to reach an ever-wider audience and gain income from a larger distribution, the society would have to look beyond simply building a vast membership; it would have to spread the magazine to a correspondingly wide circle of individuals who might never become members and who would find the magazine of value even after finding their way into the gay world. The earliest plan for an expansive distribution network was to utilize the face-to-face networks already extant within the society. Cochran suggested, "Each Area should have in it a member picked for his desire to work and ability to represent the magazine as a Circulation Manager." He concluded, "Arrangements for the placing [of] the Review on the newsstands are very important."[40] A portion of the 2,200 copies of the *Mattachine Review*'s first issue went to a few initial subscribers while the vast majority were sent as complimentary copies to potential subscribers and professionals whose attention the society hoped to attract. In addition, about 200 copies were distributed to newsstands in San Francisco, Berkeley, and Oakland with the goal of reaching a wider public. Area councils in Los Angeles, Chicago, and Long Beach, California, were each given 25 copies for the ostensible purpose of placing them in newsstands in their cities.[41]

Reading the *Review* in the Mid-1950s

Readers of the first official issue of the *Review* would have discovered in it something unique in the universe of information about sexualities. Particularly if the reader was unfamiliar with *ONE* magazine, which first appeared in early 1953, or with Donald Webster Cory's *The Homosexual in America* (1951), the *Mattachine Review* would have been almost completely incomprehensible in its subjective approach to homosexuality and in its demand that "sexual variants" enjoy the same rights as other Americans. Many readers of the *Mattachine Review* today see it as hopelessly conformist and even apologetic. Yet to read the *Review* with a critical, post–gay liberationist, post-Stonewall sensibility is to read it in a manner quite different from the way that most gay men would have read it in the 1950s. The prevailing discourse on homosexuality in the 1950s was either silence or hostility, and any conformist and self-loathing rhetoric that made its way into the *Review* would no doubt have seemed mere background noise to homosexuals in the 1950s. Accustomed to reading against the grain for the faintest hint of objectivity or affirmation in the mainstream media, gay readers of the *Review* would have been surprised by the surfeit of content that defended homosexuality, not troubled by the occasional negative reference that would merely have seemed ordinary.

Instead of closing the covers of the magazine and feeling a sense of disappointment, then, it is likely a gay man or lesbian picking up the magazine's first issue in 1955 would have read the following before setting it down: that California's vagrancy and public lewdness statutes were "an anachronism of medieval law and a menace to civil liberties," in the words of a prominent Los Angeles attorney; that, according to psychoanalyst Robert Lindner, organizations devoted to finding equality for homosexuals had a good chance of success; that one of the nation's eleven "transsexuals" spoke to a Mattachine discussion group in San Francisco about gender identity; and that, according to a report by Evelyn Hooker, "Homosexuality is not a *distinct* clinical identity," meaning that homosexuality per se does not constitute a distinct pathology.[42] Moreover, readers of the first issue would have been introduced to information about homophile organizations around the globe, addresses and activities of local chapters, and letters to the *Review* originating in six states around the United States.

In its first two years of publication, the *Review* devoted considerable space to changes in sex laws, reviews of new and classic books on sex variation, and discussions of employment discrimination against homosexuals. It also ran an incredibly prescient essay by "Carl B. Harding" introducing the radical political strategy of 'coming-out,' in which a gay man would take "concrete social action [that] can include informing carefully chosen individuals [about his homosexuality]. He can then feel himself a part of the total movement to build a world human brotherhood . . . [for] it is far more practical for each homosexual to light a candle than talk about the darkness" (fig. 2).[43] Readers of the *Review* got a sense of the larger gay world through the articles published, as well as through other elements of the magazine. Perhaps most noteworthy among these were the letters to the editor. By the end of the second year, the *Review* had published letters from twenty-two states, the District of Columbia, and Puerto Rico as well as seven countries, including Israel, the Netherlands, and Canada. Contained in the letters from gay men in the United States and abroad was a resounding confirmation of the society's goals. One man from Australia wrote, "One article in particular . . . was of help to me in overcoming the difficulty of being a homosexual. . . . But I have gone a long way since then. It is, in fact, because of the inner security which I now have that I am willing to extend a helping hand to others, if asked. Out of anguish and suffering comes compassion."[44]

Coming to expect reassuring words about homosexuality in the *Review*, readers might also have become more sharply aware of what would later be called homophobic discourse. At the beginning of 1956, one reader from New York wrote to the *Review's* editor, critiquing him for publishing an article by psychologist Albert Ellis in the November–December 1955 issue: "I had thought you acknowledged [homosexuals as] human beings, as individuals whom you were fighting for the rights of . . . Now I see that all you are doing is poking fun . . . and using us as a target for further ridicule by the public in general." He concluded, "We are not sick and don't ask treatment; we seek only understanding that we are humans as are the rest. Our sexual desires are part of our nature."[45] Between its covers, the *Mattachine Review* created a rarely before seen discrepancy: by placing a discussion of homosexual pathology (which most readers were used to) alongside paragraphs demanding full equality for homosexuals (which were new to most readers), many readers would have seen for the first time the

mattachine REVIEW

AUGUST 1956

In This Issue

Dr. Kinsey
on the Clarification of
Homosexual
TERMINOLOGY

Whom Should We Tell?
by Carl B. Harding

LUTHER ALLEN:
MORALITY versus the MORES

PLUS: ITALIAN PENAL CODE: a study in evolution
HOMOSEXUALITY: a challenge in modern America
LETTERS QUOTES BOOK REVIEWS

2 In this August 1956 edition of the *Mattachine Review,* member Carl Harding asks the novel question, "Whom Should We Tell?" Image courtesy of the GLBT Historical Society, San Francisco, CA.

juxtaposition of a counter discourse and a dominant discourse on homosexuality. The contrast between the two not only shocked gay readers with a new, progay point of view but also raised their ire to initiate a critique of unfair representations of and conclusions about homosexuals. Ultimately, it was the marked disparity in viewpoints that gave birth to a kind of homosexual political critique that might be called representational politics.[46] Moreover, the counter discourse and its defense facilitated the institutionalization of the homophile's sexual communication networks. And it provided readers with the tools to take such critiques out of the imaginary world built by a community of readers and into the everyday world in which they lived, attended churches, visited psychiatrists, worked at jobs, read the paper, and visited bars.

Struggling with Publicity

By September 1955, Call reported to the society's board that "newsstand growth had been rapid [for the *Mattachine Review*]."[47] The distribution of the magazine increased steadily during its first year of publication, climbing from about 1,000 copies with its first issue in February 1955 to over 4,500 copies for its September–October issue of the same year. Although the magazine was conceived at least in part as a journal for members, subscriptions—not all of which came from members—accounted for a mere fraction of the circulation. While subscriptions rose from 285 to 391 as 1955 elapsed, newsstand sales grew from about 1,700 to over 3,000 during the same period. This large jump was primarily due to a regular order of 2,000 copies of the *Review* from Periodical Distributors of Greater New York, which distributed the magazine to many newsstands in the mid-Atlantic region.[48] In addition to Periodical Distributors, Mattachine was building an expanding network of newsstands willing to stock the magazine: from the few that carried the first issue grew a network of twenty-three newsstands in fourteen different cities that carried the fifth issue nine months later.[49] The Mattachine Society offered retailers a handsome deal to stock the magazine, but newsstands were taking a risk by carrying it. In New York City in 1955, for instance, licensed newsstands were not permitted to sell *ONE* magazine, the somewhat more political homophile magazine published by One, Inc., in Los Angeles, and there was fear that "action may be taken to outlaw [the *Review*] because of [its] subject matter."[50] Despite potential problems, by 1956 the publishers of the *Review* understood clearly that selling to the widest public possible in easily accessible sites across the country was the one way that word of the society and its message would spread.

And, indeed, word of the society did spread. As early as 1954, the San Francisco chapter of the Mattachine Society experienced a backlash as it was embroiled in a flare-up of intolerance spurred by sensationalistic local newspaper reports that homosexuals were becoming too visible in the city.[51] Similarly, an article "authored" by the chief of the San Francisco Police Department's Sex Crimes Squad in the May 1955 issue of *Men* magazine pointed out, "The homosexuals, men and women, have their own organized group. It is called the Mattachine Society, incorporated in California on March 23, 1954."[52] After reciting several examples of the homosexual's putatively causal role in urban disorder, the article closed with the statement that as long as the Mattachine Society was "dedicated to the betterment of sexual deviates," the vice squad would continue its "harassment program" against homosexuals.[53] As it turned out, the vice chief's warning was no idle threat. In the summer of 1954, the San Francisco Police Department and the U.S. Armed Forces Disciplinary Control Board conducted a series of high-profile raids on bars and other gay sites.[54]

A little less than a year later, on 26 May 1955, the *San Francisco Examiner* reported on a new crackdown with the headline "Police Order Renews Drive on Sex Deviates."[55] Behind this antivice drive was the formation of a coalition between the newly formed State Alcoholic Beverage Control Department (ABC) and the Armed Forces Disciplinary Control Board; working independently but simultaneously was the San Francisco Police Department, which initiated a "cleanup" campaign of its own. Along with the local press, this coalition sought to renew pressure on gay bars after a supposedly quiet period when the Board of Equalization (which later spun off the ABC) considered its hands tied because of the California Supreme Court decision in *Stoumen v. Reilly.*[56] This historic 1951 decision ruled that "mere proof that homosexuals patronized a restaurant or bar . . . is insufficient to show a violation . . . warranting the suspension of the on-sale liquor license."[57] After this ruling, law enforcement agencies did not capitulate in the battle against gay bars but instead began searching for ways around the ruling that would allow them to continue closing gay bars when they became too notorious or, perhaps, failed to pay protection.

Despite press attention on the bar raids, media coverage of the Mattachine Society and other homophile groups remained virtually nonexistent in the middle 1950s. As Jim Kepner reported in *ONE* in 1956, "The press seldom mentions homosexuals except in sordid scandals."[58] And with the Mattachine Society doing everything in its power not only to keep itself beyond the taint of scandal but also to rescue homosexuals who were so tainted, the media found little reason to pay attention to the nascent organization. Indeed, not only was the homophile movement overlooked in the mass media during this period, but all aspects of the gay world not visibly scandalous were neglected as well. Instead, the only stories that made it beyond coverage in the local press—which devoted attention to bar raids and arrests for public lewdness—were pieces on the most violent and outrageous crimes ostensibly attributed to homosexuals. For instance, in 1957, the lurid magazine, *SIR*, published the article "What Makes Fairies Kill?" The short piece told in rather sensationalistic prose the tale of Harlow Fraden's murder of his parents with poison: "Poetry-quoting, cyanide-serving Harlow Fraden has committed the most revolting crime since the homosexual horror perpetrated by murderers Leopold and Loeb," referring to the famous crime of 1924 that Alfred Hitchcock later dramatized in his film *Rope*.[59] The *SIR* article admitted that both Fraden and his accomplice, Dennis Wepman, vehemently denied that they were homosexuals; the author of the article, however, surmised that a crime as brutal as patricide could only be committed by someone as deranged as a homosexual. Whether it was the Harlow Fraden tragedy in 1957, the Beekman Hill scandal in the 1940s, or the famous case of Leopold and Loeb in the 1920s, instances of horrific violent crime resulting in murder and often attributed to unbridled homosexual drives were examples of the type of information about homosexuality available to most Americans prior to the 1960s.[60]

Meanwhile, under the cover of what it began describing as the "conspiracy of silence," the homophile movement and the Mattachine Society in particular experienced great change. Among those changes were the continued power struggles within the Mattachine Society itself. By 1956 the Mattachine offices in San Francisco were clearly the hub of Mattachine activity nationwide. Having moved into a permanent space by early 1954, Mattachine San Francisco was able to establish a stable home for its activities. In the San Francisco offices were the local chapter headquarters; the *Mattachine Review* offices; and the offices of Pan-Graphic Press and the Dorian Book Service, both of which operated as the commercial side of Call's and Lucas's movement activities. Along with providing a home for the official voice of the organization through its publications, the offices also became the command center for the society's growing public relations activities. Yet with all this activity occurring in San Francisco, volunteers were still required to clear most of their actions and the content of the publications with the society's leadership in Los Angeles, which had been presiding over an apparent decline in membership since the foundation became the society in 1953.

A battle of personalities and will ensued.[61] In the end a solution was reached that left Ken Burns as chairman of the organization but also formed the new office of president, the holder of which would preside over the day-by-day operations and decisions, including those dealing with publications. At the May 1956 convention, Don Lucas was elected the society's first president.[62] Although Burns would remain on the board until the society's annual meeting in 1957, Mattachine headquarters officially relocated to the already established San Francisco offices in January 1957. The shifting of institutional autonomy to San Francisco stabilized the direction of the organization for the next decade until its effective demise in 1967. This meant that there would now be a sustained focus on, first, getting the word out and building communication networks and, then, pioneering sexual social services, in accordance with the passions of the organization's two most visible and active leaders—Call and Lucas. The lasting effect of these two activities, as we shall see, resulted in the tying of a rather strong knot, with the creation of communication networks tugging at one end and the provision of social services pulling from the other.

Obscenity Law and the Limits of the Mattachine Network

Once the dust had settled from the events of 1956 and 1957, the future looked relatively bright and busy for Call and Lucas. Call continued in the role of publications director for several years before moving into the office of president once the society's national structure disintegrated in 1960—at which point the San Francisco chapter continued on independent of and unaffiliated with other chapters around the country. Lucas served as president for one year before settling with the new office of secretary general (patterned after the organizational structure of the United Nations) in 1958. At that time, both Call and Lucas began working full-time for Pan-Graphic Press and, by extension, for the Mattachine Society—shifting tasks was as easy as moving from one desk to another. In both pursuits, Call and Lucas focused on reorienting the ways in which people communicated about homosexuality.

One method for strengthening the lines of communication among homosexuals was to provide information about other homophile publications and organizations in the United States and around the world. This was part of Call's agenda as early as 1954, several months before the *Mattachine Review* went to press, when he placed in the San Francisco Mattachine newsletter the addresses for the six Mattachine area councils that hosted the twenty different chapters.[63] Moreover, newsletters and the *Review* referred readers to the nation's other homophile organizations and publications, first to *ONE* and then, upon its founding in 1955, the Daughters of Bilitis and its publication, which first appeared a year later, the *Ladder*. In a 1954 San Francisco chapter newsletter a reader would have found a "directory of publications . . . of interest to the homophile and the sex variant [that] are published in many European countries today"; included were addresses and subscription prices of Denmark's *Vennen*, Italy's *Sesso e Liberta*, Switzerland's *Der Kreis / Le Cercle / The Circle*, France's *Arcadie*, the Netherlands's *Vriendschap*, Germany's *Der Weg*, among others.[64]

The year 1957 marked the founding of the Dorian Book Service, a company operated by Lucas, Call, and a few others that purchased and then distributed homosexual-themed books throughout the country, both directly to readers and indirectly through established booksellers. Though Dorian was not the first service of its kind (the Cory Book Service was operating out of New York intermittently since the early 1950s), it was able to build on the increasingly large sexual communication networks instituted through the Mattachine Society. Through Dorian, homosexuals and those across the country interested in a variety of sexual subjects could gain access to virtually everything published about sexual variations whether or not the bookstores or newsstands in their communities carried such controversial material. The initial list of books included fiction such as James Baldwin's *Giovanni's Room* (1956) and nonfiction such as Robert Lindner's psychoanalytic study *Must You Conform?* (1956).[65]

In early 1960, Pan-Graphic began publishing the *Dorian Book Service Quarterly*, which listed the books available for mail order, including those published by Pan-Graphic Press itself, as well as regular articles about changes in censorship laws.[66] As a publication that did not directly represent the Mattachine Society and was not bound to its strategy of representing respectability, the *Quarterly* was a bit more aggressive than its sister magazine published on Pan-Graphic's press, the *Mattachine Review*. Much of the political bite of the *Quarterly* came through the exhaustive attention it paid to the legal dramas of obscenity and censorship staged in the 1950s and 1960s. In the first issue, the *Quarterly* outlined its objectives, including its goal "to promote a 'freedom to read' movement and combat attempts at censorship. Here, the editors will cooperate with organized community groups everywhere that are active in anti-censorship work. Our policy in this field will be clear and unwavering: adult Americans shall continue to have the right to choose freely what they shall read."[67] By the fourth issue, the *Quarterly* declared that it was in support of the Freedom to Read Citizen's Committee that had formed in San Francisco to fight new obscenity laws proposed by small bands of do-gooders.[68] Under the cover of Pan-Graphic Press and the *Quarterly*, Call, Lucas, and several others were able to engage in more obviously political activities, such as challenging obscenity laws, than they were able to do with the Mattachine Society, which they insisted maintain an unimpeachably respectable public image.[69]

By seeking to end obscenity laws and to increase the distribution of all types of material dealing with sexual and gender variance, Call and Lucas through the *Quarterly* (and, more obliquely, *Sex and Censorship,* another magazine produced by Pan-Graphic) were aiding the society in its goal of creating stable and candid communication networks. As they cleared the lanes of communication of vigilant postal inspectors and local "decency in literature" committees, information—including the message of the Mattachine Society—could be transmitted more safely and reliably. Although obscenity laws were not directly challenged through lawsuits under the auspices of the Mattachine Society, the organization did extend legitimacy to that project by providing a social and political rather than an erotic context in which literature previously considered obscene might appear. In addition, Call and a few others with whom he worked closely did push the boundaries of what was acceptable in print. Although a discussion of the extensive activities of anticensorship activists is beyond the scope of this book, it is clear that it is impossible to untangle their work from the work of more cautious activists who would seize upon the newly explored and opened linguistic fields of erotic realism and sexual education.[70]

Call's begrudging respect for the law and his reticence about allowing the Mattachine Society to be too closely associated with literature and imagery that might cross the shifting line of obscenity points us to the precise type of communication network he hoped to build through the organization. He was quite aware of the varieties of networks that linked homosexuals to one another in the 1940s and 1950s, from the intimacy of love letters and the immediacy of the bar culture and gossip to the veiled yet more expansive networks fostered by contact magazines, physique magazines, and privately printed newsletters. And while Call and others at the society had no desire to disable such networks—indeed, they encouraged them on their own terms—they did hope to augment them with something entirely different. Starting with the *Mattachine Review* and continuing with Pan-Graphic Press and the Dorian Book Service, Call worked to build a stable, authoritative, and permanent network of information exchange about homosexuality and the gay world overall and to take this network to the scale of the mass media. That this network would be something different from that which came before was well understood early on. When speaking in 1954 about the *Mattachine Review,* Call argued that the "content of the publication would be entirely of a serious nature, with no emphasis whatever placed upon the so-called 'giddy' material."[71] Such material, he thought, already had outlets in chapter newsletters, in individuals' correspondence, and in direct personal communication in gay bars, restaurants, and other places that Call and other Mattachine members themselves visited frequently. Rather, they were looking to build sexual communication networks that would achieve stability by becoming removed from the obscenity battles, from the gossip of the gay community, and from the relative isolation of small friendship circles.

The homophile project was one of adding to the communication options, but it was a difficult one because it was predicated on establishing a new language for speaking about homosexuality, a language of universality and objectivity unfamiliar to many homosexuals. The "serious nature" of the new language of homosexuality that Call and others sought to interject into the overall discourse of homosexuality came from a perspective that was, in the most general terms, middle-class, white, and college-educated. Call, as a white, college-educated journalist, apparently believed in a culturally nonspecific language as the proper basis for objective reporting, which was to be the language of the *Review* but also the ideal language in which the media would address homosexuality. Yet, this language was inherently culturebound itself and thus marginally intelligible to many persons because of reasons as profound as race or as situational as sense of humor.

Along with the limitations inherent in the new language Call and others proposed, there were other ways in which the Mattachine's network was confined. While they could publicize information about changing laws, resources available for the homophile, newly published literature, and dates and locations of meetings, they felt constrained from publishing the kind of information that gay men likely most desired: personal ads; names and locations of gay bars, baths, and cruising sites; and information about how to contact publishers of pornography (especially if the circulation figures for 1950s male physique magazines are to be believed).[72]

Near the end of 1956, Call was confronted by this desire for a more personal and sexual network by a Mattachine member. Elver Barker of the Denver chapter wrote Call suggesting that the headquarters expand its goal of connecting homosexuals across the country by working with the Pen Pals Club of New York, "a correspondence fellowship for male homophiles."[73] Barker tried to sell Call on the idea by pointing out that the club was not only "a means of bringing personal satisfaction in fellowship between persons who have things in common, but [also] a means of spreading word of the Mattachine Movement."[74] Call began his reply with his answer: "My unqualified opinion about it always has been and still is—NO." This unswerving response, though, was accompanied with an extensive and complex explanation of why he thought such an endeavor would be inappropriate. First, although a correspondence club for homosexuals per se was not illegal, a club that provided for contacts that resulted in sex or in the exchange of nude photographs or pornographic material would be; in that case the courts might see the society as a procurer and thus susceptible to both state and federal prosecution. "Our prestige would topple as though a blast had occurred at the base of whatever tall or short tower of light and confidence we have thus far constructed" if the society were to be brought into a scandal involving solicitation or pornography, Call wrote.[75] Second, Call noted that because "fear is now one of our worst enemies," many members of the society would become even more uncomfortable and "immediately deduce that their names were not safe with us, but subject to exchange . . . and being given out indiscriminately." And finally, Call suggested that the society's nonprofit incorporation status as an organization devoted to research and education might be revoked if it was discovered that it was running a correspondence club, which may have been regarded as a commercial, for-profit enterprise.[76]

Call probably exaggerated the fear of some members and he seems to have forgotten that Pan-Graphic was a for-profit enterprise, but he was right to be anxious about associating the Mattachine Society with such enterprises. One of the most salacious examples of media attention gained by the society linked the organization to personal contact agencies. In the August 1958 issue of *Man's Magazine* an article describing the "Nightmare World of the Gay Man" appeared. Martin Haver, the author, portrayed a dark and dangerous netherworld populated by homosexuals riddled by guilt and a debilitating sexual desire that was made worse by the need to keep that desire secret. Providing the example of an "Arthur B.," Haver revealed that the only way for this gay advertising executive to satisfy his raging libido was to make use of an illegal contact agency that charged exorbitant "stud fees." Immediately following that scandalous revelation, Haver turned his attention to the Mattachine Society, a "semi-secret order" that "untold numbers of hidden homosexuals have joined." He reiterated his point: "As for the Mattachine Society, little is known as to how it precisely operates. But it is known that it serves countless numbers of hidden homosexuals." The implication was clear: according to *Man's Magazine,* the Mattachine existed to serve the libidinous needs of the nation's "countless" hidden male homosexuals.[77] The society survived the accusations, likely because the reputation the society cultivated was probably of higher stature than *Man's Magazine,* a drugstore tabloid, and because many other items in the article were patently incorrect, including the notion that the society was semisecret. This article and several like it stood out in the minds of Call, Lucas, and others involved with the society, demonstrating that the forces of censorship and reaction were watching them and actively attempting to dismantle the small organization or turn it into something that they did not intend it to be.

Moreover, although Call could not have known precisely the risks associated with the contact clubs, he was cautiously astute enough to realize that such a pursuit could jeopardize the society. Not long after the *Man's Magazine* article raised the specter of sexual procurement within homophile organizations, the owners of one such "pen pal" club founded in 1959, the Adonis Male Club, and dozens of its members were arrested on federal obscenity charges. In January 1961, Jack and Nirvana Zuideveld, a married and presumably heterosexual couple from Chicago, were indicted on charges of conspiring to use the mail to send obscene materials; thirty-seven others, all of whom were members of the pen pal club, also were indicted on similar charges. Of the thirty-nine indicted, thirty-six (including the Zuidevelds) either pled guilty or were found guilty.[78] The Zuidevelds took their case to the U.S. Court of Appeals, arguing that they did not commit conspiracy because they were unaware that obscene words and images circulated through the club's membership and that suspecting the members to be homosexual was not sufficient reason for them to suspect the mailing of such materials. The appellate court, however, averred, holding "that evidence on question of whether appellants intended to participate in conspiracy to transmit obscene matters through mail, in operation of correspondence club appealing to homosexual males, was sufficient to sustain their convictions, even though there was no evidence that they sent or received obscene material."[79] Thus, the Zuidevelds convictions were upheld on the simple fact that their club catered to homosexual men and the court's opinion that they should have known better than not to suspect that these men would have circulated obscene materials, especially given the context that they were readers of physique magazines.

The leaders of the society were not primarily interested in directly challenging obscenity laws, becoming embroiled in costly court cases, or participating in the legislative process to bring about reform—though they applauded and in some cases financially supported those who did do such work. While Call and other members of the Mattachine Society thought all of those strategies were necessary and even participated in them to a wider degree than most historians have suggested, they also felt no need to apologize about the path they set out for their organization. This is especially true given the very real perils associated with incorporating gay men's pleasures of everyday life into a public communication network that would be subject to greater public and legal scrutiny.[80] So, their project focused on the construction of a stable and authoritative communication network through which accurate and unbiased information about homosexuality could travel. Although this meant that they would have to eschew some of the kind of talk gay men took pleasure in and the kind of information they would find immediately useful as they sought to make sexual connections, the Mattachine leadership was able to provide an entrée into the more immediate gay world where such talk and information (about bars, baths, etc.) circulated more freely and, not coincidently, more secretively. Moreover, their strategy was designed to ensured that the lines of communication would not be compromised and that a steady and reliable stream of information would flow to isolated homosexuals around the country and the globe.[81]

Smashing the Conspiracy of Silence

Beginning in 1958 and then, especially, in 1959, the homophile movement overall and the Mattachine Society in particular appeared to break through what they had described as the conspiracy of silence. The result was greater public exposure for homophile organizations and a radically increased scale for the communication networks built through the *Review*, Pan-Graphic Press, and the Dorian Book Service—not to mention *ONE* magazine in Los Angeles and the increasing number of male physique magazines. The Mattachine Society's first real public relations coup also was the point when the tide turned in the homophile's battle for publicity.

Arguably the first significant appearance of the Mattachine Society in the alternative media came on 24 November 1958. On that day, a two-part, two-hour program called *The Homosexual in Our Society* was broadcast on the nonprofit, commercial-free, Berkeley-based radio station KPFA. On the inside fold of the printed transcript of the program, Call noted, "KPFA has often dared to air discussions on subjects which are sometimes outright unpopular."[82] According to the society, the program on homosexuality was the first feature-length program on the subject in radio broadcasting history. Though it did not hit the airwaves until November 1958, it was in the making starting in August 1957. The program consisted of two panels: the first one featured Hal Call; Mrs. Leah Gailey, the mother of a Mattachine member; and Doctor Blanche Baker, a psychiatrist. It addressed the problems faced by homosexuals. The second panel discussed society's reaction to homosexuals and featured distinguished guests such as Doctor Karl Bowman of San Francisco's Langely-Porter Clinic.

Recorded in May 1958, the first panel eventually introduced Call, the Mattachine Society, and some foundations of its philosophy to the sizable audience of KPFA and other stations in the Pacifica radio network. At the beginning of the program, listeners learned that the Mattachine Society "is an incorporated, non-profit organization that is engaged in examining and doing something about the problems that face the homosexual in our country today."[83] Call discussed the *Mattachine Review* and how it worked to promote the goals of the organization through education of the homosexual and of society overall. Call explained that the task of education was undertaken "so that he [the homosexual] may learn what he is and understand and accept himself for what he is." Call added, "We, in this work, do not stress any idea of his having a disease, or that there is necessarily a cure for it, or that there is even a need for a cure for it." Furthermore, Call advocated educating heterosexual society that homosexuals first and foremost "*are* people, and they must be accepted and understood for what they are." Although the program's moderator was at times skeptical, playing the part of devil's advocate, ultimately she exhibited considerable sympathy not only for allowing such a subject to be aired but also for enabling the speakers to do so in their own words, free from the kind of verbal harassment leveled upon gay guests of talk shows in subsequent years and decades.

In thanking the radio station for the daring program, Don Lucas wrote, "Broadcasts such as this will certainly make our job in the Mattachine Society much easier. It will help combat some of the fear which we find to be one of our biggest problems." Lucas added that fear might most efficiently be changed "by qualified persons through the great medium of radio," by which I suspect he was referring not only to the ability of radio to reach a vast audience but by the fact that it could carry the actual voices rather than simply the words of homosexuals and their allies.[84] Throughout the 1950s, the society proclaimed itself an organization of experts devoted to the problem of homosexuality, yet its leaders knew such a self-proclamation of authority would remain tenuous until society began regarding them as such. Not until the mass media, beginning with KPFA, started calling on the society to speak on behalf of homosexuals could homophiles claim an authoritative position and thus compete with heterosexual psychologists and jurists for the powerful position of expert.

While Pacifica's KPFA was clearly on the fringes of mass media, with its small network and unapologetic leftist leanings, it also was respected for its pioneering coverage of controversial social movements, which anticipated the appearance of such topics in the mainstream media. The larger distribution of information about the society through the established channels of the mass media portended important consequences for the future of the organization, the homophile movement, and eventually, the social organization of sexuality. Call reported halfway through 1958 that "the effect of this greater willingness to bring sex problems into the open is now more evident than ever," resulting in both an increase in Mattachine-sponsored public forums and in the formation of new programs designed to help the homosexual "along the lines of Mattachine aims and principles."[85] And though they would continue speaking for themselves through their own publications, the circulation of which remained steady through the late 1950s and early 1960s, it was their entry into the mass media that signaled real change—even if it was an ambiguous advance. In fact, as early as 1955, the gay author James Barr Fugate commented to the society on the occasion of the *Review*'s first issue about the treachery of entering into a compact with the mass media: "What you, and your vehicle of expression, will become is up to your collective wisdom. Whether, in twenty years, you become fresh or pedantic, effective or powerless, a guide or a pawn, is up to you. You are in the enviable position of controlling your own destiny—a position too few of us can dare to covet these days." He concluded with a prescient admonition:

> The list of your antagonists seems interminable. Not only must you face collective prudery and individual short-sightedness, but perhaps, more acutely, you will feel at times as if you are being swamped in the great commercial figures cut by your slick-coated Big Brothers such as *Life* and *Look* and similar magazines, which, as Leslie Fiedler says, "reduce all events through the camera lens to the same values and consequences—the monotone of spectacle."[86]

"The monotone of spectacle" is perhaps as good a phrase as any to describe the events of 1959. The year opened with increasing publicity about both homosexuality and the Mattachine Society. The society had recently started advertising its public forums not just by word of mouth or to its membership but to the entire interested public. It submitted short announcements to newspapers like the *San Francisco Chronicle*, student newspapers like the *Stanford Daily*, and the *Sun-Reporter*, a paper owned by a black civil rights leader and read largely by San Francisco's black population, thus reaching out into diverse populations throughout the Bay Area.[87] While publications as divergent as the *Village Voice* and *On the QT* in the first half of 1959 devoted several column inches to homosexuality—with the latter containing much accurate information about the society—the society itself was preparing feverishly for its sixth annual convention, to be held in Denver, Colorado.[88] The five previous conventions had been mostly inward-looking, dedicated either to addressing changes within the organization or to listening to speeches by sympathetic researchers and professionals. The hosts of the Denver meeting, however, were looking outward as they sought media attention. Elver Barker, known to many at the time as Carl B. Harding—a pseudonym he used because he worked in public schools—was an early member of the society when he lived in Oakland from 1953 to 1956. Barker headed back to his original home in Denver, though, after being fired from his job when his superiors learned he was gay.[89] Keeping in close contact with his friends from the Mattachine Society in San Francisco, Barker acted quickly to set up an area council in Denver and to start a new local chapter. Excited by the prospect of holding the annual convention in his hometown, Barker introduced what he called several "'radical' proposals" that would involve "certain steps some members have feared to take in the past."[90]

All of Barker's proposals focused on garnering publicity for the convention. Barker sought out attention from all the local newspapers as well as major radio and television stations in Denver. Not only did he wish to alert them to the presence of the society by distributing its published "Aims and Purposes," but also he was going to invite newspaper reporters to attend public sessions where Mattachine officers and friendly experts would present their findings. In addition, he hoped to hold a news conference at the conclusion of the convention featuring members willing to speak using their real names. Sensing that there might be some resistance to implement these proposals, which Barker submitted for approval to the board, he offered the following argument: "Only by an educational program aimed directly at the general public can our organization help abolish prejudice and halt discrimination in employment and other areas of life."[91] Although he recognized "an element of risk" in this approach, he also believed "that if such publicity were accepted by newspapers, radio and TV, it would be handled by those media in an objective and respectful manner."[92] From the public relations work that followed, it is clear that Barker persuaded the Mattachine Board to follow his plan.

Shortly after the conclusion of the convention, which ran 4–7 September 1959, ONE magazine reported, "The American homophile movement took a great stride forward toward maturity with the Mattachine Society's Sixth Annual Convention." ONE further noted that "the most surprising gain was in the matter of publicity" because of the Denver group's "effective publicity campaign." So effective, in fact, was the campaign that along with the press coverage, the Denver chapter received a number of inquiries about membership and participation. And, vindicating Barker's optimistic presumption about objective media coverage, ONE claimed,

"The result was a full and fair coverage of the convention"—indeed, that "the press coverage was revolutionary."[93]

Although those words came from the October 1959 issue of *ONE*, they were certainly written prior to 7 October. On that date, press coverage of the convention shifted from descriptive to sensational as the *San Francisco Progress*, one of the city's many neighborhood newspapers, issued the shocking headline: "Sex Deviates Make S. F. Headquarters." What followed was a classic election-time scandal report—with a twist. An upstart challenger for the mayor's office, Russell Wolden, accused the current mayor, George Christopher, and his chief of police, Thomas Cahill, of allowing San Francisco to "become the national headquarters of the organized homosexuals in the United States." The accusations contained in the article did not end there: in addition to mentioning the flourishing gay nightlife in the city—bars, night clubs, hotels, and steam baths—Wolden had an ace in the hole that provided supposed proof for his claims. According to an official publication of the Mattachine Society, which the *Progress* reproduced, San Francisco was the "national headquarters" of this organization of "sex deviates." Furthermore, the *Progress* reported that, at its recent convention in Denver, the society unanimously passed a resolution "recognizing and expressing its appreciation to Mayor George Christopher and Police Chief Thomas Cahill."[94]

That same evening, Wolden himself made a radio address in which he reiterated the charges made by the *Progress*, demonstrating that he was not afraid to involve himself directly in the mudslinging. Wolden began with the declaration, "I charge that conditions involving flagrant moral corruption DO exist here which still revolt every decent person," and closed with the promise, "I intend to continue to fight this evil development in our midst until these intolerable conditions are eliminated from our community" (fig. 3).[95] In between, he reiterated with rhetorical flourish the same specific charges introduced in the *Progress* article. Over the next two months, well over 100 articles appeared in the Bay Area's largest newspapers, and a great deal of radio and television air time was devoted specifically to the Mattachine Society's Denver convention. This explosion of press coverage caused reverberations that would be felt for years to come.[96]

Not long after the accusations were leveled, however, the scandal turned against its creators and ultimately blew up in Wolden's face. Not only did the city's mainstream, respectable newspapers not wish to engage in this particular form of yellow journalism, but with the help of the Mattachine Society and the Police Department, they soon uncovered that

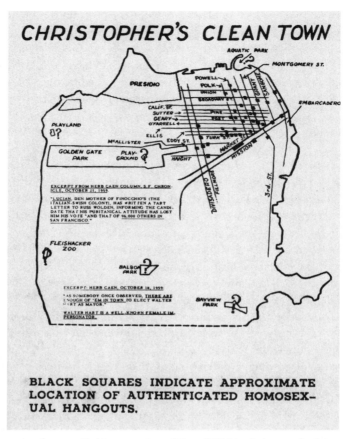

CHRISTOPHER'S CLEAN TOWN

BLACK SQUARES INDICATE APPROXIMATE LOCATION OF AUTHENTICATED HOMOSEX- UAL HANGOUTS.

3 This postcard was mailed to supporters of Russell Wolden in hopes of gaining support for his anti-vice crusade and his mayoral campaign. The postcard highlighted the locations of gay bars and other sites and thus introduced a larger public to the geography of gay San Francisco.Image courtesy of the GLBT Historical Society, San Francisco, CA.

this scandal was more manufactured than most. In fact, only a day after Wolden made the original accusations, the papers were reporting a "Mystery Man Seen in 'Smear.'" As the story grew, the public learned that a man named William Brandhove, an operative working for the Wolden campaign, had infiltrated the Mattachine Society with the express interest of stirring up a scandal—and that he himself laid the groundwork by introducing and strongly lobbying for the passage of the resolution praising Mayor Christopher. Brandhove got his way when he saw the resolution passed. Call later admitted that "Brandhove's membership was unfortunate," but the consensus of both observers at the time and those in recent decades is that Wolden made the bigger mistake.[97] In a letter explaining the situation to Wardell Pomeroy at the Kinsey Institute, Call summarized the city's reaction through the actions of the city's largest newspapers: "Two papers carried front page editorials asking Wolden to get out of the race. The third (*Examiner*) said for him to stay in so the voters could have the privilege of chopping his head off."[98] Wolden did stay in the race and, as the *Examiner* predicted, received a symbolic beheading by the voters at the polls.[99]

Once the dust had begun to settle, it was clear that the incident would be a major turning point for the Mattachine Society, the homophile movement, and the place of homosexuality in San Francisco's political culture.[100] Ultimately the newspapers were not interested in defending the Mattachine Society, for which they had no particular affection. Instead, the papers were defending the reputation of Christopher, whom they had endorsed, as well as the good name of San Francisco itself; they also hoped to distance themselves from truly sordid characters like Brandhove.[101] Still, their coverage did signal a willingness to cover the actions of homosexuals more objectively and not perpetuate the accusations. Call noted that the events marked "the first time one of our organizations has hit the news smack-dab in the middle of a city as large as this, and with such force as to bring knowledge of the society's existence home to every citizen in the community."[102] Indeed, in his first radio speech, Wolden provided listeners with very specific information about the Mattachine Society: "It operates from offices at 693 Mission Street. Pick up your telephone book. You will see the Mattachine Society . . . listed in it."[103]

In response to the dissemination of such information, many interested individuals contacted the organization. Call wrote, "The telephone has rung incessantly," and, surprisingly perhaps, "many have called seriously—to learn about the Society, and to ask for help with problems."[104] Historian John D'Emilio observed that as a result of the controversy, "it is doubtful that many gay men and women in San Francisco remained ignorant of the movement's existence."[105] Call concluded, "All in all, the Society has gained prestige from this."[106] By the end of 1959, the homophile press, which diverged on any number of subjects, concurred that the conspiracy of selective silence had been smashed and that, ironically, it was a scandal of tabloid proportions that played a key role in the shift.

For media theorist Marshall McLuhan, the mass media is defined not by "the size of their audiences" but by "the fact that everybody becomes involved in them at the same time."[107] In 1959, it would have been difficult for anybody in San Francisco not to have become involved with the Mattachine Society and the media spectacle about the city's gay world. How-

ever, beyond San Francisco and beyond readers of the homophile magazines, not only was the size of the audience not terribly large, but the
sound also was muted so that most Americans would not have heard what
happened in San Francisco.[108] Although publicity was always risky, it was
attention from the mass media that the Mattachine Society most desired.
Now more than ever, the organization's leaders were eager to gain recognition in the mainstream public sphere, feeling that this was the best way
to achieve their goals of spreading the word about the society as an organization devoted to aiding the homosexual as well as educating society
about the basic humanity of homosexuals. Whether the leaders of the Mattachine Society also were aware of their role in making homosexuality into
a public and political identity is unclear. Although homosexuality had appeared in mainstream political discourse in the past (most notably during
the investigation of the State Department for subversives in the late 1940s
and early 1950s), this spectacle and others like it reinforced the notion that
sexuality was not merely a behavior devoid of social significance. Rather,
it was something that could not be contained within the private sphere because it possessed enormous political currency that could be spent to influence people and politics.

In 1960 came the next media break that provided the society with publicity that not only spanned the country but introduced the organization
to individuals around the globe.[109] Jess Stearn, a former *Newsweek* editor,
regularly moonlighted in decidedly more marginal beats than the ones to
which the national newsmagazine generally assigned him. Already having written popular journalistic accounts of both juvenile delinquency and
prostitution, Stearn turned his attention to male homosexuality around
1959. The result of his research, a book called *The Sixth Man*, was published
in 1961 and was one of the year's top sellers, spending thirteen weeks on
the *New York Times* bestseller list.[110] Although of rather innocuous design,
the cover of the hardbound edition nevertheless promised the reader that
inside lay "a startling investigation of the spread of homosexuality in
America." A professional at sounding objective while in fact communicating very partisan opinions, Stearn's account of homosexuality in America
seemed at first glance to be fair and thus progressive for the time. A closer
examination of the prose, however, reveals that Stearn held some rather
negative beliefs about gay men even to the extent of suggesting that homophobic violence is justifiable.[111]

Although most of *The Sixth Man* detailed what Stearn saw as the alarm-
ing increase in the visibility of male homosexuals, he devoted a couple of
relatively benign chapters to the Mattachine Society. Stearn wrote, "The
Mattachine Society, a nationwide organization whose members are pre-

dominantly homosexual, asks 'sexual equality for everybody' and 'full civil rights for the world's most oppressed minority group.'" He further noted that the organization was "headquarted in San Francisco, with a charter from the state of California."[112] Recounting conversations with members in the society's New York chapter, Stearn more or less accurately summarized the views of the organization, including an observation that they were "intent on establishing that they are no different from anybody else"; that they "deplored the fact that the public automatically associated homosexuality with vice"; and that they argued "homosexuals . . . are no more of a threat to children than anyone else."[113] Clearly remaining skeptical of such claims to psychological and social normality, Stearn asked Mattachine members whether they thought they were succeeding in their goals. The quoted reply of one member accurately summarized the attitude of the society around 1960: "We feel that if we can reach a point of acceptance where we can sit down with people, like yourself, and discuss the problems of homosexuality, we have accomplished our immediate mission."[114]

Stearn, however, did not need to ask the members if they thought their message was getting out. By recounting in great detail the publicity surrounding San Francisco's 1959 mayoral election, Stearn provided the most striking example possible. Not only did readers of *The Sixth Man* learn that in San Francisco there were dozens of bars "catering almost exclusively to homosexuals" but also that the Wolden scandal had backfired in favor of the city's homosexuals and that "San Francisco's sophisticated voters gave Mayor Christopher a thumping vote of confidence at the polls."[115] "The Mattachine," Stearn continued, "feeling themselves vindicated by this reassurance of municipal government, went ahead with plans for future conventions in San Francisco."[116]

The impact of books like *The Sixth Man* and other media events was no doubt considerable. As gay scholar Jeffrey Escoffier, reflecting on the power of the popular sociology of homosexuality in the late 1950s and early 1960s, concludes, it "represented the discovery by both homosexuals and nonhomosexuals of an image of the gay social world—an imagined community," and in doing so, "closeted gay men used the popular sociology, literary, and psychoanalytic discourses to name themselves, describe themselves, judge themselves—and, by these means, to homosexualize themselves."[117] More than simply helping isolated gays and lesbians imagine an identity and community, books like Stearn's *The Sixth Man* also spatialized identity and community. By providing descriptions of places of the gay world, Stearn's stories created its geography and pointed people toward what might imaginatively be thought of as a gay homeland. So, while Stearn held much of the gay world in contempt, he quite clearly communicated that in San Francisco and New York the gay world had its own advocates and organizations that were attempting to defend and elevate the position of homosexuals in the United States and beyond.

In the early 1960s the *Mattachine Review* was continuing to reach out into the public sphere. Yet, according to statistics kept by the Mattachine Society, the *Review*'s circulation had dipped from its high point in the late 1950s. The decline in sales came at about the same time Stearn's *The Sixth Man* appeared in bookstores, and the drop continued until *The Review* ceased publication in 1966.[118] There are many explanations for why newsstand sales of the magazine declined, such as the inherent limitations of the objective journalistic language and visual presentation and the competition offered by new homophile magazines like Philadelphia's *Drum*, which not only included camp language alongside the more serious homophile rhetoric but also included male physique photographs. However, Don Lucas offered an explanation internal to the organization. According to Lucas the decline of the *Mattachine Review* at the same time as the society began appearing in the mass media was not a coincidence. "To me it just wasn't that important anymore" to spend time on the *Review*, he remembered. "Because you no longer needed to get a little magazine out to people [when information distribution] was being done on a national basis by national media by other people, whereas in the beginning, *ONE*, the *Ladder*, the *Mattachine Review* were the only ways anybody could learn anything about homosexuality."[119] Of course those who wanted to learn something about homosexuality always had more ways to access information than through the pages of homophile magazines. But Lucas was referring to a particular kind of information: the kind that was nonsensationalistic, verifiable, and widely accessible—the kind of information that was definitive of the new ways in which the homophiles sought to communicate with their own kind and the world at large.

Pioneering Sexual Social Services

Another major change, according to Lucas, was taking place within the Mattachine Society throughout the late 1950s. Not only were the organization's leaders helping the mass media to spread word in a more efficient, more widespread way than they could through their own publications, they also began working within their own organization to perform specialized functions that other social institutions were incapable of or uninterested in doing.[120] As word spread about the society, first through the homophile publications, then through local news coverage surrounding events like the annual conventions, and ultimately through publicity in the mass media, homosexuals around the country and the world did more than passively listen. Once they learned that there was an organization devoted to addressing the problems faced by homosexuals, thousands of homosexuals per year with such problems deluged the society's offices with often desperate requests for help. In what may have been an unintended consequence, increased publicity eventually transformed the society into an organization whose main task was the provision of social services to homosexuals, a pursuit they understood to be in line with their larger project of ending social isolation. Receiving telephone calls, letters, and visits to their offices, Lucas, Call, and others at the Mattachine headquarters were confronted with an avalanche of serious, sometimes life-threatening problems that they felt had to be dealt with immediately. Like black and immigrant mutual aid societies in the United States in the late nineteenth and early twentieth centuries, the society began to address serious social problems endemic to marginalized subcultures; in the process leaders pioneered new forms of activism that simultaneously addressed the immediate problems of individuals and strengthened their communities.[121] While little of this work was explicitly legislative, it anticipated those projects through a process of discovery in which activists determined precisely what areas of everyday life required political reform: discrimination in housing, employment, civil service, and military service.

During the 1959 San Francisco mayoral race controversy, Call reported that a number of people, first learning of the Mattachine Society, contacted the organization seeking help with pressing personal problems. From the local nature of that instance, though, the scale of the contacts increased exponentially as the media's coverage broadened. On Halloween 1961, for example, buried among the piles of mail the Mattachine Society received daily was a remarkable letter. "This letter might surprise you," the writer began, "for it comes from a very distant place, the Philippines." The man, writing from Cebu City, promptly explained how he learned of the organization: "I have come to know your society, The Mattachine, for I have read the book of Mr. Jess Stearns, *The Sixth Man*."[122] The letter writer claimed that he found the book "very interesting" and that, upon learning about the Mattachine, he was "thankful that an organization thus exists." He added, "I thanked God that intellectual men are born of our sex who could represent our cause to work on the justification of our sexual desire."[123] He continued with an appeal that emphasized the uniqueness of his needs by pointing out the very different circumstances in which homosexuals in the Philippines and the United States live. He said, "Being an undeveloped country, we haven't any help centers, foundations, psychiatrists, sociologists, and homosexual societies to help and rescue us from our problems . . . I'm appealing for some donations on the working literature and publications on homosexuality." He concluded on a hopeful note, "By knowing more truth, I might generate an organization in our place and affiliate it to your own." [124] By the next summer, the man had again written the Mattachine Society, this time offering thanks. In response to the man's request for information, Don Lucas had forwarded several copies of the *Mattachine Review* and had published portions of the original letter in the *Review* for others to read. The presumably gay Filipino showed the *Review* to several of his friends in Cebu City, all of whom agreed that "the magazine runs hot cake." He concluded in his second letter, "My people come to believe the existence of such society and our fight for our right to have equal place under the sun." [125]

Although the man from Cebu City was thousands of miles away from San Francisco, his requests were relatively easy to fulfill. And while the vast majority of letters, calls, and visits received by the Mattachine Society in the wake of publicity breaks were along similar lines, an important and growing number were more desperate and urgent. As early as 1958, the headquarters offices in San Francisco were beginning to experience the onslaught of requests that would thrust the organization's communications strategy into a whole new realm. Indeed, as a result of making the organization a hub within a communication network, the leaders of the Mattachine Society soon had to contend with thousands of individuals newly introduced into the networks, virtual orphans in the gay world newly visible to them. Just as scholars of social networks would predict, these homosexuals clamored for information, contacting the resource that was most easily accessible.[126] The organization's newsletter reported that during 1958, "some 300 cases of individuals seeking various types of social service assistance were handled by the national Mattachine office." [127] The issues were diverse, including needs "for legal, psychiatric, religious and employment assistance." Furthermore, "assistance was given to persons just released from penal confinement, and from state correctional mental institutions. Many veterans and their families sought ways to upgrade discharges." The newsletter added that "there has been talk of [creating] a 'Department of Social Service' . . . however, the officers have found that the Social Service Department, existing or not, is 'very much in business' right now." [128]

The leaders of the Mattachine Society responded to requests for help in one of two ways: they provided referrals to professionals or handled the problems on their own in the organization's offices. In late 1958, setting out their procedures, the leaders wrote, "Serious problems [i.e., suicide threats] are still referred to psychiatrists and clinical psychology counselors. But many times, all the caller needs is someone who can listen sympathetically, occasionally injecting a question which causes him to see his problem in a more objective perspective."[129] From the earliest days of the society, it was clear that many homosexuals would come with problems requiring greater expertise than untrained volunteers could handle. A large number of individuals requested referrals to psychologists and others in the medical profession, not to help them find a "cure" for their sexuality but to reach a sympathetic and understanding ear. So, at the board meeting in September 1954, a "standard operating procedure for securing: medical doctors, psychiatrists, and psychologists" was adopted.[130] The procedures called for lengthy interviews with each professional, asking questions such as "What is his opinion of the Society?" and "How many of his patients are sexual variants?" A full report to the board would determine if the doctor met the "minimum standards" to receive referrals. The standards required that the professional belong to the appropriate professional association, have at least two years of practical experience, and, especially, "believe in sexual equality for the variant."[131] These qualifications, which were never officially changed once adopted, reveal a great deal about the organization: it simultaneously sought the assistance of qualified and reputable professionals yet was never willing to compromise its ideals.[132] By creating a model for the nonjudgmental administration of sexual social services and by establishing a context in which such services were demanded, Lucas and his colleagues helped to push health and mental health professionals toward accepting and depathologizing homosexuality.

Not all requests for aid, though, required referrals. Ranging "from those just 'coming out' to those who are in their declining years," many contacted the society by calling, writing, or showing up at the San Francisco Mattachine offices, which they were "invited to make full use of."[133] For some homosexuals already living in San Francisco or the Bay Area, the Mattachine Society proved to be an indispensable organization where they could go for advice and help that no other organization was either equipped or willing to dispense. The society provided legal and "lay" counseling for a wide range of problems encountered by "sexual variants," including help for gay men arrested on public indecency charges as well as individuals who simply needed someone to talk to while going through the arduous process of sexual self-discovery.[134] In addition, the organization assisted gay institutions, primarily bars, with legal and other problems.[135]

The majority of homosexuals with the most pressing, seemingly insurmountable challenges, however, were not those living in places like San

Francisco where there was strength in numbers as well as nascent institutional support. Rather, the individuals who experienced greater, though still varying, degrees of isolation, invisibility, and internalized homophobia resided in towns and regions where misunderstanding family, neighbors, police, and church severely limited options.[136] In late March 1962, for instance, the Mattachine Society received a letter from "Tom Forman," writing from Owensboro, Kentucky. He began by expressing sentiments he shared with countless others: "Yesterday I had the most pleasant surprise of my life. Namely, a friend sent me 4 back issues of your publication. Until then I never knew anything such as the 'Review' existed" (fig. 4).[137] Forman explained that discovering the magazine was important because he was "one of the 'outcasts,' as we are called here in Kentucky." He used the word with more than a hint of irony but also as an accurate reflection of what his world thought of him, as he was just returning from a six-month stay at the federal prison in Terre Haute, Indiana, for he was one of the thirty-six individuals convicted in the Adonis Male Club case mentioned earlier. His life had not improved much upon release. Forman noted in his letter that in addition to finding only menial work, he felt doomed to "live in a community where 'sex' in any form is 'Verboten' and where homo's are a completely un-wanted breed."[138] After sharing his substantial problems, he got to the point: "I would like to ask if you could guide me as just where can I go to live a peaceful, happy life . . . Would San Francisco be the place[?]"[139] In this letter, Forman invoked one of the many possible consequences of being introduced into a communication network. In addition to the exchange of information, new connections would provide the opportunity for a revised understanding of one's place within the world and, along those lines, an agenda for action, which in this case Forman entertained as movement.

Don Lucas replied immediately to the wrenching letter, supplying information that elicited another letter from Kentucky, this time with more details of Forman's life filled in. Following a strict Roman Catholic upbringing in Cincinnati, years studying for the priesthood, and subsequent military service in World War II, Forman eventually married; he claimed to have had a satisfying union for fourteen years, until, "this double life caught up with me and to prison I went."[140] Months passed and despite Lucas's help and encouragement, Forman was unable to gather the funds necessary to make the journey west. Feeling that "living in this town is like living in prison," Forman's confusion and despair worsened.[141] He added, "I sincerely hope you don't mind my writing to you this way but I'm lost, I just don't know which way to turn or to whom to turn." Pleading to the one institution he knew of to help in any small way, he added, "Please let

mattachine REVIEW

7TH ANNUAL CONVENTION

September 1-5, 1960

San Francisco, Calif.

AUGUST 1960   50¢

Theme:

"Let's Change Our Outmoded Sex Laws"

(See Back Cover; Program Inside)

4 Although the masthead made it clear the *Mattachine Review* was published in San Francisco, cover images sometimes reinforced the link between San Francisco and its homophile organizations. Image courtesy of the GLBT Historical Society, San Francisco, CA.

me hear something from out there. I'll do anything to get myself established, I can't go on living with this terrible loneliness."[142] His resolve to
do something, *anything*, was evident as he concluded his letter: "I'm going
ahead and making my plans and if I can find something to do out there I'll
go ahead and come out there."[143] Of course, by "out there" he meant "out
west" to San Francisco, a place where he suspected he could find institutional support, societal tolerance, and enough anonymity to start life anew.

In response to this desperate yet not uncommon letter, Lucas lamented
"that there have been no opportunities for you to improve your situation
there . . . or to leave that part of the country."[144] Lucas did, however, send
along the name of a contact at an employment agency in San Francisco,
adding "write to him personally and mention that I have asked you to do
so. Perhaps he will be able to advise you on the employment situation and
the likelihood of getting a lead on a job that could bring you to San Francisco."[145] Although the society did not make it a policy of actively encouraging a migration to San Francisco, it did cultivate relationships with gay
male and lesbian business people in and around San Francisco who would
be willing to assist homosexuals who decided to move to the city. One of
these gay entrepreneurs was Cliff Webb of the Paramount Placement
Agency in San Francisco. Lucas remembered that the society regularly referred such requests to Paramount Placement and other employment
agencies. In fact, from September 1961 through August 1962, the society
provided 121 work hours of job referrals—in addition to 152 hours of legal referrals, 61 hours of professional referrals, and 227 hours of 'lay' counseling. By 1964, Call claimed, the caseload was "approaching 3,000 per
year."[146] Forman, as it turned out, was but one voice of many crying out
from the nation's hinterland who was able to find his way to a hub of information and, perhaps, services. Although the society was limited in the
kind of services it could provide, it intervened in the queer communicative
world and consequently transformed it by establishing itself as a place
where homosexuals could turn and seek assistance from an institution
that at least appeared to be legitimate, solvent, and professional. In so doing, the society provided homosexuals with a support structure (no matter how unstable and miniature) that they could fall back upon as they
made forays into the world as individuals, in some cases, marked by their
sexual identities.

While it is not clear whether Forman ever made it to San Francisco, he
did send Lucas at least one more letter that indicates he was thinking very
seriously of such a move, marshalling his resources to make it a reality. On
24 March 1963, he wrote that the contact at the job placement agency in San
Francisco "stated he could place me anytime . . . [so] I think I'll be able to

make it by summer."[147] He imagined that upon his arrival in San Francisco, "it sure will be wonderful to be able to . . . be among friends. I have nothing here [in Kentucky]. No friends, no one to talk too."[148] For Forman to imagine being in a place for the first time yet feel "among friends" points to the significance of the Mattachine Society's work and the societal changes it represented.

As the reputation of the society grew and as the expertise of its staff deepened, professionals started coming to it, rather than vice versa. The importance of this change cannot be overstated for it signaled a shift in the way some psychiatrists and other professionals viewed homosexuals—no longer as deviants needing a cure but individuals marginalized by mainstream society who needed the support of their own community. Lucas, who undertook most of the counseling work, remembers that in the late 1950s professionals at the state mental institutions began realizing that nonviolent homosexuals should not be confined in their wards. Seeking to ease their adjustment to society upon release, many officials approached the society asking it to help.[149] Whether the men were released from the Atascadero or Napa State Mental Hospitals, the Letterman General Hospital on the Presidio military base, or the Rehabilitation Center in Corona, California, the Mattachine counselors, led by Lucas, approached each case on an individual basis. Easing these homosexuals back into society meant dealing with mundane yet profoundly important matters: housing, jobs, and friendships. It meant, in brief, assisting them out of literal isolation and into some sense of connection with those who were perceived to be like them.

One example shows how the society's social service activities helped the transition of the formerly incarcerated back into society. Recalling this work, Lucas mentioned one "very interesting fellow."

> He was referred to me from Napa. He lived up in Napa and he'd been in Napa State Hospital for a while, but he was a complete recluse because he was so concerned about his homosexuality. He was a janitor at night where he wouldn't run into anybody, wouldn't meet anybody, in a school, in the night. And he would never come out. So he came, he talked to me. And so I took him under my wing.[150]

Acting as this man's mentor and guide, Lucas took a slow path to introducing him to the gay world, first through conversations and then by giving him a tour of a few gay bars. "I took him to the [D']Oak Room to get him acquainted with a gay bar and hopefully introduce him to somebody and get him talking with people," Lucas recalled. "Well, eventually he went flying off on his own and just had a great time. And the last time I heard anything about him, he had formed a relationship and was very happy." Lucas added that he played this role "many, many, many times, especially . . . [for] young people, very insecure young people."[151]

With the help of the Mattachine Society, the young man from Napa and numerous others like him moved from an isolated and pathologized identity to a new identity supported by a sense of community.[152] As the Mattachine Society built stable, candid, and authoritative sexual communication networks through its own publications and its work with the mass media, the officers of the organization quickly learned that information travels in several directions on such networks. Not only would isolated homosexuals around the country discover the society—often to their amazement—but they would also contact the society with everything from their opinions to pleas for help. The pleas were sometimes so grave it was clear an individual's life hung in the balance. And though the society's leaders realized early on that part of their mission would be to address the concerns of homosexuals in need of aid, by 1958 they were beginning to realize that this would be a task of utmost importance, ultimately overshadowing almost everything else they did. What began as a struggle to reach and educate heterosexuals and homosexuals about the problems of sex variation resulted in the creation of a relatively tight and far-reaching network whose traffic included not only information but also assistance and, in some cases, people as they moved to places where they hoped to find acceptance.

The activities of the Mattachine Society, however, represented only a portion of the work done by homophile organizations nationwide, and those activities only partially reflected the somewhat separate world of lesbians in the 1950s and early 1960s. The pioneering lesbian organization founded in 1955, the Daughters of Bilitis, sought to address the concerns of homosexual women and, in turn, built communication networks in some ways parallel to and in other ways radically different from those constructed by the Mattachine Society. It is to the philosophy, tactics, and history of that organization that we now turn.

CHAPTER 2

Organizing Lesbian Connections

The small group of women who came to form the Daughters of Bilitis (DOB) first met on 21 September 1955. The idea for the group, as longtime leaders Del Martin and Phyllis Lyon later recalled, originated with a young Filipina named Marie who "envisioned a club for Lesbians here in the United States that would give them an opportunity to meet and socialize outside of the gay bars."[1] The eight founders—four lesbian couples— all agreed that establishing a social network outside of the bars was important because "women needed privacy—privacy not only from the watchful eye of the police, but from gaping tourists in the bars and from inquisitive parents and families."[2] In 1950s United States, public establishments that catered to lesbians or even merely tolerated them were few and far between. Historians who have written about lesbian bars of the period demonstrate that while the few lesbian spaces that did exist provided space for socializing and nurtured forms of resistance to the outside world, the bars were far from refuges from it.[3] Rather, the sites, mostly saloons and restaurants, were quite different from the gay bars of the 1990s and first decade of the 2000s as they were attended by many types of people other than female homosexuals; some of these other visitors might include johns seeking prostitutes, vice officers looking for violations, and tourists seeking a thrill. While a few particularly brave and brazen lesbians possessed the courage and the audacity to turn such sites into places of pleasure, confrontation, and perhaps resistance, a large population of women attracted to other women were not interested in placing themselves on stage or in harm's way. For this group of women, many of whom would continue to patronize bars on occasion, there was an unmet need for places to connect with others like themselves.

The eight lesbians who gathered that late September night sought not only privacy but also a limited and tightly controlled publicity so that other lesbians may learn of the group and choose to join. This somewhat contradictory strategy meant that the organization would regularly cross the definitional line separating the activities characteristic of a private and even secret organization from the actions typical of a public group looking to advertise its message and gain new members. As a result of such crossings, the women in the organization pursued new social practices, such as when the group discussed what to name the organization. Adhering to the privacy doctrine, the founding members chose not to use a name that would immediately identify the group as lesbian-led. Yet, most members did want the organization to be identifiable to other lesbians, possibly through a code or a double entendre. To this end, one founder suggested the Daughters of Bilitis as a possible name. The name was inspired by French poet Pierre Louys's book *Les Chansons de Bilitis* (1894), a collection of erotic lesbian verse originally published as the putative translation of a work by Sappho's lover—and it was relatively well known to well-connected lesbians in mid-twentieth-century America. Years later, reflecting on their decision to adopt the name, Martin and Lyon wrote, "We thought that 'Daughters of Bilitis' would sound like any other women's lodge—you know, like the Daughters of the Nile or the DAR," to which they added, "If anyone asked us we could always say we belong to a poetry club."[4] Inscribed in the name of the organization was its somewhat contradictory approach in which the founders were guided both by principles of publicity and privacy. In this regard, the leaders would chart a moderate path to visibility in contrast to the Mattachine Society's more aggressive publicity-seeking agenda. Moreover, as we shall see, unlike the Mattachine Society, the leaders of the DOB chose a path in which they could maintain greater control over the messages distributed as well as the avenues through which such messages could travel.

Within a month of the DOB's initial planning meetings, the visions of the eight founding members began to diverge in a few fundamental ways. Soon after the first official meeting of the group in October 1955, the initial signs of disagreement emerged when a sympathetic straight woman was invited to participate in one of the group's discussions. One founder insisted that no heterosexuals be allowed to participate while others argued that beginning a dialogue with heterosexuals was one of the group's goals. Martin and Lyon later claimed that incident "marked the beginning of a long series of arguments about rules and regulations, about the degree of secrecy we had to maintain, about mode of dress and behavior, about dealing with straights as well as gay men, about the possibility of publishing pamphlets explaining our cause."[5] Upon additional reflection, Martin and Lyon remarked that half of the founders, those who came from a working-class background, "wanted a supersecret, exclusively Lesbian social club," while the middle-class lesbians "had broadened their vision of the scope of the organization" and wanted it to take on a more public, activist stance.[6] For this organization, newly born in a cultural context rife with fears about dangerous secrets and emerging class conflict between some unmarried women striving to achieve middle-class status and others from a working-class background, the disagreements appeared fundamental and "eventually led to an ultimate rift."[7] One by one most of the founders pulled out of the organization, leaving Martin (who had already been elected the organization's first president) and Lyon as the two remaining founders to stand as the pillars supporting the virtually memberless organization.

Like the Mattachine Society, which had gone through a tumultuous reorganization two years prior, the break in the DOB centered mostly on the touchy issues of whether or not the incipient organization should cross the line from private to public and how it might be done. The two women who continued to pursue the DOB idea after the early debates, Martin and Lyon, did so because of their intense desire to end the isolation they felt as lesbians as well as to assist lesbians around the country on their own journey out of isolation. Martin and Lyon remembered their first entry into the lesbian world as compromised by an utter lack of information. "When we first started living together as a couple we knew practically nothing about female homosexuality," Martin and Lyon recalled. On the one hand, "Del had read a few books—that's all there were in earlier days. She had been to a number of gay bars, which was always a twitchy experience, since police raids were common then. She had met a few Lesbians and had one previous affair." On the other hand, "Phyllis had been vaguely aware of homosexuality, but, like so many other women, never heard or thought of it in terms of the female, only in terms of the male."[8] Martin and Lyon argued that finding a way out of the wilderness of half-truths and misinformation is the most fundamental journey a lesbian has to make. Placing the creation of stable communication networks to distribute accurate information about sexuality at the center of their struggle, Martin and Lyon set out to build reliable avenues of communication. Among its foremost stated goals, the organization "would enable the Lesbian to find and communicate with others like herself."[9]

After recruiting new members, the leaders of the DOB undertook a multifaceted approach to building communication networks that were different from what had previously existed. The goal, however, was difficult to achieve considering the seemingly insurmountable obstacles they faced. While they wished to help all lesbians out of isolation, they initially rejected the idea of doing this by reaching lesbians en masse. There are many reasons for why this was so: first, while the leaders did not want a "supersecret" organization, they initially wanted to maintain control over what was said about it and who would be allowed to join. Moreover, the leaders knew that even if they wished to contact an unlimited number of lesbians the channels of the mass media would be closed to them and their message. And, further, they understood that if word of the DOB were to spread through the mass media, it would almost surely be to highlight the sensational and controversial story of the supposed threat posed by "organized lesbians." Already working within an organization whose name required decoding, the leaders of the organization decided to intervene in the already extant networks and attempt to build one that would be neither mass nor personal, visible nor hidden, but somewhere in between. In the DOB's lesbian communication network, the leaders of the organization would speak mostly for themselves, yet they would be speaking to a very limited audience. The internal constraints of both philosophy and funding as well as the external limitations of censorship and public reticence meant that the DOB would not be well publicized for several years—and would never become a household word nationwide. However, the DOB's ambivalent strategy combined with ambitious leadership still introduced the organization to a sizable group of women for whom the idea of a vast, spatially anchored lesbian community was to become much easier to imagine than ever before.

Becoming Homophile

Dorothy Martin—her friends later called her Del—was born in San Francisco in 1921.[10] Always aware of her sexual attraction to women, Martin did not have a word to name her passions until she read Radclyffe Hall's famous novel of lesbian love, *The Well of Loneliness,* in the late 1940s. In the meantime, Martin became pregnant, married her college sweetheart, and moved to the suburbs to raise her newborn daughter. This decidedly conventional path, however, was derailed when the nagging attraction she felt for another housewife in her neighborhood would not subside. In fact, the budding romance between the two women stopped only when Martin's husband discovered a cache of perfumed notes traded between the women. What began as a messy split ended in a rather amicable divorce in the late 1940s. In 1949, Martin fled further from her home, taking a job with a publishing company in Seattle.

Shortly after settling in Seattle, Martin met the woman with whom she would come to share her life, Phyllis Lyon. Born in Tulsa, Oklahoma, in 1924, Lyon moved with her family to the San Francisco Bay Area when she was young. Smart and ambitious, Lyon went to the University of California at Berkeley, where she became interested in journalism and writing for a public audience. Although Lyon dated and acted much as any coed in the early 1950s, she also advanced to the position of editor at the respected student newspaper the *Daily Californian*. Upon graduating, Lyon continued to pursue journalism, writing for a small newspaper in northern California. She then moved to Seattle and began working as an editor at the same publishing company as Martin. Martin was considerably more open about her lesbianism than was Lyon, who was only beginning to discover her homosexual desires. The two became friends and then, eventually, lovers. In 1953, they decided to return to San Francisco, near Martin's young daughter, and build a life together.

Within a few years, Martin and Lyon became two of the founding eight members of the Daughters of Bilitis. And it was in no small part due to their combined interest in and expertise at journalism and public relations that the debates about privacy and publicity surfaced in the fledgling lesbian organization. After the initial strife, Lyon and Martin were left with an organization with fewer members than when it was founded. Their first step toward building lines of communication among lesbians would be to increase membership and introduce the organization to the lesbian subculture in San Francisco as well as to isolated lesbians around the Bay Area. But the question remained: what would that step be? Considerable obstacles stood in their way. As detailed in the introduction, the paths of communication open to lesbians were notoriously few in the early 1950s. There were not many obvious lesbian bars or coffeehouses and no community centers or women's bookstores where newly formed groups could post announcements of coffee-klatches, reading groups, activist meetings, and planned political actions as there would be by the 1970s. Moreover, because the few places that did exist were often observed by the police as well as tourists, those lesbians who feared for their jobs or, in some cases, the custody of their children set about looking for alternative spaces in which to socialize. Beyond the world of bars and the word-of-mouth method, very few options for communication existed. What's more, Martin and Lyon's publicity strategy and their desire to have only who they regarded as the right people (a concept discussed below) involved with the organization meant that they were suspicious of methods for gaining additional members other than face-to-face communication or personal recommendations.

About the same time Martin and Lyon found themselves heading a virtually memberless organization, they fortuitously discovered the Mattachine Society. By late 1955, the society's reorganization tremors had mostly disappeared and its membership was eagerly pursuing its goals of expanding its size and publishing a magazine. After meeting with the San Francisco Mattachine leaders and learning of One, Inc., the sibling organization in Los Angeles, Martin and Lyon decided to travel to Los Angeles and take part in one of the largest gatherings of people active in the homophile movement yet to occur. In January 1956, Martin, Lyon, and a few other women active in the DOB attended One's Midwinter Institute and learned more about the philosophies and goals of those who had been formulating the movement over the previous five years. Also at this meeting, Martin and Lyon connected with One's Ann Carll Reid. Reid was then assisting another One member, "Marvin Cutler," who was finishing up a book-length compendium on the homophile movement that was to contain a mix of gay history, organizational histories, political essays, updates on the global homophile movement, and a blueprint for the future homophile activities.[11] If the leaders of the DOB worked quickly and assembled some information about the organization, Reid said, they too could be included in this publication. Cutler's book would not only be available nationwide, particularly to homosexuals brought together through One's own burgeoning network but it also would provide descriptive, nonsensational publicity about the homophile organizations. In other words, the book would provide publicity in the organizers' own words. This was an opportunity the DOB chose not to miss. Cutler's *Homosexuals Today* appeared in mid-1956, published on One's private press. It sold quickly and widely among the thousands of homosexuals and fellow travelers who had already learned of the movement, then still in its infancy. Represented in print and becoming known throughout the country, DOB's leadership was galvanized and ready for the public to come calling.

Included in *Homosexuals Today* was the DOB's "Aims and Purposes." Closely reflecting the goals and strategies of the other homophile groups, the DOB positioned itself as "a women's organization for the purpose of promoting the integration of the homosexual into society" by four separate yet complimentary methods. First, the organization would seek to educate the lesbian "to enable her to understand herself and make her adjustment to society in all its social, civic and economic implications"; second, it sought to educate "the public at large . . . leading to the eventual breakdown of erroneous taboos and prejudices"; third, the organization encouraged objective research into homosexuality after the pattern set by the Kinsey reports; and finally, the DOB advocated that laws be examined and changed "to provide an equitable handling of cases" involving homosexuals.[12] Years later, Martin and Lyon reconsidered their work, noting that "terms like 'integration into' and 'adjustment to' society [are] no longer viable."[13] In fact, although they sound accommodationist and even apologetic to contemporary ears, such ideas were in the vanguard in the mid-1950s, so much so that many lesbians and gay men thought those who penned them were speaking with their heads in the clouds.[14] Indeed, while some particularly visible and courageous employees and regular habitués of lesbian bars dismissed the DOB on the grounds that it was too apologetic, boring, or just not their scene, the emerging evidence suggests that another sizable population of bargoers prized their privacy and rejected the DOB because it was too public, political, and even radical.[15] Moreover, the DOB's essentially pluralist philosophy was formulated around the same time the U.S. Supreme Court offered its prointegration decision in *Brown v. Board of Education of Topeka* (1954). The atmosphere was ripe with the belief that the best hope for social equality would come with integration rather than from the isolation of groups into a world considered by many middle-class-striving lesbians to be fleeting, dangerous, and alienating. Lesbians and gay men increasingly were seeing themselves as part of this social, cultural, and political moment for the erasure rather than the construction of societal barriers.[16]

The DOB's philosophy about education that many first read in the pages of *Homosexuals Today* stands as a misunderstood yet unquestionably important guiding principle throughout the organization's life. What at first glance might appear to be apologetic reveals something quite different on closer examination. In early 1958, writing to a heterosexual couple interested in the organization, Lyon reiterated the philosophy of the DOB:

> With respect to education on the subject, our purpose is two-fold. We realize only too well that we must deal first with our own group — help them to accept themselves, discard the fears and guilt forced upon them by an unknowing public, and then channel their energies into constructive, creative, useful outlets which would be of benefit to society at large. What the public fails to realize is the great loss, through oppression, of a valuable creative potential. And that is our second problem. How to get people to realize that there is really noth-

ing to fear from us (for that is the true reason behind the prejudice—fear). That also is the reason why so many homosexuals are unable to make a satisfactory adjustment—fear.[17]

Rather than apologize for lesbian sexuality or educate lesbians to accommodate themselves to society's view of homosexuality, Lyon argued that the only way to end the so-called homosexual problem was to end the oppression of homosexuals through a widespread program of education to dispel fear. These ideas, however, were uttered in the 1950s without an established mechanism for their execution. In fact, the channels of individual and mass social education were dominated by figures such as doctors, ministers, and psychiatrists who named homosexuality an illness, a sin, and a pathology, respectively. While the picture of homosexuality drawn by experts by no measure was uniform, the general trend was one in which homosexuality was cast as a problem, the root of it being the homosexual her- or himself. Thus the experts played a role in increasing rather than lessening fear and misunderstanding of homosexuals. Lyon and her colleagues in the DOB and in the homophile movement overall knew they had to build stable communication networks within which an alternative message and new information could travel relatively unmolested. In *Homosexuals Today* in 1956, the DOB got its first opportunity to do just that.

In the meantime, the DOB focused on building a solid membership base in its hometown. Historian John D'Emilio reports that shortly after the One, Inc., Midwinter Institute, membership stood at about a dozen and the organization started to hold public meetings to attract new members. D'Emilio writes, "As Martin explained it, 'We thought it would cut down the fear. Lesbians could go there and pretend to be the 'public.'"[18] In April 1956, the organization held its first public event, a panel discussion on problems faced by gay men and lesbians, cosponsored with the Mattachine Society. As George Chauncey argues in *Gay New York,* many gay men in the early part of the twentieth century lived without the privacy found in apartments of their own or in exclusively gay bars, so they were forced to meet other homosexuals in public places like restaurants, movie theaters, parks, and city streets.[19] More than just provide a place to meet, though, public places provided space for "guilt-free" association. Although gay men might be harassed on certain streets or in parks known as "hangouts for deviates," public space in principle was open to everybody. Likewise, the forums presented by the homophile movement were public and somewhat visible to outsiders, which meant that the private identities of those present might be blurred by the performance of the public identity of a "concerned citizen" attending a public forum.

Because homosexuality was strictly regulated in public and perceived as shameful in the 1950s, wearing the mask of the well-meaning citizen with a purely intellectual or sociological interest in the subject could divert attention away from the homosexual who, in fact, attended the meetings for personal reasons. As Martin and Lyon explained, "The 'public,' of course, was comprised chiefly of homosexuals and primarily those of the female gender. . . . We reasoned that at a 'public' meeting you could hear about 'those' people and not necessarily be so identified simply by being in the audience."[20] As it turned out, slipping into a public meeting at the spacious California Hall near San Francisco's Civic Center was less worrisome to lesbians or those interested in exploring homosexuality than making what must have seemed a furtive visit after dark to a private home where the lace curtains were drawn. Thus, it was assumed that women interested in the DOB felt safer learning about the organization in a benign public setting than in a private setting where guilt by association seemed assured. Once a lesbian made it to such public discussions, she might have received additional material about the organization, such as one circular that introduced the DOB as "a home for the Lesbian. She can come here to find help, friendship, acceptance and support. She can help others understand themselves, and can go out into the world to help the public understand her better."[21] Continuing with their simultaneously private and public communication strategy, the leaders of the organization helped usher in new methods by which lesbians could communicate with one another. Far-reaching in some ways and limited in others, this agenda ultimately proved interesting for only a portion of the lesbian world, and it would be those lesbians who came to form the core of the organization.

This strategy, however, could hold little interest for people like the cross-dressing entertainers described by Nan Alamilla Boyd in *Wide Open Town* or the visible butch lesbians discussed by Elizabeth Kennedy and Madeline Davis in their study of Buffalo's lesbian community. According to Kennedy and Davis, the butch lesbians developed their "own strategy of resistance" to the everyday injustices they experienced, a strategy that entailed the creation of a tough look and manner and often meant literally fighting for spaces, like bars, in which to socialize and develop a sense of camaraderie.[22] These strategies seemed to be sufficient for the bargoing crowd until, in the late 1960s, all the gay and lesbian bars had been closed and subsequently the first homophile organization was established in Buffalo. Thus, for many lesbians (and gay men), the bar and the social world it nurtured was enough to sustain lesbian life and until that institution disappeared or was threatened, participation in a homophile movement either was irrelevant or not a high priority.

Years later, Martin and Lyon concluded, "By the end of its first year, DOB had fifteen members, only three of the original eight remaining. We decided to make an all-out push." Not only did they host monthly public discussions, but the Mattachine Society "sublet half of one tiny room to DOB" in the third-floor offices they were renting on Mission Street in San Francisco. Martin and Lyon added, "A member donated a desk [and] . . . we bought a used typewriter and filing cabinet. . . . We were in business."[23]

The Ladder Climbing from Darkness

One of the first jobs Martin, Lyon, and others performed with that type-writer and filing cabinet was to begin producing their own newsletter and magazine. While four years separated the birth of the Mattachine idea from the publication of the first issue of the *Mattachine Review,* only one short year elapsed between the founding of the DOB and the appearance of the first issue of its periodical, the *Ladder.*[24] And unlike the Mattachine Society, the DOB was not bound by cumbersome organizational rules regulating content and production. Indeed, the DOB was fortunate in its circumstances. Not only did the leaders have particularly relevant prior experience in publishing, but the Mattachine also offered the DOB use of its mimeograph machine. All the DOB needed was content and the time required to assemble and to print the magazine. However, other obstacles remained to be overcome, not least of which was financing the publication as well as distributing it to a large enough audience so that it would eventually become self-sufficient. In summer 1956 the twenty or so active participants decided to forge ahead with a magazine designed to end the perceived isolation among lesbians like themselves. Not only would the magazine facilitate wider access to the organization, it would accomplish this by providing representations of lesbianism that ran counter to what few images circulated in the mainstream public sphere in the early 1950s, images that cast lesbians as antisocial and that thus naturalized the isolation they may have felt.

Historian Lillian Faderman notes that "with the end of the war, society took a conservative turn in all areas" and that "lesbians were affected particularly by the growing interest in mandating conformity through what was promoted as mental health. It was at this time that the lesbian 'sicko' became the dominant image of the woman who loved other women."[25] "Sicko" was the colloquial designation given to lesbians by psychologists with increasing frequency and ferocity in the years after World War II. Prominent psychoanalysts of the American Freudian tradition, like Edmund Bergler and Frank Caprio, determined that lesbians were ill and in need of treatment. Bergler declared, "The Lesbian is unconsciously in search of constant masochistic pleasure; she is therefore incapable of conscious happiness."[26] As increasingly powerful and vocal arbiters of what was normal and abnormal in American culture, psychologists implied that lesbians were possessed of a psychopathic personality—and most of America listened and believed.

In San Francisco, readers of the city's dailies would have seen several of the era's most pervasive fears crystallize around the figure of the lesbian. According to Boyd, part of this image can be tied to the periodic scandals, highlighted by city newspapers, which seemed to confirm society's worst fears. One such scandal came after the raid of a lesbian bar, Tommy's Place, in San Francisco in 1954 during one of the city's periodic crackdowns on "sex perverts."[27] The *San Francisco Examiner* headlined the existence of a "Sex Deviate Ring Here" that was purportedly seducing underage girls into a life of lesbianism, prostitution, and drug abuse. Repeated throughout the country in many different locations during the 1950s, according to Boyd, such scandals meant that "the most common perception of lesbians (if any in fact penetrated popular culture) was that lesbians existed outside middle-class moral standards and that their uncontained sexuality contributed to the increased debauchery of society."[28]

Another forum where a significant number of people would encounter images of lesbians was the new mass-produced paperback novels increasingly available after World War II. Mistakenly called "pulps" by most historians and literary critics, fiction and nonfiction paperbacks revolutionized the publishing industry in the 1940s and 1950s.[29] An increasingly popular subgenre of these books began to address candidly the topic of lesbianism in the early 1950s.[30] The first paperback with significant lesbian content was Tereska Torres's 1950 novel, *Women's Barracks*.[31] The book received a great deal of attention when it became a centerpiece of a Congressional drive against "pornographic" materials in 1952. The book itself was criticized by the House Committee on Current Pornographic Materials for disseminating "sensuality, immorality, filth, perversion, and degeneracy" to the mainstream public.[32] Still, as literary scholar Kate Adams argues, the book also seemed to serve a functional purpose in the 1950s, as its "depiction of the lives of women soldiers during wartime is nothing more than a racy potboiler hiding an extremely conservative cultural message"—even to the extent that one committee member opined that it was a novel he "could love to hate."[33] Ultimately books like *Women's Barracks* were allowed to be published and drew a great deal of attention because they seemed to confirm some of America's most grotesque fears about women and the danger of lesbianism in the 1950s—that it was the cause or at least the symptom of other, more readily apparent social ills: Communism, prostitution, drug abuse, violence, and criminality overall.

With such an ominous list of ills from which they hoped to disassociate lesbianism, the members of the DOB had their work cut out. The Mattachine mimeograph machine produced the first issue of the DOB's magazine in October 1956. Although other homophile organizations helped the DOB get its start, its first mailing list was compiled solely by members Martin, Lyon, and Barbara Grier (who became known to readers as "Gene Damon," author of the Lesbiana book reviews column in the *Ladder*). Although only seventeen individuals paid for subscriptions prior to the publication of the first issue, 200 copies were mailed to the names on the list—and very few of these copies were solicited. The way in which they developed this list is telling. A portion of the names were drawn from their own address books, bringing together close friends as well as acquaintances into the new print culture group they were forming. For these women, the *Ladder* would provide a way for them to participate in the new organization and to keep abreast of the organization's activities whether they could attend meetings or not. The idea was that these women, while already integrated in the nascent lesbian world to a certain degree, would be brought in more closely and would play a key role in introducing others to this unique conception of that world. Another portion of names on the list were professional women (like lawyers and social workers) whom the leaders of the DOB assumed might either be lesbian (yet disconnected from them) or be interested in the social implications of such an organization for the status of women overall. The fact that they chose to send the first issue to those who they knew already and only extended it to professional women demonstrates from the outset the way in which they were limiting the reach of their network, that whatever their literature implied they did not seek to reach all lesbians, at least initially.[34]

While a few of those who received the first issue demanded to be removed from DOB's mailing list, Martin and Lyon remember that the response was "overwhelming" and positive.[35] "After reading your first issue of *The Ladder*, I was deeply impressed, and fully intended writing you at once," began a letter from one such reader. "Now that I've read the second issue, I simply cannot let another day go without telling you how deeply I appreciate you sending me this wonderful publication."[36] She continued, "*The Ladder* is exactly what the name implies, a way up—and out of the dark confusion and despair which so many of us live in. How rapid the climb shall be, depends on all of us, not just a few crusaders."[37] After reading two roughly printed issues with rather slight content, this lesbian caught on to the main goal and contribution of the publication: to replace isolation with sturdy lines of communication over which would travel regular and reliable information about many facets of lesbian life. Moreover, she also pointed out how difficult that task was to be. Yet, her letter also provides evidence of the ways in which the *Ladder* and subsequent efforts by the DOB would alter the methods of sexualized communication. The letter writer and the editor of the magazine were strangers to one another, yet through the conduit provided by this magazine their epistolary conversation focused on matters generally kept private, previously discussed only between close friends and confidants—particularly among the white middle-class-striving audience to which the magazine was directed.

After the publication of the second issue of the *Ladder*, the Mattachine Society's old mimeograph machine would print no more. Luckily, early DOB member Helen Sandoz worked at Macy's and had access to its printing facilities after hours. The next three issues of the magazine were printed at Macy's on Union Square, unknown to the retailer. But when the DOB leaders experienced one too many close calls with management, they sought to set up a more permanent situation, first with Call and Lucas's Pan-Graphic Press, then with another professional printer.[38] Along with securing printing facilities to get the magazine out for lesbians craving information across the states, the leaders of the DOB, aided by readers of the *Ladder,* struggled to assemble a large list of women who might benefit from such information. This agenda, however, brought them into a new territory in which the standards and methods of communication were not yet known.

In November 1956, "Mary Beals," a Women's Air Command (WAC) sergeant, provided the names of three women who she thought might be interested in the DOB and the *Ladder;* about six months later she provided another eight names and the following month another five.[39] Beals was not the only lesbian who helped usher in an almost entirely new form of social interaction among homosexuals. In supplying the DOB with the names of lesbians across the country and, indeed, around the world, individual lesbians were helping to break the hold that face-to-face relations, insular friendship cliques, and novels removed from personal connection had on the discussion of homosexuality and the exchange of information among lesbians. Thus, in building a list of potential subscribers to this lesbian publication, the DOB also was creating a sexual communication network that was not only quite candid but also was mediated by a secondary source, in this case an organization, the DOB. By mediating and facilitating this network, the DOB acted as a conduit, occupying a social role similar to that of a house party or a bar but different from those institutions because of its pretense to permanence and legality as well as because of the limitations of what could be said given its public status. Even without a physical space for lesbians to meet and exchange information, the DOB and the *Ladder* nevertheless became a hub and provided a conceptual space where lesbians could go and be relatively assured that they would find the information and even the camaraderie for which they were looking, at least within the confines of the particular type of lesbian the DOB hoped to reach.[40] Along with introducing the conceptual space of a magazine, the DOB rented office space in downtown San Francisco so that women could drop by and gain information or simply a sympathetic ear.

Another woman, who provided the names and addresses of two women and promised more, wrote that while she appreciated the magazine, calling it "a good effort and very interesting," she would much rather have been "in San Francisco for the various social events and discussions." In fact, this woman from Southern California concluded her letter by letting Del Martin know that as soon as school ended in the spring, a move might be in order, adding, "I think I should like living in San F[rancisco]."[41] Such a letter signaled an important, generally new kind of longing. Learning that something was happening in San Francisco quite apart from her own experience led this lesbian to yearn for more, for an experience she had up to that point only imagined. Accounts of the DOB discussion sessions—or, as the organizers called them, "Gab 'n' Javas"—that made it into the *Ladder* tempted the imaginations of many lesbians who had yet to experience the sociability of unbridled talk about their sexualities outside of a bar. This was particularly appealing to the lesbians who received the *Ladder*. Although by no means exclusively white, middle-class, or non-bargoing, the *Ladder*'s readers tended to shy away from lesbian bars and consequently were largely without that particular venue for discussion and commiseration. With the introduction of the discussion groups that took place in homes and other private places, we see the emergence of a form of discourse that would continue to appeal to lesbians into the 1960s and 1970s with the rise of feminist consciousness-raising groups.[42]

Speaking to the difference between the discussion groups and bar talk, "Florence Ray," a *Ladder* reader from Minnesota, stated, "We envy you there in Frisco, having the splendid opportunity to get together over a cup of coffee rather than a fifth." This lesbian, feeling disaffection with a bar culture that she felt was riddled with alcohol abuse, found in the DOB what she considered a healthy alternative. From a few thousand miles away, Ray longed to participate and "to discuss the problems that beset us and spend worthwhile time and effort in trying to find a solution rather than the intent of seeing who can drink the most and then so fortified—shake a defiant fist at the world."[43] Along with articulating difference within the lesbian world and recognizing the emergence of a new context for lesbian communication, Ray perhaps unconsciously revealed a rather unique desire for a lesbian to hold during this period. That is, the *Ladder* stimulated in her an imaginative leap of wishing to be elsewhere, to move; it was the attraction of such a place of verbal exchange—the DOB discussion group—that, in fact, inspired in some the motivation to actually move to San Francisco and participate in the real thing. The desire to move, whether they acted on it or not, certainly was motivated by forces pushing them out of their place of origin as many would cite isolation and prejudice. Yet, an apparently increasing number of women also felt the undeniable pull of a place that was home to a group of people with a new conception and practice of community to offer. This motivation did not occur only in relation to San Francisco. As will be discussed in chapter 3, stories about lesbian life in New York's Greenwich Village that appeared in paperback fiction also inspired a good many women to get up and move, thus demonstrating the emerging importance of print in shaping identity and gathering lesbians into community.

Florence Ray from Minnesota is an example of one who took such a leap in imagination and desire early on; "Jeani Gnapp" from Salt Lake City was another. Gnapp was one of the two hundred people who received the first issue of the *Ladder* in October 1956. Yet, even though she already was well enough integrated into the lesbian world to be included in that list, her subsequent response reveals the vast gulf between the immediate and the mediated lesbian worlds. Like many others, Gnapp was overjoyed with the *Ladder*. "Congratulations to the new organization on the courageous venture ahead," she wrote. However, despite receiving such a publication, she also felt she was missing something, lamenting, "I only regret that I no longer live in California and can't actively participate in your meetings and activities." She added, "I hope you continue to publish a calendar of coming events, so one may attend the functions during possible trips to California."[44] In return for opening the lines of communication, Gnapp offered Martin and the DOB information about other publications covering homosexuality. Martin's response a few days later was enthusiastic and personal, asking Gnapp to join DOB as an associate member and even providing her home address and phone number should Gnapp manage to visit San Francisco.[45]

Gnapp's response to Martin's letter, however, exhibited more gut fear than basic mistrust, as she began to question the practice of engaging in a candid and mediated discourse that had always been, in her experience, familiar and face-to-face—and consequently easier to manage and less risky. Gnapp, who was living with her brother, told Martin, "We discuss any and all the many projects each of us become enthused with [but] from the beginning he has been worried over my corresponding with and receiving material from the Daughters of Bilitis." [46] The more he shared his fears with his sister, the more concerned she became. "He fears that a list of the members could fall into the hands of those who might have the power to suppress and prosecute," she explained. Not wanting to find flaws in this new organization, Gnapp kept firing back responses, but she herself continued to doubt her security and privacy, which was of utmost importance considering that she was a schoolteacher: "How do you or any of the other members know that I or someone else who might learn of this new organization are not policewomen? How can any of us be absolutely sure that our names are safe and not subject to persecution by any number of sick laws which exist in many states even in this day and age?" [47]

Compounding Gnapp's quandary was her desire to be honest and not engage in furtive behavior around an identity for which she felt no shame. "I have always been straightforward and honest," she declared. "I sent in my real name and have used no pseudonym." Again speaking to the heart of the matter, Gnapp said she wished to help expand this new lesbian communication network but felt constrained by outside forces. "I would like to become an associate member and be able to send you other interested parties' names. Yet, I am reluctant to do so, because I have no right to endanger others." Her anxieties would be relieved, she noted, "If I lived in California [and] could investigate and allay my doubts." But it was such uncertainty and unfamiliarity that was definitive, innovative, exciting, and perhaps even revolutionary about the communication network into which she was introduced. She knew that the only other alternatives were the few options that already existed, pointing out that "too often bars are the only social meeting places." But these were far from ideal because "when such places are raided and closed, another avenue for 'hoped for' companionship and friendship is cut off." She ached for something stable and, despite her worries and misgivings, suspected that the DOB and the *Ladder* might be the solution. She concluded, "It is my hope that this organization will act as a more interesting outlet for social contact." [48]

In the second issue of the *Ladder*, there appeared an important article titled, "Your Name Is Safe." The article began, "Already, with only one issue of *The Ladder* published, we have run up against the fear that names on our mailing list may fall into the wrong hands, or that by indicating interest in this magazine, a person will automatically be labeled homosexual. This is not so." [49] Ann Ferguson, the pseudonymous author of the article and the magazine's editor, argued that readers of the *Ladder* were safe because many professionals subscribed and contributed to the magazine; because the DOB advocated "no illegal actions by anyone"; and because "the organization has obtained legal counsel on all phases of its operation, and within the very near future will file for incorporation under the laws of the State of California."[50] The real clincher, though, came a few paragraphs later: "In 1953, in the case of the U.S. vs. Rumely . . . the Supreme Court of the United States upheld the right of a citizen to refuse to reveal the names of purchasers of reading material to a Congressional investigating committee."[51] Thus, the editors at the *Ladder* were able to assert with optimistic confidence to their readers, "Your name is safe!" Two issues later, the article's author drove the point home with an unconventional obituary: "I confess. I killed Ann Ferguson . . . We ran an article in the November issue of the *Ladder* entitled 'Your Name Is Safe.' Ann Ferguson wrote that article. Her words were true, her conclusions logical and documented—yet she was not practicing what she preached. Now there is only Phyllis Lyon," the person behind the pseudonym.[52]

More than killing off a pseudonym in favor of the candor of self-identification, Lyon's decision to drop the pretense of anonymity hints at larger changes. By using a pseudonym Lyon was following in the footsteps of almost every other writer in the 1950s who wrote about homosexuality from a subjective point of view, from Donald Webster Cory to Ann Aldrich. The fact that authors used pseudonyms was well known among gay male and lesbian readers who would have assumed that the name in a by-line was not real, that it was there to protect the anonymity of the author. Moreover, many authors writing in homophile publications and in paperback books used more than one pseudonym, which invariably added to the confusion and increased the obfuscation. The ubiquity of pseudonymous books and articles meant that any homosexual, yet no one homosexual in particular, was producing the written record of the community as it was coming into being. Writing about another context, early modern Europe, historian Elizabeth Eisenstein argues that the emergence of individual authorship of texts reduced the collective authority of texts by associating them with individual authors, who were "prone to human error and possibly plagiarists as well."[53] It strikes me that in breaking from the mold of pseudonymous writer and editor, Lyon was not only introducing a new form of lesbian authorship in the *Ladder* but she was making a claim to individual rather than collective authority on the subject of homosexuality. She was not *any* lesbian, she was a particular woman, who lived in a specific place, who had a unique life history.

Gaining the reassurances from a "real," individual lesbian in both letters and in the pages of the *Ladder* provided the reassurance for which readers like Gnapp had been looking. Gnapp wrote to Martin that "many of my and other subscribers' questions were answered in this issue." Still, despite feeling relatively secure that her name was safe, Gnapp was not entirely satisfied, proclaiming, "I gnash my teeth whenever I think of my living so far from San Francisco. How badly I would like to be of direct use in this new organization." She added, "I'm tempted to check on teaching jobs or library jobs in your city."[54]

Even after Gnapp was assured that her name was safe, Martin continued to share with her ideas about the relative risks and rewards of joining the DOB. Martin wrote to Gnapp that "there is always a calculated risk in belonging to these organizations, I guess. We can't make absolute guarantees." And she further noted that "Mattachine has been in existence for 5 years and has not run into police problems. As a matter of fact, every issue of the [Mattachine] Review and all publications of the Mattachine Society are automatically mailed to the San Francisco police department."[55] The reasoning, of course, was that if the police knew what was going on in advance, they would have no cause to raid or prosecute if the homophile organizations caught the eye of the media or politicians at election time. Martin added that "there is no law against meetings that we conduct or discussion of the subject," nor is there a "law against *being* a Lesbian. The legal point comes into question with the homosexual act itself."[56] Martin did, however, acknowledge that Gnapp, as a teacher, might have cause to worry, noting that "teachers, civil service employees, and those in the military must necessarily be a little wary" because of explicit regulations prohibiting the employment of homosexuals within those lines of work.[57] Nothing seems to reassure like a meeting face-to-face, though, so Martin attempted to have Gnapp meet with a Mattachine Society member who was traveling through Salt Lake City (this never materialized) and invited her to visit San Francisco. In return, Gnapp, with her concerns mostly addressed, sent the DOB the names and addresses of two lesbians and scheduled a trip to the West Coast.[58]

By December, Gnapp's correspondence with Martin took on an even more informal appearance as she ditched the typewriter and started composing handwritten notes. In a letter that month, Gnapp wrote excitedly of her upcoming trip to San Francisco via Greyhound bus. Much of the letter, in rather hurried handwriting, was devoted to the prospect of Gnapp searching for and finding a job while visiting the coast. Speaking of Salt Lake City, Gnapp wrote with exasperation, "God, how I want to leave this town."[59] In the meantime, Don Lucas of the Mattachine Society did what his organization disavowed on the surface and put Gnapp in touch with a troubled and lonely lesbian from Cleveland named "Janis Mueller," hoping a correspondence between the two could help them solve some mutual problems, the most immediate being the pain of isolation. Gnapp, adding resolve to her idea of moving to San Francisco, in turn wrote to Mueller and "told her that all 'little' girls with wicked smiles should come and live out West—that we Westerners treat everyone royally." Not only would her social life improve by coming out West, Gnapp argued that Mueller's "chance for better employment would be better in California." She concluded, "I will continue to write and try and influence a westward movement." [60]

Gnapp herself made good on her plan of seeking work in the San Francisco Bay Area, writing her friends at the DOB in late March 1957 to let them know of her arrival in April and her appointments scheduled with the superintendents of several local school districts. Another DOB member hosted Gnapp while she visited for interviews. Gnapp ended her postcard with the hopeful closing, "We will soon live somewhere in the Bay Area." [61] Sometime by the end of summer 1957, Gnapp had moved to the San Francisco Bay Area and had achieved her goal set in motion upon reading the very first issue of the *Ladder*. [62] For Gnapp, at least, the communication networks in which she participated would no longer be mediated by unknown, distant, and potentially dangerous forces. The *Ladder* had transformed, in her mind, from a potentially dangerous weapon to a tool to reach community and, in fact, contribute to its expansion and perpetuation. In Gnapp's case, the newly emergent homophile communication networks of the late 1950s provided passage into a more immediate and personal social world guided by face-to-face relations. Yet, as we shall see in subsequent chapters, these new communication networks ultimately would impact the established communities as the reach and content of the networks expanded and as the images and ideas that circulated through mediated and impersonal channels would begin to leave an imprint upon experiential community sites.

Not all readers of the *Ladder*, however, came to the publication through a personal reference. Like the Mattachine Society, the DOB was attempting to reach out and obtain a moderate number of new subscribers—though not necessarily members—from across the country and around the globe. From the 200 copies of the first issue distributed free of charge, sales grew to 400 in 1958, then to 750 in 1960. An exact breakdown of the number of subscriptions versus those sold on newsstands does not remain, but in all likelihood about half were subscriptions, both paid and complimentary. Thus, the *Ladder* probably had a smaller newsstand presence than either the *Mattachine Review* or *ONE*. Historian Rodger Streitmatter has pointed out that newsstand sales of the homophile magazines, including the *Ladder*, were hampered by a number of forces, most especially an almost uniform unwillingness among newsstand proprietors to sell publications that might attract trouble with the law—although other factors such as the magazine's small scale of distribution also made the magazines unattractive to vendors.[63]

Considering the problems of getting newsstands to sell the magazine, one Los Angeles member of the DOB wrote to Del Martin in 1958, "Don't worry about getting turned down by a newsstand. This will work out in time. . . . As [the magazines] stand now, we have to depend upon the newsy to put them with ONE and the Mattachine Review to distinguish them, since the name doesn't imply anything. The casual browser just doesn't pick up on it."[64] But there were other factors that limited distribution, including the DOB's unease with being a fully public lesbian organization and with the *Ladder* being easily identified as lesbian. In contrast, the popular lesbian paperback fiction of the day wore covers and carried copy that shouted lesbianism, were clearly displayed on many newsstands and consequently sold quite well. The covers of the *Ladder* were conspicuously innocent, providing only very coded hints that this was a lesbian magazine.[65] One of the more blatant coded covers appeared on the April 1959 issue that featured a drawing of a somewhat butch woman, wearing slacks and short-cropped hair, eyeing another woman, wearing a pleated skirt and heels, from behind (fig. 5). The setting is easily identified as Washington Square Park in Greenwich Village, a site known to readers of lesbian paperbacks as a hub of activity in the lesbian world. Although the DOB wanted to help end the isolation of lesbians across the country, its organizers found that task rather difficult to accomplish because even when a few newsstands began to carry the *Ladder*, it was not known as a lesbian magazine to the uninitiated. This paradoxical situation meant that since a prospective reader had to know what she were looking for, few new readers would be gained from the magazine's semipublic display. Like the name of the organization, then, the covers of their magazine straddled an ambivalent line separating public from private communication. Thus, the DOB might be seen as less immediately effective in attracting the notice of women exploring their sexuality than the instances of public visibility displayed by some more masculine lesbians who, as Elizabeth Kennedy and Madeline Davis argue, "as part of the lesbian community they were recognized on the streets as women who looked 'different' and therefore challenged mainstream mores and made it possible for lesbians to find one another."[66] The two models of attracting notice, represented by the DOB and butch street visibility, could not have been more revealing in their contrasting strategies for making connections and ending isolation.

Those working on the *Ladder* recognized early on that this neither

5 One of the more blatantly coded covers of *The Ladder* appeared on this April 1959 cover which featured a drawing of a somewhat butch woman, eyeing another woman, wearing a pleated skirt and heels. Image courtesy of the GLBT Historical Society, San Francisco, CA.

obvious nor hidden presence in public space was a problem. One of these women wrote to Martin in 1958 that "I have been toying with the idea of a more sensational cover for a limited number of LADDERS for news stand sales only." "Think about it," she continued, they could "include a second run of an additional line with something like 'The Homosexual Woman's Viewpoint' or some such crap."[67] Individuals outside the DOB also suggested that the editors make the *Ladder* more visible to the public. John Jensen of the Lucien Press, distributors for the *Ladder,* asked Martin, "Why don't you put a nicely worded subtitle on your covers? Something like 'A Review Devoted To The Female Homosexual in Modern Society.'" The distributor added, though, that while "your publication is Constitutionally Protected Freedom of Expression," he had recently experienced instances of "postal inspectors get[ting] cute" and removing other Lucien magazines from distribution.[68] Although the Supreme Court decision (*One, Incorporated, v. Olesen,* 1958) that overturned the ruling declaring *ONE* obscene easily could have been applied to the *Ladder,* local authorities continued to harass vendors of homophile magazines. So, if the DOB was forced to negotiate carefully the line between circumscribed publicity and outright publicity, it was partially because the organization was doing business in an environment where censorship laws and enforcement practices were constantly shifting and not always in predictable directions.[69] Thus, while their communication strategy advocated a third and ambivalent path between privacy and outright publicity, the historical context seemed to demand it.

The editors at the *Ladder,* however, wrestled with this issue for another several years until Barbara Gittings, who began editing the magazine in 1963 from her home in Philadelphia, made the ultimate decision and added "A Lesbian Review" as the subtitle.[70] In the intervening years, a great deal had changed beyond the editorship of the *Ladder.* Homophile magazines and other anticensorship advocates had won a series of definitive victories, and the mass media had, by 1964, successfully "outed" the homophile organizations to the point that there was little use in obfuscating the true nature of periodicals like the *Ladder* and the *Mattachine Review.* Reflecting on the new sensibility encouraged by the subtitle, Gittings later said, "Adding those words to the cover helped our readers gain a new sense of identity and strength. That subtitle said, very eloquently I thought, that the word *lesbian* was no longer unspeakable."[71] Along with that, the new subtitle said to newsstand readers that communication networks had become more candid and more public. Becoming more public was always a double-edged sword, though, for while the word "lesbian" would have alerted some browsers to the magazines, it might have frightened others away from buying them in a public place. Still, by 1964, there was a net gain in the size of the audience as the distribution of the *Ladder* was approaching 1,000 copies per issue.

Chapters and Outposts

For some lesbians, the only realistic solution to ending their isolation from other lesbians was to move to San Francisco and the nascent hub of lesbian activity created by the DOB. For a great many others, however, moving to San Francisco or any other large city where a population of lesbians could be presumed was not immediately an option or even something to be desired. As a substitute for interaction in person, many of women held on tightly to each issue of the *Ladder* they received in the mail, reading it several times until the lightweight pages showed wear. Sometimes they shared the magazine with other lesbians they knew in their own town. Sometimes they read the issue alone, comforted by the notion that it takes lots of lesbians to publish a lesbian magazine and that there is safety in numbers. Like Jeani Gnapp and others who read the magazine, though, many hungered for something more. They wanted to transgress that increasingly visible line between mediated and unmediated experience; they wanted to meet and engage with other lesbians on a face-to-face basis. Moreover, they wanted to expand the options for socializing beyond bars, which if were known or did exist often were fleeting and were places that merely tolerated rather than welcomed lesbian patrons. And, besides, the core and target women were seeking an alternative to bars in the first place—they were hoping to build an alternative public institution. Even when Martin, Lyon, and a few others presided over an organization of less than two dozen members, they were actively working to start DOB chapters in other cities in an effort to quell those longings.

Without the usual literature and procedures that groups use to expand and maintain organizational integrity, in 1956 the DOB referred those interested in the organization to One's compendium of the homophile movement, *Homosexuals Today*. As already noted, outside the *Ladder*, this publication contained the most complete information on the structure and goals of the DOB, so it was used to further familiarize individuals with the organization after they had initially discovered it. Replying to a woman from Seattle who expressed interest in starting a DOB chapter of her own, Martin admitted that ideally they should meet in person, but geography prevented such luxuries. "I only wish that some of you kids in Seattle could attend some of the meetings here," she wrote. "But since you can't, I suggest that you purchase and read 'Homosexuals Today,' a book of organizations and publications now active in the field."[72] In an era when interstate travel was still cumbersome and long-distance telephone conversations an event, print remained the dominant means for individuals to communicate with each other across great distances.

The problems Martin hinted at in this exchange would come up time and again as the founders struggled to build an almost entirely new type of communication network. This evolution from candid communication solely governed by face-to-face relationships to an undisguised sexual association mediated through channels beyond one's immediate grasp required a great deal of negotiation, invention, and even courage. An article in the February 1957 issue of the *Ladder* titled "Why a Chapter in Your Area?" pointed out that "only so much can be accomplished by the printed word; there must also be the spoken word, the personal contact." The reason for this was simple, according to the article: "The therapy of group discussion of mutual problems, of talking it over with those in similar circumstances, cannot be denied."[73]

In addition to suggesting that leaders of new chapters read publications like *Homosexuals Today,* DOB national headquarters pointed out the usefulness of providing a safe, public setting for the curious to check out the organization in a nonthreatening atmosphere. Writing to a lesbian seeking to enlarge the New York chapter, Phyllis Lyon extolled the benefits of holding public forums: "Public discussion meetings held on the level of a good professional speaker with a good topic in a downtown meeting place where people come dressed up, are an excellent way of acquainting the public with the work the DOB is doing and also of meeting other potential members who might shy away from one of our more informal gatherings." Lyon added, "I really think that any new chapter should concentrate on having at least two a year—if not more." She concluded, "It brings enthusiasm to the members, stimulates their thinking, and makes the chapter and its individual members grow."[74]

Moreover, in a *Ladder* article Del Martin suggested the usefulness of such meetings: "Public discussion meetings with outside speakers . . . can be of utmost benefit not only in disseminating another picture of the Lesbian to the public but also giving the individual another slant."[75] This new "slant" would provide the public and unorganized lesbians with an image of "the lesbian" that ran counter to the dominant image as found in numerous paperback novels and sly Hollywood representations that portrayed her as self-loathing, isolated, and/or alcoholic. The leaders of the DOB felt that new chapters, through public meetings and other activities, could serve as outposts facilitating both an end to isolation and an entry into community for those lesbians who were seeking an identity that stood in contrast to the dominant, pathologized representations of homosexual women. This meant that the organization would not appeal to many lesbians who might not have recognized the new respectable image as lesbian at all, whose experience in the urban bar scene or by reading a paperback novel taught them that a lesbian was a masculine woman who attracted feminine women. But for those largely, but not exclusively, white middle-class women who were attracted to this representation of the identity, the newly founded chapters brought a little of the DOB's San Francisco to other parts of the country in the late 1950s.

Still, by 1960, with branches only in San Francisco, Los Angeles, New York, and Rhode Island and membership hovering around one hundred, the leaders' goal of rescuing lesbians from their isolation remained largely unfulfilled.[76] The reasons for this are many, but the leaders of the DOB began to recognize around 1960 that it had something to do with the paradoxically public and private communication networks they were struggling to build. For instance, in 1961, longtime DOB member Helen Sandoz wrote to Martin and Lyon to share the quandary of forging public associations based on what many considered intimate, private feelings: "Marilyn asked me gaily Saturday night if Sandy and I wanted to join her and Jearn's private friends group? Boy do I?" She further opined, speaking about the DOB, "Any good accruing to the L.A. members has been strictly on a private friends' basis anyway. I suspect it has been the same in S.F. People are built that way. If only we could have started down here with a few friends, instead of 40 unknown personalities!" She concluded, "Speaking of trust and alleviating fear in the homophile! That type of situation can only eventually aggravate fear."[77] In the late 1950s, the leaders of the DOB generally trusted only their friends or friends of friends, to become members of this ostensibly public organization and when strangers were welcomed, as Sandoz argued, it seemed to "aggravate fear" rather than quell it. Given that context, some leaders placed restrictions on who could join and become active members.

The group, then, was limited to those women who identified with—or sought to identify with—the DOB's definition of the well-integrated, respectable lesbian who looked and acted quite unlike the popular and pathologized representations of lesbians in the 1950s. As a result, gender-transgressive, or butch, women and some bargoing lesbians were dissuaded from joining the organization unless they modified their self-presentation along the lines suggested by the DOB. From all appearances, this attempt at gender-based unity, which almost surely is evidence of brewing class antagonism in the lesbian world, seemed to cut across racial lines as black women who too strove for middle-class status gained access to and a degree of acceptance within the DOB. For instance, black lesbians achieved leadership positions within the organization even though an explicit discourse of racial equality never emerged as a significant element in literature produced by members of the DOB. In 1960 Cleo Glenn, an African American lesbian, joined the DOB, worked as circulation manager from 1960 to 1963, and then was elected national president of the organization in 1964. Virtually no documentation of Glenn's life remains except the evidence of service for the DOB and a short reminiscence written by Lyon and Martin. In that short piece Lyon and Martin note that she lived in an interracial relationship, worked for Pacific Bell, and represented the DOB publicly at a few high profile events, including their 1964 convention in New York. Lyon and Martin also remembered, "At the 1966 convention in San Francisco, she was nowhere to be seen at the public forum. Although she did not say so, it apparently was one thing to be 'out' in New York and another to be 'out' in one's home state."[78] As the quote might indicate, white members of the DOB accepted black lesbians as members and leaders, but they did not actively explore the intersections of race and sexuality and thus did not develop a clear understanding of how lesbianism might have been experienced differently by women of color even if class status was shared. Consequently, the public / private communication strategy of the organization had wide implications. Not only did the strategy force the organization to define lesbianism as somewhere between public and private and thus remove clearly public lesbians (who were "public" either by their own will or because their sartorial presentation was similar to that which was represented publicly as deviant) from their definition of community, it injected class and to a certain extent race into the emerging definition of lesbian.[79]

In the early 1960s, Martin, Lyon, and other members of DOB still eager to build a large and robust network of lesbians across the country began to change their thinking about who should join. Leaders of the DOB started coming to terms with the fact that in order to reach the lonely in isolated corners of the country they would have to build a communication network that could allow unknown individuals to participate on an equal footing with the select few. By the early 1960s, they arrived at the conclusion that they could not unite masses of lesbians on a one-by-one, face-to-face basis and they would have to relinquish reticence and the control over their message and their membership. So, while the DOB in San Francisco in 1956 was likely to stay clear of visibly butch lesbians in an effort to distance the organization from public images of the pathological lesbian, by 1962 the leadership was beginning to modify this stance. For instance, when Lyon, then San Francisco chapter president, heard that the newly chartered Chicago chapter screened individuals to determine their sexuality and their commitment to the purpose of the DOB prior to allowing them to become members, she responded with forceful words: "I must admit I was rather horrified by the procedure decided upon for admitting new members." Lyon continued, "I am sure you and the rest of the Chicago members are aware that the DOB Constitution states that membership is open to *any* woman 21 years of age or older. Therefore, any woman over 21 years of age who applies for membership must be accepted as a member."[80]

Lyon's words were direct, but not without sympathy. "I think I know what you all are thinking about in trying to screen members," Lyon stated, mentioning that the San Francisco chapter originally mandated a sixty-day provisional membership, though this was never used. She added, "Over the years we have found that many people have joined DOB who didn't really fit in with the group. But we have also found that these people either dropped out, because they didn't find what they were looking for, or they began to fit in with the group!" Yet it was fear and not the politics of "fitting-in" that Lyon identified as the DOB's most persistent stumbling block. "One of the biggest problems we have in growing as an organization is the fear people feel about being associated with us," Lyon wrote, "But we have never had any trouble! The possibility of trouble does exist—constantly. But the probability is low. Anyone joining DOB should be aware of these two facts—but the possibility cannot be allowed to hamper or slow our advances." Lyon concluded:

> If you, as a new chapter, begin from the first to worry about the wrong people joining, or if you fear what may come about if the "wrong" people join, you will find that your entire life as a chapter will be hamstrung by this fear. If you, as the founding members, project your fears to new people they will also be afraid. And this fear can permeate an entire chapter, sapping its will to venture into new fields, its very will to exist . . . One of the primary purposes of DOB is to help the Lesbian. And you can only help her by allowing her in so you have the chance.[81]

This lesson was one that usually came slowly and with much consternation, as the leaders continually sought an answer to the vexed question of how to build a large and stable community across a vast geographic space while at the same time guarding the privacy that intimate relationships and a maligned identity demanded. But as Lyon's musings suggest, even though membership was open to anyone, acceptance by the membership probably had its limitations. And while DOB members displayed a willingness to accept black lesbians (even if they were not especially sensitive to the different social situations related to race), the way in which they defined their community undoubtedly had the effect of excluding lesbians who did not fit in.[82]

While some lesbians were satisfied with the level of personal communication provided by reading through the pages of the *Ladder*, and while other lesbians, desiring face-to-face contact, either started their own chapters or even moved to San Francisco, a significant number of others hoped the DOB might put individual lesbians in touch with each other. Like the Mattachine Society, the DOB received letters from readers, subscribers, and members asking the organization to share addresses of members who lived nearby, and some suggested that the DOB begin a lonely hearts or personals column in the *Ladder*. One lesbian writing as late as 1964 suggested:

> If we were really trying to help "our kind" wouldn't we do better by *providing information* thru perhaps our bookstore . . . *of places* from city to city thru-out the USA and abroad, *where one gal can meet another gal of her interests.* . . . The men have this directory already—put out by a "Mr. Larry" of *Directory Services.* . . . I know as for myself, from a small town, I find it hard to meet other gals (lesbians). D.O.B. could be one of the places we meet to form friendships. They could also provide a directory to list places much as "gay bars" where a gal could go and meet her own kind. *It is badly needed.*[83]

Like the Mattachine Society, the DOB feared the legal repercussions and refused to institute any official system for providing lesbians with the personal contacts they desired. The whole story, however, is a bit more complicated. Writing generically to "friends" at the DOB, Vancouver resident "Walli Polanski" asked for more information about the organization, then lamented that "One is entirely lost here on the West Coast of Canada as far as our situation goes. After 6 years of residing in this town, I have met either alcohol- or drug addicts. Surely there must be some decent circles on our basis." Her exclamation was followed with the hopeful suggestion: "Maybe you publish a magazine in which there is a column one could meet or contact people elsewhere in B[ritish] C[olumbia]." Moving to another place, like San Francisco, was not an immediate option for this woman, who wrote, "I feel somewhat lost in this town, but have to stay because of a good job."[84]

Though Del Martin's response to this letter has not survived, she clearly was not able to give Polanski the answer for which she hoped, only indicating that neither the DOB nor any other organization operated a service for lesbians looking to contact others like themselves. Dispirited,

Polanski bemoaned her situation, saying, "There must be hundreds of [lesbians] in a town like Vancouver, but where are they hiding? Well, I'll leave it to fate or chance"; after a six-year dry spell, her chances did not look good.[85] A few days later, however, San Francisco chapter member Billie Tallmij wrote to Polanski attempting to help. Martin forwarded Polanski's letter to Tallmij because she had once lived near Vancouver in Seattle. Tallmij wrote that Martin "asked me if I knew any kids in your area. Seattle was my stomping grounds for several years, but I am sorry to say, that although I visited in Vancouver once . . . and what a week-end it was! . . . I don't know any of the kids there." As a small consolation, Tallmij added, "Fate has a way of placing situations and opportunities on one's doorstep at the most unexpected times. And should we get any leads from your way, with Del's permission, I might write to you to get your written permission and theirs to exchange addresses." Although Tallmij gave Polanski no guarantees, she noted, "We have started several good correspondences like this. There are so many of us scattered throughout the world that it really keeps us hopping here at the office just to keep up with the letters."[86] Apparently, then, the leadership of the DOB had much difficulty navigating the divide between contacts mediated and unmediated by impersonal organizations. As with much of the work performed by the Mattachine Society, the DOB's official and unofficial procedures were not always the same. While the organization always endeavored to remain within the bounds of the law, hoping to avoid prosecution and to protect subscribers' and members' confidentiality, the leaders also selectively broke their own rules after carefully weighing the risks. Slipping between legal and illegal behavior, between nurturing secret contacts and creating candid and public communication networks, DOB organizers blazed a difficult path in the late 1950s. Yet during this period, in which they hoped to avoid overexposure, they also began to realize the power of a greater public presence and to recognize that mass publicity could do much of their most difficult work for them, a theme explored extensively in chapter 3.

By 1962 the leaders of the San Francisco chapter were arguing for greater openness and greater tolerance for any lesbian who wanted to become a member and help the organization grow and publicize its message. The tension that remained during these years, though, was the danger and dissatisfaction that arose from building relationships based on sexuality through an impersonal medium. The *Ladder* helped bridge the distance among some lesbians, and forming chapters in other cities continued the process, although both were still hampered by a limited vision that was imposed both from inside and from outside the organization. Still, many lesbians wanted more immediate participation as they came to learn more about activities sponsored by the better established DOB chapters in San Francisco and New York City, as well as about lesbian life overall. This impulse demonstrates that entry into a communication network also entails an entry into a larger social world. And within that world individuals experience a whole variety of pressures and invitations to do as the other participants in that world. The social consequences of cultural rearrangements are many. For lesbians like Jeani Gnapp, it involved migration.[87] But for many lesbians it involved either establishing an outpost in their own neighborhood or participating in a far-flung print culture, which in the late 1950s and early 1960s expanded as the mass media, along with the DOB, started talking about and to American lesbians.

Homophile Communication Networks

Throughout the 1950s and into the 1960s, a small group of gay men and lesbians worked in tandem to end the profoundly alienating experience of isolation that was shared at some point in their lives by a vast number of same-sex-desiring individuals living in the United States. Motivated by their own personal experiences and inspired by the plight of others, people like Hal Call, Don Lucas, Phyllis Lyon, Del Martin, and scores more formed and staffed organizations designed in large part to build new lines of communication among the homosexual population. Their organizations, particularly the Mattachine Society and the Daughters of Bilitis in San Francisco, and One, Inc., in Los Angeles, set in motion a program of building stable communication networks that would carry candid, authoritative, and reliable information about aspects of sexual variance to individuals across the nation and around the globe. These networks carried information about the forces seeking to keep homosexuals isolated from one another; in addition, the networks transmitted information about the burgeoning core of individuals and groups trying to end censorship and silencing, including the growing army of anticensorship publishers, civil libertarian lawyers, liberal ministers, and supportive psychologists and researchers. Of equal significance, the networks also spread word of the homophile movement itself, which further expanded the networks carrying information about homophile organizations where gay men and lesbians could go with their questions and cries for help. Moreover, the homophiles' creation of headquarters for "organized sex deviates," as the *San Francisco Progress* put it in 1959, led a growing number of homosexuals across the country to begin to see cities like San Francisco, New York, and Los Angeles not only as home to the homophiles, but also as capital cities in a newly mapped national geography.

As the homophile organizations struggled to build stable sexual communication networks, they also helped to usher in an almost entirely new mode of communication. As historians like George Chauncey and Elizabeth Kennedy have demonstrated and as I have shown in the introduction, gay men and lesbians have a long history of employing inventive means to locate and communicate with individuals of similar persuasion. These methods have traditionally been subject to a few general laws: if sexuality was spoken about candidly, the communication most likely would have been on a face-to-face level; if discussions of sexuality transgressed the boundary separating private from public utterances, the communication would have been obfuscated or coded in some manner. Throughout the 1950s, however, the homophile movement pioneered new types of communication networks in which information about sexuality increasingly was candid and public, mediated and accessible. In creating new pathways of information exchange, the homophiles opened up new possibilities of interaction even as they remained hampered by the constraints of their context and their own philosophies.

The Mattachine Society, in particular, was eager to build a nationwide organization that would eventually be an arbiter of information about homosexuality. It sought to provide scientifically and socially unbiased information about the subject of sexual variation to homosexuals and to the American public overall. However, the Mattachine Society attempted this monumental task hamstrung by a mainstream public sphere closed to such exchanges; moreover, the society was plagued by internal personality conflicts and power struggles. The organization wanted to speak to too many different groups of people while using the supposedly universal language of journalistic objectivity. Thus, the Mattachine Society placed itself in the untenable position of using the same language while attempting to speak both to the mainstream American public as well as the country's gay subcultures. The result was that not too many Americans paid attention to the group's publicity organ even while the public message of homosexuality was controversial enough to attract a much larger audience. Consequently, the Mattachine Society eventually realized that its best method of achieving publicity was not through its own outlets but by utilizing the already established and large-scale channels of the mass media. The leaders of the Mattachine Society thereby made themselves available for the media spectacle that was the emergence of homosexuality as the 1950s drew to a close. This Faustian bargain meant a substantially increased notoriety for the organization in the mass media but also a loss of control over what was to be said. Still, as the 1960s wore on, the leaders of the Mattachine Society became skilled at presenting the media with new and sometimes contradictory information that forced journalists and talk show hosts to present the story of homosexuality in America in an entirely different light than it had in the past. A particularly important example of this strategy is analyzed in chapter 4.

The work of the Mattachine Society and the Daughters of Bilitis in this regard, however, was not parallel as they diverged somewhat in theory and practice. From its inception, a tension was present in the DOB. The organization wished to rescue lesbians around the country from the loneliness of isolation, yet it hoped to do so not by creating a mass communication network but by building a network based on face-to-face contacts that would restrict participation to a certain type of lesbian—a lesbian who was ready to conform to the DOB's definition of an integrated, respectable, nonpathological female homosexual. This set the DOB apart from the Mattachine Society, whose one goal was to create a massive, nationwide communication network with very little regard for who would enter (indeed, bisexuals, transvestites, pedophiles, and transsexuals would make it into their world); it also meant that throughout the 1950s, DOB leaders had a rather conflicted relationship with the mass media, seeing it as useful to their cause but also as potentially damaging. Instead, throughout the 1950s and early 1960s, the DOB continued to devote the lion's share of its energy to its own publication, the *Ladder*, which prospered for years after the mass media had made the *Mattachine Review* superfluous. Ultimately this meant that the DOB did not court the mass media in the same way that the Mattachine Society did—a situation compounded by the fact that the mass media never went much out of its way to cover women's issues much. This resulted, then, in a less pervasive localizing of lesbian homophile activism in places like San Francisco and New York than had occurred for gay male identities. The mostly white middle-class-striving lesbians who participated in the DOB tended to shy away from the mainstream public sphere as they paid more attention to the private channels of communication, nurturing their own personally cultivated grapevine. As the relative quiescence of the 1950s disappeared in the din of the 1960s, however, the DOB was no longer able to retain a close hold on the particular kind of lesbian sexual communication networks it idealized. The leadership realized that the split public / private approach was problematic and learned that the mass media was beginning to pay attention. As a result, the leadership decided that it must begin to devote attention to the image of lesbians and the representation of the DOB in the mainstream public sphere. Indeed, as the 1960s came into full bloom, the lesbian grapevine that the DOB had so carefully mediated would soon become a mass phenomenon.

PART 2

The Homosexual Revolution in the 1960s

Introduction

> The shock of recognition! In an electronic information environment, minority groups can no longer be contained — ignored. Too many people know too much about each other. Our new environment compels commitment and participation. We have become irrevocably involved with, and responsible for, each other.
>
> Marshall McLuhan, *The Medium Is the Massage* (1967) [1]

"Once upon a time in America we pretended that sex did not exist. Now we scream its existence to the rooftops," or so declared R. E. L. Masters in this introduction to his 1962 book *The Homosexual Revolution*.[2] Among the most striking changes regarding sexuality in the United States, Masters concluded, was that homosexuality had become part of the national discourse and that a homosexual revolution was set to occur. Although the book heralded a revolution in American sexual mores, it neither ignited that revolution nor was it particularly revolutionary in its own right. Nor was the book the first of a burgeoning genre of pseudo-social-scientific studies of homosexuality in the United States—that distinction should go to either Donald Webster Cory's *The Homosexual in America* (1951) or Ann Aldrich's *We Walk Alone* (1955). Masters's book also was not the most popular of the new genre; a bestseller published by Doubleday, Jess Stearn's *Sixth Man*, outsold *The Homosexual Revolution* and its predecessors. And neither was Masters the first author to spend time researching within the gay world then growing more visible in American cities and the homophile organizations headquartered there.

Masters's "exposé," as the dust jacket labeled it, did however encapsulate all of the developments in the flourishing literature on homosexuality designed for wide public consumption. Moreover, *The Homosexual Revolution* was probably the most cerebral, sensitive, in-depth, and prescient of the popular American studies of homosexuality published in the first half of the 1960s—even if it remained absolutely comfortable in its standpoint of heterosexual privilege.[3] More than notable content, though, *The Homosexual Revolution* is an important if symbolic watershed in the question of communication medium; it provides a typical and popular example of the kind of publication that introduced homosexuality to the mass-mediated public sphere in the early 1960s. *The Homosexual Revolution* was just one of dozens of publications in an increasingly crowded field populated by hacks, self-proclaimed authorities, and a few authentic experts on the subject. The explosion in widely disseminated material on homosexuality during this period forces us to consider not only the content of these publications but their sheer number and scale of distribution making an information-packed discourse newly available to a much wider audience. Writing at the dawn of the 1960s, Masters reported, "An enormous amount of homoerotic literature has been published and/or made available in this country throughout the 1950s and up to the present." Masters seemed aware that his book was part of this trend and that it would only gain steam throughout the 1960s. He added, "Books—scientific studies, popularizations of science, propaganda tracts, novels, collections of short stories, plays poetry, and other forms and varieties—have rolled from the presses in an unceasing and rather incredible torrent."[4]

This massive increase in publicly available literature about homosexuality was only one reason why Masters declared a homosexual revolution to be at hand in the United States. In virtually every chapter, Masters argued that this revolution was not an accident and was not being left to chance, stating that "in fact some powerful, more or less hidden forces are constantly working in [*sic*] behalf of just such an eruption."[5] He exposed these powerful forces as the organizations of the homophile movement: the Mattachine Society, the Daughters of Bilitis, ONE, Inc., and a few smaller organizations just emerging like the League for Civil Education. Indeed, Masters's publisher assumed the reading public already would know of such organizations, mentioning the Mattachine Society on the cover of one paperback edition of *The Homosexual Revolution* without any definition or explanation.[6] Moreover, Masters revealed that as a number of the homophile groups were headquartered in San Francisco, the city gained the "informal designation as America's Capital of Queerdom."[7] More than establishing the location of a queer capital, though, Masters contributed to the mapping of a national homosexual geography with his explicit references to regions, cities, neighborhoods, bars, parks, community centers, and other sites. His descriptive mapping named not only capitals, but meccas, retreats, outposts, hinterlands, borderlands, and colonies.

According to Masters, the sum of the events he described was that society could expect to see a drastic shift in American sexual mores as homosexuals became more visible, as sexuality-based communities grew in size and power, and as the previously silent millions of homosexuals emerged into public space and began to populate the gay world. Although Masters almost certainly overestimated the power of the combined forces of the homophile movement, he accurately pointed out that it was providing services for homosexuals, laboring on behalf of homosexuals, and working with the media to change the representation of homosexuals. According to Masters, the confluence of massively increased publicity with an energized and expanding movement that sought to make the most of that publicity resulted in an entirely new social situation. The final outcome of this "quiet revolution" would be the transformation of American sexualities and sexual subcultures.

Whenever historians argue that published words and images can inspire a revolution, critics invariably and oftentimes legitimately contend that the news media does not create but merely recognizes what already exists. Lesbian writer Marijane Meaker, writing as "Ann Aldrich" in the book *We Two Won't Last* (1963), countered Masters's prognosis, asserting, "I think there is no such thing as a homosexual revolution, but simply (and because of new investigations into *all* our archaic legislation) more dissemination of information about an already existing large homosexual population."[8] What becomes clear, however, after gaining a familiarity with the great abundance and diversity of information that appeared during the period as well as benefiting from the knowledge of what came to pass is that Meaker was both correct and incorrect in her assessment. Yes, the media disseminated information about an already existing population, as she claimed. But she was incorrect in downplaying the influence that such information could and in fact would have upon the millions of Americans who, as she wrote, are so lonely and isolated that they write her letters "by the hundreds . . . asking if I know anyone to whom they can write. . . just one homosexual with whom they might have a friendship."[9] While the media did not create homosexual community, it did greatly expand awareness of it in both general and very particular ways. And, following McLuhan, expanded awareness precipitated mutual participation and responsibility.

As the subsequent chapters will make clear, the expanding coverage of the homophile organizations and homosexuality overall is largely attributable to significant innovations in the American news and culture industries from the late 1950s into the early 1970s. In many ways propelling this change was the introduction of television to the vast majority of Americans in the 1950s. As television was becoming the dominant medium through which news and entertainment reached the American people, other media struggled to keep pace largely by seeking to provide what primetime television could or would not.[10] From *Life* magazine to nighttime radio and from Hollywood films to local newspapers, media outlets in competition with television gave Americans increasingly extended peeks into the arenas of deviance, illegality, and activism that television executives and censors refused to broadcast into the new American hearth—the television room. According to Masters and numerous other observers, coverage of homosexuality proved to be one way in which photojournalists, radio talk show hosts, and paperback authors could set themselves and their products apart from what appeared on television. As the news and culture industries began to cover homosexuality regularly and candidly during this period, the producers, photographers, and writers looked to the past as well as the present to help them as they formulated stories. In the past they found evidence of homosexuality as a grave social problem that touched everything from childhood education to international espionage; in the present they focused on current manifestations of the "problem" along with individuals and organizations that offered a wide range of remedies. That most journalists, in particular, consulted the same experts and institutions meant that not only was the story of homosexuality cast in "pro" and "con" terms but that through repetition a narrative of homosexuality emerged in which certain patterns of identity acquisition, community building, political organizing, and geography making were established as normal and predictable. These narratives of people and places became the lens through which the American public learned about homosexuality as well as the lens through which individuals exploring their sexuality came to understand themselves. The following two chapters take Masters's pronouncements from 1962 seriously and build on and complicate them. The chapters examine the entry of homosexuality into the mass media; the role the publishers, journalists, photographers, and homophile organizations had in enabling this development; and the impact such developments had upon the options available to homosexuals as they sought others like themselves and as they searched for the meaning of that quest.

CHAPTER 3

Building the Lesbian *Grapevine*

From love letters to small-circulation newsletters, from words exchanged at a bar to information shared in a Daughters of Bilitis (DOB) discussion group, lesbian communication networks existed on a limited scale before the 1960s. Individuals may have gathered together in small groups, but even the largest and most geographically dispersed of these would have been based primarily on a traditional ideal of community whereby individuals knew one another by sight and could communicate by word of mouth. And in the rare case when a connection was made through a less traditional means of communication, fear and suspicion tended to dominate the exchange, at least until adequate reassurances could be made.

By the 1960s, though, the character of lesbian communication networks already had undergone dramatic changes. With the increase in literature that dealt with lesbians, primarily in paperback books, not only were American men given a steady supply of erotic fiction, but countless women around the country were exposed to ideas and information that previously were forbidden or at least well hidden. Moreover, during the early 1950s the lesbian bar gained cultural currency. When the bar was expressly situated in New York's Greenwich Village, as it was in so many novels, the previously amorphous ideas about lesbian geography became concrete and, for those with the mettle and resources to travel, those ideas might become the basis for experience. Similarly, although it was a small and fledging group, the DOB succeeded in linking hundreds of lesbians across the country with one another and gathering them into a distinctly modern communication network that was mediated through print and, consequently, imagination, rather than sight, sound, smell, and touch. As a result of such innovations in communications, as limited as they were, the lesbian world gained in visibility and it expanded in reach; and the lines linking lesbians became both more robust as well as further reaching. These trends accelerated quickly when the mass media entered the fray in the latter part of the 1950s, adding the important dimension of mass scale to the transformations already afoot.

With greater attention being directed to the lesbian world, most especially through representations of the emerging iconic institutions of the lesbian bar and the lesbian organization, communication networks transformed in significant ways. Because of an increase in the circulation of information about the lesbian world and the construction of new gateways through which individuals could gain access to it, the character of connection and isolation in the lesbian world changed. Not that lesbian isolation expanded or contracted noticeably during the period, but lesbians (or those curious) increasingly gained the understanding of the varying degrees to which they were connected to other people like themselves. With the expanding awareness of the possibilities of connection also came the broadening understanding of one's proximity to other lesbians and to lesbian community. For many, this realization translated into a feeling of isolation and, consequently, the sense that they should seek out and connect with other lesbians, whether by moving to cities, participating in an organization, meeting a friend, exchanging letters, or simply reading a book or magazine.

The possibilities open to women who sought to connect with the lesbian world, however, were not limitless and they were not entirely of their own making, although those seeking contacts did invest a good deal of imagination and exerted inestimable energy in their quest. The literature of the day made it clear that two of the more visible and accessible pathways that women might travel as they sought to connect with others like themselves were by seeking out and then visiting a lesbian bar and by learning about and then participating in the activities of the DOB. The reason for the predominance of these two options is the frequency with which they appeared in public discussions of female homosexuality during the period and in the memories shared in oral history interviews in years since. Yet, another reason is that mentions of the lesbian bar and the DOB elicited some of the most sensational and memorable representations produced during the era and that discussions of the two institutions provided the public with contrasting narratives of lesbian life. Moreover, the publicity achieved by the two institutions provided lesbians, or those simply curious, with two options for connecting with others they perceived to be like themselves. The lesbian bar, according to most descriptions, was set in New York's Greenwich Village, and it was revealed as a place of mixed joviality and pain, surveillance and escape, alienation and inclusion, in which patrons from all walks of life participated in an almost exclusively gay world populated by lesbians butch and femme. The DOB, in contrast, was revealed through the contents of its magazine and the activities of its members associated primarily with the headquarters chapter in San Francisco. Wherever they came from, though, the lesbians in the DOB were striving for life as members of the respectable primarily white middle class that eschewed the bars, although they too created and lived in an almost exclusively gay world.

For the women who were engaging in the process of identification or who already considered themselves homosexual, these contrasting narratives pointed toward different paths by which they may travel while becoming lesbian or by which they could connect with others who so identified. That lesbians would travel such paths was not inevitable, but these representations provided some of the few signposts available to lesbians (whether part of the lesbian life or not). Reams of correspondence and other documentation further reveal that many women did connect to the lesbian world through these mostly unintentionally prescribed pathways—and that the expanding knowledge of the location of certain gateways to the lesbian world translated into an expansion of those worlds. Yet, the two gateways—the lesbian bar and the lesbian organization—were accessible to divergent populations and they attracted different kinds of women. Not only did various groups of women have access to different physical and conceptual spaces, but they had access to spaces that turned out to be somewhat in contrast to those desired by male homosexuals. Although both the DOB and lesbians bars were situated within cities, there were ways in which both negated the city and encouraged lesbians not to look to urban enclaves or their own communities—theirs was a queer world that by the early 1970s would be defined by distance and by connection in extraurban surroundings.

The lesbian bar and the DOB appeared in a whole variety of literary, psychological, sociological, and journalistic explorations of lesbianism, but they received their fullest, most complex treatment in what arguably were the era's most widely read nonfiction portrayals of female homosexuality, Ann Aldrich's series of nonfiction paperback originals (1955–1963) and Jess Stearn's book *The Grapevine* (1964).[1] Among the many factors making these books significant is that they reached hundreds of thousands of readers, while earlier forms of communication (like the *Ladder* and information passed by word of mouth) could reach only a fraction of that population. Moreover, as a result of gaining a larger audience and capturing in prose many key elements of the lesbian experience typical of the era, Aldrich's and Stearn's books would, by the late 1960s, enjoy a kind of cultural authority on lesbian life.

Mass-Mediated Lesbians

If the image of the lesbian "sicko" dominated representations of female homosexuality during the 1940s and early 1950s, by the late 1950s and into the 1960s new and sometimes contrasting images appeared, augmenting those already in circulation. While arrested development theories of lesbianism still were disseminated in professional journals and in popular culture during the period, they were both enhanced and complicated by additional information and ideas. According to the new literature of the day, the lesbian was more often seen in the context of her world and less prominently on a psychiatrist's couch or interned in an asylum for the insane, though, of course, these images remained. For instance, in "queen of lesbian 'pulp'" Ann Bannon's first book, *Odd Girl Out* (1957), readers were treated to the somewhat familiar lesbian setting of a women's college. Yet, the book was not written as a startling exposé or a psychological case study. Rather, it was a romance between young and attractive women. Surely the affair between the two women ended by the close of the novel and heterosexuality was at least in part reaffirmed, but Bannon also allowed one of the women to escape to New York's Greenwich Village, probably *the* key site of lesbianism in the late 1950s. This perspective was continued as a central theme through much lesbian paperback fiction published between 1952 and 1966. In the late 1950s, then, Americans were provided with an augmented image of the lesbian that highlighted both the social structure of the lesbian world along with the erotic elements of that world—elements that were deemed safe for consumption by heterosexual men of the era.

The reasons for this shift in lesbian representation are perhaps more important than the content of the shift itself. Of the many reasons for the change, perhaps the most important is simply that more was being said by a wider diversity of people in a larger number of media. From the second half of the 1950s through the early 1960s, accounts of lesbianism appeared in fiction and nonfiction paperbacks; professional journals in the fields of sociology, psychology, medicine, and social services; "fringe-time" radio and television; mass- and small-circulation newspapers; mainstream and alternative magazines; popular sociological studies; and plays and films. As will become clear later in this chapter, each of these different media tended to offer distinct representations of lesbianism, and each were burdened by varying mandates of self- and outside-imposed censorship as well as by the demands and expectations of the particular audiences of each venue.

That there was a simple increase in the frequency of candid representations is attributable to several factors. For one, formal and informal barriers to presenting images of and information about homosexuality began to fall in the 1950s. A few key U.S. Supreme Court decisions largely affirmed the right to distribute homosexual and homoerotic materials through the mail, including the 1958 decision, *One, Incorporated, v. Olesen*, which overturned a lower court decision declaring *ONE* magazine to be obscene.[2] Yet self-censorship and informal barriers to publication had long been a greater threat to representations of lesbianism than legal censorship, at least since a New York court refused to ban Radclyffe Hall's *Well of Loneliness* in 1929.[3] Although the paper trail left by informal and self-imposed censorship is rather skim, the increase in representations suggests that cases of extralegal censorship also declined in the 1950s. Still, to read about lesbianism in a mainstream magazine or in a novel published by a respectable publisher would have been rare in the 1950s. The fact is that the majority of representations of lesbianism appeared in relatively new media, most particularly in paperback originals (or "pulps") and, to a lesser extent, late-night radio and television talk shows—all media which were designed in a way that accommodated more risqué material. Although various decency-in-literature committees and antismut leagues were active throughout this period, by the late 1950s the tide seemed to be turning toward a greater societal tolerance of and, indeed, interest in information and stories about sex. In fact, one of the most vocal groups of people arguing on behalf of a more robust discussion of sex and sexuality were those professionals working in psychology and medicine who hoped to direct the national conversation on the subjects. Psychiatrist Edmund Bergler, author of *Homosexuality: Disease or Way of Life?* (1956), borrowed terms (but not pleas for tolerance) from the Mattachine Society and lamented that there existed a "conspiracy of silence" about homosexuality; and prior to Bergler, both Frank Caprio and George Henry each complained about the paucity of information and discussion of homosexuality.[4] Although few of these professionals expected the increased chatter about homosexuality to result in increased tolerance of it—quite the contrary, in fact—they did argue on behalf of the expert's opinion in influencing public opinion. As a result of the changed climate of opinion as well as the altered media landscape, editors and publishers in the mainstream media began including references to homosexual people and the places they frequented in articles about a variety of subjects and started to ask their reporters and authors to come up with feature stories and book manuscripts addressing the phenomenon. Thus, by the middle 1960s, lengthy discussions of or complete articles about homosexuality appeared in national publications like *Life, Time, Newsweek, MacLean's,* the *New York Times, Sports Illustrated,* and *Holiday;* in regional publications like the *Washington Post,* the *Denver Post, Chicago Daily News, Philadelphia Magazine* and many more; in addition, CBS News produced an hour-long television special on male homosexuality in 1964, although it did not air until 1967.[5]

The vast majority of the mainstream journalists focused on the lives and lifestyles of male homosexuals, but many included at least passing references to lesbianism. And when the journalists did mention lesbianism, they often did so in a way similar to the more gregarious authors of paperbacks and late-night talk show hosts. That is, they examined lesbianism through the contrasting lenses of the lesbian bar and the lesbian organization.

Ann Aldrich's (Not So) Lonely Groves of Lesbos

In 1951, the newly founded subsidiary of Fawcett Publications established to publish paperback originals, Gold Medal Books, issued a book that its editor thought of as a women's war story. It was called *Women's Barracks.*[6] Shortly after the book was published, however, the editors at Gold Medal not only realized that they had a massive hit on their hands (the book eventually sold over three million copies) but that it attracted readers not primarily due to its wartime setting but rather because of its depiction of lesbian love affairs among women serving during wartime. Moreover, through the piles of mail received from readers hungry for more stories in this vein, the editors were shocked to learn that a large number were from women who were attracted to other women and were hoping that the press would publish more books like it. The first lesbian paperback original, then, was an accidental birth, but the second one would not be. Among the most prolific, widely read, and influential of those authors who built upon the foundation established by Torres's *Women's Barracks* was a writer by the name of Marijane Meaker, better know to readers through her many pen names, including, most importantly, "Vin Packer" and "Ann Aldrich." As Packer, Meaker wrote the early and important paperback original, *Spring Fire* (1952), a novel about sorority sisters at a midwestern college who pursue a romance that ultimately ends in heartbreak that was a major success in its own right, selling at least 1.5 million copies.[7] Over roughly the next two decades, she followed with nineteen additional Packer novels, a few of which dealt with homosexuality. Not long after the success of *Spring Fire*, Meaker proposed to her publisher that she write a nonfiction exploration of lesbianism from a subjective point of view, because she too was a lesbian. Meaker's editor was intrigued, and he gave her the go ahead. Writing as Ann Aldrich, Meaker eventually wrote four books as well as edited an anthology on lesbian life in the United States in general and in New York in particular. Like the fictional lesbian paperbacks that preceded them, the Aldrich books sold extremely well as each book went into a third or fourth printing of 400,000 copies.[8]

Aldrich's first book, *We Walk Alone through Lesbos' Lonely Groves* (1955) was both an addition to the established genre of nonfiction writing on female homosexuality as well as a radical departure from earlier studies (fig. 6). Aldrich wrote in the foreword, "This book is the result of fifteen years' participation in society as a female homosexual . . . I am convinced that the opinions and viewpoints of the lesbian herself are as valuable in arriving at conclusions about her nature as are those proffered by the psychiatrist, sociologist, anthropologist, jurist, churchman, or psychologist"—that the view of the "insider" was a necessary augmentation of the view of the "outsider."[9] In making this argument and in offering a book based upon subjective experience, Aldrich placed her study in the distinctly modern tradition of works that sought to enlighten the public about problems of identity not through scientific discourse but through a subjective one. It was this impulse that inspired foundational twentieth-century critiques such as W. E. B. DuBois's *Souls of Black Folk*, in which the author asks, "How does it feel to be a problem?" as well as James Weldon Johnson's novel, *The Autobiography of an Ex-Colored Man*.[10] Moreover, this impulse was shared by Donald Webster Cory (Edward Sagarin) when he wrote *The Homosexual in America* in 1951—a book celebrated as the first non-fictional account of male homosexuality written by a self-acknowledged homosexual in the United States. Indeed, Aldrich remembers that it was Cory's book that inspired her to write her own subjective account of female homosexuality. All of these authors, Aldrich included, had tired of hearing outsider experts offering opinions and issuing prescriptions on issues relating to a cultural group of which they were not members. In response to the pronouncements from above, those who had been studied and examined began to produce their own subjective studies and examinations. Along with being part of this American literary and sociological tradition, Aldrich stepped out of convention by becoming the first self-acknowledged lesbian to write a nonfictional account of lesbian life in the United States. Moreover, Aldrich published this generally serious study in

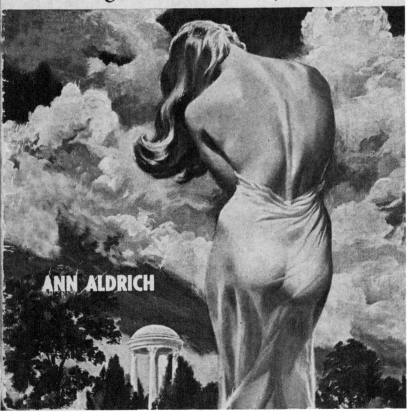

6 The cover illustration of Ann Aldrich's debut 1955 book helped introduce the reading world to the image of a sexy lesbian, alone in a mythical Greek setting. The text of the book, however, focused on lesbians gathered in the modern metropolis. From the personal collection of the author.

the unconventional context of the paperback original. Usually host to westerns, crime thrillers, and romance novels, the paperback original provided a rather queer fit for a serious albeit subjective account of lesbianism.

Still, the queer fit proved to be a rather good one as *We Walk Alone* was just the first of four successful books that Aldrich would publish for the paperback house, Gold Medal, in the 1950s and 1960s (a fifth book was published by another press in 1972). Because of the tantalizing style of subjective explorations as well as the easy accessibility of mass-distributed paperbacks, Aldrich's books could be expected to be used for very personal purposes, much like homosexual readers had done with books like *The Well of Loneliness* and others detailed in my introduction. The personal tone and the wide distribution of Aldrich's studies made her books particularly conducive for readers who were seeking help in the process of self-definition and who were seeking locations in which to connect with others like themselves. In other words, the Aldrich books uniquely provided the means through which a woman might participate in a communication network and thus set out on a journey of self-discovery. Any process of identity making, though, would be filtered though the images on the cover and the words on the page.

After encountering Aldrich's "coming-out" in the book's foreword, readers of *We Walk Alone* were taken on a tour of the lesbian world in sixteen thematic chapters, ranging from a review of psychological theories to lesbians in history, from lesbians in Greenwich Village to those in Paris, and from married lesbians to the parents of lesbians. In this book as well as those that followed, Aldrich's style was not so much that of the objective journalist or the reflective diarist but was closer to what has been called reportage, which, according to literary scholar Elizabeth Francis, "blended journalism with the storytelling devices of fiction"; in a recent interview, Aldrich concurred, describing her approach as based on "casual observation . . . [and] a fiction-writer's facts."[11] Aldrich's particular style of reportage vacillated between straightforward reporting and reconstructed dialogue among lesbians. Although only two chapters focused specifically on lesbian bars, much of the reportage in other chapters was set in or around bars, thus making those places lynchpin sites in the composition of lesbian life in the United States (and Europe), at least according to Aldrich.

Aldrich painted a relatively complex portrait of the lesbian bar in *We Walk Alone*. Lesbians bars, according to Aldrich, were to be found is most major cities; some of the bars catered to mixed clientele while others, generally more hidden to the outside, were woman-only establishments. Because of the clear illegality of the latter type (in New York, for instance, bar owners were forbidden from allowing two or more homosexuals from entering their establishment at the same time), such exclusively lesbian bars would have had a brief life expectancy; yet, once such a bar was shut by police action, another was sure to open within a month or two.[12] In all of her books, Aldrich focused on New York City, and through her examples she suggested that most lesbian bars were located in Greenwich Village. In such places "the whole world is gay," a "no man's land, filled to overflowing with female homosexuals." The lesbian bar was the kind of place where "dark corners hide the hand-holders and the couples who kiss each other lightly, furtively—for even [the bar] must know some discretion, must be wary of a possible disguised member of the vice squad in their midst." This furtiveness took its toll, Aldrich argued, for the "gay life for the female homosexual, as lived in the gay bars and cafes of the world, is a lonely, harassed, and depressing life." However, as Aldrich made clear, it was a particular breed of lesbian who patronized such establishments, those who adopted butch or femme styles. In lesbian bars, Aldrich wrote, "The butches move through the room like little boys who are old enough to wear long pants, but too young to shave. The feminine lesbians, made up of chorus girls, flirt with them, tease them, touch the collars of their shirts with long red fingernails."[13] Although she described the behaviors of the patrons in great detail, she offered much less help to readers who wished to identify the bars in particular. For none of the bars mentioned, which she claims were sketches of actual sites, did Aldrich use the real name. And further, even though she changed the names of the bars, she engaged in additional acts of coding—but they were acts that might have taught readers how to find the bars in question. While Aldrich printed the name of the bar with a mixed clientele, the Blue Room, she named the exclusively lesbian only as M's. Although she hid M's well, she nevertheless revealed that exclusively homosexual bars often could be found by visiting intermediary places like the more visible Blue Room and asking around or listening for verbal cues, thus providing her readers with a hint about the lesbian communication network as it operated on the streets and in the bars of New York City.

In her second nonfiction study, *We, Too, Must Love* (1958), Aldrich covered much the same territory as she did in her first but focused more specifically on New York and upped the quotient of storytelling through dialogue. She also continued to reveal the lesbian world through the lens of the Greenwich Village lesbian bar, this time, however, augmented by chapters focusing on Uptown lesbians who only visited but did not frequent the bars. In this book, too, Aldrich mentioned two bars, one of which attracted a mixed clientele, while the other was exclusively lesbian. In a recent interview, Aldrich noted that she invented the names for the bars (the

Dock and Three Flights Up) to disguise and protect the real bars (P-town Landing and Seven Steps Down, respectively). Moreover, she noted that in the case of one lesbian bar, "You could walk right by it without knowing it was there. There is no sign outside; there are no lights visible to the street. It is in the basement of a corner building, and save for the people going in and out, it does not look like a bar or restaurant."[14] In another case, Aldrich mentioned that an exclusively lesbian bar had to pay protection fees to the police and, when political pressure was on, the lesbian waitresses in the bar were forced to ditch slacks for skirts. Along with a sustained emphasis on the furtiveness associated with lesbian bars, Aldrich in We, Too, Must Love also focused on what she perceived as antisocial behavior, most particularly alcoholism. Still, Aldrich included stories and offered conclusions of her own that complicated a simple depiction of lesbian bars.

The response of readers to these books is not so easy to gauge, in part because of the question of who read the books, in part because of the difficulties in recovering their thoughts. Scholars have claimed that although the vast majority of lesbian paperback fiction was purchased by heterosexual men as erotic literature, the books eventually gained a sizable lesbian readership. The scholars further claim that the lesbians who read paperbacks not only were quite adept at reading for lesbian romance while ignoring the unhappy (for lesbians) endings. Lesbian readers also favored books that were apparently written by lesbians and that treated lesbianism overall in a sympathetic light.[15] I think it reasonable to assume that readers of lesbian paperback nonfiction were at least as diverse as readers of fiction, for not only might they have appealed to lesbians and heterosexual male readers, but others like relatives of homosexuals and social service professionals might have been drawn to the books. Further, documents reveal that lesbian readers of nonfiction were similarly capable of reading the books selectively, appreciative of representations they liked but critical of those they did not, as discussed below. This is further confirmed by Aldrich herself, who included selections from a few letters written by her readers in subsequent books.

Writing three years after the publication of her first book, Aldrich claimed that she had received well over six hundred letters in response to that book, the majority of which were from women. The letters that were reprinted in her books revealed a high degree of emotion, confusion on the subject of homosexuality, and according to Aldrich, were a "testament to a more appalling fact than that of people's obvious misery and frustration—to the fact that on so serious a subject as homosexuality there is no one to turn to but a person whose name one copies down from the cover of a book on that subject."[16] Although Aldrich unfortunately did not save any of the letters she received, the correspondence she reprinted included letters from parents concerned that a daughter might be lesbian, from men who would have liked to a meet a lesbian or had been in a relationship with one, and most prominently, from women who called themselves lesbian or who thought they might be one.[17] The letters from the final group varied in situation and tone: some berated Aldrich for emphasizing the lives of unhappy and poorly adjusted lesbians, others applauded her candor in exposing the pain that comes with gay life. Many, however, shared a complaint and, consequently, a common request. The complaint was that there existed a lack of information on the subject of homosexuality and, if the letter writer knew such information was out there, that the lines of communication linking individuals to the information were too few and too tenuous. Although some of these letters blamed what they regretted as a fall into sexual perversion on the paucity of information, others sought to remedy the situation by seeking out information or someone with whom to correspond. Whether the correspondents wanted homosexuality banished or they desired an easier life for homosexuals—and letters from both perspectives were included—all pinpointed increased and better communications about homosexuality as the means to achieve their goals, and Aldrich's books were seen as a step in the right direction.

Aldrich's response to these women demonstrates the power held by a widely read author to influence the flow of information and even to help some people manage that information. Yet, her responses to the readers also highlight the constraints imposed by the mass media upon the exchange of information. In explaining some of the appeal of her books in a recent interview, Aldrich said her "books were resource books. A lot of the mail I got was from people wanting to know where the bars were in New York, where they could live, where I had lived. You know, they wanted to know how to get to New York and how to get to these bars." As a lone author rather than an activist or social service provider, Aldrich was not entirely prepared for this kind of mail and was not fully equipped to handle it. She eventually received so much mail that she decided to respond only to letters that included a direct question—or to readers who hinted that they might be in serious emotional or psychological trouble. To those asking about bars in New York, Aldrich said, "I told them where they were. I told them most cab drivers know where lesbian bars are." However, Aldrich recalled that when it came to lesbian bars information was of the moment and, as far as settling in New York, information was only so useful. She remembered, "I said the bars that I can mention to you now probably won't be there by the time you get to New York. And I told them not to come to New York and expect to be part of bar life and look for a job at the same time because it was too risky."[18]

Offering her readers a place to stay or a personal introduction to the scene certainly was out of the question, but with no organization or group of professionals (with the exception of a few psychologists) to refer these women to, Aldrich's only option was to provide them with information that likely was out of date, to offer hints about how to find new bars, and to suggest to her readers that they stay put and perhaps not seek to make a connection with the lesbians described in her books. So, while Aldrich reached a much larger lesbian audience than the members of the DOB could ever dream of reaching, Aldrich also was not as well equipped to handle the requests and offer help in the same way as was the DOB. Consequently, while the mass media opened up possibilities for connection to a larger population of women interested in exploring lesbianism, the information itself was unmoored from any institution through which it could be managed and made into something rational and useful. Certainly a number of Aldrich's readers who either did not heed her advice or never asked for it in the first place moved to New York and other large cities looking for places like the Dock and Three Flights Up. Some of these women probably found what they were looking for, while others left the city unfulfilled.[19] But they came to the city with images and expectations in their minds that had been shaped in part by the words of people like Aldrich who could provide descriptions of the lesbian world but not much more.

Perhaps because Aldrich focused primarily on the lesbian bar scene and on New York City, she did not mention the DOB in her writings until 1960, when she wrote an essay about the *Ladder* in the collection she edited called *Carol in a Thousand Cities.* However, prior to Aldrich writing about the DOB, members of the DOB had, since 1956, been discussing Aldrich's books and publishing their thoughts in the *Ladder.* While a full discussion of the long dialogue between members of the DOB and Aldrich is beyond the scope of this book, it is worth knowing that members of the DOB were developing an idea of representational politics that was in part spurred on by readings of Aldrich.[20] After reading Aldrich's first two books and discussing them with other members of the DOB, Del Martin published an open letter to Aldrich. In it, she wrote, "With the publishing of your two books you have become a rather prominent spokesman for the Lesbian," but then quickly shifted tone, writing, "Your intentions are admirable, Miss Aldrich, but somehow we feel that you have not reached your objective." Martin's point of contention was based on the question of representation, contending, "The cross-section of Lesbian life which you have depicted may be likened to a similar study of heterosexual life in which only the Skid Road characters and the well-to-do are delineated," to which she added succinctly, "Your sampling is just not very representative."[21] The fault of Aldrich's book was, according to Martin, that she only reinforced stereotypes and that she failed to present positive portrayals of lesbians, like, for instance, depictions of DOB members, who Martin thought might elicit a better understanding of lesbianism by the mainstream public. Martin followed the open letter with a personal one addressed to Marijane Meaker, the woman behind Ann Aldrich. In the letter she introduced herself and the DOB and suggested that they initiate a dialogue in order to forge common strategies and goals. Aldrich never responded directly to the open letter or privately to the personal letter. However, in her books *Carol in a Thousand Cities* and *We Two Won't Last* (1963) Aldrich included many pages on the DOB and the *Ladder.*

Although Aldrich devoted a good deal of attention to lesbian bars in *We Two Won't Last* (*Carol in a Thousand Cities* was a collection of essays primarily by writers and psychoanalysts on lesbianism), the DOB and the *Ladder* emerged in her post-1960 books as a prime site of lesbianism that to a certain degree stood in contrast to the lesbian bar. Like the lesbian bar, though, the DOB was treated both critically and complexly by Aldrich. In her 1960 chapter-length review of the *Ladder,* which focused on fiction rather than analysis or news, Aldrich took on the magazine from several angles but most plainly expressed disappointment in the quality of writing and in the way in which lesbians were represented. Three years later, she expanded her analysis of the organization, writing, "It is fortunate that a lesbian organization has not only survived, but grown, for the DOBs are a well-meaning group, and their aims (breakdown of unfair legislation and taboos, research projects to study the variant, dissemination of educational literature on the homosexual theme, etc.) are worthwhile ones."[22] Yet, while she expressed appreciation that an organization existed to help the lesbian, she also felt that the DOB had become too powerful, that other journalists had cast the DOB as synonymous with and representative of lesbianism overall. Aldrich wrote, "Clearly, the DOBs are fast becoming a major voice, if not the sole organized voice, of the lesbian in this country. This has both fortunate and unfortunate aspects," adding that widely read authors like R. E. L. Masters have "depended almost entirely on the Daughters of Bilitis as representatives of female variance." Aldrich concluded, "Suffice to say now that the DOBs are a well-meaning and dogged little band, but they are about as representative of the majority of female homosexuals as T. C. Jones, the famed female impersonator, is representative of womankind."[23]

While Aldrich did not like the ways in which the DOB portrayed lesbians and sought to speak for them as a group, she mediated between her readers and the DOB in a way somewhat different from how she responded to readers interested in New York City bars. After Aldrich published her first essay on the *Ladder* in 1960, she started receiving mail from women interested in that magazine and the organization that published it. Aldrich recently remarked that "even though I despised that magazine. . . I did recommend *The Ladder*" to readers in the same way that she revealed the names of lesbian bars to readers.[24] However, the important difference between lesbian bars and the DOB was the instability of the former and the relative permanence of the latter. While the lesbian bar as an institution was remarkably persistent, individual sites were not; in contrast, the DOB was an incorporated nonprofit organization located in San Francisco with a few chapters around the country. In her books, Aldrich played an important role, along with authors of fiction like Ann Bannon, in spreading word that in places like Greenwich Village lesbian bars could be found. But because of the fleeting nature of those places, the link between readers and bars was rather tenuous and fraught with obstacles. Aldrich, though, helped to establish more robust links in the lesbian communication network when she connected her readers to the DOB simply by mentioning the organization in her books as well as through forwarding letters and sharing addresses with the organization.[25] As this happened, the mass media of paperback originals became an important mediating force in the realignment of the lesbian world and in the establishment of new kinds of connections available to women seeking to make contact. Although the DOB critiqued Aldrich for falsely representing lesbianism and Aldrich critiqued the DOB for doing the same, they were engaged in the shared project of representing lesbianism both to the mainstream American public and to isolated and connected lesbians. While Aldrich then (and now) critiqued the DOB from a variety of angles, by 1963 she came to a position that the organization served a purpose and within the confines of that purpose Aldrich was willing to offer a little help and serve as a hub in the larger lesbian communication network.

The question of lesbian representation and communication networks becomes perhaps even more vexed when considering what was one of the most popular and controversial books on lesbianism and probably the greatest public relations coup for the DOB prior to 1966: the publication of Jess Stearn's 1964 nonfiction book, *The Grapevine*—which sold well in both hardcover and paperback. Through this book, the DOB extended the communication network it had so carefully begun constructing upon the face-to-face relations of lesbians in the middle 1950s. The complex and sometimes surprising story of the creation, content, and reception of Stearn's *The Grapevine* demonstrates the power of manufactured media events to transform societal assumptions and to continue the dialogue initiated by writers like Ann Aldrich.

The Lesbian *Grapevine*

What is the lesbian grapevine? According to Jess Stearn, author of *The Grapevine*, it was the underground network populated by women who loved women (see fig. 7). Instead of being isolated in secrecy and silence from the outside world, Stearn discovered, "many were part of a vast, sprawling grapevine, with a secret code of their own." This was a highly elaborate world, where, according to Stearn, "on Thursdays, for instance, multitudes of lesbians throughout the country wore a special color of dress to identify themselves to other secret lesbians. In New York, Los Angeles, and San Francisco, the cognoscenti wore green; in Chicago, they chose yellow; in Connecticut, it was pink. The day itself was known as Sweet Thursday."[26] Stearn added, "Many lesbians even had a special vernacular. The phrase 'coming out' ironically indicated a lesbian's sexual debut; being 'brought out' reflected the same result."[27] As Stearn learned about the complexities, rituals, and language of the lesbian grapevine, he also discovered its vast size: although "lesbianism was by no means the province of the big cities alone," lesbians tend "to lose themselves in the anonymity and excitement of a teeming metropolis."[28] Although written in the somewhat fictionalized tone of reportage and while probably overestimating the size and scope of the lesbian grapevine circa 1964, Stearn's book is notable not only for recognizing the importance of lesbian communication networks but also for playing a role in transforming them.

Stearn became well known among homophile activists following the publication of his 1961 best-selling book on male homosexuality, *The Sixth Man*. As a popular journalist and a former associate editor at *Newsweek*, Stearn possessed an unusual amount of media savvy. His books reveal his ability to discuss subjects of great controversy while keeping himself above the fray. For someone who had authored books on juvenile delinquency, prostitution, and homosexuality, Stearn comes across to readers even today as generally objective and balanced. That he made an attempt for balance is one reason why he was so appealing to homophile activists who were used to reading works that were more obviously judgmental. So, following the publication of *The Sixth Man*, Stearn became something of a regular on the homophile lecture circuit, appearing at public discussion sessions held by local chapters and conventions sponsored by the national

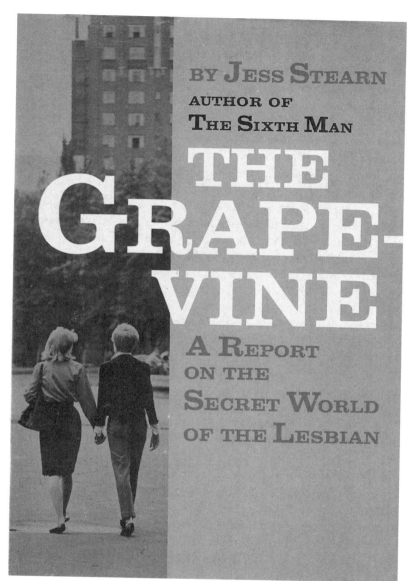

BY JESS STEARN
AUTHOR OF
THE SIXTH MAN

THE
GRAPE-
VINE

A REPORT
ON THE
SECRET WORLD
OF THE LESBIAN

7 The cover to the hardbound edition of Jess Stearn's 1964 study *The Grapevine* juxta-
poses slightly sensational copy ("The Secret World of the Lesbian") with a nearly banal
image of an apparently lesbian couple walking hand-in-hand in a public park. From the
personal collection of the author.

organizations. Stearn's first appearance at a Daughters of Bilitis function was at the group's 1962 biennial convention held in Los Angeles, where he spoke on the subject of the lesbian in the mass media.[29]

While presenting to the audience of DOB members and fellow travelers, Stearn provided an answer to the question of whether the lesbian was being represented at all in the mass media. Stearn agreed with other panelists that she was not (or not nearly enough), but he didn't lay all of the blame on journalists or publishers. Instead he claimed, "One of the reasons we don't have any material is the Lesbian herself," who, he asserted, "was reluctant to reveal herself."[30] Furthermore, he lamented that journalists were presented only with the exceptional or outrageous lesbian, thus preventing them from getting a reasonable cross section of the population. But Stearn also was aware of limitations. Newspapers and magazines, he claimed, probably would not be willing to write about lesbians in any detail, making books the most likely venue for publicity. Moreover, he was defensive about the ability of outsiders (i.e., nonlesbians) to make a contribution on the subject, claiming success was merely "a matter of empathy." "As a reporter you try to put yourself into the other person's problem," he said, "regarding him as a human being instead of a case history."[31] Presenting these ideas before the DOB biennial convention, Stearn not only articulated his thoughts about the representation of lesbians in the mass media but also asserted the credentials he was trying to establish as he prepared to write a new book, which this time would focus on lesbians.

A month later Stearn headed for New York, where he was to appear at a panel discussion sponsored by the New York chapter of the DOB and the Mattachine Society New York entitled "Homophile Organizations in the Public Spotlight." At the panel, Stearn shared more of his ideas about the representation of the lesbian in the mass media. According to the *Ladder*, Stearn suggested that "a conventional image should be conveyed to the American public. The Lesbian, to be made palatable, must appear to be as normal as 'the girl next door.'" Not all on the panel, however, were in agreement. Randy Wicker, for one, challenged Stearn, arguing "that *all* types of homosexuals should be presented to the public from the most respectable to the most flamboyantly disrespectful."[32] By this time not only had Stearn made the decision to write a book about lesbianism, he also had issued a public declaration of how he would go about doing it: that the DOB was going to represent the lesbian as the "girl next door" and, by extension, it would be contrasted to the lesbian who was to remain in his writing unconventional and strange.

The leaders of the DOB were excited about the prospect of gaining additional media attention, yet they were wary enough to remain suspicious of Stearn and smart enough to handle him with kid gloves. By 1962, Martin, Lyon, and the rest of the women active in the DOB were right to be cautious when dealing with journalists and authors. As the experience with Aldrich had made clear, declarations of camaraderie aside, exposure entailed an exchange between the gains of publicity and the pains of critique. Martin, author of "Open Letter to Ann Aldrich," perhaps knew best that such relationships could also be aggravated, so she attempted both to cultivate an easygoing, friendly working relationship with Stearn while impressing upon her colleagues in the DOB the need to treat him with the kind of respect one would give to a person in a position of considerable power. Early on, however, this somewhat humiliating yet politically astute position caused some tension within the DOB.

Writing to Marion Glass of the DOB's New York chapter, Martin summed up the activities in San Francisco then turned to the topic of Jess Stearn's recent visits with members of the organization. She wrote that he "doesn't seem to think the New York group has been very friendly or cooperative" and added, "Whether you like him or not, Marion, he is going to write and publish a book on the girls. And it doesn't hurt to try to present another approach to the subject. Be politic, gal!"[33] All relations between the DOB and Stearn, however, were not conducted on pins and needles. Reporting to Martin and Lyon on the progress of the book in December 1962, Stearn wrote that it "is coming along well, and I have done three chapters dealing directly with the DOB." Stearn also shared with Martin and Lyon his account of the New York public meeting in which he found himself debating Randy Wicker about the ideal media representation of homosexuals. In the discussion, Stearn suggested that the organizations should present a conventional image but, Stearn noted, Wicker "seemed to take umbrage at this point of view, declaring that the worst as well as the best should be presented to the public." "My point," Stearn added, "that the public already believes the worst—and only the worst— seemed to be regarded as the maunderings of senility."[34]

Although Stearn did not make explicit what he meant by the "worst" of the gay world—did he mean sex criminals or merely lesbians who frequented bars?—he revealed his position that there was indeed a "worst" and a "best" in the gay world. Interestingly, this perspective dovetailed, to a certain extent, with the beliefs of the DOB—a fact Stearn surely must have known. Stearn and the DOB, then, shared a media strategy and, as a result, engaged in fruitful collaboration. As part of this arrangement, Stearn wrote to Martin and Lyon, "I would like you girls to see these chapters, and if I get out to California in the next few weeks, will try to arrange to meet you somewhere out there."[35] Stearn hoped that Martin and Lyon would think of themselves as meaningful participants in the creation of his book. Yet, as his reference to the forty-something Martin and Lyon as "girls" suggests, Stearn also carried with him many of the assumptions male heterosexuals held of women, not to mention lesbians, in the 1960s.

Like Ann Aldrich, Stearn was a quick and prolific writer. Having begun research on the book in the summer of 1962, he informed Martin and Lyon in March 1963, "The great epic is near some state of completion." Moreover, he seemed to be quite pleased with his work, even sharing some praise of his work with Martin and Lyon, though through his characteristically circuitous path of another's voice. "It was reviewed by the Doubleday attorneys the other day, and their comments were certainly revealing. One of the attorneys had the feeling that I had condoned this heresy by appearing sympathetic to the problem."[36] The real point of the letter, however, was to ask Martin, Lyon, and DOB national president Jaye Bell if they would meet up with him while he was in Los Angeles in April. "Then you can read the whole [manuscript]," Stearn said proudly, "which I would like very much for you to do."[37]

The relationship between Stearn and Martin and Lyon appeared to blossom over the next few months. Sometime in April, Martin and Lyon read the six chapters of Stearn's manuscript pertaining to the DOB and were for the most part "greatly impressed." "In this book," Martin wrote to Stearn, "You are not just an outsider with an 'open mind' reporting on what you see. You do not just have a rapport with the lesbian." Instead, she told him, rather curiously, "You have empathy, you *are* the lesbian." Indeed, Martin even went so far as to say to the author, "You have had a love affair with each one of us." Whether Martin's words reflected her true feelings or whether they were offered in a strategic move is difficult to tell.[38] What is certain, though, is that Martin placed herself squarely between Stearn and members of the DOB who were suspicious of his methods and motivations; indeed, by speaking metaphorically of her love affair with Stearn and the idea of the "Oneness" of "the male-female principle," she placed herself between the heterosexual man and the lesbian woman.[39] By removing herself from the position of a defensive member of the DOB, a lesbian supposedly swayed by subjective emotions, Martin positioned herself as both the outsider and the insider. In doing so, she offered a number of critiques and suggestions for revision. Handling Stearn with care, careful not to let him think his authority was being usurped by the group he presumed he was helping, Martin hoped she was seen by Stearn as a detached observer. Martin, then, cast herself in much the same role that communication networks played in social mediation: filling in the gap between the public and private spheres, acting as a portal through which information flowed from and to different directions.

The same day Martin wrote the fawning letter to Stearn, she reported on her activities to the DOB governing board and chapter presidents. Martin began by mentioning that she and Lyon had been allowed to preview the portions of Stearn's book pertaining to the DOB and both were "very pleased" with the "excellent treatment" accorded to the organization. Martin, however, went further and spoke to the issue of whether a man could empathize with lesbians. "One of the contentions in the panel discussion at the 1962 Convention was whether or not a man could write *the* book about the Lesbian," Martin recounted. "From the part which we have seen, we personally feel that not only can a man do the job, [but] that the man is Jess Stearn." However, Martin noted that *the* book would not be solely affirming, that it would portray all aspects of the lesbian world and that this might strike some members of the DOB as sensationalistic. So, Martin warned, "While the book, if it is to be a true report on the subject, will include the seamier side, it does have the balance we have all wished for." Before signing the letter with the closing, "With new hope for the future," Martin concluded, "Certainly we feel that the book should boost DOB inquiries, membership and LADDER subscriptions. Others have done this for us with much less favorable reports"—a likely reference to the Aldrich books.[40]

The Daughters of Bilitis as a Lesbian *Grapevine*

The Grapevine hit bookstore shelves a little over a year and a half after it was first conceived. If the nonfiction lesbian paperbacks of Ann Aldrich focused on the lesbian world in and around Manhattan, then Stearn's book (and Masters's that preceded it) departed from that model by taking a more national perspective. This is noteworthy because it marks an important shift in the representation of homosexuality: from this point forward homosexuality was spatialized and, further, often localized according to a more complex national geography. Stearn's study would make stops not only in New York but also Los Angeles, suburban America, Chicago, and, most especially, San Francisco. Indeed, if Aldrich's books took New York lesbian bar or house-party culture as the center of the lesbian universe, Stearn (again, following Masters) placed homophile activism and the DOB in particular at the heart of the lesbian's present and future—although he too wrote about Manhattan. Overall, Stearn's book succeeded in presenting an alternative narrative of lesbian life in the United States with

San Francisco competing with New York for the title of capital and the DOB challenging the lesbian bar as its core of activity and philosophical fountainhead.

The book opened in a manner characteristic of the era: like male homosexuality, lesbianism was a social problem. Although included as an assumption rather than a declarative statement (at the time one would have to make a strident declaration that lesbianism *wasn't* a social problem), the book proceeded not only to detail the problem but to offer a potential solution. The "lesbian problem" already had been presented well by Aldrich and others: lesbians were too mannish, they disliked men, they were violent, they hung around bars and drank too much, they were pathological, they refused to fulfill their "natural" role, their psychological development was incomplete, they were in danger of corrupting youth, and finally, they were to be pitied and given proper treatment to "cure" the problem. According to Stearn, this was how he initially approached the subject of lesbianism and lesbian individuals. Yet, in the book's first chapter he admitted, "It soon became apparent to me, as I got on with my research, that my original view of the lesbian, which was shared by so many males, had been completely erroneous. Where I had thought of lesbians as mannish, hostile figures, I soon discovered that some of the loveliest women in the world were lesbians."[41] His first introduction to this previously unseen type of lesbian occurred at the DOB's 1962 biennial convention. For Stearn, members of the DOB for the most part embodied a new form of lesbianism that would help end the "lesbian problem" in the United States.

That the DOB might help end the "lesbian problem," however, sounds more than a little ominous. The old method for solving the "lesbian problem" was vividly communicated by psychiatrists like Edmund Bergler who hoped to shock lesbians onto the road to heterosexuality. However, rather than ask how the lesbian can be "cured," Stearn proposed an entirely separate set of questions:

> How to find somebody they could love who could love them? How to avoid giving unnecessary pain to families or precipitating a direct break? How to function socially—and in their jobs—without provoking suspicion? What to do about whatever yearnings they might have for children—and to how to bring them up? How to handle the men who insist on insinuating themselves into their lives?[42]

According to Stearn, then, the "problem" of "the lesbian" was not the question of sexuality itself but how homosexuals should best manage the deep rift that separated them from the rest of society. Over the next several hundred pages, Stearn recounted his private visits with members of the DOB, his observations of a "Gab-n-Java" session, his impressions of the DOB convention, and his opinions about the *Ladder*. In the end, Stearn reached the conclusion that not only had the DOB appropriately recast the "lesbian problem" but that they had also supplied a reasonable solution.

According to the DOB, by Stearn's accounting, the first problem faced by lesbians was isolation. Stearn's first lengthy account of the DOB in *The Grapevine* was through his observations of a "Gab-n-Java" held at Martin and Lyon's house in the summer of 1962. A lesbian Stearn described as a "pretty blonde" said, "Once you find out . . . that you're not the only lesbian in the world, it makes all the difference." Stearn added that "the "difference,' of course, was that she no longer felt alone—or left out . . . in California she had finally found herself, and now for the first time she was 'living.'" In another chapter,"The Lace-Curtain Lesbian" (who we might call the "closeted" lesbian), Stearn recounted the sad tale of the lesbian whose sense of privacy and propriety made it very difficult for her "to communicate with another lesbian, her very nature often working against her taking the first step." While having lunch with one such "lace-curtain" lesbian, Stearn mentioned attending a DOB convention. The lesbian replied, "I think that's the most hysterical thing I ever heard of . . . What are they trying to do, change society?" Stearn said he "suddenly felt defensive about the D.O.B." and explained to her "that it gave them a purpose, and that getting together privately as they did, they didn't have to frequent bars and run the risk of humiliation and exposure. They can meet in surroundings of their own choice and talk things out . . . It seems to have some therapeutic value."[43]

Once providing the small membership and discussion group as an alternative to isolation as well as to the perceived pitfalls of the lesbian bar as a site of socialization, Stearn shared what the DOB was going to do about the other problems lesbians encountered on their road to contentment. The first step, according to Stearn, was to extend the small discussion sessions and the idea of a lesbian membership organization to a more public organization, which would drop the scale of isolation drastically. One way in which the DOB was said to accomplish this was through holding gatherings, like its 1962 convention, at which Stearn was a speaker. Stearn set the scene: "They looked like a ladies' auxiliary of some typically American organization—more so perhaps, like a militant women's group, which they actually were," adding that "save for an extremely short haircut here and there, there was nothing to suggest that any of the women were lesbians."[44] Stearn's account of the convention included anecdotes that showed the reader both joyful and pitiful, proud and self-effacing, con-

frontational and apologetic moments of the conference: from the funda-
mentalist preacher who delivered a condemning sermon and then stormed
out disgusted when Lisa Ben, "songbird of D.O.B.," entertained the con-
ventioneers with a stirring and hopeful Sapphic song. What is clear after
reading this chapter on the convention is that the DOB succeeded in creating an open, public dialogue on lesbianism; though, in 1962, this "open"
conversation meant that dissent and condescension would define much
of the exchange. While the small discussion groups provided lesbians with
a relatively safe space to discuss their "problems," the public forum of a
convention brought those issues out into the open, both allowing a larger
group of lesbians to participate and also enabling lesbians to query heterosexual experts and opinion makers about what exactly should be done
to remedy the so-called "lesbian problem."

The following chapter picks up with the DOB biennial convention, but
Stearn cast his net more widely by considering the whole of the DOB's activities as the nation's largest lesbian organization. Early in the chapter
Stearn formally introduced the organization, its history, and its goals to his
readers: "Launched in San Francisco in 1955 by eight women who were
tired of congregating in lesbian bars, the D.O.B. has proved a happy re-
volving door for hundreds wanting to do something about their lesbianism." That "something" was to achieve a sense of comfort and even pride
with their sexuality. Stearn added, "Besides helping lesbians to understand themselves, the D.O.B. has embarked on a program of educating the
public about the average lesbian. Ignoring stigmas and taboos, they have
ventured on television and radio, submitted to interviews, and compiled
surveys, helping reporters and social scientists seeking information about
the lesbian."[45] Publicity was only one goal of the DOB, according to Stearn.
Along with modifying (and augmenting) the public representation of lesbians, the DOB sought to reach isolated lesbians around the country and
provide them with the knowledge that an organization such as the DOB
exists and is willing to help them.

Stearn concluded the chapter by providing a test case: was the DOB's
increasing public presence having the desired effect? "During the D.O.B.
convention," Stearn wrote, "I was given an indication of how the group
uses the mass media to win acceptance for lesbians." The president-elect
of the Los Angeles chapter was to appear on Paul Coates's television program, which had an estimated several million viewers. Stearn claims to
have watched the interview in the company of a friend's grandmother,
who served as his barometer of public opinion. While watching the interview the grandmother vacillated among expressions of disgust, shock,
and disbelief, concluding at the end of the program: "You can't tell who's

decent any more." Though he didn't offer his own conclusions, Stearn seemed to suggest that changing minds in this fashion might be futile. But heterosexuals were only one of the DOB's intended audiences; the other was lesbians themselves. Stearn noted that "in DOB circles, the interview was considered a great triumph," quoting a DOB officer as saying, "It gave the girls a sense of accomplishment—and status—and was a symbol of acceptance." [46]

Stearn's final extensive chapter on the DOB discussed the *Ladder* and its role as a kind of communication intermediary between the small, closed discussion groups and the potentially dangerous and compromising forays into the mainstream public sphere. Stearn began by drawing a picture, albeit a rather overstated one, of the bustling atmosphere from which the *Ladder* emerged monthly: "A small office in downtown San Francisco is the Singapore of the lesbian world. It is the crossroad of lesbian news and views, the distillery of virtually all thought and activity in the lesbian grapevine. It is the headquarters for *The Ladder*, a publication by lesbians for lesbians." [47] Although its reach was by many factors less than major city newspapers or television programs like Paul Coates's show in Los Angeles, Stearn reported that the *Ladder* "is sold on the newsstands in the larger cities where homosexuality is regarded with indifference, and it is sent through the mails, its right to be heard defended by a recent ruling of the U.S. Supreme Court." [48] Stearn told his readers that the circulation was no more than a few thousand, though readership undoubtedly was larger and that those who did get their hands on a copy would find a plethora of information about the DOB in particular and the lesbian world in general.

Stearn added that one of the most interesting and popular sections of the *Ladder* was the Reader's Respond letters which, according to Stearn, reflected "the spread of the lesbian grapevine from Alaska to Florida, from the rockbound coast of Maine to sunny California, where a flourishing grapevine has been wryly dubbed another 'grapes of wrath'"—referring to the impoverished migrants blown out west during the dustbowl, motivated in large part by the California dream. Along with discussing the *Ladder* as a pioneering communication medium, he evaluated the content of the magazine, relaying its discussions of marriage, religion, parenting, paperback book publishing, poetry, and politics. "By orderly expansion," Stearn concluded, "*The Ladder* plans to spread its message of kinship throughout the world." [49] By the end of the chapters about the DOB, it is clear that Stearn's message to readers around the country was that San Francisco's DOB stood at the center of a new communication network much in contrast to the lesbian world of bars on a Greenwich Village side street as depicted by Aldrich, Bannon, and others. And, the architects of that network were not only interested in reaching out to the public to change their minds but even more fundamentally to reach isolated lesbians and provide them with the knowledge that they were not alone. Arming lesbians with that information enabled them to enter into a network at a point where they could continue the process of connecting to the lesbian world, or at least the portion of that world inhabited by the upwardly mobile crowd in the DOB.

Localizing an active and visible lesbian presence in San Francisco, however, was not the only mapping of identity Stearn did in *The Grapevine*.[50] Unlike Aldrich's emphasis on Manhattan, there is little hard-and-fast consistency to Stearn's sexual geography of the United States, but some trends do appear. In New York, again, Stearn tended to highlight the lesbian underworld in a manner not so different from Aldrich's nonfictional exposés. In one typical (and cliché) tale, a "superb beauty of eighteen" left her parents' home in New Jersey "because of her family's strictness." Soon she was drawn into the treacherous world of Greenwich Village lesbian bars and then disappeared. She returned to the storyteller about a year later but had changed drastically in the interim: "The features had changed. Her skin was coarse, her eyes dull, her hair unkempt. Even her nails were dirty," and if spoiled beauty was not enough, Stearn reported that "on her slim, rounded arms he saw the telltale needle marks. Not yet twenty, she was already a drug addict and a prostitute." While Stearn included the typically sensational examples, he also produced a more complex portrait of a Greenwich Village lesbian bar that he claimed to have visited. Although Stearn wrote that "many gay bars were often fronts for . . . sinister activities," the main focus of his chapter on lesbian bars was how they were places of entertainment, comparing them to the famous Stork Club more than once because of drink prices as well as the uniqueness of the entertainment offered. Claiming that "in some bars it was often hard to distinguish the sights from the sight-seers," Stearn established the subjective position from which he revealed the lesbian bar to his readers: as a straight male tourist.[51] Although Stearn steered mostly clear of a thoroughly negative portrayal of the Greenwich Village lesbian bar, he did so at the cost of transforming the lesbian patrons into a spectacle rather than as subjects with their own humanity.

If according to Stearn New York provided an example of the spectacle of lesbianism, Los Angeles and Hollywood in particular were home to many lesbians engaged in a search for the good life that often ended at the bottom of a bottle or sunburned on the beach. Stearn claimed, "It is almost as though lesbians flourish in the Pacific air; the beaches up and down the rock-crested shores of California are alive with them, and they converge on Hollywood, the happy haven of stardom, beauty, and idiosyncrasy." The attractions, however, were not without their risks, according to Stearn, as "only a bare minority manage to get into the film industry, but many revel in just being on the fringes."[52] After introducing lesbian after lesbian who had been caught up in the fantasy and false consciousness of Hollywood's romance and glamour, Stearn concluded, "I thought of the broken marriages, the shattered lives, and the heartbreak so characteristic of Hollywood. There seemed to be no end to the trail of tragedy."[53]

If New York and Hollywood spelled tragedy, despair, and self-delusion for the lesbian, San Francisco, again, was some sort of peculiarly hopeful haven for lesbians in Stearn's formulation. In addition to the chapters on the DOB, the attractions of California and San Francisco in particular appeared throughout *The Grapevine*: the place is noted for its easygoing populace ("People seem easier and more understanding when they're not fighting the weather"); its tolerant social atmosphere ("It was warm and receptive"); and its supposedly relatively benign police force ("It was so difficult for a lesbian to get arrested in San Francisco").[54]

The nation's sexual geography, according to Stearn, was highly differentiated by region and city. Although the movement of women to (and away from) cities as part of a journey of sexual exploration cannot be attributable to Stearn's writings, he was in a good place to report on a somewhat revised geography as it was beginning to emerge—and report on this change with commentary that let his readers know he valued a certain kind of lesbian geography over another. Indeed, the problems suffered by lesbians seemed to be either exacerbated or solved depending on where they decided to live out their desires and identity. In fact, it is quite clear that Stearn knew he was employing this literary device. Not only did it make for a highly symbolic story, but it supported his own contention that the resolution of the "lesbian problem"—which included self-loathing as well as supposedly antisocial behavior—was best approached by San Francisco's DOB. "All we try to do," Stearn quoted a leader of the DOB, "is to help the individual recognize his [sic] own worth as a human being, and thus direct the wasted energies of antisocial hostility toward more productive goals."[55]

As a postscript, Stearn relayed the story of one lesbian who continually referred back to the lesbians in San Francisco during their conversation: "What do you think of the girls out there? . . . Don't you get the impression, particularly in San Francisco, that the girls out there are smarter and more sophisticated?" Stearn thought, "I had been favorably impressed by the San Francisco chapter of the Daughters of Bilitis, especially the leaders, who seemed a stimulating, enterprising group living interesting, productive lives while seeking to do some good." The girl concluded, "You see? . . . I knew the girls out there had a lot more to them."[56]

Reading *The Grapevine*

Stearn's 372-page book differed from earlier popular treatments of lesbianism because it was published by Doubleday rather than a publisher of paperback books like Gold Medal, which had overseen the publication of Aldrich / Packer and Bannon's books, which were rarely reviewed and advertised in the popular press. While Doubleday was not then among the most respected publishing houses, it did introduce popular lesbian nonfiction in hardcover to the public, a gesture that signaled the coming of literary respectability to the topic. Moreover, it meant that the book would gain greater public attention because it would have a publicity budget and an author unbridled by the cloak of anonymity who was willing to tour with the book. And as a hardcover book, newspapers and magazines would be more likely to review it, further increasing its publicity. And while *The Grapevine* was less widely reviewed than Stearn's *The Sixth Man*, it was more widely reviewed than other nonfiction accounts of lesbianism, including Aldrich's paperbacks and the more "scientific" studies of female homosexuality.[57]

Library Journal, the standard publication used by librarians to determine what books they should order, described *The Grapevine* as a study of the "aberration" of lesbianism written "for the general reader." The review noted that the book was a follow-up to *The Sixth Man*, and "like the previous volume, *The Grapevine* is readable and superficial, but has compassion and a full measure of masculine curiosity." The review mentioned that Stearn "interviewed many women, chiefly in bars, visited the homes of some Lesbians, and was a speaker at a convention in Los Angeles of The Daughters of Bilitis, their national organization."[58] The review ended with a recommendation that libraries that had purchased *The Sixth Man* also should add *The Grapevine* to their collections.

Not all reviews were as basic as that which appeared in *Library Journal*. In *Book Week*, Midge Decter offered an analytical review of both *The Grapevine* and Gael Greene's *Sex and the College Girl* (1961). Decter noted that while Greene was more intelligent in her approach, "Jess Stearn, if he is more traditionally newsy and solemn than she, manages, nevertheless, to avoid several of the pitfalls of writing informatively about homosexuality—most notable among them being the temptation to assembly-line psychology." Yet, Decter claims, "both Gael Greene and Jess Stearn, and their books, operate from the same unspoken assumption as is made by writ-

ers who deal only in sexual sensationalism—that there is something ultimately mysterious and unmanageable in the relation of women to sex."
She argued that both of these books perpetuate the myth that grave danger lies in the unleashed libido of women. She read Stearn's book as a tale
of what can happen when women capitulate in the battle of the sexes and
turn to their own sex for love and sensuality. "The one thing that all of [the
women in Stearn's book] reveal, however, is that lesbians, far from being
sexual deviates," Decter noted, "are merely retreating back to a point of
girlishness from which grown-up life in the world cannot really make its
full and painful demands on them."[59]

In addition to publicity from book reviews, *The Grapevine* gained
greater attention when Stearn took it on the road. In early 1964, Stearn told
Martin and Lyon that "Doubleday says they are planning a big summer
[publicity] campaign, as they like the book much more than *The Sixth
Man*."[60] The publicity tour got off to an early start at the end of February
when Stearn appeared on the notorious all-night Long John Nebel radio
show, broadcast out of New York City.[61] This show was followed by Stearn's
appearance on Robert Kennedy's ninety-minute radio show, *Contact*, in
Boston in May, then on Vincent Tracy's talk show on WOR in Boston.[62]
That Stearn was able to tour the country's burgeoning talk show circuit
with his book—likely financed by his corporate publisher—is another
reason that *The Grapevine* ultimately gained fame and exerted influence
alongside the lesbian paperback originals best remembered today because
of their colorful covers and titillating copy.

The Grapevine not only reached well into the mainstream public
sphere but also became known to innumerable lesbians throughout the
United States. Distributed by Doubleday in a hardbound edition and by
MacFadden-Bartell in paperback editions, the book was moved through a
massive and well-established communication network. Still in print at
least until 1970, *The Grapevine* was more visible than the DOB's publications. And, further, while it might not have achieved as large an audience
as did Aldrich's books, it did win a longer-lasting presence in the public
sphere owing to the legitimacy provided by being published in hardcover
and because of its many subsequent reprintings. Consequently, Stearn's
picture of the DOB was more extensively disseminated than the organization's own direct self-representation.

Moreover, the book also augmented the story of the DOB by placing it
in the overall narrative of the "lesbian problem" and thus alongside other,
more familiar, manifestations of the lesbian world of the 1950s and 1960s,
most especially the lesbian bar. These competing narratives gave members
of the DOB and readers of *The Grapevine* a great deal to talk about and in

the process enabled them to further articulate their identity and map out an alternative sexual geography to the one established throughout the 1950s in the pages of lesbian paperback fiction and nonfiction.

In January 1964, a month in advance of publication of *The Grapevine*, the *Ladder* published a lengthy review of the book laden with words of praise like "absorbing," "blockbuster," "excellent reportorial work," "brave," and "masterful"—all words notably absent from the magazine's reviews of the books by Aldrich, a lesbian peer.[63] In addition, the reviewer also noted that the book would probably become a best seller simply because it was the first book about lesbians to be published by a major house as opposed to a publisher of paperbacks like Gold Medal. In particular, the reviewer singled out the chapters on the DOB for applause, claiming, "Mr. Stearn is particularly effective in detailing the aims of DOB, describing also its work, its difficulties, and its successes." Reading the work as it was apparently intended, the reviewer pointed out that the chapters on the DOB "offset the dreary pictures presented in other parts of the book. For the ever-present 'bar-crowd' . . . are all interviewed—the butches, the prostitutes, the neurotics, the delinquents and so on."[64] The reviewer thus pointed to the perceived gap between bar lesbians and the DOB and lauded Stearn for recognizing the differences and for praising the DOB's approach.

"Gene Damon," who usually wrote for the *Ladder*, penned a brief review of *The Grapevine* for the *Mattachine Review* in October 1964. Damon echoed many of the conclusions that had appeared in the *Ladder* several months before, "Despite the inevitable inclusion of the dregs of society, there is much of real value." Again, Stearn was applauded for "his lengthy chapters about the DOB and their publication, *The Ladder*." Overall, according to Damon, "He manages the almost impossible 'marriage' of sensational subjects with objective reporting." She added that "he did a better job than he perhaps realizes, and the kind of publicity this creates for the groups in general is not to be purchased. You can't buy a better press than an obvious bestseller with a sympathetic tone." Recognizing the role of the DOB in the production of this book and their successful handling of Stearn, Damon claimed, "There is no doubt that the little groups of homosexuals are accomplishing for their own people the main aim: the focusing of a national spotlight on the problems of living a homosexual life in a hostile society."[65]

Several years after the publication of *The Grapevine*, Martin and Lyon remembered, "After Jess Stearn's book *The Grapevine* was published, the Daughters of Bilitis was deluged with phone calls and letters."[66] Some of those letters made it into the pages of the *Ladder* while others remained hidden in the DOB's archives. In fact, some letters arrived prior to the publication of the book, expressing anticipation and in some cases ordering the book from the DOB book service in response to advance word and reviews. Though many letters came from lesbians already involved in the DOB's communication network, numerous others came from lesbians who heard about the organization for the first time in the pages of *The Grapevine*.

Many of those who wrote to the DOB did not necessarily share the *Ladder*'s evaluation of the book. In April 1964, for instance, one reader wrote, "Mr. Stearn did not do an honest job of reporting. If he had, he would not have thrown the content of the book completely out of balance by giving the lion's share of attention to couples who are obviously psychoneurotic and making a mess of their relationship." The reader did grant that the publicity the book gave to the DOB was important, as "a great many lesbians across the country will find out about DOB and *The Ladder* via this book."[67]

One such letter read: "Dear Madam: I am sincerely asking for your help. I obtained your address (finally!) via a rather circuitous route: reading *The Grapevine* . . . bolstering up *all* my courage and calling Mr. Jess Stearn on the telephone. It is he who gave me your address." The woman, who was from Washington D.C., quickly got to the point: "Finding a D.O.B. chapter in Washington D.C. would—I know—be too much to hope for . . . Therefore, I am only asking you—*please!*—to send me the address of your New York City chapter." Cognizant that the DOB was not a lonely hearts club, she nevertheless hoped that the New York chapter might put her in touch with other lesbians living the D.C. area so she "could be (for the first time in my life!) open and honest, unashamed—in a word—myself." Once assuring the DOB that she was over twenty-one years of age, she admitted that her letter "sounds melodramatic, but knowledge of your existence has truly given me new hope. I am *begging* you not to let me down now."[68] In a few short days, Del Martin responded to the letter. She told the woman about the upcoming DOB convention in New York in June; gave her the address of the DOB's New York chapter, enclosed the current issue of the *Ladder*, and told her "there is a Mattachine group in Washington, D.C.—though its membership would be predominantly male, it may be helpful for you to get in touch with them." Martin concluded by reassuring the formerly isolated lesbian: "You will find that you are far from 'alone.' When Phyllis and I first started the DOB in 1955, we knew only a handful of girls. Now we know them all over the world!"[69] As this exchange reveals, in the decade since its founding, the DOB succeeded in creating a network that was qualitatively and quantitatively different from the kinds of networks that had linked lesbians in years past. Surely, the DOB's network did not quite match Stearn's hyperbolic description of a "vast, sprawling grapevine," but with the combination of Aldrich's and Stearn's books there can be little doubt that the processes by which women could connect to the lesbian world underwent dramatic shifts and innovations.

Over the next several months, the DOB received similar letters from a number of women—many of whom, incidentally, had difficulty locating the DOB because Stearn neglected to print its address in his book. Such letters took the DOB's sexual communication network to another level, linking the journalistic forces of production to a mass audience with the DOB standing as intermediary, helping direct the flow and content of information in both directions. As such a visible and authoritative intermediary in this game of representation and public introductions, the DOB was becoming on a limited scale what Stearn called the "Singapore" of the lesbian world for both the media and lesbians around the country: it was a center of activity and a hub of information—although it certainly was not alone in serving this function, it was uniquely far reaching and media savvy. Alongside the iconic Greenwich Village lesbian bar, which could be located but not named or pinpointed in the literature, San Francisco's DOB newly became a real and imaginary destination of lesbians who wished to do everything from timidly gaining information to intrepidly seeking out community.

The Lesbian Grapevine and the National Imaginary

As the months and years passed after its original publication, *The Grapevine* started to achieve an even greater public influence than is evident in book reviews and in the letters of isolated lesbians alone. As one of the most visible books on lesbianism published in the United States in the early 1960s, *The Grapevine* became a kind of Rosetta Stone upon which subsequent writers relied to unlock or perhaps further obfuscate the mysterious world of Lesbos for a popular audience. Between 1964 and the end of the decade, *The Grapevine* was quoted, cited, or simply referred to in many publications by other authors. In fact, the references were so widespread that the book can be said to have played in important role in the formation of the United States public's collective imagination about lesbianism overall from the mid 1960s through the beginning of the next decade.

Stearn's book, along with some of his conclusions and anecdotes, appeared in many of the literally countless putatively nonfiction paperback studies of male and female homosexuality published in the period. The books were generally published by small, fly-by-night presses yet received a vast regional distribution around the time of their appearance. Though these paperbacks often were among the cheapest, most ephemeral, and, judging from the titles and covers, most salacious items yet produced by publishers, the quality of their prose and research actually varied a great deal. Whether they were the trash they were advertised to be or surprisingly sensitive and progay treatises, the paperbacks all commonly referred back to the most popular and hence most authoritative studies of homosexuality earlier published. Favorite among these were Donald Webster Cory's *The Homosexual in America,* Frank Caprio's *Female Homosexuality,* and, of course, the two Kinsey studies.[70] However, by the middle 1960s, paperback authors were citing with increasingly frequency the books of Jess Stearn, *The Sixth Man* and *The Grapevine.* Some of the paperback books, like Lee Dorian's *The Other Men* (1966), Tor Erikson's *The Half-World of the American Homosexual* (1966), and Donald Gilmore's *Soixante Neuf: A Study of Oral-Genital Sex* (1968), mentioned *The Grapevine* as a reliable source, suggesting the reader look there to learn more about lesbianism.[71]

Other books, however, consulted *The Grapevine* more extensively, both quoting from the book and citing it as an authoritative—if not the authoritative—book on female homosexuality. For instance, on the first page of her introduction to an anonymous (and possibly fictitious) lesbian's memoirs, Doris Hanson notes, "Very few books touch on what has sometimes been called *the hidden disease.* Lesbians are reluctant to talk about themselves and until the publication of Jess Stearn's *The Grapevine,* no comprehensive picture of the lesbian problem in present day society was available."[72] In still other books, authors cite *The Grapevine* on authority of its central thesis: that there exists in the United States a network of communication and sociability populated by lesbians. For example, in his book *The Young Homosexual,* Lee Dorian writes, "The Lesbian grapevine, as Jess Stearn has pointed out in his famous book, 'The Grapevine,' works just as efficiently as the male homosexual's grapevine, with tentacles in every large city!"[73] Similarly, in *The New Homosexual Revolution,* author Ken Worthy draws much of his argument from Stearn, writing that the defining factor of the coming homosexual revolution was the expansion and publicizing of homosexual communication networks. Worthy defers to Stearn's *The Grapevine* on several occasions, often quoting at length from the book.[74]

Along with the references to *The Grapevine* and its central thesis about the astonishing growth of communication networks, the paperbacks presented other information, most particularly frequent and at times lengthy discussions of both the DOB and of San Francisco's lesbian world—often with those two themes explicitly linked. In addition to the several paperback books mentioned above, an even larger group of books further linked San Francisco and the DOB with an emergent lesbian community. The references ran the gamut from brief mentions, such as that which appeared in Matt Bradley's *Faggots to Burn* (1962) to more extensive (and objective) coverage in Roger Blake's *The Homosexual Explosion!* (1966).[75] What remains consistent in the innumerable paperback books on homosexuality published throughout the 1960s is the attention paid to growing lesbian communication networks and the portrayal of the DOB and San Francisco very near the center if not precisely at the center of those systems, thus marking a shift from the dominant representations of the 1950s that placed that center in the bar culture of Greenwich Village.

Ann Aldrich's books too left their mark, but in ways that are much more difficult to document than with Stearn's book. Unlike *The Grapevine*, Aldrich's books were not reviewed outside of the homophile press, they didn't stay in print for several years, and while the books received the occasional mention by a subsequent writer they weren't mentioned in the dozens of books and articles as was *The Grapevine*. While it is difficult to trace the legacy of Aldrich's books through the paper trail, after browsing secondhand bookstores, interviewing lesbians active in the 1950s–1960s, and reading accounts of how lesbians treasured their "under the mattress library," it is almost certain that Aldrich's books were kept privately and continued to influence their readers on a personal level.[76] The are at least two reasons for the different ways in which *The Grapevine* and Aldrich's books left a legacy. First, Stearn published his book in hardback while Aldrich's were paperback originals. Along with factors cited above (e.g. reviewed vs. not reviewed), paperbacks were designed to be disposable, to literally fall apart after just a few readings, but hardback books were made to stand the test of time; while Aldrich's books were destined for the dumpster, Stearn's book was slated for the permanence of the library shelf.[77] Second, and not unrelated to the first point, is that Stearn possessed the privileges of his race, sex, and sexuality; as a self-identified white heterosexual man, he no doubt was granted a measure of authority by subsequent writers who also considered him objective as a consequence of his social distance from his subject. Aldrich, in contrast, identified herself as a woman and as a homosexual, factors that might have been held against her by many male journalists who wrote about lesbianism in the second half of the 1960s. Combining these two factors, medium and gender, provides a plausible explanation for why *The Grapevine* achieved a greater visible historical legacy than Aldrich's books, which, interestingly, were read by more people when they first were published.

The Sprawling *Grapevine*

As information and image layer on and reinforce each other a critical mass of widely dispersed intelligence emerges. This is what happened with the reputation of the Greenwich Village lesbian bar and with the emergence of the DOB as a geographically specific organization by the early 1960s: for those who had access to any information about lesbianism, whether on the television or radio or in books and newspapers, it became clear that one of the most distinctive developments of the early 1960s was that lesbian bars were complex sites characterized by often contradictory descriptions and that there existed an organization that was equally complex which sought to help lesbians gain self-esteem through association with their own kind. What's more, those with access to the media who were lucky enough to run across a publication or program with the right information would have learned with very little exception that Greenwich Village was rife with lesbian bars and that an organization, the DOB, kept its headquarters in San Francisco. For those with the means and desire, such information proved incredibly attractive, enough so that they might just marshal their resources and move to another location, thus contributing to the further realignment of the sexual geography of the United States. Although anecdotes abound, the experience of one young lesbian proves emblematic.

Carol Seajay, an assumed name, was born in 1950 in Kalamazoo, Michigan.[78] The most important early influence in Seajay's life was the Girl Scouts. Introduced to the organization at a young age, Seajay was attracted to the Scouts because they allowed and enabled her to do things for herself, to achieve a measure of self-sufficiency. Moreover, while participating with the Scouts during the school year and at summer camp, Seajay was able to put some distance between herself and her family while building a new, homosocial family with other Scouts and with troop leaders and camp counselors. As it turned out, the Scout summer camp she regularly attended was something of a lesbian hotbed, though an exceedingly discreet one. And as Seajay matured and became a more independent member of the Scouting world, she started to recognize that many of the women around her were lesbians, even if she did not yet possess the vocabulary to name that identity. Coming to terms with her own romantic sexual desires, Seajay slyly fought her way into the counselors' web of lesbian relationships.

Seajay remembers that her discovery of the lesbian world was facilitated not only by the unspoken and somewhat furtive relationships of the women around her but also by her discovery of lesbian literature. In 1967, when she was a junior in high school, Seajay remembers an intriguing incident leading to her discovery of both the lesbians around her and the larger lesbian world beyond her town. One afternoon a group of high school–aged Scouts found themselves in the room of one of their leaders, who was away at the time. While in the room, Seajay spied a book on the shelf to which she was almost mystically attracted. Though the cover of the book had been removed, she could read the title from the spine. It was Ann Aldrich's *We, Too, Must Love.* Apparently, Seajay was not the only teenager in the group who noticed and was attracted to the book: when she made a move to borrow it surreptitiously, she discovered to her amazement that someone else already had lifted it. As the carload of young women left their leader's house, one of them threw down the gauntlet, asking, "Who took the book?" Seajay recalls that her friend Tina admitted to having taken the book. Over the next few weeks, Aldrich's paperback made the rounds as everyone in the circle read it and quietly marveled. Some of the group spoke about it and searched out other Aldrich titles as well as books mentioned by the author, among them *The Well of Loneliness.*

For Seajay, the Aldrich books had a profoundly important impact. Not only did they introduce her to the one easily accessible source of published material about lesbianism—the mass market paperback—but, she remembered, they also "really opened up that there was a world . . . there was New York, there was San Francisco. You could go to those places." Still, as an astute and aware reader of the Aldrich books, Seajay was not overly impressed with the image of the lesbian world portrayed by the author. Aldrich's lesbian world, in large part, was dominated by images of Greenwich Village and of "dark smoky bars and alcohol" where lesbian relationships were often violent and always short-lived. An idealistic teenager, Seajay was looking for something better. Then, shortly after reading *We, Too, Must Love,* Seajay came across references to the DOB and the *Ladder* in Aldrich's later books and even found a bound set of issues of the *Ladder* in one of her scoutmaster's apartments. Learning that the DOB was located in San Francisco and that it published the *Ladder,* Seajay immediately reached a conclusion: "What I knew from the magazine was there were enough lesbians in San Francisco to publish a magazine."[79] Moreover, the lesbians of the *Ladder* were far more attractive and powerful to Seajay than the alcoholic lesbians in Aldrich's books. "I remember," Seajay said, "one of the copies of *The Ladder* I saw pretty early on was kind of a profile of a woman on a tractor, a very strong image" (fig. 8).[80] Having done plenty of tractoring herself, Seajay saw herself reflected in the active, self-determined images presented on the covers of the *Ladder.*

This was 1968, however, and Seajay was only eighteen. She graduated high school and attended college nearby, but kept the notion of San

The Ladder
a Lesbian Review

75¢ 12/7-8

MAY- JUNE 1968

8 This self-confident lesbian on the cover a 1968 issue of *The Ladder* gave a young Carol Seajay an image of lesbian self-sufficiency and esteem that she could identify with. Image courtesy of the GLBT Historical Society, San Francisco, CA.

Francisco foremost in her mind. As the next few years passed, her original image of the city as home to the DOB and lots of lesbians was augmented by the city's burgeoning counterculture and its famously beautiful surroundings, ideally suited for a graduated Girl Scout who still loved the outdoors. At age twenty-four, Seajay finally packed her bags and moved to San Francisco. When she arrived, Seajay contacted the DOB, but by then the moment for that organization had passed and she decided not to become affiliated with the organization, even though it helped bring her out to the city; rather, she became deeply involved with lesbian feminism, especially as one of the founders of the feminist bookstore, Old Wives' Tales, in 1976.

The relative influence of authors and journalists, publishers and distributors, and organizations and bars in the transformation of sexual communication networks is difficult to measure. However, it is undeniable that the confluence of the lesbian bar, DOB, the *Ladder*, lesbian paperbacks and books like *The Grapevine* exerted genuine power over the public's imagination about the place of sexuality in 1950s and 1960s America and about how isolated individuals might make their way into worlds previously hidden to them. The legacy of the explosion of nonfiction works about lesbianism published starting in the late 1950s and continuing throughout the 1960s, particularly through Aldrich's series and with Stearn's *The Grapevine*, was the shifting of sexual communication networks into what must be called a mass phenomenon. As was shown earlier, lesbian communication networks have a long history, dating back to the early twentieth century and before. In the 1950s, with the aid of organizations like the DOB, lesbian sexual communication networks started to mature, become more permanent, and become much more public. Throughout the 1950s, however, even the DOB was unable—and perhaps not entirely willing—to nurture the networks so that an ever larger population would be able to join them, draw on their resources, and contribute additional information to them. As evidenced by the several examples provided in this chapter, it was not until the DOB entered into an uneasy and always unpredictable relationship with the mass media and its agents—journalists, authors, publishers—that lesbian sexual communication networks started to become mass in scale and thus subject to the vagaries of mass culture.

CHAPTER 4

Publicizing the Gay *Life*

In the early 1960s, with the so-called conspiracy of silence becoming but a memory for homophile activists, homosexuals even more actively sought to speak for themselves and to expand the ways in which they could communicate with one another.[1] Standing in uneasy relation to the press, members of homophile organizations pursued the difficult path of encouraging the media's coverage of homosexuality while simultaneously attempting to influence the kind of images that would reach the vast American public. For their part, editors, journalists, and photographers asked homophiles to open up the gay world to them but then mostly failed to communicate the complexity of that world once they were given access to it. The mass media, even with the aid of homophiles, tended to represent the gay world in highly stylized and often spectacular ways. As with lesbians, the bar and the homophile organization emerged in the 1960s as the two most widely used lenses through which the American public would see the world of male homosexuality. Through these two portals the public was invited to enter into the gay male world. While some readers kept their distance and merely skimmed the articles and glanced at the pictures, others eagerly joined in.

The result of one particularly innovative exchange between the mass media, the homophile movement, and gay male community itself came with the article "Homosexuality in America," published in *Life* magazine in June 1964.[2] Once the magazine hit the newsstands it immediately became a media event. Word of its publication spread fast, and people rushed to purchase the magazine. According to a number of sources, the issue sold out in less than two days in San Francisco, Los Angeles, and other large cities.[3] The issue sold nearly 7.3 million copies to a substantially wider readership nationwide and gained even wider circulation when it was published almost simultaneously around the globe in *Life International* and *Life en Español*.[4] Recognized by homophile activists at the time and by historians subsequently as a watershed event in the representation of homosexuality in the mass media, the feature at once symbolized the end of the conspiracy of silence and marked a real milestone in the content and scope of media coverage about the subject.

Philadelphia's popular homophile magazine, *Drum*, reported that "1964 was not only the Year of the Great Republican Demise, but it was also the Year Magazines Discovered Homosexuals"—which was in no small part attributable to the *Life* essay.[5] The year also was a high-water mark for popular sociological literature on homosexuality, such as Stearn's *The Grapevine*, which helped expand and complicate public opinion on the subject.[6] In many ways typical of several articles published in the first half of the 1960s, "Homosexuality in America" also broke several barriers in its content, use of the medium, and scale of distribution. The article was published at a fortuitous time and place, allowing it to leave its stamp on American culture—and San Francisco in particular—in a way few offerings of the mass media have before or since.

The combination of forces surrounding and creating *Life*'s "Homosexuality in America"—the editors at *Life*, homophile organizations, gay bar managers and patrons, and *Life*'s millions of readers—further influenced a shift in the national imaginary that included differentiating the gay populations of various places, from New York's Greenwich Village denizens to Los Angeles's beleaguered and hunted homosexuals to San Francisco's citizens of what was heralded as the nation's "gay capital." With detailed stories about homosexuality starting to appear in family publications like *Life*, individual gay men and lesbians could expect to begin receiving regular, stable, and increasingly reliable information in the mass media not only about homosexuality in generally but about specific homosexual communities and organizations. For many men and women who considered themselves homosexual though isolated from others like themselves, this explosion of information invited them to think about the relationship between their identity and place, and it allowed them to imagine places where homosexuals lived and where inward identifications could be expressed publicly in a community. Moreover, the article introduced to a wider audience the idea that identity and community could be built upon same-sex attractions and sexual experiences. As the national imaginary about sexuality shifted and a growing number of individuals became enmeshed in newly mass communication networks, the contours of an American sexual geography were drawn in sharper relief.

Mainstream Journalism "Discovers" Male Homosexual Community

"Homosexuality in America" did not emerge out of the ether. In addition to the media coverage already discussed, *Life*'s first major foray in the topic of homosexuality had two immediate and important precedents in the United States.[7] The venerable *Harper's* carried the essay "New York's Middle-Class Homosexuals" in March 1963. This was followed in December by a front-page article on homosexuality in the *New York Times*.[8] While each article restrained its conclusions to particular times and places, the *Harper's* essay and the *New York Times* story both covered new ground. In particular, they exemplify the particular moment when the media establishment was coming to terms with homosexuals as persons (rather than simply as criminals or psychopaths—or psychopathic criminals) and as constituting a distinct community (rather than as individuals isolated and alone because of their putative antisocial behavior).

The articles began with numbers and demographic estimates and moved onto considerations of "gay" individuals—all varieties of "them." William Helmer's article in *Harper's* introduced the then-rather novel idea that "the varieties of actual behavior among homosexuals are endless." And although he admitted that his article "undoubtedly oversimplified them," he proceeded to dissect gay identity along lines not unfamiliar to us today. Helmer devoted paragraphs to gays from Greenwich Village and the Upper East Side, butch lesbians, drag queens, "Negro" gays, the "homosexual bourgeoisie," the "flaming faggot," "S-Ms," transvestites, "sex maniacs," and bisexuals—"a kind of mulatto in gay life."[9] The result of such differentiation has been the journalistic creation of people who, while still defined by their sexuality, nevertheless are individualized to a greater degree, shown to be distinct within the whole, and sometimes even antagonistic toward one another. This media representation of more individualized homosexuals stands in marked contrast to the perspective popular in the preceding decades that it was pointless to categorize varieties of homosexuality because homosexuals were merely one of the most common manifestations of "sexual perversion." By interviewing homosexuals in groups and one-on-one, as both Doty and Helmer did, the journalists were compelled to draw a picture of homosexual individuals.

A shared stigmatized status frequently nurtures a sense of community.[10] *New York Times* writer Doty made similar observations in his 1963 piece on homosexuals in New York City. He noted the trend in "treating" homosexuality was that while "homosexuality is not the preferable condition, . . . there's nothing morally wrong with it . . . [and] one has to make the best of the situation" and that "out of this desire to make the best of it grows a gay community with a social structure specially adapted to homosexual needs."[11] This idea, that something called a "gay community" actually existed, was probably the most noteworthy conclusion of these essays. In years prior, homosexuals and other so-called sex perverts may have cruised certain streets, attended outlaw clubs, or visited notorious resorts, but they did not constitute a relatively self-perpetuating "community" according to the media and folk knowledge. The notion that homosexuals formed into communities was made intelligible by the journalists because they cast community in geographic terms: community was not simply a relationship, it was a place. In the early 1960s, such spatialization of homosexuality was a quietly radical notion. Consider the impact the following statement may have had on an individual only vaguely aware of homosexuality as a behavior, let alone an identity: "A New York homosexual, if he chooses an occupation in which his clique predominates, can shape for himself a life lived almost exclusively in an inverted world from which the rough, unsympathetic edges of straight society can be almost totally excluded."[12] Furthermore, although later activists and historians have challenged journalists for unfair treatment of homosexuals, these authors largely introduced the trend of including the perspectives and sometimes the words of gay men and lesbians, some of whom were activists.[13]

While these two articles set the tone for subsequent pieces, they still had one foot in the past. The journalists' reporting was done in a style similar to the beat reporters of the 1940s and 1950s who wrote for the local press about the problems caused by hometown "queers." Local newspapers had been covering and uncovering the dalliances of local deviates throughout the twentieth century—albeit in intermittent and prurient ways. Aside from catering to the public's salacious appetite and editors' desire to sell papers, the reporters' stories often brought about a rather introspective if public conversation: What is wrong with our town? Why have so many undesirables chosen to live here? And, of course, what can be done to get rid of them? This is precisely how the 1959 San Francisco mayoral scandal was presented in city newspapers. Although Doty and Helmer helped popularize new ideas about identity and community, they did so in the decidedly traditional mode of focusing on the problem of homosexuality in their hometown, New York City. They did not extend their analysis to homosexuals in other places and did not attempt to place their hometown in a larger, national frame.

Life Gone Gay

The *Harper's* and the *New York Times* essays are worth mentioning for still another reason. As media scholar Edward Alwood writes of the *Times* article, it "became something of a guidepost for other media. Reporters and editors at other publications, who had been uncertain how to cover the subject, found they could more easily do so now by pointing to the *Times.*"[14] Among those watching the emergence of homosexuality as an attention-grabbing topic were the editors at *Life,* who took both inspiration and information from the 1963 *New York Times* and *Harper's* essays when they formulated a contribution of their own to the new genre.

The editors at *Life* struggled to stay one step ahead of the curve through-out most of the 1960s. Although *Life* was the venue where many Americans first learned about the growing forces of postwar cultural dissent, from the Beat's rebellion against conformity to the pop art of Andy Warhol in 1957, it was not the first place either of these phenomena appeared in print.[15] So while *Life* was rarely the first to introduce a topic into America's living rooms, the editors did cover controversial topics, and the magazine was an outlet where contentious words and images exhibited their obvious vitality in contrast to the conventionality of America's recent past. This was partly attributable to a generational shift in *Life's* editorial hierarchy. Ralph Graves, an assistant managing editor at *Life* in 1964, remembered that at that time he, along with three other editors, were new to their positions, were relatively young, and were eager to prove themselves.[16] The combined atmosphere of youthful energy, the widely held belief in the value of a good story, and the magazine's emphasis on news told through photographs explains the magazine's most important overall legacy: that it contributed key images to the construction of American memory of the 1960s.[17] The images that Americans retain in their memories of that decade's assassinations, political victories and defeats, cultural revolutions, and wars quite often were published first in *Life* magazine. According to cultural historian Wendy Kozol, *Life's* "photojournalism was uniquely situated in the postwar period to represent the intersection of national politics and culture" as it was nestled rather auspiciously between the age of print journalism and the age of television. It thus straddled the divide between the "rise of the image and the fall of the word," in the words of media theorist Mitchell Stephens.[18] As the definitive magazine of photojournalism, *Life* was a medium particularly suited to its historical context.

Life's medium was its message, providing the best approximation of the era's dominant communication processes.

In late February 1964, writer Paul Welch, from the magazine's Chicago bureau, and freelance photographer Bill Eppridge traveled to the West Coast to conduct interviews and take photographs in San Francisco's gay world.[19] Institutions like to speak to institutions, so once arriving in San Francisco the journalists contacted the local homophile organizations, the Mattachine Society and the Daughters of Bilitis.[20] In doing so, the reporters followed in the footsteps of a number of other journalists before them, including those working for *Harper's* and the *New York Times,* who sought the "official" opinion of the homosexual world. The task for the reporters from *Life,* though, was different in one key regard: they were to return to Manhattan with difficult-to-obtain photographic evidence of the gay world.

At the Mattachine Society offices, Eppridge and Welch sat down with Hal Call, president of the Mattachine Society. Years later, Call remembered the eventful meeting: "People from *Life* magazine contacted us and wondered if we could help them get a photographic representation of the homosexual community in the San Francisco area." He added, "It had to be authentic news, not staged, because *Life* was a news magazine."[21] But Call and others involved with the Mattachine Society had an agenda of their own, an agenda that when put into action would blur the line between "authentic" and "staged." Call, who once had been a reporter and even owned a newspaper, knew from experience that a reporter's informant can have the upper hand in an exchange, particularly when the source stands between the reporter and a world generally not open to the prying eyes of the media—like the gay world in 1964. So, instead of seeing the *Life* reporters as potential trouble bringing unwanted bad publicity, Call saw opportunity to influence the conversation on homosexuality. He thought that if he could give the reporters from *Life* a good story, the magazine likely would publish it, and with an article in *Life* the selective silence surrounding homosexuality might forever give way to endless dialogue.

Call knew, however, that publicity was a risky move. After all, the media had a well-deserved reputation for tending toward for the sensationalistic. Would the reporters from *Life,* then, discover homosexuals to be mostly average people deserving of basic citizenship rights or perverts constantly engaged in immoral and debasing behavior with children in public, deserving of surveillance if not prison terms? Would greater media attention result only in more bad press? Call concluded, "Even bad press was good to have," gambling that silence was a more risky venture.[22] Silence would keep homosexuals out of the public sphere, out of the discourse on human rights, and beyond the pale of law and justice; silence would leave gay rights to the whims of extortionists, corrupt law enforcement officers, and the unpredictable mass hysteria like that which brought about the sex crimes craze of the late 1940s, of which Call had been a victim.[23]

Call had more specific goals than ending the silence associated with homosexuality; he also sought to influence the kind of representations that would appear in the mass media. He thought that by helping the *Life* reporter and photographer, he also might place new gay icons on the stage, possibly challenging heterosexuals' preconceptions and providing homosexuals with role models possessed of strength, self-determination—and perhaps even sex appeal.[24] These new icons would show a side of male homosexuality that was largely absent from previous mass representations, yet closer to the Mattachine Society's ideal representation: middle-class as opposed to elite or impoverished; law-abiding rather than criminal; well-adjusted instead of insane; integrated rather than isolated; and, most especially, masculine and not effeminate.[25] Moreover, Call thought that by helping the *Life* reporter and photographer, he also might introduce more homosexuals to the larger gay world and bring them into the extensive networks his organization was engaged in building.

Tellingly, Call's goal of increasing homosexual visibility was more closely aligned with the needs of the *Life* reporters than with those of most gay men and lesbians in San Francisco, who were more concerned about police harassment and job security at that time. Indeed, by helping the *Life* reporters gain access to various sites in the gay community—such as homes, businesses, homophile headquarters, and of course, bars—Call was seeking to build a bridge between the gay community and the media, which meant a journey into relatively uncharted territory. He wanted to see if he could forge a symbiotic relationship between the two: on the one hand, journalists would gain access to stories about the shocking gay world and surely sell some magazines; on the other hand, the gay community would gain a measure of access to the mass media that might increase the scale and visibility of their world and educate the public about the subjective "truth" of homosexuals. In this context, the *Life* reporters likely were cognizant that barriers would be broken by surreptitiously bringing the gay bar, gay men, and even gay sexuality into America's living rooms through the pages of its most popular family magazine.[26] For their part, Call and his colleagues also knew that there would be consequences—that asking gays to publicize their bars, their organizations, and themselves, also would mean asking them to give up the privacy that so many treasured.[27] What perhaps no one completely realized was the degree to which homosexuals and heterosexuals would soon be compelled to participate in the gay world whether they wished to or not. In March 1964, these worlds dramatically collided at San Francisco's Tool Box bar.

The Men of the Tool Box

Located at the corner of Fourth and Harrison, in the area of San Francisco alternatively known as South of the Slot or South of Market, the Tool Box was in a largely industrial part of town.[28] Housed on the first floor of the dingy Hotel Harrison, the Tool Box opened in May 1962 as a gay motorcycle bar and became popular soon after opening as San Francisco had seen virtually nothing like it before.[29] Funded by a group of Los Angeles investors, the bar was to be a northern home to the southern California–based gay motorcycle clubs like the Satyrs and the Oedipus as well as the indigenous clubhouse for the Warlocks, a San Francisco–based motorcycle club. As the home to these clubs, the bar was at the center of the kind of immediate social and sexual networks described in the introduction.[30] That is, the bar was a place the reputation of which spread mostly by word of mouth; where individuals met face-to-face; and where the community present had an immediate, absolutely familiar and almost familial aspect. Indeed, Tool Box employee Mike Caffee remembers that the bar "was kind of a clubhouse" where "as people would make the bar their own [they] would bring things in . . . a lot of cartoons, jokes, and things like that . . . and we'd staple them up on the wall where they could be read."[31] Eventually, the walls of the bar themselves became a canvas, a self-portrait of the group as they created their own very closely knit subculture. Caffee said, "You could know everybody, just about, in town who was into that scene." He added that "at one point [we] made up a list for a party, we were having a private party at the bar and we wanted to invite the regulars, and our list came up to 300 people for which we had the list of their names, addresses, astrological signs, and sexual proclivities."[32]

The most notable feature of the bar was a black-and-white mural of masculine men whose features were borrowed by the artist from photographs in the sports pages of newspapers and from men's clothing illustrations in department store catalogs. However, the human dimension of the bar was striking as well, as most patrons were participants in the emerging gay motorcycle subculture and they performed the exaggerated masculinity of that world familiar to anyone who has seen Marlon Brando in *The Wild One*, proudly wearing leather jackets and caps, blue jeans, dark sunglasses, and at times, a menacing sneer.[33] Hal Call, who was familiar with the bar and the mural not only because it was already one of the city's most popular gay bars but also because he knew several people involved with the bar, realized in a moment of inspiration that the bar, its mural, and the bar's patrons would provide the perfect antidote to media images of powerless and emasculated homosexuals.[34]

Not encumbered by a desire to distance his organization from the bar culture, Call contacted the bar's current manager, Bill Reque, who he had known since attending Mattachine Society house parties in the 1950s, with a request.[35] Bringing reporter Welch and photographer Eppridge to the bar on a weekday evening, Call asked if Eppridge could photograph the bar.[36] Though Reque recalls that gays at that time, including him, "didn't like the attention of the media one damn bit," he offered little resistance when Call asked if the photographer from *Life* could take pictures inside the bar.[37] Reque said that Eppridge could photograph inside the bar if permission was granted by the owners in Los Angeles and if the *Life* team respected the bar patrons privacy by agreeing not to reveal the identity of anyone without his prior consent.[38] Although he agreed to be interviewed by Welch, Reque did not want his name to appear in the article, nor did he want to be anywhere near the bar when Eppridge would return to take the photographs. While Reque was more concerned about protecting his own identity than that of the bar, Call nevertheless remembered that when he first approached the Tool Box and another popular San Francisco gay bar, the Jumpin' Frog, "They were both reluctant."[39]

The reticence of gay bar owners about publicizing their establishments and of some people being identified as homosexual in print in 1964 is logical considering that, though legal breakthroughs were imminent and the authorities were putting less pressure on gay drinking establishments (though inconsistently), gay bars continued to be raided and their owners and patrons arrested on charges ranging from keeping a disorderly house to solicitation to lewd conduct.[40] In fact, only a few months before Welch and Eppridge arrived in San Francisco, the Black Cat Café lost its liquor license after a protracted legal battle, forcing the legendary establishment to close its doors. And only two years prior to the Black Cat's loss of its license, San Francisco witnessed its largest gay bar raid ever at the Tay-Bush Inn.[41] Still reeling from the embarrassment suffered after the exposure in 1960 of an extortion ring operated by members of the San Francisco Police Department and the State Department of Alcoholic Beverage Control who demanded payoffs from owners of gay bars, the city's law enforcement agencies placed the city's gay bars, restaurants, and baths under withering scrutiny. So harsh was the crackdown, in fact, that about half of the city's gay bars were closed in 1961 due to police action, according to historian John D'Emilio.[42] Thus, a decision to allow the interior of a bar to be photographed as a gay bar was an extremely risky venture for both bar owners and patrons in 1964. Because the photograph would be published in a national magazine, the risk increased exponentially.

In addition to raising serious concerns about the physical and legal safety of bars and patrons, the opening up of such quasi-private spaces that had been built, protected, and even fortified by gay men and lesbians signaled a shift in the way both homosexuals and the society in which they lived conceived of the relationship between private and public, closed and open, and secret and known.[43] Concerned about their ability to accommodate the requests of the *Life* reporters and dogged by worries about the possibly costly results of overexposure, Call and his colleagues became increasingly aware of the tricky navigation of the public-private divide in which they were engaged. Acting as intermediaries between the mass media and the gay community, the homophiles worked to build a bridge between the two. The question remained, of course, whether beneficial traffic would flow in both directions.

Whether those involved with the Tool Box had thought about the issues in those terms, most had encountered difficulties arising from their private sexuality becoming public knowledge. Mike Caffee and Bill Tellman, both employed by the Tool Box, had been hunted down and removed from the armed forces as young recruits when, after investigating, the military had learned that each had engaged in homosexual sex. Shortly after being discharged from the service, both Tellman and Caffee made their way to San Francisco. Despite being labeled as an undesirable by the navy, Tellman first found work in the restaurant business but landed a job at San Francisco's prestigious Sutro and Company, coming in through the backdoor provided by a temporary employment agency. Caffee, however, claims he was not as lucky, that the dishonorable discharge branded him with the indelible mark of a deviate and thus made him unable to find any permanent or satisfying work. Upon arriving in San Francisco, Caffee looked up the Mattachine Society, hoping it would help him find work and get set up in the city. The Mattachine Society never found Caffee a permanent job, but Call did employ him on a part-time basis to do typesetting and layouts for Pan-Graphic Press. Through his participation in the city's small gay motorcycle subculture and by hanging out at the Tool Box, Caffee was hired in 1963 by Chuck Arnett, who was then managing the bar. Chuck Arnett did more than just manage the bar, however: he held court there. Arnett was known throughout his immediate world not only as a convener of the scene but also for his sexual prowess and artistic ingenuity—he painted the famous Tool Box mural.[44]

Such was the culture surrounding the Tool Box, a site that might be seen as a microcosm of San Francisco's several gay scenes, intimate and idiosyncratic but overlapping. When Eppridge gathered the bar regulars—including Caffee, Tellman, and Arnett—to pose in front of the mural in February 1964, not only were two very different groups of men meeting face to face, but two very different cultures were, too: the public culture of the respectable mass media and the private world of a gay bar met in this moment where the gay world was literally giving up its privacy in exchange for mass publicity. It is curious, then, that when Eppridge and his assistant gathered the bar regulars to pose in front of the mural, there was not more apprehension on the part of the young, leather-clad men, for there seemed to be so much at stake. Eppridge promised that their identities would remain secret and that their images would be obscured, but he could make no such promise for keeping private the bar itself and the unique subculture it fostered.

By all accounts, the shoot took less than an hour. Before Eppridge jetted off to his next assignment, he showed the men gathered a small Polaroid photograph similar to the image that was destined to be published in *Life*. The men in the photo would have had to squint to see themselves in the crowd beneath the looming mural. All agreed that the picture was innocuous and that it would not bring any of them recognition. But the image that eventually appeared in the magazine was significantly larger than the Polaroid the young men had been shown. Indeed, once the photograph was published, several faces could be seen, a few men claimed to be recognized, and most gained some sort of recognition. But individual recognition was only the most immediate consequence of the photograph and feature that would profoundly affect individuals' lives, the fate of the Mattachine Society, the gay world of San Francisco, and the image of the male homosexual in the mind of America.

San Francisco Pictured Inside the Gay *Life*

Anticipating the Republican national nominating convention, the editors at *Life* chose as the cover story for the 26 June 1964 issue a picture essay on Pennsylvania governor Bill Scranton, who was at that time vying with Barry Goldwater for the Republican presidential nomination.[45] Unlike the subsequent international and Spanish-language editions of *Life*, "Homosexuality in America" was not mentioned on the cover of the American edition and did not appear until page sixty-six, as the sixteenth of nineteen items listed in the table of contents. The essay was nestled between a short photo-essay on Oregon's Republican governor Mark Hatfield and a visit with Nancy Ames, a barefoot, folk-singing debutante. The placement of this groundbreaking article near the end of the magazine makes it look like

9 The opening spread for "Homosexuality in America" created a tableau well remembered by many gay men who first saw it in 1964. LIFE Magazine © Time Inc. 1964. Used with Permission.

an afterthought, yet I think that its location follows a logic also used by homophile organizations: for discussions of homosexuality to reach a large audience yet occasion few antihomosexual outrages, they should be presented as neither fully public nor furtively private. By placing the article in the least conspicuous location in the magazine, the editors were hiding the article in plain sight.

Few words have the power to capture the attention of an audience like "sex." Arguably, "homosexuality" possesses a similar—if not greater—ability to attract notice. It is all the more remarkable, then, that upon opening *Life* to the spread on pages sixty-six and sixty-seven, most readers might first notice something *other than* the title of the article, "Homosexuality in America" (fig. 9). Competing with the words is an image printed across the two-page spread. The image, of course, was what came from the early afternoon photo shoot at the Tool Box in late February 1964. As far as I have been able to uncover, this photograph is the first picture of the interior of an authentic gay bar to be published in any mainstream magazine in the United States.

The opening image of the essay performed a great deal of cultural work. One noticeable element of the photograph is the mural looming over the crowd. Each of the twenty-five or so faces in the mural is an anecdote—and antidote—in the larger story about homosexuality in America. Some of the men in the mural look at each other, eyebrows raised in gestures of inspection and interest; others look directly out from the mural and into the crowd, turning the viewer into the object of their attention and attraction. The mural presents masculine men; but in 1964, masculinity included men in suits and ties as well as the emergent gay archetype—or clone—clothed in a tight white t-shirt worn underneath a leather motorcycle jacket.[46] An even closer inspection of the mural reveals a curious sight: a woman and her male companion, both wearing dark sunglasses, briskly heading for the door, avoiding eye contact both with the crowd of men and with the viewer. The image says that this is a masculine and homoerotic place.

From the mural, the reader's gaze moves down to the actual "brawny young men in leather," as the editor's introduction describes them. Most of the bar patrons are arranged in a circle, with a gap at the front left open to draw in the viewer of the photo, who in effect becomes the final member of the group. Not only have readers been allowed to look inside a gay bar, but they have been situated inside the bar, facing the entryway, and even possibly engaged in a conversation or cruising with the other men in the bar. The six men in the foreground of the photo may be speaking with each other, but they also are clearly participating in a highly sexualized ballet, as eyes, cigarettes, and beer bottles are placed in sexually suggestive positions.[47] The image and its erotic choreography may well have aroused readers' imaginations—or it may have offended readers, prompting them to turn the page or close the magazine. Yet, the impact of the image makes looking away difficult as the reader likely felt compelled to consider the spectacle of homosexual masculinity.

Certainly the most prominent photograph in "Homosexuality in America," the Tool Box image was only the first of several shots featured by Eppridge, who also provided images from New York and Los Angeles. The reader, however, makes two more stops in San Francisco before moving on. The additional images from San Francisco at once augment and complicate the representation of the city's gay world provided by the Tool Box photograph. Later in the article, another popular San Francisco bar appears in black-and-white (see fig. 10). The Jumpin' Frog, like the Tool Box, was a high-volume beer bar, but unlike the Tool Box it was not known for its performance of masculinity; instead it was a crowded and cruisy saloon where the patrons gathered on Monday nights to drink cheap beer and watch campy classic films like *The Women* and *All about Eve*. The *Life* photograph shows a crowded, smoke-filled room, with a movie projected on a screen at the far end of the bar, attracting the attention of the assembled men in a scene that looks not at all unlike a military barracks on movie night. Although the caption claims that night's movie to be *Some Like It Hot*, a film "in which Tony Curtis, Jack Lemmon wear women's clothes," the actual photograph captures another, unidentified film. Perhaps the editors at *Life* added the movie's name to add a certain queer mystique to the setting. Even as the patrons at the bar are anonymous, shown only from behind or in silhouette, they are presented as average, jovial people who are, in the words of the headline above the photograph, building "a society of their own."[48]

The final San Francisco image that made it into the pages of *Life* was a small photograph of Hal Call (as in fig. 10). Like the Tool Box spread, this picture of Call was groundbreaking, for it was one of the first photographs published in a popular American magazine of a self-acknowledged homosexual who was identified as such with his permission. Like the masculine Tool Box crowd, Call looks unlike the image of homosexuals most Americans held in their mind. In a word, Call looked average. Representing the new homosexuality, Call was not an easily identified exotic creature but instead an icon of normative masculinity: he looked like one's neighbor, boss, father, or husband.

The three photographs of San Francisco's gay world in the *Life* article presented the city in an unprecedented light—even for that reputably liberal city. From the evidence of the photographs, San Francisco possessed a diverse and flourishing gay nightlife where sexual partners, friends, and maybe even lovers might be found; and it was a city where, as evidenced by Call, homosexuals owned small businesses and ran organizations for the benefit of other homosexuals. But, perhaps most important, the representation of San Francisco is notable for what is absent; that is, the gay world of San Francisco was missing police harassment, a homophobic populace, sexual criminals, and all else that contributed to the supposed loneliness and alienation experienced by homosexuals. The article, however, did present these images of gay life, which appear rather strategically, it seems, in the photographs taken in New York and Los Angeles.

Life Photographing Place and Identity: New York and Los Angeles

Turning the page from the Tool Box photograph of masculine homosexuals, the reader is next presented with his inverse: the fairy. In fact, both of the photographs taken in New York City present images of the fairy, locating in Greenwich Village this effeminate, stereotypical, easily identifiable, and even comforting homosexual (fig. 11). The most prominent image carries the caption: "Two fluffy-sweatered young men stroll in New York City, ignoring the stare of a 'straight' couple. Flagrant homosexuals are unabashed by reactions of shock, perplexity, disgust." Indeed, the picture of two young men sauntering away from the viewer through the definitively public Washington Square Park in their tight pants, elaborately coiffed hairdos—one wearing feminine sneakers, the other pointy-toed slippers—is a bit head-turning. But that breed of homosexual, the fairy, was the image of homosexuality that most heterosexuals were familiar and comfortable with in 1964.

Heterosexual readers of *Life,* along with their proxies, the straight couple in the photo reacting to the two passing queens, might have expressed disgust, but there was little that was intimidating about the two homosexuals—who are seen only from behind. As Vito Russo points out, "Sissies were yardsticks for measuring the virility of the men around them." Similarly, George Chauncey argues that in New York earlier in the century, "The spectacle of the pansy allowed men to confirm their manliness and solidarity with other men by distinguishing themselves from the pansy."[49] The other photograph from New York City in the *Life* article only served to confirm these observations: it portrays a mannequin inside a Greenwich Village shop window dressed, as the caption says, in "the colorful, off-beat attention-calling clothes that the 'gay' world likes." Again, according to the iconography employed by *Life,* New York City was home

10 Images compete with each other and with the lively prose typical of *Life* magazine in this spread from "Homosexuality in America."
LIFE Magazine © Time Inc. 1964. Used with Permission.

The 'Gay' World Takes to the City Streets

by PAUL WELCH

In New York City, swarms of young, college-age homosexuals wearing tight pants, baggy sweaters and sneakers stroll and gather along Greenwich Avenue in the Village. By their numbers and by their casual attitude they are saying that the street—and the hour—is theirs. Further uptown, in the block west of Times Square on 42nd Street, their tough-looking counterparts, dressed in dirty jackets and sneakers, loiter in front of the shabby bookstores. Few of the passers-by recognize them as male hustlers.

• By Chicago's Bughouse Square, a small park near the city's fashionable Gold Coast on the North Side, a suburban husband drives his car slowly down the street, searching for a "contact" with one of the homosexuals who drift around the square. A tonjeatt on Chicago's vice squad explains: "These guys tell the wives they just going to the corner for the evening paper. Why, they even come down here in their slippers." Ten blocks north of the square is the haven for homosexuals, which parallels Hollywood Boulevard, festering with prostitutes and homosexuals. Two men approach one another tentatively, stop for a brief exchange of words, then walk away together. In the shadows that reach out beyond the streetlights, the vignette is repeated again and again until the last homosexual gives up for the night and goes home.

Homosexuality—and the problem it poses—exists all over the U.S. but is most evident in New York, Chicago, New Orleans and San Francisco, New Orleans and Miami. These large cities offer establishes homosexuals a certain protection, plenty of opportunity to meet either homosexuals on the streets, in bars or at private homes, and, for those who seek it, complete anonymity. Here tolerance—and, where it is abetted by the "straight" world—is more prevalent than in smaller communities. Where the "gay" world flourishes and provides so many social compensations, even the persistent pres-

sure of anti-homosexual police operations can be endured. Also, in the large cities these professions favored by homosexuals—interior decorating, fashion design, hairstyling, the dance and theater—provide the most numerous job opportunities.

Homosexuals can find some or all of their advantages in many parts of the U.S. but, because of its reputation for easy hospitality, California has a special appeal for them. In the city of San Francisco, which rates as the "gay capital," there are more than 30 bars that cater exclusively to a homosexual clientele. The number of these bars changes from week to week as about 18 months) Some bars, like the Jumpin' Frog, are "cruising" (pick-up) bars. What such cruising young men in tight khaki pants. They spend their evening standing around (there are few stools in "cruising" bars) drinking inexpensive beer and waiting. As each new customer enters, the 10 or 12 dozen young men before reaching his place at the bar. Throughout the evening there is a constant turnover of customers as contacts are made and two men slip out together, or individuals move on to other bars in search of better luck. As closing time—2 a.m.—approaches, the pressure grows as the tension heightens. It is the "frantic hour," the now-or-never time for making a contact.

In contrast to the "cruising" bars are the "gay" cocktail lounges, some of them just off the lobbies of the city's better hotels. They are frequented by local businessmen and out-of-town visitors plus occasional innocent heterosexuals alike.

A step or two down from the cocktail lounges are the "gay" bars where a single personality draws the customers. Until a closed recently, the Bickridge was one of the town's most popular because of José Sarria, who entertained regularly on Sunday afternoons. Sarria would up his routine—an appropriately witty "emotional" ending in full "drag" (dressed and made up like a woman) and shouting in the audience: "All right, you retiñe queens, on your feet!

United we stand, divided they'll catch us one by one!" As San Francisco's self-styled "Nightingale," first has achieved a certain notoriety in his capacity as tour city-county supervisor and polled almost 6000 votes.

In San Francisco's Tenderloin, off Market Street, are the bottom-of-the-barrel bars whose patrons and misfits of all kinds hang out. The hard-applied clientele includes dope pushers and users, male and female hustlers, Some of the customers have been "busted" (arrested) at least once. Here one finds the most flagrant of homosexuals—the "queens," with orange-red lipstick, eye shadow and mascara, worn by men who dress as women. There may be a man or two in "drag," a few Lesbians, some "gay" prostitutes, drunks and cheap con men.

On another far-out fringe of the "gay" world are the so-called S & M bars (S for sadism and "M" for masochism). One of the most dramatic examples is in the warehouse district of San Francisco. Outside the entrance stand a few brightly polished motorcycles, including an occasional tableau to lend the bar the accent is on leather and sadistic symbolism. The walls are covered with photos of motorcycle racers, men in black leather jackets. A metal collage of motorcycle parts hangs on one wall. A cluster of men stand—dangles from the ceiling. Over the raucous jukebox and the screams of the revelers. "Down with sneakers!"

"This is the architecture side of homosexuality," says Bill Plunkett, past owner of the bar. "We throw out anybody who is too swishy. If one is going to be homosexual, why not be a giant to do with women of either sex? We don't go for the giddy kids." A Madison touch on that philosophy is the neon sign in the room; chains on the wall, the

CONTINUED

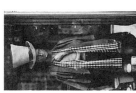

The window of this New York Greenwich Village store which caters to homosexuals is filled with the colorful, off-beat, attention-calling clothes that the 'gay' world likes.

A homosexual site a pad in Los Angeles' Pershing Square, where homosexuals meet in town make contacts. A few who frequent it are male prostitutes but most just seek company.

Two fully-sweatered young men stroll in New York City, approving the wares of a 'straight' couple. Flagrant homosexuals are unwelcomed by markers or shock, passively, disgust.

66

to the fairy, the gender-ambiguous male mascot of urban culture who was to be disdained, pitied, and grudgingly tolerated in return for the spectacle that he created.

According to *Life*, if the homosexual was familiar and perhaps even comforting in New York City, he was dangerous and disorderly in Los Angeles. The first picture readers saw of Los Angeles's gay world came with the following caption: "A homosexual sits on a rail in Los Angeles' Pershing Square, where homosexuals new in town make contacts. A few who frequent it are male prostitutes, but most just seek company" (fig. 11). The young man, who like his fairy brethren in New York is seen only from behind, is apparently identified as homosexual because of his sartorial presentation (pointy, polished black shoes and tight pants) as well as the context of Pershing Square, known in 1964 as a gay cruising spot. But unlike the Village queens, the Los Angeles homosexual was looking for trouble and possibly engaging in prostitution. The theme of sexual disorder is carried through to one of its logical conclusions in a few of the photographs that follow.

With the bold banner over two images proclaiming, "In a Constant Conflict with the Law, the Homosexual Faces Arrest, Disgrace," *Life* shows the reader the bait, "a policeman in tight-pants disguise on a Hollywood street," and the unfortunate homosexual who took it hook, line, and sinker. In the accompanying photo (not reproduced here), according to *Life*, the "decoy officer and partner lead handcuffed homosexual away in Hollywood." Since all faces were obscured, the caption added, "When arrested for soliciting, he burst into tears." And if public cruising in Los Angeles did not result in arrest, the pictures in *Life* suggested that it often ended in despair and disappointment, as a small photograph of the crowd outside a gay bar communicates: "On Main St. in Los Angeles, the 'frantic hour' comes when homosexuals face their last chance for a pickup that night."

The scenes of public cruising and its consequences are augmented by two additional pictures from Los Angeles, which stand in clear and curious juxtaposition to each other (see fig. 10). Both images are portraits: one is of Barney Anthony, the notoriously homophobic owner of the West Hollywood bar Barney's Beanery; the other is of Don Slater, the smart and sober editor of the Los Angeles–based homophile magazine, *ONE*. That both Anthony and Slater are white men from Los Angeles is where their similarities end. The vehemence with which Anthony hated homosexuals is made obvious by the misspelled sign he placed over his bar: "Fagots — Stay Out." The caption below the photo allowed Anthony to articulate his feelings more clearly; he said, "I don't like 'em . . . They'll approach any nice-looking guy. Anybody does any recruiting, I say shoot him. Who cares?" One person who did care was Slater, a man *Life* readers encountered in a crisp white shirt and dark tie, hair neatly combed, looking businesslike and eminently competent. While the photo of Anthony clearly contributes to the image of the disorderly, even dangerous life lead by homosexuals in Los Angeles, a slightly different portrayal emerges when considering the sum of the photos. Disorder and danger define the lives of Los Angeles homosexuals, according to *Life,* but perhaps the heterosexual world is as much to blame as the traditional culprits, homosexuals themselves. The combination of a semiliterate and belligerent barkeep and a police force that dressed its attractive young officers in tight pants to lure homosexuals seemed to say that homosexuals were not the only Americans suffering from pathology, that many heterosexuals in Los Angeles were themselves a bit too obsessed with the "homosexual problem."

One commonality that emerges when considering all of the photographs, however, is that *Life*'s picture of homosexuality in America was exclusively white and male. According to Wendy Kozol, "Despite the magazine's inclusive claim, depictions of 'America' and 'Americans' were limited [and] presented a particular image, based on dominant social norms of gender, race, class, and sexuality, as representative of national identity." [50] Thus "Homosexuality in America" contained no images of lesbians or gay men of color, but then again, a substantial editorial on the 1964 Civil Rights Act in the very same issue failed to make any mention of the gendered element of that legislation that made women a protected class. [51] Moreover, a photo-essay from May 1963 that featured writer and civil rights activist James Baldwin, also quietly known to be gay, failed to make any mention of his sexual identity alongside his racial one. [52] This focus on the singularity rather than the intersectionality of identity is typical of the era and thus provides some context for understanding why the publishers of the homophile press, following the example of the mainstream media, rarely considered issues of race or class alongside the topic that concerned them most, sexuality. By the middle 1960s, then, *Life* was beginning to deconstruct universalizing tendencies, but it still had a long ways to go. While *Life* was willing to acknowledge that America was a diverse place by revealing its gay worlds as well as several other minority or alternative cultures, it was not yet ready to discuss levels of difference within that diversity, thus perpetuating one of the pitfalls of pluralism.

Mapping Place and Identity in *Life*'s Text

In a magazine famous for its photographs, the text portion of the articles often receive short shrift, both from readers of the day and from historians decades afterward. And while the photographs make "Homosexuality in America" a cultural landmark, the text itself is important in that it adds specificity and depth to many of the people, places, and themes that are visually represented. Like the photographs, a picture of the gay world emerges in prose that is highly differentiated by geography. In particular, New York City almost disappears in the text, Los Angeles is even more narrowly and frighteningly represented, and San Francisco becomes more complex.

Similar to earlier journalists who "exposed" homosexuality, *Life* reporter Paul Welch began by revealing America's worst kept secret: "Homosexuality—and the problem it poses—exists all over the U.S. but is most evident in New York, Chicago, Los Angeles, San Francisco, New Orleans and Miami." Adding that although "these large cities offer established homosexual societies to join, plenty of opportunity to meet other homosexuals on the streets, in bars or at house parties in private homes," San Francisco nonetheless still "rates as the 'gay capital' [with] 30 bars that cater exclusively to a homosexual clientele." Among the San Francisco gay bars Welch discusses are the Tool Box and the Jumpin' Frog. While the opening photograph places the Tool Box squarely at the center of the gay world, the text relegates it to a "far-out fringe" of the gay world as one of "the so-called S & M bars" where gay men explored the line between pleasure and pain. After providing a description of what the reader can plainly see in the photograph, the article quotes a "Bill Ruquy," actually Bill Reque, then manager of the Tool Box: "This is the antifeminine side of homosexuality. We throw out anybody who is too swishy. If one is going to be homosexual, why have anything to do with women of either sex?"[53] But for all the displays of masculinity and the apparent attempts to intimidate "all those screaming faggots [in] fuzzy sweaters and sneakers," Reque reveals that the Tool Box was "probably the most genteel bar in town." A bar that did not come across as so genteel, according to Welch's description, was the Jumpin' Frog, a place where heterosexual standards of courtship and sexual restraint were flouted with abandon. Welch noted that the establishment, located on Polk Street near the city's Russian Hill district, was a "pickup" bar "filled with coatless young men in tight khaki pants" spending "the evening standing around (there are few seats in 'cruising' bars), drinking inexpensive beer and waiting." Focusing on the waiting and the cruising, the reporter attempted to draw a picture of the loneliness of gay life: "As each new customer walks into the dimly lit room he will lock eyes with a half dozen young men before reaching his place at the bar. Throughout the evening there is a constant turnover of customers as contacts are made and two men slip out together." It is ironic—and significant—that Welch's sensationalistic prose hardly comports with the contradictory image of the Jumpin' Frog provided by Eppridge's photograph. And while Welch's text followed many of the same themes presented in Eppridge's pictures, at times a dissonance emerges between prose and photo. This friction likely encouraged multiple interpretations among the several million readers of "Homosexuality in America."

Despite the occasional dissonance between image and text, Welch and Eppridge worked together closely while assembling the article; in most instances, the reporter-photographer team would travel together to each interview or location shoot, with one photographing the scene while the other interviewed the participants.[54] Although very little of the interview made it into the final article, Welch spent a great deal of time speaking with Hal Call, who told him much about the goals and accomplishments of the Mattachine Society. Readers of the article learned:

> The homophile groups actively conduct programs to increase public understanding of homosexuality in the hope of getting more sympathetic treatment, particularly from law enforcement agencies . . . In San Francisco . . . the Mattachine Society operates much as a social agency: it helps homosexuals find jobs in the city, gives them legal advice when they get in trouble with the law and serves as a liaison with police and health departments.

In addition to reading about the Tool Box, the Jumpin' Frog, and the homophile movement, readers also learned much more about the city's gay world, including the variety of bar cultures—from the Tenderloin haunts of queens and lesbians to sophisticated hotel cocktail lounges "frequented by local businessmen." Moreover, the article contained paragraphs describing drag queen José Sarria's shows that ended with the exhortation, "All right, you nellie queens, on your feet! United we stand; divided they'll catch us one by one!" The article also mentioned Sarria's history-making run for the San Francisco Board of Supervisors in 1961.

The textual representation of San Francisco in Welch's article both confirmed and complicated elements of Eppridge's photographic story. Welch's words added a perspective that was distinctly of the moment, including rhetoric that was meant to sting homosexuals and reassure heterosexuals of their superiority. But his words also contributed important information about which the photographs could only hint: that San Francisco had a large number and variety of homosexual gathering places (the text also pointed readers to their locations), that the city was home to organizations and individuals committed to fighting for homosexual rights; and that the city was arguably the nation's "gay capital."

When Welch got around to discussing Los Angeles, his prose agreed with Eppridge's visual characterization of the metropolis as home to disorder and danger in the gay world. Welch boldly proclaimed that "the antihomosexual stand taken by the Los Angeles police is unswervingly tough" and that they went so far as to publish an "educational" pamphlet which warned, "What the homosexuals really want is 'a fruit world.'" Even more revealing than the police department's war of words was the battle it waged on the streets "to deter homosexual activity in public." Again, in this case Welch's description mirrors Eppridge's photographs, as the writer included the transcript of a lengthy discussion between a presumably homosexual man and a police decoy who attempted to entrap the gay man into solicitation. The scheme did not work in this telling, but the police officers were quick to brag of their successes in other instances. Welch's reporting leaves the reader with a feeling similar to that produced by Eppridge's photographs: in Los Angeles the homosexual may be disorderly, but an unenlightened heterosexual society is only making matters worse.

The article closed with a consideration of the changing legal situation for homosexuals. The paragraphs discussed the influence of the Wolfenden Report—"the famous statement on homosexuality made in 1957 by a British governmental committee . . . [which] recommended that Britain changes its sex laws so that 'homosexual behavior between consenting adults in private no longer be considered a public offense.'" Welch also mentioned the redraft of the Illinois penal code based on recommendations from the American Legal Institute, "which, in effect, says that a person's private sex life is none of the law's business." Other topics included "sex crime" scandals in Florida, the Department of Defense's exclusionary policy against homosexuals, and the role of the American Civil Liberties Union in agitating for an end to the exclusion of gays from the civil service. Welch concluded his lengthy essay: "Today, as homosexuals become more visible to the public, there is a need for greater knowledge about them."[55] Though insipid and predictable, Welch's conclusion is an indication that Call's hope for objective research and education had, by 1964, become a mainstream platitude.

Americans and "Homosexuality in America"

Hundreds of thousands, if not millions, of readers of "Homosexuality in America" absorbed the article with great interest. According to statistics kept by *Life*, the issue generated 783 letters to the editor with 494, or 63 percent, addressing "Homosexuality in America."[56] Of those, 36 percent praised *Life* for its coverage, 21 percent were critical of the article, and 43 percent wrote with general comments.[57] If the letters published in the 17 July 1964 issue of the magazine are at all representative, opinions were anything but mild. The readers critical of the article were quite vocal in their expression of disgust. One man from Brooklyn wrote, "Having traveled around the world and met all kinds of people, I cannot consider myself a prude, but your article on homosexuals nauseated me. *Life* should have enough good stories not to have to write about topics which other folks never discuss in polite society."[58] Similarly, a woman from Austin, Texas, proclaimed, "Sodom and Gomorrah were both destroyed for these very sins which are an abomination unto the Lord. I hope harsh restrictive measures will be continued, so that if such practices persist at least they'll be in private where our youth won't be exposed."[59] It is interesting to note that all critical letters reprinted in the Letters to the Editors section based their critique on their feeling that *Life* magazine had transgressed an important private-public boundary. And the letter from Austin, Texas, also appealed to the sanctity of the private-public boundary in her hope that homosexuality, at the very least, be confined to the private sphere.

The biggest worry of those policing homosexuality, that it was entering the public sphere, highlights the pivotal effect of this article and others published in the first half of the 1960s upon American culture. Americans with antihomosexual attitudes were most disturbed by the fact that homosexual communication networks were coming into view: what had formerly been unstable and underground was by 1964 thrust on the public stage where all Americans not only could participate but in a certain sense were required to.

Voices of praise—177 in all—also made it to the *Life* editors. A large number of the favorable letters were written by sympathetic heterosexuals and/or irate civil libertarians—both groups were aghast that extensive public resources were being used to police what was in their estimation a small, persecuted, harmless minority. One such man wrote, "I say let's step hard on such activities where children are involved or force or violence is used." "But as a taxpayer," he added, "I revolt against the spending of such huge funds for harassment and entrapment of those keeping such activities indoors *if* on a consenting basis among adults. That police entrapment conversation in L.A. was absurdity at its height."[60] The theme of the encroachment of law on civil liberties was touched on by other readers as well, such as a woman from Peoria, Illinois, who wrote, "Your statement that many states have laws prohibiting sexual acts that cannot possibly result in procreation seems to be infringement upon private parts of our lives that the government has no right to enter into." She continued with this declaration:

> I and many of my friends use the new birth control pills. Therefore, our sexual activities cannot possibly result in procreation while we are taking our pills. According to this law we are criminals. Why should law enforcement agencies have the power to examine the sexual lives of individuals? I deny that the government or anyone else has the right to examine my personal life or that of any other person.[61]

The *Life* report on the letters, however, noted, "The preponderance of response to the article is from 'practicing homosexuals,' many of whom, 'for obvious reasons,' sign themselves anonymously."[62] If the two gay readers' letters reprinted in *Life* are typical responses, it would be wrong to categorize the gay reaction as either praise or condemnation. One anonymous letter sent from a reader in Pacific Grove, California, read in part, "The homosexual contributes to society and would make an even greater contribution if he could live without fear. When you must stand on guard all of your life, much of your energy must go toward this instead of spending energy on life itself. I am a practicing homosexual . . . who lives as near to normal a life as possible under society's yoke." He continued, "I would love the day I could write a letter like this openly, using my name without fear. My community respects me and has accepted me. But if they knew of my inner life all this could be shattered. Your article was an important contribution to understanding."[63] The pain of silence is palpable in the words published by *Life*, even as edited as they likely were. While the reader ended by praising the article, he clearly was concerned that it had gone only so far in communicating the unnecessary difficulties experienced by many homosexuals who knew themselves from within but felt forbidden by society from expressing those inner, private feelings in a public, open manner. Another reader was more explicit in his criticism: "As a practicing homosexual it was not easy looking at Bill Eppridge's photographs and admitting that I was a part of this life. Though accurate, it was not a pretty picture . . . For obvious reasons I cannot sign my real name."[64]

In both of these responses to "Homosexuality in America," the specter of the private-public boundary is raised as the readers lament the degree to which, as homosexuals, they are forced to live double lives and to keep their sexuality secret, private, and, in the increasingly common language of the day, closeted. Again, the scale and the medium of the discussion has as much to do with the lifting of the curtain of invisibility—the transgressing of private into the public—as does the content of what is being said. The fact that *Life* magazine, with its legitimate voice and tens of millions of readers, decided to broach the topic of homosexuality meant that untold numbers for the first time not only would receive information, but that they also would read it and understand it differently; by 1964, it was fast becoming a legitimate topic of discussion, even in "polite" conversation.

San Franciscans, Homophiles, and the Consequences of Publicity

A few days after the *Life* article hit the newsstands, San Francisco scribe Herb Caen penned in his column:

> LIFE MAGAZINE just published a spread on homosexuals in America, and tabbed S.F. as the capital ('Queen City' might have been a more apt title, but skip it). As Joe Finocchio once said: 'If they ever organized, they could elect Walter Hart Mayor,' and that wouldn't be the worst thing that ever befell us. At least they and their associates have a gift for improving rundown properties around town . . . and maybe we should unleash 'em on the whole city.[65]

Caen, who showed little reticence in including bits about homosexuals in his daily column, seemed to be pleased with the attention *Life* directed toward his hometown. In a sense, *Life*'s characterization of San Francisco as the nation's "gay capital" both confirmed and perpetuated the image of the kind of city Caen thought—or hoped—San Francisco to be. For Caen, a "Queen City" presided over by a famous female impersonator like Walter Hart might just have provided the antidote for the runaway redevelopment and "modernization" that was erasing the streets and sights of old San Francisco. Caen was not only a popular columnist, though; he seemed to articulate the social tastes and manners of San Francisco's cosmopolitan gentry and citizenry. If Caen could turn a potentially damaging characterization of his city into a ribald if backhanded compliment, so could most San Franciscans.

Guy Strait, a San Francisco publisher and sexual libertarian, however, was considerably less euphoric about *Life*'s contributions.[66] In *Citizen's News*, his newspaper that served the bargoing gay community, he wrote, "We must say that this article was about the most unoriginal work that we have ever seen." Yet, Strait was aware that it was the medium more than the message that was at issue, proclaiming, "Only because it appeared in LIFE is there any reason to consider it."[67] He concluded, "With this 'break-

12 Guy Strait's "Heterosexuality in America," published in July 1964. From the personal collection of the author.

thru' we can expect to see more and more national publications investigating the situation for surefire boosts of their newsstand sales."[68]

Parody rather than vitriol, however, was Strait's most effective form of critique. In the 20 July 1964 issue of *Citizen's News,* Strait offered his own report on the *other* sexuality in America—he called it "Heterosexuality in America" (fig. 12).[69] The four-page satire of text and pictures began much like "Homosexuality in America," but with a twist: "These healthy young men and women in their gray flannel suits and cocktail dresses are practicing heterosexuals. They are part of what they call the 'straight world' which is actually not so straight and narrow, but often crooked and twisted, sordid and sadistic."[70] Mimicking *Life'*s opening photograph of butch gay bikers in the Tool Box, Strait's first picture contained the following caption: "The group to the right is a posed picture of active, practicing heterosexuals who wear white robes and make a show of masculinity and scorn effeminate members of their world"—the picture is of four Ku Klux Klan members in full hooded regalia.[71] By replacing the Tool Box men with the KKK, Strait introduced the thorny issue of race into his satire. Drawing from cues in the rest of his parody, it seems plausible that he did so to point out that while masculine gay men might discriminate against effeminate men, the heterosexual world was by no means above prejudice, as the example of the KKK made abundantly clear. Less clear was whether Strait might also have been satirizing the apparent whiteness of the gay world by highlighting racial exclusivity among homosexuals as well as heterosexuals. The parody continues for another several pages, often critiquing the more salacious aspects of the *Life* article by simply replacing the word "homosexual" with "heterosexual" as well as adding new dimensions, such as with the photo of a female prostitute carrying the caption, "The straight world takes to the streets . . . Actual photo of a five-dollar prostitute hustling a John on a Broadway side street."[72]

This outrageous parody did not go unnoticed. *San Francisco Chronicle* columnist Merla Zellerbach devoted an entire column to the piece with the headline, "Odd News about Heterosexuals."[73] She said, "It's a take-off on last month's Life article about homosexuality in San Francisco . . . Editor Guy Strait, who masterminded this piece, feels pleased with his work."[74] But, she noted wryly, Strait was "disappointed by the reaction, 'A lot of homosexuals didn't dig it,' he sighs. 'They thought I was being serious. One fellow even said to me, 'Honestly—ALL heterosexuals aren't like that!'"[75] At any rate, by this point, parody layers upon parody to the degree that readers could not possibly have known what was straight—so to speak. When asked about "Heterosexuality in America," Tool Box bartender Bill Tellman said coyly, "I've learned not to believe everything I read."[76] Such responses demonstrate that the reaction of many San Franciscans to the "odd news" about their city was an urbane nonchalance, as local opinion makers saw the city's newly revealed national reputation as something to laugh at and not to take seriously. This view points toward the source of the city's famed tolerance of queers: that is was rooted more in a bemused fascination rather than a staunch support of equality.

Yet, Strait's piece and the reaction to it tell us something about political critique as well. A few short months after Strait's satire appeared, Susan Sontag published her famous "Notes on 'Camp.'"[77] Sontag's fifty-eight notes touched on almost every manifestation of this sensibility rooted in artifice. And though Strait's satire exemplifies many principles of camp as outlined by Sontag, it betrays a very important point: "It goes without saying that the Camp sensibility is disengaged, depoliticized—or at least apolitical."[78] In its playfulness, bad taste, and acumen with inversion, "Heterosexuality in America" embodies a camp sensibility; by adding a political critique, the satire augments and transcends the kind of camp Sontag knew. Heterosexuals who gained or sought "expert" status on the question of homosexuality, like author Jess Stearn and journalist Paul Welch, came to be easy targets for critics like Guy Strait. Strait was able to offer an alternative reading—a queer reading—of the *Life* article simply by highlighting the "outsider" status of Welch, by pointing out that Welch merely created a piece of camp by taking himself and his subject matter too seriously and with no irony and by mistakenly assuming that as a heterosexual he was above reproach. By employing the tactics of camp, Strait gave sophisticated readers of the *Life* article a rather clear political statement of how homosexual society differs very little from heterosexual society and how the difference, if any, lies primarily in its representation. Strait further realized that Welch's article was as much about what heterosexuals thought about themselves as what they thought about homosexuals. By placing a mirror before Welch's words, Strait introduced a new form of critique that called into the question the validity of heterosexuals' opinions of homosexuals by highlighting the double standard of morality used against homosexuals. From the new mass sexual communication networks, then, grew new forms of content and a new political sensibility.

Moving Through *Life*

The publicity received by the Mattachine Society, the Tool Box and Jumpin' Frog bars, and the overall gay world of San Francisco had the effect of advertising the city to many isolated homosexuals nationwide; and in many cases the advertisement was alluring enough to encourage a number to move about the country and to San Francisco in particular. Some of those who moved at that time claim that the article introduced them to the ideas that same-sex desire had a name—"homosexuality"—and that homosexuals formed into specific yet distinct communities in places like New York City, Los Angeles, and San Francisco. Many of these men—and they mostly were men—also noted the important role played by the homophile organizations by providing a face to "the homosexual," by introducing them to homosexual communication networks, and by helping them make their way out of what they said was isolation and into the communicative world of gay publications, bars, and specific enclaves in certain cities.[79]

As a consequence of *Life*'s coverage of the world of resources—cultural, political, social, and sexual—available in San Francisco, the Mattachine Society received several hundred requests for information and some very explicit pleas for help.[80] Of the many who called, visited, or wrote the Mattachine Society, a few letters received following the publication of "Homosexuality in America" survive, allowing us to glimpse the kind of reaction the article generated, the Mattachine Society's response, and how this media event helped transform the nation's sexual geography. These letters in many ways are similar to those the Mattachine Society received throughout the 1950s, but with two key differences. First, the letters came from around the globe and from isolated points within the United States, thus providing evidence for the ever-expanding international scale of sexual communication networks. Second, a close reading of the letters reveals that their authors possessed a different kind of imagination of place as well as an understanding of the wide-ranging consequences of new forms of communication networks.

The correspondence ranged from simple requests for information about the organization to pleas from individuals seeking to move to San Francisco. A minister from Macon, Georgia, composed a letter of the former type. He wrote, "After reading about your organization in the June 26th issue of 'Life' magazine I decided to write you and find out more about your organization and your monthly publication. Would you please send me information concerning subscription to your 'Mattachine Review.'"[81] This simple request, though, also occasioned what reads like a tearful, explosive confession:

> I am a young Minister . . . and I need help . . . with myself, and with those to whom I seek to minister. I do not understand myself in relation to my being in the ministry because I too am a Homosexual. There is no one I can confide in . . . no one to listen. No one knows. Even telling you . . . someone I don't even know is a hard thing to do. I hope your paper will offer some answers to many of the questions I have.[82]

While historian George Chauncey overturned the notion that the lives of homosexuals in New York prior to World War Two were ruled by the dictates of invisibility, isolation, and internalized homophobia, the minister from Georgia felt painfully isolated and invisible even in 1964—although the evidence of the letter and the courage it took to write it indicate he was challenging the internalization of society's disapprobation.[83] The minister from Macon reveals to us that overcoming invisibility and isolation were individual as well as larger historical processes; while connecting to other homosexuals was easier in some periods and more difficult in others, the process always has been dependent upon the individual's varying access to information dispersed in historically specific networks of communication.

In 1964, *Life* magazine published versions of "Homosexuality in America" in its global sister publications, *Life International* and *Life en Español*.[84] Several readers of *Life* outside of the United States wrote letters to the Mattachine Society not unlike those of their brethren in America. One man, a "native Indian" from Gujarat State, wrote, "Mr. Hal Call, Kindly excuse me for having taken the liberty of addressing this personal letter to you. I came to know about the Society from the *Life International* magazine of July 1964. I very much like the aims and objectives of the Society from what I could know from the magazine."[85] Even while reaching across international borders, the man from India still was quite concerned about privacy, constantly appealing to the need for "confidentiality" and emphatically requesting that Call "*not to send post cards.*"[86] He ended with his main request: "I shall be pleased to get in touch with two or three members of your Society . . . I should be obliged to you if you will let me know whether there are any of your past or present members currently in India. I hope you understand and appreciate my anxiety to get in touch with gay men. Kindly help me and reply immediately."[87] In this case, the globalization of the mass media that began in earnest around the same time as the publication of "Homosexuality in America" demonstrates how scale and reach means something much greater than simply a bigger audience.[88]

With readers of *Life* present in numerous countries around the globe, some even reading "Homosexuality in America" in their own language rather than English, the idea of San Francisco and a few other cities as "gay capitals" must be taken much more seriously. The internationalization of this kind of information, which just a few years before was limited to readers of tabloid magazines, FBI reports, and privately printed guidebooks, must have had a profound impact on the national, even international, sexual geography. San Francisco, in particular, moved from being one city among many that harbored a gay population to occupying center stage. Less than three years after the publication of "Homosexuality in America," media theorist Marshall McLuhan observed, "The new electronic interdependence recreates the world in the image of a global village."[89] As the world shrank, it took less and less imagination to project oneself into other places, communities, and identities; that a modern "gay" identity began cropping up in places like Macon, Georgia, not to mention India, owes a great deal to media constructions like San Francisco as a gay capital— the idea that homosexuality was anchored in specific locales at the same time that the material and cultural distinctions of place were becoming less pronounced.

Back in the United States, the *Life* essay was reaching deep into America's cities, towns, and farms, inviting people not only to imagine their sexual identity in a different manner but physically and figuratively to move from one identity to another and from one community to another. One man writing from Marietta, South Carolina, in early August 1964 stated the case eloquently: "Dear Mr. Call: I am a young man twenty-one years of age and I am a homosexual . . . I live in a small southern town where everyone knows everyone. There are no known homosexuals in this area that I might contact." He continued, "I cannot risk to proposition anyone for fear of ruining my reputation. My relatives are very religious and to them sodomy is an abomination unto the Lord. No one understands."[90] The young man was isolated, but with the information provided by *Life,* the gay world was no longer invisible. He resolved, "I've decided that I must remove myself to another environment where I would have ample opportunity to meet other homosexuals and lead a new life as I want to lead it. According to an article in the June 26th issue of Life Magazine, titled 'Homosexuality in America,' the city of San Francisco is the 'gay capital' of this country. I feel that this is the place for me."[91] But moving was expensive, particularly for a young man just finishing his education two thousand miles away. He admitted:

> I realize the fallacy of attempting to go [to San Francisco] at the present time with my almost non-existent funds. According to this . . . article your organization is partly devoted to helping homosexuals find jobs in your city. Perhaps you could be so kind as to help me also. If I should move to San Francisco I would need a job and a place to stay upon my arrival. I wonder if you could fix me up . . . It takes practically every cent that I earn to live on but perhaps I could save the amount that I would need.[92]

There is no record whether the young man from Marietta ever made it to San Francisco or exactly how Call responded to the letter, but other cases help us reconstruct a rather plausible picture of the transformative role played by media spectacles like the *Life* article, which helped to realign and perhaps strengthen lines of communication connecting queer people and places.

In June 1964, at the age of sixteen, Walter Wedigo Watson found a rather boring-looking *Life* magazine waiting in his parent's mailbox in West Monroe, Louisiana. On the cover were the bland stares of the Scranton family. Upon leafing through the issue, however, things started heating up, first with the piece on "Russia's Rockettes." Then, a few pages later, Watson turned to a ten-page article that would change his life: "Homosexuality in America." Watson remembered, "It totally blew me away . . . that article opened my eyes [and] hit me like a ton of bricks, I mean, it was right in front of me!"[93] The contents of the article itself exerted a profound impact on Watson, just at the age of his sexual awakening. Admittedly a sexually precocious teenager, Watson was practicing a rather polymorphously perverse sexuality. He remembered that he thought homosexuality was defined by oral sex between two men; and so, while he had been practicing anal sex with other boys for years, he did not consider himself a member of the stigmatized "homosexual minority." Watson recalled, "Now you have to keep in mind, I wasn't clear on [whether I was a homosexual] because I hadn't done oral sex up to this point, so I wasn't sure if it included me."[94] The *Life* article changed all that, refining his notions of what it meant to be homosexual: "I came to the conclusion that it had to [mean me] because I was definitely attracted to men . . . The article made it very clear that homosexual men . . . were [men] attracted to other men. They didn't go into graphics about oral sex."[95]

Concluding that he, too, was homosexual, Watson mustered his courage and decided to contact the "social service" organization he had read so much about in the article. Watson was unable to recall whether he wrote or called the Mattachine Society in San Francisco, but he did remember what he said and that he received a reply: "I remember the letterhead [from the Mattachine Society], I remember that distinctly. And I pretty much [remember what I said] in the letter. I must have talked about how lonely I was and felt I was the only one. You know, the word gay was not used then so I probably used . . . homosexual."[96] In his correspondence with the Mattachine Society, Watson also asked to be put in touch with other gay men as well as with the gay world through copies of the organization's magazine. The Mattachine Society provided Watson with all of this: the organization sent him copies of its publications (probably the *Mattachine Review* and *Town Talk*); a list of bars in Louisiana; and, most importantly, contact with other gay men looking for pen pals. Watson engaged in a lengthy correspondence with about six or eight gay men of various ages across the country. He remembered that through the letters, he was exposed to many aspects of the gay world: glossy male physique photographs; political and cultural magazines like San Francisco's *Vector*; and, more generally, news from around the country that lifted his feeling of loneliness, that he was "the only one." Through "Homosexuality in America," Watson found the door to the gay world, and though he lived in the same small Louisiana town for another decade, he eventually moved to San Francisco, seeking a refuge from "the unhappy living there because of the closet situation."[97]

Although he did not approach the city's gay world through the Mattachine Society, one man provides a revealing example of an individual directly and immediately influenced by the images of San Francisco he viewed in *Life*. A resident of Columbus, Ohio, David Barnard was what the neighbors euphemistically would call "artistic." While in high school, administrators discovered he was gay and sent him to a psychiatrist to help him "solve" the problem, but the experience only encouraged his entry into the gay world. While visiting the psychiatrist's office at Ohio State University, he discovered the campus's gay cruising scene, and soon was engaging in trysts before and after his appointments. Aside from the euphemism, Barnard genuinely was artistic, interested in painting, dance, and theater. It was his interest in the arts, as well as his desire to get out of Columbus for the summer, that sent him to London in July 1964 at the age of twenty-six. And it was while in London that an issue of *Life International* on a newsstand in Oxford Circus caught Barnard's eye. Unlike the American version, the cover of *Life International* did provide readers with a hint of what they would find inside, with the slightly salacious teaser "The Secret World of the Homosexual Grows Bolder and Broader" emblazoned on the top corner.[98]

After purchasing the magazine, Barnard remembers "getting on a red double-decker bus and going upstairs because there's not as many people there" so he could read it in private.[99] However, because Barnard suffered from dyslexia, "reading" meant looking at the pictures rather than "reading" the words. In fact, he claims that he never actually read the article and instead allowed the powerful photographs to tell him *Life*'s story about homosexuality in America. Predictably, the one image that leaped off the page, landing solidly in his imagination, was Eppridge's opening photograph of the patrons at the Tool Box bar. As Call and the regulars at the Tool Box had hoped, the masculinity of the men in the photograph was powerful enough to completely alter Barnard's image of homosexuality. "The *men!*" Barnard exclaimed, remembering how appealing and mysterious they appeared in the *Life* photo. That was July 1964. In August he returned to his life in Columbus, where he resumed teaching art—but it took only one small reminder about San Francisco before he packed his bags and moved out west.

In early April 1965 the San Francisco Ballet stopped in Columbus, Ohio, on its tour of the United States. On that evening, in Mershon Auditorium on the campus of Ohio State University, the ballet staged a long program that included a performance of the ballet, "LIFE: A-Do-It-Yourself-Disaster." Created that January, "LIFE," according to San Francisco Ballet historian Cobbett Steinberg, is "credited with being the first pop art ballet."[100] As such, "LIFE" communicated the same fascination with cultural artifacts and societal changes that appeared in other works of pop art. The libretto, written by Herb Caen, touched on the quandaries of mass communication ("never has there been so much Communication, never have people been less able to communicate"), mass consumption ("Her legacy is a mountain of supermarket sales slips, but there is no Safeway, only a

Hardway"), and the popular fascination with drugs ("if rope makes you think of hemp, and hemp of marijuana, you're getting the idea").[101] The ballet was divided into four parts: incipiency, virility, maturity, and resignation. The second of the four parts was what attracted the attention of Barnard. "Virility," wrote Caen, "is fraught with sex and violence, and all the other good things of life." In the ballet, a "tender and lyrical love theme" celebrating the happiness of a young heterosexual couple is interrupted by "harsh lights, dissonance, motorcycles—danger on two wheels, violence in four leather jackets."[102] The four men in leather jackets, who looked eerily like the gay men in the Tool Box photo, encircled the couple (fig. 13). Photographs from the production show the four leathermen from behind with the letters "H – A – T – E" on their jackets as they assumed a sexually aggressive pose. In the ballet, the four dancers then go in for the kill; the girl survives, the boy does not. Looming above the leather-clad ballet dancers was a large skull and crossbones, with the letters S and M filling the eye sockets.

Seated in the audience, Barnard witnessed the collision of his two worlds on the stage that night. The San Francisco Ballet's critical take on the menace of "virility" that preys on conventional heterosexuality reminded Barnard of the gay bikers of the Tool Box featured so prominently in Life magazine. The tableaux of art meeting life, of ballet meeting homosexuality, sealed his fate, and within a few months Barnard found himself in San Francisco, both working for the San Francisco Ballet and engaging in the city's gay night life—and, as it happens, getting to know Arnett and the other Tool Box regulars who appeared in the famous photograph. For people like Barnard, Life's "Homosexuality in America" and its resurrection in 1960s popular culture clearly removed homosexuality from the domain of doctors, psychologists, and ministers; it was newly an artifact of culture to be celebrated and commented on in the public sphere. Reflecting on "Homosexuality in America," Barnard concluded, "It was everything in getting me here [San Francisco]!"[103]

Regardless of whether any of these men, most of whom contacted the Mattachine Society after reading about it in mass-market publications like Life and The New York Times, moved to San Francisco, all of the letters and memories provide examples of individuals coming into previously inaccessible homosexual communication networks. Through such coverage in the mass media and through the initiative of isolated homosexuals to reach beyond their immediate world and find others they imagined might be like themselves, a massive realignment of homosexual networks of communication and connection occurred with far-reaching implications.

13 Four menacing, sexually aggressive leathermen prey on conventional heterosexuality in San Francisco Ballet's production of the 1965 pop-art ballet, "LIFE: A Do-It-Yourself Disaster." Photograph by Stephen Frisch. Image courtesy of San Francisco Performing Arts Library and Museum. © Stephen Frisch. Used with Permission.

Because of the frank content and massive scale of distribution of "Homosexuality in America," the Mattachine Society was bombarded with requests like those from young Walter Watson. Call and others involved with the organization initially were ecstatic with the article's success in introducing the organization to millions of Americans. For example, at the meeting of the newly formed East Coast Homophile Organizations in September 1964, the delegates unanimously approved a motion praising *Life* for its "pioneering" article on homosexuality.[104] The Daughters of Bilitis's publication the *Ladder* reviewed the article in July 1964, announcing, "LIFE magazine finally did it! The June 26 issue features 14 pages of pictures and text on 'The Homosexual in America.'" The *Ladder* added, "The pictures, of course, are sensationalistic for the most part, showing several bar and cruising scenes. The text shuttles between traditional prejudices and all shades of informed opinion, leaving the reader to draw his own conclusions. On the whole, the *Life* write-up is surprisingly objective and far-ranging."[105] The writer for the *Ladder* also pointed out some of the limitations of "Homosexuality in America": "As always, those homosexuals who are quiet-living, constructive people get short shrift in the article. Most sensationalistic touch was the big chunk of space devoted to depicting police entrapment techniques in Los Angeles." "One, Inc., and the Mattachine Organizations copped pictures and mentions, but DOB was overlooked (despite interviews at our headquarters office) in favor of a male-oriented spread," the DOB member wrote.[106] Still, the DOB's reporter appreciated *Life*'s nod to fairness: "Most unexpected and up-to-the minute tack was the denunciation of the recently released report on homosexuality put out by the New York Academy of Medicine. LIFE called the report '. . . just another example of the confusion and downright ignorance that surround the entire subject of the nature, cause, and extent of homosexuality.' Bravo!"[107] The *Mattachine Review* announced that *Life*'s "Homosexuality in America" did as much as anything in recent memory to smash the "conspiracy of silence" about homosexuality.[108]

Hal Call, Don Lucas, and others involved with the homophile movement were pleased that their plight was finally receiving media attention on a mass scale and that the attention it was receiving showed signs of "objectivity"—what they thought to be a momentous step on the road from condemnation to acceptance. Moreover, Call and others were satisfied that they and their organizations played no small part in the way the topic was formulated and presented. Yet the proclamation by the *Mattachine Review* was not without its caveats, the most important of which was that with success came a crisis: simply put, the small, financially strapped organization no longer could accomplish all the activities it had done in the 1950s and early 1960s now that the scale of need had increased so dramatically. Indeed, the problems were evident with the *Mattachine Review* itself, which in its heyday of the late-1950s was a monthly magazine, but by 1964 was appearing only irregularly. In fact, there was no issue published immediately around the time of the *Life* article; the next issue bore the date April–September 1964. In that issue, Call admitted, "Great difficulty continues to characterize the struggle for the existence of the Mattachine Society."[109] The *Review* indicated that letters from members and subscribers asked, "What's happened and why? Is Mattachine on the skids? Is its future clouded with doubt?"[110] Although Call replied that "Mattachine isn't on the skids," in reality the Mattachine Society was nearing the end of its active life.[111] However, as we shall see, the leaders continued to work but focused less on building communication networks, which they thought the mass media was doing quite satisfactorily, and more on serving in an educational capacity and providing services to homosexuals in need newly introduced to those networks.[112] Moreover, around the same time the article appeared, the organization spawned or was replaced by a second wave of more specialized homophile organizations, including the League for Civil Education (founded in 1961), the Tavern Guild (founded in 1961), the Society for Individual Rights (founded in 1964), the Council on Religion and the Homosexual (founded in 1964), the Imperial Court system (founded in 1965), and Vanguard (founded in 1966)—a transformation that was at least partly attributable to the increased need discovered through expanded publicity.[113]

Writing about the events of 1964, Call noted, "In the past year, it is probable that Mattachine has moved faster than at any time in its fourteen-year history. From placing emphasis on in-group problems and education, it has evolved into a type of project where major concern has had to go outward to the general public like never before."[114] Indeed, the remaining records of the Mattachine Society as well as recollections of several individuals involved reveal that in the first half of the 1960s, the organization experienced exponential growth in its activities. Summarizing these activities, Call wrote, "Mattachine has been called upon by church, university and public health groups on many occasions in the past 12 months to speak with authority about the homosexual in our midst, and to give its views on how modern society can understand him and his problems."[115] From an organization that originally sought to have experts speak on behalf of homosexuals, the Mattachine Society now was being asked by experts—whether in the mass media, the academy, or the government—to speak as experts about homosexuality. Such newfound public visibility and institutional respectability proved ominous for a small, poorly funded organization like the Mattachine Society. With success, according to Call, "has come an equally increased onslaught of individuals locally, from Northern California, and from all over the U.S. seeking answers to pressing individual problems—from lay counseling, to veterans affairs, to finding jobs, and so on. This caseload is now approaching 3,000 per year."[116]

In chapter 1 we learned of the scope, content, and impact of the social service work of the Mattachine Society during the 1950s and early 1960s. The group still was engaged in such activities in 1964, but the consequences changed as the scale increased. The entry of the Mattachine Society into the mass media—particularly with the intensive coverage in *Life*—produced many of the results for which homophiles had been working: the formation of a national and even international network of homosexuals with contacts based on service, education, politics, and activism. The Mattachine Society helped initiate a shift in the homosexual world as it made the transition from *gemeinschaft* to *gesellschaft*—a shift from a world convened primarily through face-to-face relations to one more likely to be mediated by larger social institutions such as the press and service organizations. One important outcome of this shift was that groups like the Mattachine Society and One, Inc., and places like San Francisco and Los Angeles would stand at the center of a vast sexual communication network.

As a facilitator of this shift, the Mattachine Society was overwhelmed by the torrent of letters and pleas for help and by the media's demand for experts. Call wrote, "When *Life* magazine hit the newsstands June [26] with its 9-page article of essays and photographs on 'Homosexuality in America,' Mattachine was scarcely able to cope with the flood of phone calls and letters it generated."[117] At the time, the Mattachine Society had only about two hundred dues-paying members and two full-time paid office staff, including managing secretary Don Lucas. Call's disappointment is understandable as he reasoned, "With this fantastic workload, one would expect that funds to make the daily operation possible would also come in. But this has not been true to the extent necessary for Mattachine's continuation on a minimal service basis."[118] And worse, Call mused, "Even though *Life* correctly stated that insufficient funds was one of the great problems of the organized homophile groups, response to alleviate that plight has been almost nil."[119]

Speculating about the reasons for this state of affairs, Call noted that "no answer seems possible, unless we lean upon the tired old analysis of the problem we have struggled against for years—fear among those who do not understand themselves, and outright selfish apathy on the part of those who have it to give, but just don't care a hoot."[120] A reason Call did not mention is that individuals could have been concerned about becoming a member of a homosexual organization for fear it might jeopardize home, family, or job. Potential members, moreover, may have been alienated by the organization's contradictory stance as a private social service agency, a public membership organization, and a public relations and publicity engine rolled into one. In addition, the Mattachine Society's political philosophy did not keep pace with the times, nor did the organization adequately capitalize on its established relationships with bar owners and patrons and the networks that they had created. Nevertheless, the Mattachine Society, as the recipient of massive publicity, experienced difficulty transforming visibility into institutional longevity. Already overworked by the variety of social service and educational activities the group undertook, Don Lucas, Hal Call, and others at the Mattachine Society experienced the publicity of the gay *Life* initially as a victory but ultimately as an insurmountable challenge. Inundated by competing demands, the employees and volunteers in the organization decided to prioritize immediate aid to troubled homosexuals and educational outreach to professionals, thus allowing other functions to fall by the wayside, even permitting the demise of the *Mattachine Review*—the publicity organ that had introduced thousands to the organization in the first place but by 1964 seemed superfluous to its publishers.[121]

A Gay Capital in the National Imaginary

As part of this process, San Francisco ceased being one point among many and became a gay capital—a symbolic homeland of an identity and a city that was a haven for institutional support unknown in most American cities. Borrowing a theme from Benedict Anderson, such a shift in the national imagination about homosexuality and about San Francisco—and about homosexuality in San Francisco—represents a more indirect, less immediate impact than the letters and memories that document the experience of homosexuals who turned their attention to San Francisco during 1964, seeing it as the gay capital, as a place where they wanted to move or visit.[122] This long-term change in the national imaginary is more difficult to document even as it is more pervasive and likely more consequential than the verifiably immediate and direct outcomes.

In the months and years following the publication of *Life*'s inquiry into the world of homosexuals in America, national newsmagazines and network television came through with their own versions of "Homosexuality in America."[123] After 1964, the media coverage of homosexuality increased exponentially as did the distribution of information about the locations and institutions of the gay world. Although *Look,* which was in direct competition with *Life,* and *Time* had been working intermittently on articles about homosexuality since the late 1950s, it was not until later in the 1960s that the results of their research were published.[124] The content of *Look's* "The Sad 'Gay' Life," *Time's* "The Homosexual: Newly Visible, Newly Understood," and *Esquire's* "The New Homosexuality," provide evidence of the power of *Life's* "Homosexuality in America" to influence the national imagination.[125]

Look editor Jack Star's "The Sad 'Gay' Life" was published in January 1967. In the two and a half years after *Life's* "Homosexuality in America" had landed on the newsstands, America had gone through massive social disruption, and the images of revolt were changing as quickly as the philosophies of those challenging "the establishment." From the civil rights movement of the Southern Christian Leadership Conference to the fight for Black Power led by the Black Panthers, from Berkeley's free speech movement to the Weathermen's millennial rhetoric, and from the bearded beats to the counterculture of Haight-Ashbury's hippies, style changed along with substance between the mid- and late 1960s. The new image of the masculine male homosexual popularized in "Homosexuality in America" in 1964 similarly became dominant by the end of the decade. The opening page of the *Look* spread featured a photograph with the caption: "This tough-looking man, left, is an admitted homosexual. He is Jerry Read [Reed], 35, a former Los Angeles public relations man" (fig. 14). The full-page close-up shot of Reed's face shows him to be the definition of a new masculinity: with a stern look and chiseled features, Reed wore dark sunglasses, an earring in his left ear, and a leather cap decorated with pins commemorating gay motorcycle outings. Reed not only looked a great deal like the men in *Life's* Tool Box photo, he in fact was one of the men in the photo. Whether or not the *Look* photographer actively sought to track down any of the Tool Box regulars, one was found and subsequently featured as the dominate image representing the American homosexual in the 1967 *Look* article.

The text of the "The Sad 'Gay' Life," as the title suggests, was somewhat less balanced than *Life's* coverage three years before, concluding, "Society does have a right to make its own rules, even if the rules are harder on homosexuals than heterosexuals."[126] Still, despite the differences in the tone of the media's awakened attention to homosexuality, there remained some important similarities in content. One such commonality was the focus on location, thus perpetuating the notion that the gay world was a geographically specific phenomenon. Again, following *Life* and several other

14 "Admitted" homosexual Jerry Reed, who also was featured in *Life*'s 1964 Tool Box photo, here represents the new male homosexual for *Look* magazine in 1967. Photograph by Douglas Jones. From the personal collection of the author.

publications by that time, San Francisco was portrayed at the center, as evidenced by the description in the first paragraph of drag queens sauntering down San Francisco's Market Street.[127]

Two and a half years after the *Look* spread and over five years after *Life*'s seminal photo-essay, *Time* visited the subject just months after the riots at the New York gay bar called the Stonewall Inn, which, according to some historians, touched off the gay liberation movement. Following precedent, *Time* featured San Francisco in the first two paragraphs.[128] Within those paragraphs, readers learned that homosexuals were preparing to elect an "Empress" of the gay community at a massive Halloween ball and that, all counted, there were more than 70 gay bars in that city of fewer than a million inhabitants. Moreover, hovering over the first page of text,

HOMOSEXUALS WATCHING OLD MOVIES IN SAN FRANCISCO GAY BAR

BILL EPPRIDGE—

The Homosexual: Newly Visible, Newly Understood

AN exclusive formal ball will mark Halloween in San Francisco this week. In couturier gowns and elaborately confected masquerades, the couples will whisk around the floor until 2 a.m., while judges award prizes for the best costumes and the participants elect an "Empress." By then the swirling belles will sound more and more deep-voiced, and in the early morning hours dark stubble will sprout irrepressibly through their Pan-Cake Make-Up. The celebrators are all homosexuals, and each year since 1962 the crowd at the annual "Beaux Arts Ball" has grown larger. Halloween is traditionally boys' night out, and similar events will take place in Los Angeles, New York, Houston and St. Louis.

Though they still seem fairly bizarre to most Americans, homosexuals have never been so visible, vocal or closely scrutinized by research. They throw public parties, frequent exclusively "gay" bars (70 in San Francisco alone), and figure sympathetically as the subjects of books, plays and films. Encouraged by the national climate of openness about sex of all kinds and by the spirit of protest, male and female inverts have been organizing to claim civil rights for themselves as an aggrieved minority.

without a dishonorable discharge if their background is discovered.

Some 50 homophile organizations have announced their existence in cities across the country and on at least eight campuses. Best known are the Mattachine societies (named for 16th century Spanish masked court jesters), and the Daughters of Bilitis (after French Poet Pierre Louÿs' *The Songs of Bilitis,* a 19th century series of lyrics glorifying lesbian love). W. Dorr Legg, educational director at Los Angeles' 17-year-old ONE, Inc., claims, "I won't be happy until all churches give homosexual dances and parents are sitting in the balcony saying 'Don't John and Henry look cute dancing together?'" Radical groups such as the Gay Liberation Front chant "Gay power" and "Gay is good" and turgidly call for "the Revolution of Free and Frequent Polysexuality."

Last week's report to the National Institute of Mental Health (TIME, Oct. 24) urged legalization of private homosexual acts between adults who agree to them.* It was the latest sign that the militants are finding grudging tolerance and some support in the "straight" community. The Federal Appeals Court in Washington, D.C., for example, has responded to a recent case by declaring

Homosexual organizations across the country run discussion groups and record hops. A San Francisco group known as S.I.R. (Society for Individual Rights) organizes ice-skating parties, chess clubs and bowling leagues. Nor is it necessary for a homosexual to join a homophile organization to enjoy a full social life: homosexuals often are the parlor darlings of wealthy ladies ("fag hags"). Marriage in these circles can involve a homosexual and a busy career woman who coolly take the vows for companionship—and so that they can pool their incomes and tax benefits for a glittering round of entertaining.

SEDUCTION AND SODOMY

Homosexuals with growing frequency have sought the anonymity and comparative permissiveness of big cities. It is this concentration of homosexuals in urban neighborhoods rather than any real growth in their relative numbers that has increased their visibility and made possible their assertiveness. According to the Kinsey reports, still the basic source for statistics on the subject, 10% of American men have long periods of more or less exclusive homosexuality; only 4% (2% of women) are exclusively homosexual all their lives.

15 In 1969 *Time* magazine reprinted a five-year-old photograph of a long-closed San Francisco gay bar in order to offer an iconic image of homosexuality in America. Image courtesy of Time, Inc.

the editors of *Time* decided to borrow one of the famous images published in its sister magazine *Life* in 1964 (fig. 15)[129] The image they chose to republish was of the interior of San Francisco's Jumpin' Frog bar; *Time* added the caption: "Homosexuals watching old movies in San Francisco gay bar."[130] That the Jumpin' Frog had been closed for five years did not seem to matter to the editors at *Time*. Rather, they likely selected the photograph for its iconic quality, a status it had achieved when first published in *Life*. Combining an image of the interior of gay bar with its setting in San Francisco seemed to define homosexuality in America to the arbiters of the national imaginary.

A month after *Time* republished *Life's* five-year-old photograph, *Esquire* magazine printed a lengthy and sensationalistic article on "The New

Homosexuality."[131] And though the editors claimed this to be a new look at the subject, it was in fact one pioneered, in part, by *Life* five years prior. Directly below the headline of the *Esquire* article was the following warning: "Look, Mack, this is a red-blooded, all-American, with-it faggot you're talking to. Show a little respect." Opposite this quote was a photograph

16 Photographer Larry Couzens convinced these two men who were active in the New York gay leather scene to go with him to Long Island to create images of the new male homosexuality. A roving patrolman, however, did not find the pair amusing and pulled them over. Couzens captured the scene in this candid shot. © Larry Couzens. Used with Permission.

of the possible setting of the declaration (fig. 16). Two "red-blooded, all-American, with-it" faggots, dressed in leather and leaning against their motorcycle, talking to a police officer, who had presumably pulled the pair over because of the curious sight of a two men riding a motorcycle with a poster announcing "Just Married" and several tin cans attached to the rear fender. The text of the article begins with the rather prescient statement: "Pity: just when Middle America finally discovered the homosexual, he died." The author wrote "died" but went on to make it clear that he really meant transformed—from a "curio-shop proprietor with an uncertain mouth, wet basset eyes, a Coppertone tan and a miniature Yorkshire, who lives in a white and silver Jean Harlow apartment, [and] mourns Judy," into a "guiltless male child of the new morality." [132] While *Esquire*'s Tom Burke essentially was correct to note that important changes were taking place in the formation and public manifestation of gay identity, he failed to acknowledge that America's perception of the homosexual as simpering fairy began to change years earlier. *Life* had presented the revised, "new morality" homosexual in 1964, and other media had introduced him even earlier, though to smaller audiences. But Burke's *Esquire* piece did accurately, if also hyperbolically, announce that a new kind of homosexual was coming to dominate not only the gay world but also heterosexual society's image of it.

The Men of the Tool Box Redux

While Hal Call and Don Lucas were busy responding to the torrent of correspondence following the publication of "Homosexuality in America," the men of the Tool Box bar were struggling with the consequences of publicity as well. Not only did just about every gay man residing in the Bay Area want to visit the newly famous bar, it also became a prime attraction for the rising tide of gay tourists visiting the city. What was already a busy bar on weekends now drew crowds throughout the week. [133] Not all were pleased, however. For instance, the absentee owners were forced to sell the bar once they realized they could no longer keep the bar staffed and stocked to keep pace with the increase in business. [134] And the regulars who had made the bar their semiprivate clubhouse began seeing caricatures of themselves walk through the door. These new patrons, however, were different from the originals in one key regard: while they dressed the part well enough, most did not own motorcycles and therefore were considered inauthentic. Within a short period of time, the first group of bartenders, managers, and patrons left the Tool Box behind just as that scene exploded, spawning not only new bars, but laying claim to an entire neighborhood of San Francisco, South of Market—which, by the middle 1970s, was one of the most densely populated gay enclaves on the planet. Thanks to the initial publicity and the long-term legacy of the *Life* article, San Francisco's gay world not only increased in size, but it was built with the images and ideals migrants and tourists learned first through the media and only secondarily through their experience.

These thousands of young men were coming out and constructing their lives around their gay identities, and moving to urban gay ghettos like the several that existed in San Francisco by the late 1960s: the South of Market District, Polk Street, the Tenderloin, North Beach, and soon the Castro. For the most part, they were following a model, though not often consciously, that looked much more like the media's representations of the masculine Tool Box gays in San Francisco than the gender-transgressive fairies in Greenwich Village or the desperate and disorderly aging homosexuals in Los Angeles that had been offered as counter-examples in the *Life* article. As both a symbol and a direct product of the changing representation of homosexuals in the middle 1960s, *Life*'s "Homosexuality in America" stood at the center of an immediate and long-term transformation of sexual communication networks, the effects of which would alter the ways in which both heterosexuals and homosexuals connected with the gay world, which, in the process transformed its institutions both large and small.

PART 3

Do-It-Yourself into the 1970s

Introduction

With all the attention paid to the mass media by homophile activists, journalists who covered the gay scene, and most anybody who picked up a magazine or listened to a radio talk
show and was exposed to the spectacle of homosexuality in
the 1960s, one might suspect that discussions on the role of the
mass media monopolized conversations about homosexuality
in the period and that it acted as the main conduit through
which information about homosexuality flowed. While the entry of the mass media into homosexual communication networks certainly resulted in important changes, it merely augmented the already established networks but did not destroy
or even weaken them. Indeed, with mainstream magazines
and paperback books advertising sites and organizations in
the gay male and lesbian worlds that previously were hidden or had trouble getting publicity, the networks of lovers,
friends, and acquaintances nurtured in places like lesbian bars
and gay male organizations expanded to include more members from ever-diversifying backgrounds. In short, the adop-
tion of homosexuality as a topic of mainstream conversation
in mass culture did not make face-to-face connections among
homosexuals less likely—if anything, it made such meetings
more likely. Still, along with simply directing homosexuals to
gay male sites (as did *Life* magazine) or to lesbian organiza-

tions (as did Ann Aldrich), the mass media's coverage of homosexuality influenced the ways in which individual lesbians and gay men would pursue new ways of connecting with others like themselves. In the two chapters that follow, I tell the stories of a handful of gay men and lesbians, influenced by mass and alternative media and imbued with a do-it-yourself ethos, who took on the task of strengthening the queer lines of communication as a personal goal. The results of their projects, begun on kitchen tables and in art classes, would eventually mimic and, perhaps, surpass the influence of the mass media in their ability to disseminate information about homosexual people and places and connect those people and places within a robust and somewhat independent communication network relatively unmoored from corporate, commercial media.

Do-it-yourself, or DIY, is a folk philosophy that calls for those with the ideas to learn the means of production and to execute the project largely without the aid of direct paid assistance. Although DIY has gained an enormous amount of cultural currency in recent years with the appearance of home (and everything else) improvement cable television shows and networks (including one called the DIY Network), the development of this cultural sensibility was a long time in the making. Some scholars have traced the emergence of a DIY impulse back to the eighteenth century with the popularization of "self-help" manuals aimed at the newly emerging white middle class.[1] Historian Steven Gelber dates the appearance of a widely adopted DIY cultural current around the beginning of the twentieth century as a function of both the emergence of the suburban white middle class and the attempt by men to remasculinize their domestic physical environment through the development of craft-oriented skills and the completion of home improvement projects.[2] Although self-publishing and the distributing of homemade magazines and books have a much longer and better-studied history than the DIY impulse, both pursuits are built on the premise that things made with one's own hands will come out the way they were intended to be and that larger cultural institutions are unwilling or incapable of producing things that are tailored for a specific fit, whether it be a tongue-in-groove or a group of people.

As the twentieth century wore on, a middle-class DIY sensibility melded with a somewhat subversive trend in self-publishing and resulted in a thriving underground or alternative press in the United States. One of the best-studied examples of a self-conscious DIY impulse within the world of publishing is found in the flourishing of "little magazines" beginning in the early twentieth century.[3] The publishers of these small-scale literary publications, like the *Little Review* and *Masses*, endeavored for quality and produced the magazines as a critical response to the emerging mass culture of movies, radio, and photojournalism. Both the DOB's *Ladder* and the Mattachine Society's *Mattachine Review* were marginally a part of this trend, but both were produced by individuals who previously had a great deal of experience in publishing and who were very hopeful that their publications would become popular and accepted by the mainstream; rather than critiquing or moving away from mass communications, the homophile publishers hoped that their publications would inform and become part of mass culture.[4] The underground press of the 1960s, however, rejected the mainstream impulse and instead sought to speak to specialized groups and to foment change according to a variety of mandates and ideologies.[5] In the 1960s, just as the first homophile publications were beginning to gray from middle age, a new generation of gay male and lesbian do-it-yourselfers emerged on the scene.[6] These young gay men and lesbians produced a whole variety of publications, from bar guidebooks to arts journals, from resource directories to explicit pornography, and they did so in a manner that both borrowed from as well as rejected elements of the new mass media coverage of homosexuality. Although produced by hand, with the labor of friends and family, and on a shoestring budget, these publications blended publicity, commerce, and activism in a very forthright manner, largely without the complications the affected the homophile organizations whose nonprofit status and lofty goals made the element of commerce an uncomfortable fit with other motivations. And though these publications were begun with very modest means and almost entirely unstated or vaguely ambitious goals (in contrast to the clearly articulated agenda of the homophile movement), they grew into extremely popular and long-lasting forms of communication and media upon which homosexual communication networks could be built and could grow.

The following two chapters unearth two examples of DIY homosexual communication networks, but readers soon will see that their differences are at least as pronounced as their similarities. As with parts 1 and 2, here I have provided separate chapters detailing gay male and lesbian communication networks. While the previous parts point out a good number of parallels along with a substantial list of differences between the gay male and lesbian experiences in constructing and navigating networks, the contrasting elements become much more fundamental in this final section of *Contacts Desired*. I focus on the DIY publishing impulse arising from the culture of gay male bars (as manifested in gay bar guidebooks) in comparison to a similar drive that emerges within the context of lesbian feminism (as it appears in feminist magazines). Although gay male activism of the liberation era (1969–1973) is mentioned in the pages that follow, it does not take center stage in my analysis. My explanation for this is a simple one that both confirms as well as revises the earlier work of historians. The goal of this book has been to uncover and examine the most significant communication innovations of an era—the homophile movement–created networks of the 1950s, the mass media–influenced networks of the late 1950s and early 1960s, and the DIY networks of the late 1960s and early 1970s. In the overall context of gay male history, the communication innovations surrounding the expansion of gay male bars warrant more attention than the radical gay liberation movement which flourished for a brief period of time. This, of course, does not mean that political activism played no role in determining the fate of gay male bars or culture during the period. It did—and I detail some of the connections in the following chapter. But, it played a supporting role to the commercial imperative adopted by small-scale gay entrepreneurs (such as bar owners) that kept the bar a central institution in gay male life throughout the period. The opposite is the case for lesbianism in this period in which alternative institutions and places replaced, or attempted to replace, the bar as the hub of communications and community formation in the lesbian world. For lesbians, the influence of feminism on the lives of women across the country provided a powerful conduit through which information about lesbianism could travel into places and on a scale unheard of in previous decades. For both gay men and lesbians in the late 1960s and early 1970s, the desire to connect with their own through channels they themselves constructed was a cultural and political imperative; but, when considering the overall landscape of homosexuality in the United States, a sharp divide began to appear between gay men and lesbians with regard to the precise nature of those channels and the sites to which individuals would be directed.

CHAPTER 5

Assembling a *Lavender Baedeker*

The do-it-yourself impulse has always been a prominent one within the context of sexual communications and the circulation of sexual information and imagery. From the elicit photographs of the late nineteenth century to the "Tijuana Bibles" of the 1930s, from the reprints of classic erotic novels in the 1920s to the photostatic reproductions of erotic drawings in the 1940s, a good deal—if not the greatest proportion of—sexually explicit material produced before the 1970s in the United States was what I call do-it-yourself.[1] It was not produced by established publishing companies or professional photographers and not disseminated by large commercial distributors but rather reached its audience by and through the hands of loosely knit networks of individuals hoping to evade enforcers like the police, postal authorities, and copyright lawyers. Of the many reasons why the production and circulation of sexual information and imagery remained a DIY operation for so much of the twentieth century, the punitive eyes of police, the FBI, and postal authorities were perhaps the most pervasive and convincing. Although the circulation of information about specific sites where homosexuals gathered was not necessarily subject to the same kinds of censorship as erotic imagery, because such information identified places (especially businesses like bars and baths) deemed illegal after the end of Prohibition in the 1930s by any number of laws and regulations the information itself was intimately intermingled with the policing apparatus of the state.[2] As a consequence of this close proximity between illegal sites and illicit data, the circulation of information about queer sites was largely hidden from the mainstream press and publicly eschewed by the homophile organizations and thus was left to do-it-yourselfers to elevate the circulation from word-of-mouth to a wider sphere.

Still, despite the barriers to publicity, homosexual gathering spots have been listed publicly with varying frequency and varying degrees of accuracy since at least the nineteenth century. Such spots were referred to in news reports on bar raids; they were mentioned in gossip columns in newspapers; and they were discussed in the pages of sexology journals.[3] In each case, however, the information was burdened with some kind of limitation: it warned the reader away; it was coded and thus required decoding; or it was located in hard-to-find publications read primarily by specialists. By the 1920s in New York and by the 1930s in San Francisco, however, publications that sought to expose the underbelly of America's cities also began to offer their readers the precise locations of sites that, if not an outright gay bar, might have tolerated a mixed clientele. For example, the 1939 guidebook *Let's Have Fun in San Francisco* listed the tourist-oriented but gay-attended cabaret Finocchio's, which was recommended for its "rather naughty" female impersonator revue.[4] However, during this period the information that was provided generally was rare, unreliable, vague, and often condemnatory—at least in contrast to what would come in the 1960s and 1970s.

The situation began to change and in dramatic ways by the middle 1950s. For instance, although One, Inc., the Mattachine Society, and the Daughters of Bilitis provided social services and performed public relations on behalf of homosexuals, none of the organizations directly publicized homosexual gathering spots with the exception of the addresses for the organizations' offices and the locations of meetings or conventions. Among the reasons for this is that the leaders felt constrained by the climate of the 1950s in which bars frequently were raided and homosexuals often arrested.[5] Thus, the leaders thought it would have been unwise to circulate to the public the names and addresses of gay bars or other establishments. Although homophile publications did not name specific locations, they did influence the cognitive geography of the gay world. Among those several thousand homosexuals who came across the *ONE, Mattachine Review,* or the *Ladder* in the 1950s, many would have concluded—and rightly so—that Los Angeles, New York, and San Francisco were centers of gay activism and, by extension, also were home to a sizable and perhaps powerful homosexual population, perceptions that became more prevalent and complicated in the 1960s with the attention of the mass media through the work of people like Ann Aldrich, Jess Stearn, and the editors at *Life* magazine.[6]

Activism, Commerce, and Guidebooks, 1954–1963

Recent years have witnessed a virtual explosion of serious historical and sociological writing on tourism.[7] Scholars have found that rather than being a diversion from the main themes of American history, the study of tourism can provide important insights into consequential themes like the formation of national identity and the construction of race- and class-based social boundaries. Moreover, this literature has brought to the fore a whole new genre of source material: the guidebook.[8] Guidebooks, like the celebrated WPA publications of the 1930s, have long been mined by historians for the abundance of factual information they contained about the location of particular sites and the characteristics of cities and their neighborhoods. Only recently, however, have scholars begun to show how tourist guidebooks were, according to Marguerite Shaffer in *See America First*, part of a tourist discourse "central to the development of a nascent national culture in the United States."[9] Along with contributing to the cultural understanding of what America was *writ large,* the authors of the guidebooks played an important role in presenting specific and intelligible geographies of the United States. In writing about and revealing the idiosyncratic details of particular places, whether cities or specific sites, guidebook authors actively engaged in the construction and distribution of knowledge about place. The readily comprehensible knowledge that they created was, for the most part, not disinterested knowledge. That is, the information offered was designed to elicit responses of desire among the readers—most obviously, desire to visit and desire to experience a place or, in reverse, to avoid it. As sources, these guidebooks offer a compelling view into the complex processes through which cultural constructions of place interact with and influence the social histories of individuals as they acquire identities and the social histories of groups as they form into communities. Moreover, guidebooks—or, at least, gay guidebooks—were compiled as both small-scale do-it-yourself projects and as collaborative works in which the line between author and reader was quite permeable. Tracing the emergence of such a form of communication demonstrates how social networks transformed the ways in which information circulated and knowledge was established.

Although handmade listings of gay bars and other queer sites may have been passed around from person to person for decades prior to the

1960s, the first one I know of was compiled sometime in the early to middle 1950s.[10] Titled *Gay Girl's Guide to the U.S. and the Western World*, little is known of this guide to gay male life other than it was hand-assembled, privately printed, and sparingly distributed. A little more, however, can be gleaned from a surviving copy, the third edition printed in 1957.[11] Interestingly, the contents of this guidebook were much more expansive topically, if more limited in quantity, than the strictly bar and business books that flourished in the 1960s and 1970s. In addition to listing a little over eight pages of gay-friendly bars located in the United States and abroad, the *Gay Girl's Guide* included under the subject heading, "Where to Make Contacts," several pages naming cruising sites around the country (such as parks, movie theaters, and baths). Moreover, the *Gay Girl's Guide* not only helped homosexuals locate particular sites, but also instructed them on what to do, how to speak, and what to avoid while visiting those places by printing a "Gayese-English Glossary" and a rather lengthy bibliography. Among the more surprising contents of the guidebook were brief but relatively explicit sections on sexual "techniques" and venereal disease. The sexual candor contained in these two sections leads me to believe that the *Gay Girl's Guide* was never very widely distributed, as its contents almost assuredly would have made the distributor susceptible to obscenity charges if the U.S. Post Office came across a copy. Indeed, the editor instructed the owner of the booklet to keep it under wraps, writing, "Obviously, don't go leaving the booklet around for your mother, landlady, Sgt. or CPO, as the case may be, to look into. Keep it always in the envelope or otherwise suitably concealed."[12]

Around the same time the first edition of the *Gay Girl's Guide* appeared, members of the Mattachine Society produced a compilation of bar names and locations. Although the leaders of the organization were not interested in and were not capable of advertising gay sites to the wider public in their publications in the 1950s, they did provide information to trusted individuals within their own circles based on the recognition that there should be a distinction between information intended for the general public, for homosexual strangers, and for gay friends. In this context of carefully managed flows of information, the Mattachine Society collected the names of bars and privately—even secretly—printed the list. Recalling this directory, Hal Call, longtime president of the Mattachine Society, remarked:

> In 1954, we mimeographed a directory of gay bars on the West Coast, from San Diego to Seattle. There were about 35 on the list. We num-

bered the sheets of paper and we signed out the numbered copies for
people to fold up and put in their wallets. They signed for them because we did not want the list to get into the hands of the police. It was
that sensitive a matter in those days. We had only about fifty copies.
That was all we dared to print.[13]

So, the Mattachine Society's bar directory was not a public document and
would only go so far to remedy the isolation of homosexuals, but in a limited fashion it helped strengthen communication networks and, by extension, community though the distribution of cautiously assembled information to a small group of Mattachine Society members and friends.

After *The Gay Girl's Guide,* the first guidebooks published in the United
States that were available for purchase and thus distributed to individuals
unknown to the publisher appeared in the late 1950s. Among the first, if
not the first, such guidebook was called *Le Guide Gris,* or the Grey Guide
(fig. 17).[14] First issued in 1959 as a privately printed list, this guidebook,
perhaps predictably, revealed the locations of gay sites in most countries
of the western world *other than the United States.* The motivation for producing the guidebook, according to its creator Bruce Baird, was "the first
time I went to Europe . . . I knew there were gay bars, but I didn't know
where they were, nobody else did, there were no lists, there were no publications." Finding bars in unfamiliar territory, he said, "was really a white
cane thing, tapping around and finding things."[15] Europe, perhaps even
more so than the United States, had a vibrant homophile movement that
hosted organizations that published their magazines in many countries.
By word of mouth, Baird had learned either during or prior to his visit to
Germany that a magazine published out of Hamburg called *Der neue Ring*
contained within its covers a few pages of listings of bars and hotels. The
listing did not explicitly describe the sites as gay (some like Harry's Bar in
Venice were not), but the context of the publication made it clear that an
evening's companion, or at least some gay camaraderie, might be found in
one of the places listed. Baird claims that he picked up a copy of *Der neue
Ring* at a bar called Kleist Kasino in Berlin and used the listing inside the
magazine to help him locate other bars as he traveled throughout Europe.
Yet, Baird remembers, the brief listing left a lot to be desired. "This was really in the primitive days of gay communications," he said, "half of the
things were out of date anyway." And though the listings in *Der neue Ring*
would help him locate the right neighborhood with gay bars, if not a
precise bar, he still thought there was room for improvement. So, Baird
started taking notes, jotting down names of bars and their addresses and

17 *Le Guide Gris* by Brice Bard (Bruce Baird) was one of the earliest published guidebooks to gay bars and other sites. He assembled the first edition by collating pages of
listings at his kitchen table; for this edition (1968) Baird enlisted the services of a professional printer. Image courtesy of the GLBT Historical Society, San Francisco, CA.

making note of some of the characteristics of each bar. When he returned
home, Baird typed and mimeographed his findings and distributed the
stapled, homemade guidebooks to a few friends.[16]

The response to the rather obliquely named *Le Guide Gris,* meant to
reference the famous *Le Guide Bleu* travel books, was extremely positive.
Baird distributed the first copies to his friends, but soon he received requests for copies from friends of friends as well as complete strangers.[17]

Baird did not produce the guidebooks with the intention of making a profit or turning it into a business, rather he assembled them simply to make the European (and later worldwide) vacations taken by himself and his friends more enjoyable through easier access to other men for companionship and sex. The initial response, however, told him that there was an unmet demand for this kind of information. Indeed, he had discovered that his gay male friends and acquaintances were numerous enough to form what might be called a market.[18] Fortunately, Baird worked as a teacher in the Oakland school district, so he had summers off and could spend a good deal of time traveling European cities, staying in inexpensive pensions, and learning about new bars and sites and revising information he had on older ones. During his subsequent trips he began to draw little maps that would help American travelers, unaccustomed to the "medieval cow path" style of urban design, navigate European cities. As the popularity of the guidebooks increased, so did the scale of production. From mimeographing and stapling the first edition himself, he solicited the assistance of others to assemble later editions. Indeed, Baird remembers he sought the help of his mother for the assembly of one edition, which they did by hand-collating pages while walking around his kitchen table.

By sometime in the middle 1960s, Baird's do-it-yourself project went into the next phase when it was published by Pan-Graphic, the press owned by Hal Call and Don Lucas of the Mattachine Society, and distributed through the Dorian Book Service (also owned by Call and Lucas), Guy Strait's publications (*LCE News* and *Citizen's News*), and through an ad hoc mail-order service run by Baird.[19] Moreover, as the guidebook gained additional readers and it achieved wider distribution, readers started to assist Baird in the collecting of information by correcting mistakes from previous editions and by offering dispatches from places around the globe that Baird had yet to visit, including locations in Africa, the Middle East, and Asia.[20] This exchange demonstrates the relation of print to communication networks and the importance of scale when considering milestones in the circulation of information. It also points to the way in which the gay market began first on the small scale of independent entrepreneurs seeking to satisfy the desire for information and, initially, not by media corporations seeking to name and segment a new consumer population. This example of entrepreneurship from below suggests that as commerce began in the gay world, it did so as an attempt to sidestep and/or undermine corporate capitalism and thus provide an alternative, community-oriented model for linking commerce with the activism of creating connections.[21]

Still, the achievements of these earliest guidebooks were hemmed in by their limited distribution, by their focus on sites outside the United States,

THE
LAVENDER
BAEDEKER

VOL. 1   NO. 1 $2.00

18 The cover of the first edition of *The Lavender Baedeker* (1963) featured urban phallic imagery; inside the covers appeared one of the first widely available and commercially distributed listings to gay bars in the United States. Image courtesy of the GLBT Historical Society, San Francisco, CA.

and by the implicit whiteness and maleness of the sites. The credit for breaking the barrier of publishing, advertising, and distributing the first guidebook to gay bars in the United States must go to another individual. In mid-1963 Guy Strait (born Elmer Guy Strait) published *The Lavender Baedeker* (fig. 18).[22] Although he worked with the Mattachine Society for a short time in the 1950s, he formed a competing organization in 1961, which he called the League for Civil Education. Despite their quarrels, which could be quite virulent and public, Strait and Hal Call had many traits in common; for instance, both were journalists and both believed that strengthening homosexual networks was the surest way for their community to gain stability and power. That Strait and not Call was the first to produce and publish a guidebook to gay bars in the United States, though, probably is attributable to Strait's closer relationship with San Francisco's bar culture: for a time he was allied closely with José Sarria, the presiding queen of San Francisco's gay world in the late 1950s and early 1960s. Moreover, in 1961, Strait published the first bar-oriented newspaper, called at various points *LCE News, Citizen's News,* and *Cruise News and World Report,* the last of which ceased publishing after the threat of legal action from *U.S. News and World Report.*[23]

Another motivation behind Strait's decision to publish a guidebook is closely tied to the context in which he lived and worked, in particular, the rapidly changing status of San Francisco's gay institutions in the early 1960s. As Nan Alamilla Boyd persuasively argues in her book *Wide Open Town,* a series of events between 1959 and 1961, including the repeal of vagrancy laws and the formation of a protective organization by gay bar owners and employees (the Tavern Guild), strengthened the legal position of gay bars in San Francisco.[24] These events influenced the attitude of activists in San Francisco, enabling them to begin thinking about the gay bar in different ways and perhaps encouraging them to project localized changes that were happening onto a nation filled with towns and cities that did not yet have an established gay community or comparable homosexual institutions. As a result of the city's unique culture of activism and commerce, individuals began to question the necessity of distinguishing information according to intended audience; their new ideas had lasting consequences when they began offering the names and addresses of gay bars for purchase and, thus, relinquishing control over how that information would be used by the public of strangers.

Although the full story of the origin of Guy Strait's *The Lavender Baedeker* is lost to history, the memories of a man who helped to assemble the first edition of the guidebook shed some light on this remarkable tool for queer connectivity.[25] Gerson Goodkind was born in Chicago during the Great Depression. After a stint in the military, he moved to San Francisco in the mid-1950s and immediately began to participate in the city's nascent gay bar scene. Among the friendships he developed, one was with Jim McGinnis, better known in the gay world as "Hazel," José Sarria's accompanist at the Black Cat Café. McGinnis, in turn, introduced Goodkind to the League for Civil Education and its director, Guy Strait, who had just worked with Sarria on his 1961 campaign for a seat on the San Francisco Board of Supervisors and who was well known in the San Francisco gay scene as the "Senator." Strait had learned that in a few months Goodkind was going to depart on summer-long tour of the United States and Canada on his newly purchased Harley-Davidson 74 FLH and he wanted Goodkind to help him gather information for a gay travel book that he then was assembling. Already planning on visiting as many gay bars and cruising sites as he could find, Goodkind readily agreed, even though it meant he would be obliged to check out places, like piano bars, where he wouldn't ordinarily go (he was an early participant in the masculine gay motorcycle scene). Goodkind claims that Strait already possessed a list of gay bars throughout the country that he was to use when compiling his more detailed list. That such a list might have existed says that for those well connected and in the know, a degree of information existed about the geography of the gay world in the early 1960s. Yet, because this knowledge remained out of public circulation, its impact was minor until someone would take the risk of publishing and distributing it. Strait's publications were known around the San Francisco Bay Area for revealing previously unpublicized things about the gay world—although often in the coded language best known to gay men—such as the location of t-rooms (or public sex sites), the recent actions of the police and liquor agencies, and the gossip of goings-on internal to the gay community. Moreover, his publications carried dispatches from New York, written by renegade homophile Randy Wicker, and a column he called the Roving Report, which detailed the ins and outs and openings and closings of the gay bar scenes in San Francisco and Los Angeles. Revealing the names and locations of gay bars around the entire county was simply a matter of taking the next step for Strait.[26]

Like Bruce Baird, Goodkind was a schoolteacher who liked to travel during his summer vacations. Unlike Baird, Goodkind preferred to travel around North America on his motorbike, visiting places as unfamiliar to himself as Berlin was to Baird. Goodkind remembers that he departed San Francisco the evening of June 15th, which was the last day of school and the first day of his summer vacation (fig. 19). He packed his saddle bags and "made a diamond-hitch with ropes and had a suitcase that wrapped inside a side-zipper sleeping bag" which he attached the rear of the bike. Just before leaving town, he stopped to say goodbye to his buddies at his favorite bar, the Tool Box, which had opened a year earlier (but still a year before *Life* magazine paid a visit). Over the next eleven weeks, Goodkind remembers covering 11,000 miles and visiting 26 states and 2 provinces in Canada. While on the road, Goodkind visited numerous bars, restaurants, and hotels that were purported to tolerate a gay clientele. Along the way, Goodkind found Strait's list of gay bars to be almost worthless. In addition to the many bars that had been closed, Goodkind discovered that a few

19 Using a camera timer, Gerson Goodkind took a self-portrait in front of Mount Hood in Oregon shortly after setting out on a round-the-country journey in which he collected a good portion of the information that would be included *The Lavender Baedeker.* Image courtesy of Gerson Goodkind.

addresses and bars simply did not exist. However, being resourceful and eager to meet new people and find new places, Goodkind was nevertheless able to come up with a substantial list. Although Strait had also obtained information from other sources as well as his own research, Goodkind contributed a good deal of material on cities and sites that otherwise would not have been known and thus not included in the guidebook, which was first made available to the public in mid-September 1963.[27]

Reading *The Lavender Baedeker* and *The Address Book,* 1963–1965

While Guy Strait crossed an important barrier of communication in publishing *The Lavender Baedeker,* he continued to manage information about gay sites in a strategic, deliberate manner. Strait called his guidebook *The Lavender Baedeker* because of what it would evoke as well as what it might keep hidden. Specifically, "lavender" had long been used as a signifier for homosexuality, and "Baedeker" was the well-known name of the popular

European tourist guidebook; combining the two told many that this little book was a compendium of previously forbidden information.[28] Of the original Baedeker guidebook from 1833, Strait wrote, "prior to this [travel guide] all information regarding places to stay and to eat were rumors and misinformation." By calling his guidebook *The Lavender Baedeker*, Strait associated the historical significance of the original with his own. Indeed, in the introduction to the first edition of his guidebook, Strait wrote, "We have set out to compile a list of little known places whose reputation has previously been passed by word of mouth," and in so doing revealed his hope that the era of information about gay sites guided by rumor, misinformation, and the inconsistency of the spoken word soon would come to an end.[29]

In 1963, Strait shifted the boundaries of information, but he did not obliterate them. Indeed, he called his guidebook *The Lavender Baedeker* and not something more obvious, like "gay bars in America," because the title required the reader to engage in an act of decoding, which provided a thin line of defense against those who might use the book for other than its intended purpose. Indeed, we know this to be a gay bar guidebook today primarily because of accounts of its production and reception; the introduction, the title, and the entries contained within the book adhere to the tactic of plausible deniability: no bar is called homosexual specifically and the preface only offers the hint that "some of these places are not exactly the type of place that you would take your maiden Aunt."[30] Also important to note is that such obfuscations used by gay men would have limited the audience of the information to particular kinds of homosexuals, especially those who were male, white, and native English speakers. So, while Strait's guidebook took an important step toward mediated candor, it continued to use time-honored communication strategies popular among gay men that were designed to obfuscate and encode rather than entirely lay bare.

By the time Strait was assembling a second edition of *The Lavender Baedeker* in 1964, Hal Call of the Mattachine Society and his friend Bob Damron, a San Francisco gay bar owner, were working on a guidebook of their own, which they would call *The Address Book*. Like Strait, Damron and Call offered their publication with both commercial and activist motivations: the books were expected to turn a profit because they contained information largely unavailable elsewhere *and* they would ease the feeling of isolation felt by many homosexuals, particularly those living in small towns and rural areas.[31] Moreover, it was just about this time that the leaders of the homophile movement and gay entrepreneurs began to consider the ways in which commerce and activism might aid one another.[32] Surely those involved with the homophile organizations already understood the intimate relationship between the ability to raise funds and to operate their organizations, but until Call and Lucas founded Pan-Graphic Press, money generally was raised through donations rather than explicitly gay commercial activities. After Pan-Graphic, however, activists began to tap the emergent gay market as a source. In September 1964, Guy Strait wrote an article on the "Gay Dollar" in which he offered an early inventory of how much money homosexuals spent on an annual basis and he hinted at (but didn't fully develop) the idea that social power might come with purchasing power. The first step and "the primary need," Strait argued, "is for a channel of communication and an advertising media wherein the homosexual can be addressed as such and told that certain merchants would like to have his business." [33] Strait's idea, it seems, was that along with building a network through which information could circulate, homosexuals also should construct a network through which their dollars moved but also in which their dollars remained, thus providing for a stable financial foundation for advocacy-based institutions like *Citizen's News.* In basing an activist strategy on the circulation of money, however, Strait did not consider how this might have excluded homosexuals with little income from participating in the gay movement, thus making it difficult for that population to influence the overall activist agenda.

Borrowing the methodology for gathering information pursued by Baird, Strait, and Goodkind before him, Damron spent several months a year traveling coast to coast, visiting as many gay bars as he could find and building relationships with their owners and patrons. [34] In so doing, Damron played a role comparable to guidebook compilers like Karl Baedeker and the WPA researchers. First, like other authors of guidebooks, Damron assumed the role of an information broker. By gathering hard-to-access information and by offering it to a public who desired it, Damron assumed a position of power over both the source of the information (the bar owners) as well as those who would eventually purchase it; in emphasizing some elements while downplaying others, he could shape a particular image of a site and the people who went there—and he could and did do it in ways that benefited his own best interests as the eventual owner of several popular gay bars and restaurants in San Francisco. Moreover, the guidebooks of Damron and others demonstrate how the publication of seemingly mundane, practical knowledge about distant and otherwise hidden places can transform into a socially significant body of knowledge.

The content of these earliest published guidebooks was very similar— and very simple. For example, the first edition of *The Lavender Baedeker* contained twenty-four pages of listings of and advertisements for gay or gay-friendly bars, restaurants, and lodgings.[35] These listings were sorted by state and further by city. Other than the name and address of a site, the earliest guidebooks provided no description of the place other than the implied information that it was a gay site—a definition that itself was undergoing important changes during this period, as we shall see.

Beneath the surface of the simple factual information contained in the guidebooks published prior to 1965, however, a number of consequential cultural shifts began to take place. First, the actual production of the guidebooks reveals something about the mindset of those who assembled and published them. Most basically, the fact such books were produced demonstrates that Baird, Strait, Call, Damron, and others imagined the gay world to be expansive, established, and spatially anchored in the early 1960s. To undertake the project of cataloging gay sites not only in one town or region but throughout the entire country and even the entire world suggests an ambitious vision on the part of the compilers. It suggests that they knew there were gay sites in small towns and large cities and that the commonalities they shared were far more important than their differences— that at the base these were places where men could meet men and women could meet women for friendship, companionship, and sex. This image of the gay world shared by the compilers shows that they believed a sort of gay nationality existed but was waiting to be discovered by its members; by cataloging and mapping this nation, the publishers of these guidebooks not only told gay men and, to a lesser extent, lesbians where they could find others like themselves, but they provided them with evidence of the larger world, indeed the quasi-nation, in which they lived.[36]

Perhaps even more remarkable than the fact that these gay men could imagine such an expansive gay world is the fact that they thought they could publish very specific information about it given the contextual constraints of that era. Their willingness to undertake such a project has much to do with the fact that they lived in and were active in an established gay subculture like the one that existed in San Francisco.[37] In the late 1950s and early 1960s, gay bars in San Francisco were undergoing important transformations that made these sites much less likely to be raided by the police or closed by the Alcohol Beverage Control Board. Moreover, although the gay bar existed as an institution since at least the 1930s, it was in the early 1960s that we see the emergence of the contemporary gay bar as a place that had an almost exclusively gay clientele, was owned, managed, and run by homosexuals, and was advertised in gay publications designed to attract gay patrons. By the early 1960s, then, the contemporary gay bar was without the kind of ambiguity that characterized many bars frequented by homosexuals prior to the 1950s as well as some bars outside of urban areas into the 1980s.[38] Recognizing these changes that were happening in San Francisco well before most other cities, Strait, Damron, and the others thought that lists could be compiled and published without causing trouble for the owners or patrons of the bars.[39]

In addition to advertising the names of bars, then, the publishers of the guidebooks were exporting the very idea of a gay bar, consequently helping to remove the definitional ambiguity of bars that for decades had been frequented by male homosexuals along with male and female prostitutes, bohemians, mannish women, wealthy slummers, misdirected tourists, and men who might have sex with men but who cannot be called "gay" or even homosexual—much like Walter Watson was before he came across the *Life* magazine article in 1964. Evoking the characteristically euphemistic style of speaking in the early 1960s, Gerson Goodkind recently explained how this labeling process worked in practice. "I'm sure that there are a lot of places listed that were [based on] one time contacts," Goodkind said. "That somebody went there and made a contact, a friendly contact one time and there was no other report of a similar occurrence. So, if a place is friendly to you, then you might report it to a person who was collecting information and it may not be friendly to anybody else." In other words, the threshold for a site to be included in *The Lavender Baedeker* or any of the other early listings of gay bars was rather low—and it certainly did not have to meet today's definition of a gay bar. For example, if Goodkind visited a rural roadhouse once and happened upon a sexual liaison in the toilet of the establishment, he might have suggested the site be listed in the guidebook although the bar would have been unrecognizable then (or now) as a gay bar. Goodkind continued, "Anything that would be used to identify a gay club to include it in *The Lavender Baedeker* would no longer be appropriate today because it was more suggestion than it was actual fact."[40] Indeed, the changing characteristics of a "gay bar" as hinted at by Goodkind were the subject of some discussion at this time, as evidenced by an article by Guy Strait called, simply, "What Is a Gay Bar?"[41] Strait argued for a clarification of the term based on the situation that "the best-known homosexual pickup spot in the United States is the Men's Bar of the Waldorf-Astoria in New York City. Yet this is not a 'gay bar.'" What was the difference between bars in which homosexual contacts might be made and a gay bar? According to Strait, gay bars were places where gay men did not have to speak in euphemism or subtleties but where they had "freedom of speech" and freedom from self-censorship. More importantly, though, in "pickup spots" and "gay bars" "there is a variance in the understanding of homosexuality itself." In the mixed sites, "you will find a married man from the suburb who strays from his ordinary bed only from time to time . . . The pickup spot patron merely wants to go to bed sexually—the gay bar cruiser is looking for the possibility of a lover."[42] Although we might take issue with how Strait defined a gay bar, both Goodkind and Strait were aware of an emerging dissonance as the idea of a "gay bar" was becoming a clearly understood cultural concept while at the same time many men who were not "gay" continued to go to bars that also were not "gay" to find male sexual partners.[43]

Along with their impulse to identify bars where men could find sex with other men and call those places gay bars, the considerable work of producing, advertising, and distributing guidebooks suggests that these gay men thought there to be a sizable audience of gay tourists, business travelers, and even people looking to move who were willing to buy the guidebooks. This suspicion of an audience, of course, began as a hunch but after the initial noncommercial forays into the genre by Bruce Baird and then the for-profit projects of Guy Strait and Bob Damron, it became clear there was a huge unmet demand. Although distribution statistics have not survived, the fact that by the end of the 1960s scores of such guidebooks were being published is further evidence for the demand. While travel is a theme in much gay literature before the 1960s, the idea of a gay tourist industry is an artifact of the 1960s.[44] As places like San Francisco and Los Angeles were evoked in the mass media as gay capitals by the middle 1960s, homosexuals began not only to move permanently to these places in large numbers but also to visit them as tourists and experience their unique sights and sounds as temporary, fantastic interludes in lives that for many were only nominally gay.[45] Living, working, and even owning gay bars and restaurants in San Francisco, the producers of the guidebooks witnessed, commented upon, profited from, and further encouraged this increased circulation of queer information and queer people, resulting ultimately in a rising tide of migration and tourism.

Along with all that the guidebooks reveal about the mindset of those who compiled and published them, we might also speculate how they may have influenced the ideas of those who purchased and used them. Because evidence is scarce and subject to the vagaries of human memory, it is difficult to generalize upon what homosexuals might have known about the people and places of the gay world beyond their immediate experience. But we can be relatively sure that their knowledge and their way of knowing changed in important ways throughout the 1950s and 1960s in relation to the innovations in communication networks detailed in previous chapters. In *Gay New York,* George Chauncey wrote about what was likely the most sophisticated and knowledgeable population of homosexuals in the

U.S. before the 1940s. Many of the gay men he discussed claimed to have had a common history, a collective knowledge of locations where they could socialize, and a shared yet distinct language that was ill-understood by outsiders.[46] Yet, despite all that these gay men knew, their knowledge of the national extent of the gay world likely would have been limited by their own experiences, by what they learned by word of mouth, and by the few items they might have come across in a scattering of books and magazines. Not until the early 1960s with the publication of the guidebooks could a national sexual geography be known with any specificity—and a specificity that could be known on a mass scale.[47] Take, for instance, this example—an ad for *The Lavender Baedeker* Strait placed in his own San Francisco–based newspaper, *Citizen's News* (fig. 20). The full-page ad on the back page described *The Lavender Baedeker* as, "a guidebook to 600 interesting places in the United States. The most complete and up to date ever published. The result of thousands of letters and cross-checking."[48] He added that it could be ordered by mail through his offices in San Francisco or was available for purchase at a number of locations not just in San Francisco but scattered throughout southern California and across the country in cities like Seattle, Washington; Oklahoma City, Oklahoma; Columbus, Ohio; Daytona, Florida; and Calumet City, Illinois. Although it came upon the heels of *The Lavender Baedeker, The Address Book* reached an even wider distribution, being advertised in the pages of *The Mattachine Review* and *Town Talk* and sold through the Dorian Book Service and at numerous bars, restaurants, and newsstands.[49] Even more important, though, by 1968 *The Address Book* was distributed through the mail-order arm of Calafran Enterprises, Damron's publishing company that specialized in producing and distributing photos and magazines featuring male nudes.[50]

The effect of reading the guidebook and reading about the distribution network set up to sell it must have been profound for those gay men who purchased it in the middle 1960s. When such information was distributed candidly and to a wide audience in *The Lavender Baedeker* and *The Address Book,* gay readers might have imagined themselves no longer participating in a secret society but instead taking part in a kind of alternative yet mass culture. Moreover, the users of the guidebooks would have learned that gay world was so wide and dispersed that it could never be known in its entirety, that the accumulated knowledge of it was enough to fill a book—albeit a rather slim one in 1963. This change would bring to the gay world both the safety, along with the cultural segmentation, of consumer-oriented mass culture—thus fulfilling the goals of the homophiles and leaving a legacy that activists continue to wrestle with today.[51]

20 Advertising his *Lavender Baedeker* in his own newspaper (*Citizen's News*), publisher Guy Strait created an ad that effectively communicated that the publication was a guidebook to gay bars in the United States without ever printing "gay bar" in the copy of the ad. From the personal collection of the author.

How to be Gay / Where to be Gay in the Late 1960s

Like many other arenas of American social life in the 1960s, change was rapid and dramatic in the gay male world.[52] After 1967 the landscape of primarily gay male institutions in San Francisco had shifted considerably. Although the influence of the Mattachine Society had been declining in recent years, in 1967 the organization departed its offices on Mission Street for a fresh start at a new location on Ellis Street, in San Francisco's Tenderloin district. Don Lucas had since departed to pursue social services as part of President Johnson's War on Poverty programs, while Hal Call further intertwined activism and commerce when he opened up what was probably the nation's first gay bookstore, the Adonis Book Store, around May 1967.[53] In addition to offering a large library of books dealing with sexuality, the Adonis sold physique magazines, erotica, homophile publications, guidebooks, musical recordings, and even gay-themed greeting cards, most of which previously had circulated only through mail-order shipments. Although the leaders of the Mattachine Society no longer played the same roles as they had done from the mid-1950s, other individuals in different organizations had taken up the slack and had established themselves as community leaders by 1967. As Bob Damron and Guy Strait presided over their own small commercial and quasi-activist enterprises, still others, like Bill Plath, Bill Beardemphl, and George Mendenhall, pursued a less-commercial, more community-oriented agenda through organizations like the Society for Individual Rights (SIR).[54] A full history of SIR is beyond the scope of this book, but it is worth mentioning that this organization by 1967 became the largest U.S. gay organization in the years prior to the Stonewall riots of June 1969 (as well as for some time after the riots). A few reasons for its success include that it established what is commonly regarded as the first gay community center in the United States, which was located just off Market Street in San Francisco, and that it published *Vector*, a magazine that linked the homophile movement and the larger population of gay men who read physique magazines and bar-oriented newspapers and successfully bridged the pre- and post-Stonewall years. While the Mattachine Society was much more supportive of gay bars than most historians suggest, the formation of organizations like SIR, with their very close links to the bar scene, mark an important transformation as bar owners and homophile activists considered their battles to be nearly one and the same—at least in San Francisco.[55]

The extent of change in the gay world between 1965 and 1972 is further evident in the evolving content of the guidebooks, in the increasing number of different books published, and in the expanding scale of their use and distribution. For instance, I have found just four U.S. gay guidebooks published prior to 1965: *The Lavender Baedeker,* the *Address Book, Directory 43,* and the *Guild Guide* (later the *International Guild Guide*), the last compiled by H. Lynn Womack, a publisher of physique magazines in Washington, D.C.[56] Even prior to the eruption of gay activism following the Stonewall riots, dozens of new guidebooks to gay bars and other sites appeared, such as *In Scene, San Francisco Scene, The Lavender Guide, Golden West Gay Bar Guide, Barfly West* and *Barfly East,* and the *International Vagabond World Travel Guide.*[57] And by the early 1970s scores of such guidebooks were available, many of which were published in San Francisco, New York, and Los Angeles, but others were running off presses in cities like Minneapolis and Hartford in the United States and Toronto and Vancouver in Canada.[58]

In addition to the increasing number and availability of books through a distribution network that included mail order and adult bookstores, their content is also worth examining. The most interesting modification to the guidebooks was that as early as 1965 a few of the books started to differentiate the listings by brief, descriptive codes. In the 1965 edition of Damron's *Address Book* most names of sites were followed with codes in parentheses; the codes were explained (but not fully decoded, as we shall see) at the beginning of the guidebook. For example, a "D" indicated that dancing was permitted; a "G" signified that "girls," likely meaning lesbians, frequented the bar; "PE" meant "pretty elegant" (although some readers may have made decoded it as "Piss Elegant," a derogatory term for upwardly mobile gays) and the guidebook suggested that men wear a jacket and a tie; "RT" was decoded as "rugged types," but those already in the know would further recognize the "RT" as an initialism for "rough trade," or masculine male prostitutes; and, similarly, "S-M" was explained to mean "some motorcycle," although those in the life would have recognized the letters also to stand for "sado-masochism."[59] Bob Ross, a gay publisher and friend of Damron, explained, "the gay lingo is self-defining amongst our community and at that time the straight community had no idea of what our references were to or for. And so [Damron] was able to get away with a lot by coding it—if people picked up the books in those cities they wouldn't know what the shit meant."[60] Moreover, the fact that the coding system became ubiquitous and nearly uniform in the different guidebooks published after 1965 suggests not only that there was some sharing and/or theft of ideas, but that the system of categorization was an idea whose time had come.

Although experienced bar patrons, especially those in large cities, likely already created mental notations similar to those offered by Damron and other guidebook compilers, the publication of the explanations in the guidebooks provided in print a quasi-official taxonomy of diversity within the gay world. While these explanations accounted for gender and, eventually, racial difference, the vast majority of the descriptions differentiated sites according to what might be called "lifestyle" preferences.[61] The recognition of such differences not only named and recorded what previously primarily had been verbalized and thus casually remembered, it also succeeded in complicating notions of homosexual identity and community and situating those notions in the inhabited spaces of bars, baths, hotels, restaurants, and the like. These more complex descriptions of identity and community, of course, had their roots in the lived experiences of people like Damron, Baird, Goodkind, and Strait, who had collected information and compiled the guidebooks. Again, like the motivation to name bars publicly in the first place, the decision to begin differentiating them by type is attributable in part to the fact that the compilers were active in the gay bar scene in a place like San Francisco. In the middle 1960s, as the guidebooks and other sources indicate, a good number of towns and most small cities had at least a few bars where members of the same sex might gather, build friendships, and find sexual partners. In towns and cities with only one or two gathering spots, the bars would have attracted the full diversity of the homosexual population in a given area, including but not limited to upwardly mobile gay men and lesbians, butch-fem lesbians, gay motorcyclists, young queens, elderly aunties, and those who simply were curious.[62] The bars also might attract a much wider clientele of individuals who cannot be classified as homosexual but who might tolerate homosexuality or even engage in homosexual sex. In San Francisco, New York, Los Angeles, and a few other large cities by the early 1960s, however, these diverse groups each had a bar they could call their own—and in some cases, more than one. For instance, the first edition of *The Lavender Baedeker* listed a single bar for Jackson, Mississippi, the Cellar, which purportedly catered to a variety of types hailing from a wide geographic area.[63] In comparison, the 1965 edition of *The Address Book* lists almost sixty bars for San Francisco, including two women's bars, three S-M bars, five bars featuring drag shows or female impersonator revues, and two bars that attracted a "pretty elegant" crowd.[64]

While instituting new categories of identity within homosexuality, the new guidebooks also acknowledged more recognizable categories of difference like gender and race. When asked about the nature of the relationship between Damron and the lesbian community, Gina Gatta, the current publisher of the Damron guidebooks, told me that the guidebooks of the 1960s and 1970s were held in rather low regard by many lesbians because they contained so few listings of lesbian bars.[65] Indeed, the listings that did appear were categorized in a rather sexist manner as "girls'" bars until 1980 at which point they were described as "ladies'" bars; not until 1984 did the Damron guidebook begin using "lesbian."[66] Bob Ross, Damron's business associate in the 1960s and 1970s, claimed that Damron did visit lesbian bars on his jaunts around the states but frequently was asked by owners and patrons not to list their bars for fear they would receive unwanted visits from the police or other men who might harass them.[67] Regardless of the ultimate reasons for the lack of information, lesbians had for many years a more ambivalent relationship with publicity. Similar to the ways in which the leaders of the Daughters of Bilitis managed communications, women associated with lesbian bars in the 1960s and 1970s were more committed to keeping in their own hands the distribution of information about their community. They generally did not trust either the mass media or gay male–run media to publicize information about lesbian sites in a manner that would be sensitive to the different situation of female homosexuals.[68] So, lesbians took on the task of building social networks in a distinct way and, predictably, they produced rather different results, which will be detailed in the next chapter.

The acknowledgement of racial difference in most guidebooks took even longer to appear and was even more muted than gender difference. The first year in which the Damron guidebook provided racialized descriptions was 1970, when the code "B" for "Blacks predominate" appeared.[69] Throughout the 1970s, however, few listings were said to be places where "Blacks predominate." For instance, in Damron's 1970 edition San Francisco was said to have no "B" bars, while Los Angeles and New York City, cities with substantially larger black populations, had two and one bars, respectively, where "blacks predominated." Thus, although the inclusion of such a description challenged the notion that no homosexuals were black and no blacks were homosexual, the lack of listings provided evidence that the racial divide was as important a barrier within the gay world as it was outside of it.[70] The small number of "B" listings in the *Address Book,* however, is somewhat mysterious considering that, according to those who knew him, Damron had many lasting relationships with black men and made it a point to visit predominantly black gay bars on his travels around the country.[71] Like Damron's lack of coverage of lesbian sites, then, it is unclear whether the relative invisibility of sites frequented predominantly by races other than whites is attributable directly to neglect, discrimination, a paucity of such sites, or requests on the part of bar owners and patrons to remain unlisted. Consequently, like the situation of lesbians, it is evident that homosexuals of color—of both sexes—had a more ambivalent relationship with the public sphere of mass and alternative media than did white gay men, meaning that the guidebooks probably played a less important role in the mapping and the coalescing of the black gay world than in the larger gay world marked by its whiteness.

These brief descriptors became a nearly uniform feature of the scores of guidebooks produced by small presses and do-it-yourselfers and thus reveals a trend toward standardization and specialization in the gay world that both reflected and, arguably, influenced the established bar scene. But, as Elizabeth Eisenstein argues in the context of the original printing presses, "Concepts pertaining to uniformity and diversity—to the typical and the unique are interdependent . . . One might consider the emergence of a new sense of individualism as a by-product of the new forms of standardization. The more standardized the type, indeed, the more compelling the sense of an idiosyncratic personal self."[72] If the same were true of gay guidebooks, which for the first time instituted standardized descriptions of diversity within the gay world, it might be argued that those publications simultaneously allowed homosexuals to see how and where they fit in the gay world—and how and where they did not; it provided them with the opportunity to identify with a portion of the gay subculture but also with the possibility of failing to identify with any of the particularities in the gay world as it was being parceled and its parcels were named. As new subgroups within the gay world began to emerge, they were almost always absorbed within the categorization schemes offered by the various guidebooks, thus legitimating certain kinds of difference within the gay world. In the late 1960s and early 1970s, gay liberationists and lesbian feminists could be absorbed under the category of "hip" or "hippies," thus naming those groups as part of the overall mosaic of the gay world while, perhaps, neutralizing their critique of that world, placing them as yet another selection in the market of bodies and lifestyles. Although the respect and the political rights accorded to various class, gender, race, ethnic, and lifestyle groups within the gay world has been quite uneven, a recent (2001) edition of *Damron's Address Book* listed about twenty-five different categories describing what kind of people could be expected to patronize a particular establishment. Thus, in publications initially designed to ease the strains of communication in a loosely knit information network, we can see the eventual institutionalization of a queer form of pluralism within the gay world. This pluralism is queer not only because of the non-normative sexual and gender identities listed but because the complexities went well beyond race or gender and expanded into social categories not found in the mainstream heterosexual world.

At the beginning of the 1960s the geography of the gay world, to the extent that it existed at all, was only incompletely known—and it was only incompletely knowable. Due to a convergence of events and personalities, however, there existed by the early 1970s a homosexual geography that not only was known to some people but that also was knowable to an increasingly sizable population through the scores of guidebooks, newspapers, and magazines that carried sometimes very specific information about gay sites. And while mass circulation periodicals like *Life* played an important role in establishing main themes and general ideas, one cannot deny the importance of handmade, do-it-yourself guidebooks produced first by Bruce Baird, Guy Strait, and Bob Damron. Lending credence to the cliché that necessity is the mother of invention, the early gay guidebooks filled a need that was unattended to by the professional homophile organizations and by the corporate mass media. The compilers' approach to resolving what was essentially a problem of communication came from their own experience rather than the somewhat political and ideological motivations of the homophiles and from the primarily economic stimulus felt by the editors and journalists working within the context of the mass media. Still, although the compilers and publishers of the early guidebooks were inspired by the very basic desire to ease the task of connecting, they were not untouched by activist or commercial motivations. Strait offered *The Lavender Baedeker* alongside (and advertised within) his newspaper *Citizen's News,* which repeatedly and loudly demanded an end to police harassment of gay bars and attempted to get homosexuals to organize into an identifiable voting and spending bloc. Damron compiled *The Address Book* with the help of the Mattachine Society's Hal Call, who saw in the guidebook another front in the overall movement to end isolation among homosexuals by shattering silence about homosexuality and improving communications within the gay world. Because the market eventually dominated over activist and public service motivations, entire groups, especially lesbians and homosexuals of color were relegated to secondary status within this network. Yet a large number of lesbians in the late 1960s and early 1970s would not have noticed the elision as they were busy pursuing connections in a rather separate context.

Shaping an "Amazon Network"

While guidebooks produced by gay men became a do-it-yourself (and later commercial) publishing phenomenon by the early 1970s, not a single lesbian bar guidebook was produced until around 1973, a full decade after the first edition of Guy Strait's *Lavender Baedeker.* The absence of a published guidebook, however, did not mean that lesbian bars did not exist or that information about bars and other sites did not circulate. Neither did it mean that lesbians were uninterested in strengthening their communal bonds or that they lacked the do-it-yourself ethic possessed by some gay men. Rather, in the decade in which bar guidebooks produced by gay men gained in popularity, a portion of the fledgling lesbian community picked up on some of the goals established by an earlier generation of lesbian activists and produced their very own robust communication networks through which a large quantity of information flowed. The Daughters of Bilitis continued with their program of building a strong national lesbian communication network through discussion groups and conventions, through the publication of the *Ladder,* and through the support of chapters around the country. While the so-called golden age of the lesbian pulp paperback was over by 1965, new novels by lesbians along with new editions of older works continued to be published and distributed to women around the country who read them as they wrestled with their sexual desires and identities. Lesbian bars, too, continued to play an extremely important part in the landscape of female homosexuality; although they did not proliferate at an equal rate as gay male bars during the same period, exclusively lesbian bars continued to open and, in some locations, remain open for longer periods of time owing to the gradually stabilizing legal status of such establishments in many cities around the country (which is not to stay that lesbian bars also were not surveilled, harassed, and closed during this period).[1]

But by the mid-1960s a new and extremely important force began to influence the lesbian world from Greenwich Village lesbian bars to the San Francisco offices of the DOB. That force was the emergence of second-wave feminism, and with it came an invigorated interest in establishing a separate lesbian community and in reaching isolated lesbians and drawing them into that world. Although the seeds of second-wave feminism were sown in the 1950s, the first milestones were achieved in the first half of the 1960s, including the publication of Betty Friedan's *The Feminine Mystique,* the issuing of the *Presidential Report on American Women,* and the passage of the Equal Pay Act—all of which occurred in 1963. The promise as well as the failures of these developments culminated in the founding of the National Organization for Women (NOW) in 1966, which was established to address economic and legal inequalities suffered by women.[2] NOW achieved immediate success more in organizing women around the cause of gender equality than in bringing about legal or economic change (although they made strides in these areas as well). Betty Friedan, one of the driving forces in the organization, noted that the early organizing efforts benefited from an already extant "underground feminist movement" among professional women living in Washington, D.C., and other cities.[3] Through these "underground" networks grew an institution in which women could meet one another, sharing the common goal of the betterment of themselves and other women. With very few exceptions—the DOB among them—women were without such institutions through which they could make connections based on their identity as women (or, for that matter, lesbians) in the 1950s and early 1960s.

The formation of organizations like NOW and, even more, the radical feminist consciousness-raising groups a few years later signaled an important shift in the communication networks of women in the United States overall. Such organizations and groups provided countless thousands of women with the opportunity, indeed the imperative, to connect with others to discuss problems they had previously considered personal in a context that highlighted their universality and their political dimensions. The impact of this shift would be felt in the most profound ways by women who would eventually come out as lesbian. Along with the exclusively lesbian groups that emerged in the late 1960s and early 1970s, the feminist consciousness-raising group provided for many women a safe space in which to verbally explore their sexual rejection of men and attractions to other women, although some women of color and working-class women would later critique these institutions as white and middle-class. As a result, the previously massive gulf between white heterosexual women and white lesbians could be much more easily bridged as the two sexualities—along with the many that were curious and willing to experiment—came into close contact with one another. Gone were the days when women who were exploring their sexual desires had extremely limited options for places in which to do so. Although homophobia certainly was present in feminist groups and organizations (along with a degree of insensitivity to racial differences), with the emergence of the second-wave options for connecting with other lesbians or similarly inclined women expanded exponentially.

Along with a boom in feminist and, later, lesbian-feminist organizations and groups, the early 1970s witnessed the emergence of vast movement in feminist publishing, from books to newsletters and from magazines to newspapers.[4] Between 1967 and 1976, several hundred books were published in the United States from a feminist or women's rights point of view.[5] During the same years, likely between 600 and 800 different feminist (many of which were lesbian-feminist) newspapers and magazines appeared in women's and alternative bookstores and made their way to readers through nascent feminist distribution networks.[6] Moreover, there were an untold number of newsletters produced by members of women's community centers, college women's studies departments, women's health centers, feminist organizations, mothers' collectives, feminist bookstores, and so on. With the exception of very few magazines, like *Ms.*, none of the publications had a very large readership. Rather, the significance of these small-scale periodicals resides in the number that appeared and how many women not only were reading them but also contributing to their production as writers, artists, editors, publishers, and distributors. Although not the earliest or even the most influential lesbian-feminist publication, *Amazon Quarterly*, initially published out of Oakland, California, beginning in 1972, was among the first and certainly became one of the most influential publications to promote a lesbian-feminist perspective on the world and help women who considered themselves both lesbian and feminist (and less explicitly white and middle-class) to connect with one another in conversation and collaboration.[7]

From Lesbian Homophiles to Lesbian-Feminists

The gap between the heightened presence of the DOB in the mass media in 1964 and the appearance of the first issue of *Amazon Quarterly* in 1972 is an important one both in terms of years and, even more, in terms of social change and innovation. Although many of the influential personalities and events from this period came from and/or transpired on the East Coast, the changes experienced by the members of the DOB in San Francisco— and changes in the organization itself—are illustrative and anticipatory of larger, even national, trends.

After the coverage in Ann Aldrich's books, Donald Webster Cory's *The Lesbian in America*, Jess Stearn's *The Grapevine*, and numerous newspaper features, magazine articles, and radio and television talk shows, the DOB and its publication the *Ladder* went through a period of growth that culminated in 1966 with the conference held in San Francisco called "Ten Days in August." The conference was really several events rolled into one, the two most important being the DOB's fifth biennial convention and the second meeting of the North American Conference of Homophile Organizations (NACHO). NACHO was a federation that formed the previous February which sought to bring the roughly seventeen disparate regional groups together in order to work on common goals, including ending discrimination against gay men and lesbians in the military and civil service and addressing the harassment of gay bars and publications, to cite a few areas of action.[8]

About the combined DOB-NACHO conference, usually contrite and dismissive Guy Strait wrote, "Never before in the history of the organized homosexual has any organization or group of organizations ever presented such a list of distinguished speakers, panelists and subjects."[9] Strait, also prone to hyperbole, in this case did not underestimate the prominence of the speakers and the visibility of the conference. Alongside such regular homophile allies as psychologist Evelyn Hooker, panels featured San Francisco municipal court judge Joseph Kennedy; Willie Brown and John Burton, both elected to the California State Assembly; Stefan Mason, the editor of the *UCLA Law Review*; representatives of the San Francisco mayor, district attorney, public defender, and police chief; and prominent liberal ministers including Reverends Ted McIlvenna, Cecil Williams, and Lewis Durham. Moreover, the conference received extensive coverage in all the major San Francisco newspapers and local radio and television news programs, as well as in the growing homophile press. Far more than words, these early meetings of liberal politicians, civil servants, and ministers with members of the homophile community portended important advances in civil rights that would come over the next decade in California.[10] In many respects, then, the conference in August 1966 represented the culmination of much of what the San Francisco homophile community had been agitating for during the past decade—at least on a local and statewide level.

Along with signaling achievement, the conference also pointed out to some attending an increasingly noticeable failure of the male-dominated homophile movement. As the focus on reforming laws relating to sexual behavior and the dominance of male panelists may hint, issues of interest to lesbians in particular, and women in general, were hard to find on the program.[11] As a result of such elisions, cracks started to form in the already precarious alliance among women and men in the homophile movement.[12] The emerging critique of lesbian invisibility within the homophile movement occurred just as feminism began to reemerge as a powerful force in American society.[13]

As feminist groups provided a fertile soil in which lesbianism could grow, members of lesbian organizations, meaning primarily the DOB, started to move toward feminist and away from homophile activism. Sarah Boslaugh argued that when Helen Sandoz assumed the editorship of the *Ladder* in November 1966, after the departure of Barbara Gittings, "the idea became expressed that [lesbians] in fact had more in common with other women and should make their alliances with them" rather than with gay men, thus opening a dialog that continues to dominate feminist discourse today: the intersectionality of subjectivity.[14] Moreover, less than two years later, Del Martin and Phyllis Lyon joined NOW and simultaneously relinquished their roles as officeholders in the organization they cofounded, the DOB. In that year, Martin also spoke about "The Lesbian's Other Identity": woman. In the speech, reprinted in the *Ladder,* she argued that the DOB "needs to broaden its identity and make another alliance treaty with such women's organizations as NOW" and suggested that DOB members also join NOW, for which she provided an address and other information.[15] At the end of Sandoz's term as editor of the *Ladder* in 1968, longtime contributor Gene Damon (Barbara Grier) took over. With Damon as editor, the *Ladder* continued to move toward feminism and away from homophile activism. Yet, Damon continued to feel constrained while operating under the auspices of the DOB, a lesbian rather than explicitly feminist organization. With the help of her lover, Rita Laporte, Damon physically moved the *Ladder* to their home in Reno, Nevada, where they continued to edit and publish the magazine as an independent, lesbian-feminist periodical. The magazine continued to thrive until its demise in September 1972 when it reportedly collapsed under the weight of a quickly growing list of readers who subscribed to the magazine but were not charged enough to keep the periodical afloat.[16]

At the time that the *Ladder* closed shop, its readers were left without a comparable national magazine that explored the intersections of lesbianism and feminism. But with the explosion of radical feminist organizations, some of which espoused lesbianism as a political practice, the production of a vast and increasingly accessible feminist discourse held lesbianism as a central point of discussion. Books like Kate Millet's *Sexual Politics* (1970) and Shulamith Firestone's *Dialectic of Sex* (1970) were widely publicized and sold thousands. Anthologies like *Sisterhood Is Powerful* (1971), edited by Robin Morgan, and *The Black Woman* (1970), edited by Toni Cade Bambara, spread word of an ideologically and geographically diverse and growing movement. Mary Thom reported that "By the summer of 1970, every major national magazine had done its cover story on feminism" and, after a sit-in protest by a group of feminists, the conventional *Ladies Home Journal* even published an eight-page supplement on feminism that was produced by feminists.[17] Moreover, a number of magazines, newsletters, and circulars appeared that, although short-lived for the most part, contributed to the circulation of ideas and information about feminism. Perhaps the most mainstream and, likely as a consequence, the most visible of these was the magazine *Ms.*, which first appeared in late 1971 as a supplement in *New York* magazine and then as an independent publication in July 1972. Historian Ruth Rosen writes that in its early years, *Ms.* "had an astonishing reach," part of which was measured in distribution, but its reach also was evident in the impact it had upon readers, thousands of whom wrote heartfelt letters to the editors. Rosen claims that, "like an early electronic bulletin board, the letters section of *Ms.* functioned as a national consciousness-raising group . . . here was where women learned they were not alone."[18] For the readers of *Ms.*, then, learning that they were not alone was a central element of consciousness-raising. Of course women knew that they were not alone as women, but many felt alone as women who experienced discrimination, who had had an abortion or used birth control, who were dissatisfied with the roles of wife and mother, or who felt lesbian desire. Thus, publications like *Ms.* introduced readers to a world in which there were other women like themselves who had similar problems and were actively searching for solutions. Although the solutions proposed ranged from the modestly practical to the ambitiously radical, central to all of them was the impulse to remove oneself from isolation in the masculine world to sisterhood in a feminist one—at least temporarily by joining a consciousness-raising group or reading a feminist magazine.

Some feminists thought the separation of women from the male world temporary and ultimately not for every woman, while others began to articulate a theory and practice of lesbian separatism. The precise origin of lesbian-feminism is difficult to pin down because it came from a variety of sources virtually simultaneously. However, it is undeniable that the "Lavender Menace" action of May 1970 marked a turning point where women previously involved with the liberal feminist organization NOW, the lesbian organization DOB, and radical feminist groups like the Redstockings collaborated to make lesbianism a front-burner issue for feminists across the ideological spectrum.[19] Ranking alongside events like the Stonewall riots in the memories of feminist activists, the Lavender Menace action was a carefully orchestrated "zap" of the Second Congress to Unite Women held in New York City.[20] The conference became the target of lesbians within the feminist movement because movement leaders like Betty Friedan and Susan Brownmiller had taken to calling homosexuality among feminists a "Lavender Menace" and a "Lavender Herring," respectively. Because the organizers of the First Congress to United Women in 1969 had decided not to list the DOB as a supporting organization and because the program of the Second Congress had failed to include any lesbian issues or speakers, that high profile event became the target of a group of about forty well-organized lesbian activists. On the day of the event, the lesbians, who called themselves the "Lavender Menace" and wore t-shirts emblazoned with the same slogan, rushed into the convention hall and took over the podium and proceeded to turn the plenary session into a large consciousness-raising session on lesbianism.

In preparation for the action, several women gathered and began drafting a statement that would be printed and distributed to the women attending the Second Congress. The result was the ten-paragraph manifesto, "The Woman-Identified-Woman"—a widely circulated document that provided one of the first and perhaps the most eloquent articulations of lesbian-feminism.[21] In arguing that a lesbian "is the rage of all women condensed to the point of explosion," the authors, who referred to themselves collectively as the "Radicalesbians," linked lesbianism with a feminist impulse thought to be shared by all women: the dissatisfaction with the roles thrust upon them by men and the desire to break out of those roles in a movement of liberation. Yet, for a document that has been remembered for its tendency to universalize and desexualize lesbianism, the authors made it clear that they were not attempting to change anyone's sexual orientation. Rather, they argued that if women were going to rid themselves of male ways of thinking, like treating other women only as sex objects, they may want to "withdraw emotional and sexual energies from men, and work out various alternatives for those energies in their own lives."[22] Based upon this growing sense that for women to liberate themselves they must withdraw from men, whether emotionally or physically, the theory and practice of lesbian-feminism began to spread. Moreover, in adopting this perspective, developed most forcefully within the context of lesbian-feminism, feminists began to turn away from an engagement in radical politics as practiced by the New Left and move toward an instrumental separatism, which is a key component of what historian Alice Echols calls "cultural feminism."[23] Within a few short years after the "Lavender Menace" action, lesbian-feminists began to draw up plans for a separate lesbian nation (as Jill Johnston did in a largely metaphorical way in her book *Lesbian Nation*).[24] This plan for a separate lesbian nation included discussions of women-only cultural institutions, rural communes and city houses, and businesses. Moreover, some lesbian-feminists even initiated inquiries into the possibilities of human reproduction without men and without sperm.[25] By 1973, then, the practice of lesbianism and the theory of feminism had become one in the minds of many women.

An Amazonian Network

At the same time that gay men were gravitating toward urban meccas and generally avoiding areas considered backwaters, many lesbians were developing a critical view of urbanity and were struggling to build their own communities outside of and/or independent of America's largest cities where gay ghettos were located. Although an antiurban, back-to-the-country strain was present in the counterculture of the 1960s, the articulation of an extraurban perspective found its fullest expression in the lesbian-feminist movement of the early 1970s.[26] These ideas already were circulating in feminist print culture, perhaps most notably—and notoriously—in Jill Johnston's *Lesbian Nation* (1973), a collection of her essays from the *Village Voice*. Moreover, a number of contemporary magazines and newsletters, including *Country Women* (1973–1979), *Leaping Lesbian* (1977–1980), *Rubyfruit Reader* (1976–1978) and *Lesbian Connection* (1974–present), discussed the benefits (along with some of the hardships) of the nonurban life and also helped those who chose that life to connect with one another and share ideas.[27]

On occasion an article appeared that addressed the urban / nonurban divide directly. *Cowrie,* a short-lived lesbian-feminist magazine from New York City, produced an issue devoted to "Amazon Architecture" and "Amazonian growth" outside of the "urban network" (fig. 21).[28] Along with the accompanying drawings, the stream of consciousness text made clear that

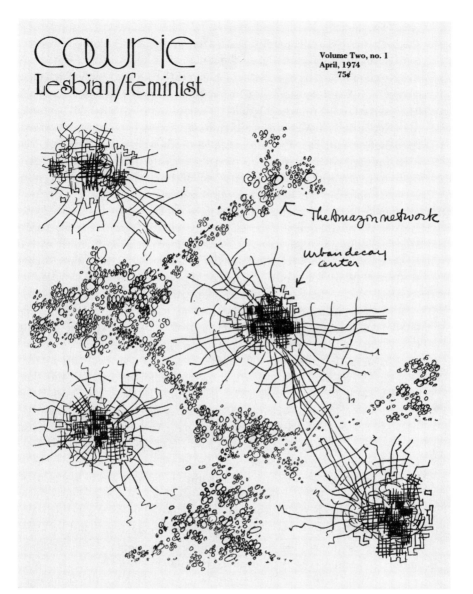

cowrie
Lesbian/feminist

Volume Two, no. 1
April, 1974
75¢

The Amazon network

urban decay center

21 This conceptual map on the cover of *Cowrie,* a lesbian-feminist publication, imagines an "Amazon network" thriving in the spaces between the centers of urban decay. Image courtesy of the GLBT Historical Society, San Francisco, CA.

once "women can stop giving birth to male babies" and once the World Trade Center "will fall apart," an "Amazon Community" would grow and flourish in the "spaces between the cities while they decay"—and that these spaces would be filled with new institutions like a "Skills Exchange Center," a "Multiple Mothers Cluster," and a "Kids Liberation Center." The basis of this new world would be what might be called an "Amazonian Network." This explicitly lesbian-feminist network, however, seemed burdened with a definitional contradiction: how could a close-knit yet wide-ranging community be formed that rejected the urbanist, mecca-building mentality espoused not only by male homosexuals but also by others like bohemians, artists, and political radicals who sought out one another in the hopes of creating a critical mass of people like themselves? The answer to this quandary is found in articles like "Amazon Architecture" and in publications like *Country Women*—that a lesbian-feminist world need not rest upon spatially defined communities. Rather, the lesbian-feminist network could be built and could be robust without being tied to specific neighborhoods, cities, or regions; the lesbian-feminist network could be established through the interaction of close-knit and small-scale lesbian communities (including as few as two, or maybe even one person) linked with others through newspapers, magazines, newsletters, collectives, distribution networks, telephone calls, live music festivals, conferences, and pen-pal clubs. Among the more important publications that came out of this milieu—and, indeed, sought to nurture it—was *Amazon Quarterly*, which was founded in 1972 by Laurel Galana and Gina Covina.[29]

Galana and Covina were in many ways typical of the lesbian-feminist generation. Galana was born in Fort Lauderdale, Florida, in 1946 and was raised by her working-class parents near Cape Canaveral. Galana remembers that religious fervor and an affair with a bohemian girl in high school enlivened her youth, but that her parent's meager resources and modest education limited the choices available to her even though she was a bright and talented teenager. Not until she graduated high school did she learn the procedures for applying to college, but she was eager to leave her home and try something new. So, she moved to Tallahassee and enrolled in summer school at Florida State University, where she stayed until she finished her bachelor's and master's degrees in literature a very short four years later, in 1968. While a graduate student, Galana gained a reputation for working hard (she remembers primarily being motivated by her desire to be apart from her husband) and, as a result, was given the honor of editing the school's literary annual. Although Galana claims that she was so apolitical at the time that she didn't even know who was running for president that year, she soon became the center of a controversy that would introduce 1960s radicalism to that Southern campus. As editor of the journal, Galana accepted an essay for publication written by a student who also was a veteran of the Vietnam War. In the essay, which was about the soldiers' experience of war, the student used the word "motherfucker" several times. Galana accepted the word as part of legitimate literary expression, but the campus printer and, subsequently, the administration had a different take; their response was censorship.[30] Within very little time, the campus was embroiled in a battle over censorship that Galana likened to a late-60s version of the University of California, Berkeley, free speech movement.[31] The wave of protest galvanized the nascent leftist and counter-culture students and faculty on campus and even spawned a three-week-long sit-in in front of the administration building. For Galana this was one of the major turning points in her life: after speaking before the crowd of students and faculty and spending night after night camped out with the other protestors, she came to the realization that much was wrong in her personal life as well as in the world. Following the protest she returned to her husband only once—to retrieve her personal items—and then immediately moved in with a group of students she had recently met.

Galana graduated shortly after the events at Florida State and soon headed with a new boyfriend to the Tuskegee Institute where she taught literature and composition. Even though she was raised and educated in the South, Galana claims that she had no significant interaction with blacks prior to teaching at that historically black college. Soon enough she realized that her cultural ignorance and her white skin made her an inappropriate choice as an authority figure over a group of students who had recently experienced the assassination of Martin Luther King, Jr. While at Tuskegee Galana also continued to feel the pull of places outside of her native South, most particularly from San Francisco, where she remembers Walter Cronkite regularly reported to the nation about a new generation that was doing things very differently. It was in the summer of 1969 that Galana and her boyfriend (by then, she claims, their relationship was largely asexual) packed their car and drove to San Francisco. However, by the time they arrived in the city they realized that they were two years too late for the Summer of Love and found much despair and wrecked lives on Haight Street. After a drug-related murder in their apartment building, Galana and her boyfriend moved across the bay to Berkeley, where they found precisely the scene that they had been looking for. While in Berkeley, Galana joined the party scene, worked with the newly formed Berkeley Tenants Union, and most importantly, started participating in a feminist consciousness-raising group. With several of the women from the group, Galana started to work on the recently founded radical feminist newspaper, *It Ain't Me Babe* (1970–1973). Through the consciousness-raising group and the newspaper, Galana explored feminism, read many of the publications and manifestos as they were circulating, and began to think about her long-standing attraction to women in both a political and an explicitly lesbian sense. She recalls that she did not identify specifically as lesbian before she met Covina, but she had discussed it with other women and felt sure that she was moving in that direction by the time 1971 rolled around.

Like Galana, Covina never participated in the lesbian bar scene and did not consider herself a lesbian until she met Galana, saying, "I came out with her."[32] But, by contrast, Covina was not involved with the counterculture and feminism like Galana, who was several years older. Covina was raised in suburban southern California and remembers that she never felt quite at home in that place where a nice tan was prized above creative expression and the creativity that did exist was associated with mass-produced movies, not the kind of folk and craft-oriented art that she admired. What did attract her interest was what she imagined northern California to be. Along with "the whole hippie" scene in San Francisco, Covina recalls that at seventeen she liked that "there were more trees left in Northern California. It's greener. There are more people who appreciate that. There are more people who are really [living] in relation to the place."[33] When she left high school in 1970 and received a scholarship that would pay her to attend college anywhere in California, she immediately chose one in which she could study arts that was located in the northern part of the state: the California College of Arts and Crafts (CCAC) in Oakland. During her first semesters, Covina studied broadly but especially liked to include the natural environment in her art, making what she described as "pre-Andy Goldworthy type things." Not long into art school, Covina went to the Women's Place Bookstore, which was located across the street from CCAC, to look at listings for rooms for rent on the bulletin board. She responded to one that promised a room in a big house for reasonable rent. When Covina knocked on the door of the house in Oakland, it was Galana who answered. Although neither had publicly declared their lesbianism or engaged in an adult, sexual relationship with another woman, within a few months they expressed their attraction to one another and almost immediately were sharing a bed—and a life—together.

While radical feminism and the counterculture were relatively new to Covina, Galana already had been involved with radical feminism and with putting together a feminist publication. But once the two met and started to pursue a relationship, they became more deeply committed to lesbian-feminism, especially through editing and publishing *Amazon Quarterly*, which was subtitled "A Lesbian-Feminist Arts Journal." When asked about how the magazine came about, Covina recalled that she and Galana "had been looking for a while for various projects to involve ourselves in . . . and in some way to bring what we wanted to do in the arts into the world, and to be able to be fully present with ourselves as lesbians in that endeavor."[34] After "a two-month pursuit of 'art' in the 'peaceful solitude' of 'the country'" in the hot and dusty Sierra foothills during the summer of 1972, Covina and Galana returned to their home in Oakland with piles of manuscripts and drawings but had no one to share them with and no place to publish them. Covina wrote, "After two months of speaking to no one but each other, we found that in the city we were really just as isolated—Where were the artists and writers who were working out of a sensibility similar to ours?"[35] As Galana put it, a lesbian arts magazine would be a "fish hook" that they could use to catch other women like themselves. "We knew that out there in the world must be other women who, like us, were trying to create new ways of living based on their woman-identified perceptions. And we guessed that many of these women were as isolated as we were. We would spread the tantalizing bait of *Amazon Quarterly* across the waters, and see who came to nibble."[36] Before they reached out into the turbulent sea across the states, Covina and Galana first tried to make connections in their own backyard. They visited the bulletin board at the local women's bookstore to see if any other women in the area might be interested in participating in the project. Soon enough they connected with a women's writing group and persuaded several of the participants to contribute stories, critical pieces, poetry, and visual works to the anticipated publication.[37]

As planning progressed, Covina and Galana must have felt burdened by the amount of work it would take to get the magazine assembled and published let alone distributed. But this burden surely was lightened by the prospect that they might just be able to contribute to the growth of a lesbian sensibility in the arts in particular and lesbian community overall. They also gained inspiration from learning about Margaret Anderson and from reading recently reissued editions of her *Little Review*.[38] Along with a supply of food stamps, more practical assistance came from women already active in feminism. Gene Damon, then editor of the soon-to-be defunct *Ladder,* agreed to help Covina and Galana get started by sending an announcement to subscribers that a new magazine was soon to appear that they could subscribe to just as the *Ladder* was ending. The ambitious publishers also sent letters to well-known feminists requesting assistance. Robin Morgan, editor of the popular anthology *Sisterhood Is Powerful,* donated $200 from the proceeds of that book to Covina and Galana's cause;

and poet Adrienne Rich also donated cash.[39] They also received a grant from the Associated Students of the University of California, Berkeley, which paid for the printing of the first issue. Another source of funding that started pouring in were prepublication subscriptions—four hundred in all, most of which came from former readers of the *Ladder*.[40] But more than provide necessary start-up capital, the instant base of subscribers, according to Covina, immediately gave *Amazon Quarterly* "a pretty broad spattering of people all across the country who didn't have any other way to connect with each other, or any kind of lesbian community to connect to that was not just their local bar if they even had that."[41] The subscriptions, which came well in advance of the first issue, put pressure on Covina and Galana to produce a worthwhile publication; the prepublication subscriptions also established a clear link between the new generation of lesbian-feminists with their predecessors in the lesbian homophile movement. Advertisements placed in the fledgling but relatively mainstream and widely distributed *Ms.* magazine shortly after the second issue of *Amazon Quarterly* were designed to introduce the magazine to what Covina described as "the next generation."[42]

Even with the investment of feminist supporters and with the faith of hundreds of subscribers behind them, the process of producing *Amazon Quarterly* was still a do-it-yourself operation that was conducted on a table in the publishers' basement using a rented IBM Selectric typewriter as the primary tool. In an interview, Covina fondly recalls that assembling the magazine was a labor of love and that each of the women had to learn a great deal about the printing process, which, as I'll discuss, they later passed on to their readers. They learned how to operate the Selectric and to work with different typefaces; they learned the basics of graphic design; and even though the printing costs of the first issue were paid for, the stapling and cutting were not, and as Covina remembers, "the printer let us come in, and showed us how to work the machines and let us do it ourselves. The very first one, we actually did all that."[43] More than simply doing what had to be done, their enthusiasm and willingness to produce the magazine themselves grew from the feminist imperative of female self-sufficiency, thus placing a do-it-yourself ethos at the center of lesbian-feminist practice.

The first issue of *Amazon Quarterly* appeared in fall 1972. The editors explained their goals with reference to communication and community, terms that would have been familiar to lesbians struggling with the task of building community and overcoming barriers to communication—even if they already were living in relatively well-connected places like the San Francisco Bay Area. They wrote, "We are calling this an arts journal in the sense that art is communication. The standard we want to maintain is not arbitrary: we simply want the best communication from lesbians who are consciously exploring new patterns in their lives."[44] While the magazine included poetry and drawings, stories and criticism, the art of communication informed most everything *Amazon Quarterly* published. Galana ruminated in the first issue, "As I look back on my life I see·that what I have desired and looked for more than anything else is good conversation."[45] Contributing to the theme present in much lesbian-feminist writing that moving to the city often fails to solve the problem of isolation, Galana added, "I decided I must leave the South to find what I wanted. I came to Berkeley four years ago. I have found it occasionally, but still I am in contact at this moment with only a very few people who have any interest in conversation."[46] Despite fruitless attempts to find "good conversation," Galana remained hopeful that *Amazon Quarterly* might just be the desired venue for exchange and connection. In the following two issues, Covina and Galana continued to emphasize that their main goal was to establish a dynamic network through which ideas and information could circulate; importantly, the network would involve not only writers and editors but also readers. They wrote, "We want *Amazon Quarterly* to become a real communication among women wherever the magazine reaches—both the communication and the 'wherever the magazine reaches' are in large part up to you."[47] More than speak to the idea, Covina and Galana listed the names and addresses of other lesbian-feminist publications, like *Lavender Woman* (Chicago) and *Lesbian Tide* (Los Angeles), and published an ever-increasing selection of letters from readers. By the time the second issue appeared, the circle of women engaged in a "good conversation" moderated by Covina and Galana numbered in the thousands with over a thousand copies of *Amazon Quarterly* distributed to a larger readership nationwide.

In the May 1973 issue Covina and Galana announced "a marvelous dream."[48] Unlike many a "marvelous dream" from this radical era, however, theirs was realistic and soon came to fruition. They wrote, "We want to do a very special fourth issue devoted to our readers, about our readers, and with you." "How?" they asked. "By meeting you, talking, and sharing some time together," they answered. Covina and Galana proposed to travel the perimeter of the United States, dipping occasionally into Canada, to see the country and meet its lesbians. They figured that they could make the trip if a few readers helped to subsidize it and if their '61 VW Beetle could survive the journey but also if readers of *Amazon Quarterly* would offer to host them in the cities and towns they planned to visit. More specific than their desire to produce a "reader's issue," Covina and

Galana wanted to test and, in all likelihood, overturn the popular notions people held about lesbians in America—that they were rejected by men, that they were lonely and full of regret, that they engaged in "role playing" and were either butch or femme. Their motto for the trip, as they put it, was "All preconceptions AWAY!"[49] Preconceptions, however, were political constructions, and it was a political act to attempt to transform or overthrow such widespread cultural notions. While Galana, for instance, was raised in a working-class family and never achieved what might be called middle-class status, she never identified with what has been called the "working-class" butch-fem bar culture. She always viewed that option for expressing lesbian identity as an undesirable one, perhaps because of the negative stereotypes of it that circulated in the mainstream public sphere and instead wanted to live within and introduce other women to the lesbian-feminist world.

Although Covina and Galana "begged, borrowed, and nearly stole enough money to make the trip," travel around the country they did in the summer of 1973. They reported that in response to their request, they received an overwhelming response—about three hundred invitations from lesbians in the United States and Canada to visit or stay. Ultimately, they visited about fifty of these women "in places like Birmingham, Alabama; Windham, Maine; and Vancouver" and from "every conceivable lifestyle from California to Florida, from Texas to Toronto"—and they covered about 12,000 miles in the process.[50] A supporter even donated a Volkswagen camper van for their trip, but Covina remembers that it didn't do much better than their VW Beetle would have done because it "didn't make it either, its engine fell out twice during the trip. [Although] some form of it made it all the way around [the country]."[51] Because they spoke with and, indeed, interviewed dozens of lesbians from a wide diversity of backgrounds, their impressions were varied, but generally they found that lesbians across the country, like themselves, were committed to replacing isolation with connection and silence with communication. They wrote, "We found that many women who have everything to lose are coming out of the closets, starting rap groups, setting up lines of communication to help other women out of isolation."[52]

Once they returned from their adventure, Covina and Galana began readying a special double issue devoted to their journey and the readers they met (fig. 22). When the issue appeared, it contained a great deal of information, numerous anecdotes, and several first-person accounts drawn from their travels. Along with an essay in which Galana provided her impressions, sociologist Deborah Wolf completed a statistical analysis of the interviews conducted with lesbians across the country by Covina and Ga-

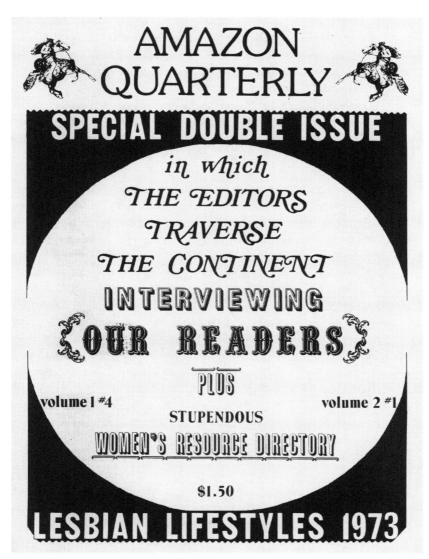

AMAZON QUARTERLY

SPECIAL DOUBLE ISSUE

in which

THE EDITORS

TRAVERSE

THE CONTINENT

INTERVIEWING

OUR READERS

PLUS

volume 1 #4   volume 2 #1

STUPENDOUS

WOMEN'S RESOURCE DIRECTORY

$1.50

LESBIAN LIFESTYLES 1973

22 *Amazon Quarterly* publishers Gina Covina and Laurel Galana drew upon the visual archive of the *Farmer's Almanac* to create the cover image for this late 1973 issue of their magazine. Image courtesy of the GLBT Historical Society, San Francisco, CA.

lana.[53] Wolf found that most interviewees were well educated and came from middle-class backgrounds but that their income and occupation levels were lower than their parents; she speculated that both structural inequalities as well as personal choice were the culprits.[54] The interviews also revealed that many of the lesbians had previously been married to men and that a strong majority, seventeen out of the twenty asked, had been or currently were participating in a feminist group. Beyond the statistical impressions provided by Wolf, the editors included transcripts of several interviews they conducted—a larger number of which later were published in the *The New Lesbians* (1977).

A sizable portion of this issue was devoted to an extensive "Resource Directory" compiled by Covina and Galana through their own research but also by flouting copyright and borrowing from listings in other publications.[55] The directory, which the compilers allowed to be reproduced by other feminist publications, contained listings for the United States and Canada (with a few notices for groups in Europe). It listed women's resource centers; counseling groups; organizations; university centers; health clinics; switchboards; coffeehouses and bookstores "with a significant lesbian-feminist collection"; women's art co-ops and organizations; women's liberation bands and music labels; women's / lesbian theaters and performance troupes; journals, newspapers, and magazines (including, for example, *Country Women, Dykes and Gorgons, Libera, Lesbian Tide, Sisters,* and many more); producers of feminist radio, video, and film; printing presses; lesbian bars (a total of eleven were listed); and other "important resources" like books, manuals, and the contact information for the Liberation News Service. By offering the resource directory, Covina and Galana not only were trying to help ease lesbians out of isolation but to get their sisters to take an active part in building their own communities.[56] Covina wrote, "It'll take many of us, ultimately all of us, to create the woman-centered culture that has to start in each of us and spread through small communications like *Amazon Quarterly.* We invite / implore you to participate in whatever ways you can in this process of communication."[57] Covina, then, asked her readers to recognize that reading a publication like *Amazon Quarterly* was merely a beginning, a means to an end; although participating in the community of readers might provide for some "good conversation," it could not bring out a larger cultural transformation in which women, and lesbians in particular, created an alternative culture. Yet the goal of creating an alternative culture, one built on nonmainstream, nonpatriarchal communications, was the basis of the new world that they wanted to create. In an important sense, then, the means (publishing *Amazon Quarterly*) also was the end goal: a lesbian network or what we might today call a virtual community. And herein lies the difference between the communication networks of the female homophiles and the lesbian-feminists. The female homophiles, although ambitious in their context, limited their goals to establishing networks where none existed before, while the lesbian-feminists of *Amazon Quarterly* and their sister publications used those foundations to pursue an alternative culture and society that need not be run by the rules of the established order. The lesbian homophile networks, then, were largely instrumental and nonideological. The lesbian-feminist networks, in contrast, were the ideological basis of the social movement in which they originated; they were the raison d'être of the movement itself. It is on this basis in which the story of lesbian-feminist communications intervenes in the larger history of communications and media in the United States at the beginning of the 1970s.

In placing an alternative communications network at the heart of their ideology and program of action, Galana and Covina—and their cohorts—rejected the changes then afoot in the larger context of communications in the United States. While these women may have accepted the conclusions reached by thinkers like Marshall McLuhan about the degree to which electronic (and thus corporate) media had become an extension of man's ability to see, know, and feel, they also rejected the inevitability of this shift and critiqued its desirability.[58] Yet their critique of the ways in which mass media was extending into the social body was much more complex than a simple rejection. After all, many lesbian-feminists hoped publications like *Amazon Quarterly* would develop into extensions of the close-knit culture of women's communities, but on a vastly different scale and in a way that would ensure the control of women rather than corporate media over the network. So, while Covina and Galana hoped to establish a separate communication network and alternative culture, their ideas were enabled in part by a context in which a greater social impact of various media was being articulated and presumed. Thus, McLuhan's idea of the media as a quite literal "extension of man" must have been reviled by many lesbian-feminists who wished to insulate themselves from such infiltrations. But many such women, Covina and Galana included, nevertheless pursued an ideological program that was based on similar ideas, such as advocating (and pursuing) a media-driven extension of feminist culture.

In 1974, the editors of *Amazon Quarterly* provided additional means through which lesbians could contribute to the process of community building by establishing new lines of communication. The first bit of inspiration Covina and Galana provided was through a series of three articles by Galana instructing *Amazon Quarterly* readers in the do-it-yourself arts by teaching them "How to Make a Magazine."[59] The first and second installments discussed in great detail the process of making a magazine, from textual and graphic layout to the basics of graphic design and the use of a variety of fonts to the options for printing. The third and final installment focused on methodologies for distribution. Galana suggested that ambitious publishers of fledglings distribute their magazines through a variety of means, including subscriptions, libraries, bookstores, wholesale distribution companies, and feminist distribution companies. She also advised that publishers of a new magazine follow the example of *Amazon Quarterly* and advertise in publications with large feminist (but not necessarily lesbian) readerships like *Ms.* and *Off Our Backs* in order to spread word and gain name recognition. Finally, Galana wrote that perhaps more than needing another publication, "we long for the day when there will be a widespread women's distribution system." Although she noted there already existed "First Things First, a national fe-mail order house and there are a few local networks," the creation of national magazine distribution company would be a "fantastic opportunity to both create jobs for women and spread women's culture [that] has not been explored very thoroughly to date."[60]

During their round the country journey, Covina and Galana met a lesbian couple in Florida who shared their hopes for connecting lesbians and extending lesbian culture. In subsequent correspondence, the couple proposed an idea to Covina and Galana: the creation of a correspondence club through which lesbians might be able to connect with other lesbians in their own backyard or around the country. Although Covina and Galana were warned not to get into "computer dating" because of its sexual implications, they eventually decided to sponsor it under the auspices of *Amazon Quarterly,* provided that those who participated were legal adults. In July 1974, an ad appeared for "Connections," a lesbian pen-pal club run by women associated with *Amazon Quarterly.* The copy read, "If you would like to contact women who share your interests, we will try to help . . . Let us know if you want to meet women in your area, women anywhere living in communes, women in the arts, women with children, women just coming out, etc.—make up your own categories."[61] By November, the editors claimed that about three hundred women had chosen to participate in "Connections." Whether or not Covina and Galana or the couple from Florida who managed "Connections" knew it, the era had passed in which pen-pal clubs were a particularly dangerous project and one that was avoided by all homophile organizations. Because of the changes in obscenity laws and in the way in which they were interpreted by the courts, correspondence clubs were under much less scrutiny and less threat of legal action than they had been in the 1950s and 1960s. In fact, gay men, heterosexual swingers, cross-dressers, and lesbians made contact clubs a regular staple of their communicative repertoire through which they located others for sexual and / or romantic liaisons. Through *Amazon Quarterly,* then, Covina and Galana established a lesbian-feminist communication network, but more than that they contributed to the grounding of feminism by pointing out—in practice—that the network was the means as well as the desired ends.

The New Lesbians: Expanding the Amazon Network

In *The New Lesbians,* Covina and Galana's 1977 book based on the interviews they conducted while circumnavigating the country, twenty women explained what feminism meant to them and the changes they hoped it would bring about. Although their ideas ranged widely, many focused on the concept of "community." When asked by Covina what she most wished for, Alix Dobkin, a lesbian folksinger, responded, "I would wish for a communication network among women, where I could get my music distributed, records, publications, everything, get to each women's community without going through men." [62] Dobkin's hope, at its base, was a sentiment shared by a vast number of lesbian-feminists in the early 1970s: the desire to construct lines of communication through which feminists, and lesbians in particular, could share ideas and connect with one another. Writ large, this trend in creating a women-identified female culture was the result of a cultural turn in feminism, which according to historian Alice Echols resulted in the dominance of "cultural feminism." [63]

Cultural feminism, according to Echols, entailed the creation of "alternative women's institutions" and insisted upon "women's essential sameness to each other and their fundamental difference from men." [64] More than define cultural feminism, however, Echols holds it up to scrutiny and critique, arguing that its ascendance around 1973 spelled the doom of radical feminism and consequently enabled the discourse of liberal feminism (emanating from NOW) to reign as the primary public voice of feminism. And while I agree with Echols that the emergence of cultural feminism occurred around 1973, with lesbian-feminism as its most acute manifestation, I would not say that this brought down radical feminism, which had by then run its course and was beginning to shrink on its own accord due to defections, departures, internal disputes, burnout, and, in Echols's words, "the eruption of difference." [65] The "ascendance of cultural feminism," like that practiced by Covina and Galana, liked that hoped for by Alix Dobkin and others, was primarily the result of the emergence of a major upswing in lesbian-feminism—which, still, was heavily influenced by general socialist (or at least social democratic) ideas such as a critique of hierarchies and a belief in collectivization. It is not that most radical feminists were seduced by cultural feminism, then, but that many lesbians became feminists and many women who joined feminist consciousness-raising groups were coming out as lesbians. While Echols is partially cor-

rect in asserting that "cultural feminism succeeded in large measure because it promised an end to the gay-straight split" amongst feminists, it
would be more accurate to say that with the emergence of cultural lesbian-
feminism the gay-straight split approached irrelevance—lesbian-feminists
seemed more interested in building their own community than critiquing
women who failed to join in.[66] It was the emergence of lesbian-feminism
and the desire to construct lesbian-feminist communities, many of which
espoused some form of separatism, that resulted in the dominance of cultural feminism.

The reason that community formation and the elaboration of a women's
culture appeared to be the main activity in the early 1970s, rather than radical (e.g., Marxist or anti-imperialist) politics per se, is that the multitudes
of women "coming out" understood in a very personal way the relationship between their gender and sexual identities and chose a form of living
that would nurture those aspects of their lives.[67] Moreover, it also was this
primary mode of understanding through sexuality that precipitated rifts
among lesbian-feminists along lines of race and class, especially because
working-class lesbians and lesbians of color (and working-class lesbians of
color) felt excluded from the community in which they wanted to be acknowledged and included. We must not overemphasize, then, the effect
that radical manifestos, whether from a leftist or cultural feminist perspective, would have upon the thousands of women who came to participate in the lesbian world in the early 1970s. From my reading, most
lesbians were a rather practical lot of women who certainly considered
themselves feminist but whose idea of feminism lay primarily in the immediate goals of ending their sense of isolation and locating others like
themselves. Once these women located those networks, whether through
reading a newspaper or joining a commune, the political and economic
issues undoubtedly became more important, but they were secondary—
both temporally and ideologically—to the task of locating and then joining a network of similarly inclined women. It is for this reason that lesbian-
feminism became a mass movement that, arguably, surpassed the relative
influence of a radical political critique in the gay male world which took a
more commercial path to community building, as detailed in chapter 5.

The women's voices in *The New Lesbians* did not just help articulate the
hopes of lesbian-feminists, but the production and distribution of the
book, along with *Amazon Quarterly* before it, helped to lay the groundwork
for the hoped for "communication network among women." Along with
inviting their readers to join "Connections," the correspondence club, and
instructing them about how to make their own magazines and get them
distributed, Covina and Galana joined others around the country as they

enlarged and institutionalized the more informal communication networks that already existed. In particular, through *Amazon Quarterly*, they sought to link isolated, community-based networks with the goal of creating a national one. Covina remembers, "We were realizing just from the response that we felt suddenly we were in this remarkable position of being in contact with the women who were all over the country." The already extant network established by the *Ladder* certainly helped, but once the first issue of *Amazon Quarterly* was published, it began to spread into new places and points of distribution. Although few lesbian community centers existed at this point in the United States, scores of women's centers and women's studies departments did. And, as Covina said, "women's centers were . . . a good way to find lesbians." Tapping into this emerging feminist network, Covina and Galana sent copies of *Amazon Quarterly* to these various centers in an effort to build a national lesbian network. The result was immediately gratifying. "Between those things, we had, right away, readership that was really spread all over the country and Canada," Covina remembered. The appearance of *Amazon Quarterly* also coincided with the birth of the women's bookstore as a cultural trend, which Covina and Galana capitalized on by compiling the names of the bookstores and ultimately getting their magazine sold through these stores.[68] By the time they had completed their travels around the country in 1973, they knew of thirty women's bookstores or bookstores that had a significant lesbian-feminist collection. Although they worked to create a lesbian-feminist distribution network, Covina and Galana were not hemmed in by lesbian exclusivity. Rather, they found many alternative bookstores that would carry *Amazon Quarterly*, and they even used the distributor, New Left Publications, to get their magazine into additional venues.[69]

The publishers of *Amazon Quarterly* were not alone in working to establish a separate lesbian culture through the building of women's institutions and communities.[70] In fact, a great deal of sociological research conducted in the first half of the 1970s documents the integral relationship among communication, community, and feminism. A number of feminist sociologists and anthropologists spent a good deal of time in the early 1970s researching lesbian-feminist organizations, communities, and communes as they were forming and dissolving.[71] Although a complete review of the literature is beyond the scope of this book, it is worth noting some themes common to the various studies: lesbian-feminist communities tended to operate outside of the mainstream; their communalism and antihierarchical beliefs dominated group culture; constant communication was necessary to maintain the networks, which were somewhat anarchic, meaning authority and community standards were informal, shifting, and to a certain extent verbal; and the groups were intensely local but viewed themselves as part of a larger cultural trend, which brought up the contradictions of space discussed above. These points, which were plainly present in the lesbian-feminist literature of the day and which come up in oral history interviews, point to the dominance of an abstract lesbian conception of space that was much less defined by meccas, capitals, and outposts—in general quite dissimilar from the occupations of Euclidean space typical of gay men. The reasons for this are many and complicated, but they must include the widespread disidentification with lesbian bars among the mostly white, well-educated lesbians who took active roles in organized lesbian endeavors from the DOB to the publishing of lesbian-feminist magazines in the 1970s.

Indeed, another way in which the creators of *Amazon Quarterly* followed in the footsteps of people like Del Martin and Phyllis Lyon was their lack of affinity with the lesbian bar culture and, along with it, their political critique of butch-fem roles, or what they called "role playing." In recent interviews, both Galana and Covina claim that they rarely went to lesbian bars and when asked about the subject in general, said that they didn't have much to contribute to the historical record. In distancing themselves and their work from the culture of lesbian bars, however, they also were removing those sites from a communication network that was designed to map a lesbian geography and from the list of options where lesbians might be able to meet other lesbians. This move sets lesbians apart from gay men who, while at times critical of certain behavior in gay bars, still considered them to be the central institutions of gay male life. While the resource guide that was published in *Amazon Quarterly* named a total of eleven lesbian bars in the United States and Canada, the vast majority of listings were for places like women's centers and bookstores; the editors made clear that lesbian-feminists would do better to find community in feminist institutions rather than bars. Among the many reasons that there were no guidebooks to lesbian bars published before 1973, one of the most compelling is that there existed a larger gulf between political lesbians engaged in publishing and lesbians who frequented bars than in the gay male world where people like Guy Strait and Bob Damron who had bridged the divide in the 1960s.

But if lesbian resource listings are any guide, the cold war began to thaw around 1972 when several publications associated with the emergent lesbian-feminist press movement started to list lesbian or women's bars along with the places like women's centers and coffeehouses. Publications like *Echo of Sappho* (New York), *Portcullis East / West* (Los Angeles), and *Lavender Woman* (Chicago) each contained combined and sometimes extensive lists of women's centers, gay liberation organizations, hotlines and switchboards, and lesbian bars; *Lavender Woman* even went as far as to provide comparative ratings according to categories like prices, quality of drinks, and the attitude of owners of bars in Chicago.[72] While the gay male bar guidebooks focused more on the type of people who frequented each bar and what sort of entertainments were available, the lesbian listings tended to focus more on the relationship between sites and the practice of feminist politics; as editor of the *Lavender Woman* survey wrote, "Hopefully these surveys do serve and continue to serve the Chicago lesbian community in helping to end our oppression in the only institutionalized gathering places now available to us. Hopefully, also, the gay bar owners will pay attention to these surveys and make changes that seem appropriate."[73]

This spirit was carried through to the publication of the first guidebooks to lesbian bars and other sites, which included *The Gay Girl's Guide* and *Gaia's Guide*.[74] The editors of the first edition of *The Gay Girl's Guide* (1974), which was compiled from both London and San Francisco, began with the impressive assertion that "there are over 700 listings in this little book, including: Bars, Clubs, Organizations, Discos, Meeting Places, Community Centers, Religious Groups, Bookstores, Hotels, Restaurants, Social Services, Newspapers and Magazines." But, they immediately added the caveat: "Alas! Not all of these are frequented by Gay Ladies *Only*. Truth to tell—there simply are not 700 such places in the world today. So what we've really got now is a spectrum" from women-only sites to mixed ones.[75] Like the gay male guidebooks, the producers of *The Gay Girl's Guide* pointed out that while they endeavored for accuracy they could not promise it; instead, they asked their readers to share their intelligence, writing, "So, if we've guided you to a place that was so bad it almost sent you rushing back to your dangerously violent husband—why not write and tell us so that we can strike it off in future years?"[76] Although there was less information on bars in lesbian publications and guidebooks than in most of their gay male counterparts, such places were listed and, thus, should help us remember that lesbian activism and bargoing were not necessarily contradictory activities. Ultimately, in these publications there was more emphasis on the various options for connecting with other women than dictating to those women precisely where they meet up.

The development of lesbian-feminist communities in the early 1970s was powered in large part by an ethos of communication that prized the project of circulating information through their world; but, like the communication network pioneered by the DOB, the Amazon network veered away from channels of the mass media and sought to establish its own, both through the conventional means of word of mouth but also through travel, do-it-yourself publications and newsletters, and eventually, through extensive listings of sites that included lesbian bars. According to lesbian-feminists like Gina Covina and Laurel Galana, shaping an Amazon network was not only an important feminist task, it would come to be recognized by many as the ultimate goal of their movement. In arriving at this conclusion and in exerting a massive amount of individual and group energy in seeking to achieve it, lesbian-feminism in the early 1970s in many ways represented the pinnacle not only of the do-it-yourself ethos, but of the long movement of transforming homosexual communication networks begun in the early 1950s by the homophile organizations.

The Study of Sexuality in the Internet Age

Contacts Desired was researched and written in a period that roughly coincided with the emergence and popularization of a new medium of communication: the Internet. As should have been clear in everything from the language and concepts employed to the very thesis of this book, the historical and communicative context in which it was produced is an essential factor in shaping what it has become. Rather than write a summary conclusion (for that the reader should revisit the part introductions), I offer this epilogue to provide a glance, ex post facto, at how the ongoing revolution in communications influenced the conceptual thinking that went into making this book. More important, though, I want to reflect upon what *Contacts Desired* reveals about communication innovations in the past that might help us better understand some of the changes that are taking place today.

The book originated as a dissertation that was written for the University of Southern California History Department, but was largely conceived, researched, and written in San Francisco between 1995 and 2004. In those years I witnessed San Francisco at the height and then the nadir of the now infamous and ridiculed dot-com boom. Talk of a new communication medium, the Internet, was everywhere, and its direct and residual effects were being felt very close to home. For one, the immediate economic changes made it very difficult for a graduate student to continue living in a city where both commercial and residential rents were skyrocketing and vacancies virtually nonexistent; and while I eventually was priced out of the city, the good fortunes and high-paying jobs of a few people close to me meant good meals out on the town and more than a few trips to the opera. It was a time of extremes. Casual and expert observers alike were attributing the apparent economic free-for-all to the birth of the Internet. Within a very short period of time, however, the economic bubble burst, but five years later the influence of the Internet on American society, politics, and culture is arguably stronger than ever.[1] It was in this context that I read the provocative accounts by Robert Darnton, Marshall McLuhan, Manuel Castells, and others of how an assortment of media exert varying yet always profound influence upon society (not to mention being exposed to a new breed of interdisciplinary scholars whose studies of networks provide insight into the structures of systems like the media).[2] And further, the ideas of McLuhan, Darnton, and Castells encouraged me think that it is not always the content of the media that stirs people to action but also the particular medium in which the information travels that alters the historical context and makes new realities possible.

Media critic and 1960s and 1970s pop culture icon in his own right, Marshall McLuhan wrote eloquently and imaginatively about consequential media changes in a book published in 1964 but reissued by MIT in 1994 for readers in the Internet age, *Understanding Media.* There McLuhan claimed that the power of "electric speed in bringing all social and political functions together in a sudden implosion has heightened human awareness of responsibility to an intense degree." This heightened awareness of responsibility was driven by an increased knowledge that people of differing regions, classes, ages, races, and sexualities could no longer be segregated and isolated as they had been in the past. The boundaries that isolated these groups from one another and that isolated members within each group began to disintegrate in part because of the changing communication media. Or, as McLuhan asserted from his own subjective position as an educated white male, "It is this implosive factor that alters the position of the Negro, the teen-ager, and some other groups. They can no longer be *contained,* in the political sense of limited association. They are now *involved* in our lives, as we in theirs, thanks to electric media."[3] Although his ideas certainly were evocative, the fact that McLuhan wrote these sentences in the same historical period in which there appeared to be a transformation in queer representation gave me an idea—might it be that novelty in the representation of homosexuality was not to be found in the content of a document that emerged as a key element in my study from very early on, the *Life* magazine article "Homosexuality in America"?

Might it be that the uniqueness of that article was to be found rather in the photojournalistic magazine in which it was published and its expansive scale of distribution? Was it the medium of *Life* magazine rather than the print on its pages that made the article so memorable and, thus, signaled historical change to so many people who came across it at that time and since? I began to think that the reason people remembered the article so vividly and ascribed to it a transformative power was not only what it said but also that it was published in the most influential mass circulation family magazine of the era.

Thinking along these lines helped me come to terms with just what had changed in the history of homosexuality over the twentieth century. While some historians are interested in what remains the same, which institutions and practices date back the longest, I have been most interested in change, especially in relation to the history of San Francisco, a city some claim to have been a sort of gay mecca since the early days of the Gold Rush when an instant city was populated mostly by men and where middle-class standards of sexual propriety held little sway. Confronted with this highly dubious but widely accepted notion, I began to question whether San Francisco had always already been a gay mecca. Reading in the history of homosexuality taught me that the vagaries in the history of gay identity made such a designation historically unlikely. I asked, then, what had changed and why had it gone unnoticed? Observing the Internet and reading thinkers such as McLuhan and Darnton helped me realize that change in San Francisco's gay world was both obvious and hidden—that while one might be able to find evidence of the appeal of San Francisco to homosexuals or the presence of homosexuals in the city prior to the 1940s, the references that did exist were few and far between. While historians have expertly uncovered evidence like cultural archaeologists, many focused on the intriguing and rare nugget rather than the absences, silences, and overall paucity of evidence as the most revealing element to be examined. Change then was not to be found primarily in how San Francisco was represented but it was possible to uncover significant change in the media in which the representations were distributed and in the size, scope, and even diversity of the audiences who witnessed those representations. According to this logic, there existed a substantive difference between a period (the early twentieth century) in which one of the only mentions I found of San Francisco and homosexuality together came in an appendix to a privately printed book to an era (the 1970s) in which the city and the sexuality had been paired so regularly that people used the city as a euphemism for homosexuality.[4]

In my own life, too, the influence of medium, and, related, of scale, was a matter of consideration. I remember longing for more information about homosexuality than what was readily available while in high school (I already had come out to a few people), but finding very little—partially because of a fear to ask or look for it, but also because it was often difficult to locate. Now, of course, the problem comes not with locating information, but from sorting through the vastness of the information available at one's fingertips. For example, a search of Google in December 2004 for the word "gay" retrieved 135 million pages! Similarly, "lesbian" pulled up 54.1 million pages; "homosexual" retrieved 40.6 million; "queer" fetched 4.75 million; "dyke" uncovered about 3 million; and "homophile," a term used largely by historians, even brought up nearly 17,000 pages. I would guess that the word "homophile" was not printed more than 17,000 times in the fifteen-or-so-year period in which homophile magazines were in print. While *Contacts Desired* did not seek to chart the history of gay male and lesbian communication networks after the early 1970s, it is clear to me that the emergence of the Internet is yet another chapter, perhaps a particularly long and significant one, in the narrative of gay male and lesbian history presented here. After all, the pairing of "gay" with "San Francisco" retrieved 5.3 million pages through a Google search.[5]

More than inspiring me to seek out thinkers who theorized about and studied the history of communications, writing about networks in a period in which many claimed a revolution in communications was brewing gave me a vocabulary to describe the elements of communications relating to medium along with content. While the spate of neologisms reached epidemic proportions in the late 1990s and led many (including myself) to call for a moratorium on "new words" related to the Internet, I must admit that I looked forward to Sunday mornings and the opportunity to read William Safire's musings on language (but not on politics) because the bounty of new words provided such a meaty dish to feast upon. Not all of the words in vogue, however, were new. Many were recycled from older contexts into newer ones. Words such as "portal," "link" (often with "hyper-" as a prefix), "network," "space," "webs," "hubs," and so on came into regular usage as people struggled to describe the structure of the Internet and help new users "navigate" (another such word) the new virtual environment. As I started thinking about the pathways upon which information traveled and the various portals through which gay men and lesbians might access that information, the new language of the Internet not only provided a descriptive language, it also proved useful by continually directing my attention to the structures of communication. In examining those structures, it became increasingly evident to me that the ways in which people access information can be as important as the content of the information itself.

If there is one point I have hoped to make within these pages, it is that information circulates rather than being handed down and that knowledge creation is a dynamic and unpredictable process. Such was the case with this book. While the booming Internet may have provided a context for me to look at the structures of communications and may have provided a vocabulary useful for describing changes in medium, what I was learning about sexual communication networks in the past also began to influence my understanding of communications in the world around me.

Although innovations in communication networks are emphasized in *Contacts Desired*, I tried to make clear that older and established forms of communication persist alongside newer ones. Even as countless thousands of homosexually inclined women read lesbian paperbacks in the late 1950s, many thousands of women (some of whom read paperbacks) continued to visit bohemian or lesbian bars where they met women who sometimes confirmed, sometimes challenged the pictures of lesbians drawn by novelists. For those who read the novels and went to bars, however, a new sort of internal dialog must have occurred as they made such comparisons between the experienced and the mediated; as a result, sometimes they found the literary or, perhaps, the lived experience wanting. I suspect that the resulting dissonance inspired some of these women to look for something better or simply newer, to improve their world and their experience of it in some way. Similarly, although thousands of men were aroused by the picture of gay cruising inside the Tool Box bar provided by *Life* magazine, images in magazines, whether family-oriented or pornographic, did not replace the lived experienced of cruising in a bar or on the streets. Yet, I think future research would offer evidence that the experience of cruising was changed and in important ways by the visual representation of it by magazines beginning with *Life* in 1964 and the published listings of cruising sites beginning with the *Lavender Baedeker* in 1963. For example, cruising became more infused with a context in which homosexual behavior also meant homosexual identity; thus, while greater publicity meant more people might participate, it also meant that participation might be limited to a more particular group of people. Not only do established forms of communication or, in this case, "connecting to" persist, but they will be transformed by new and newly dominant ones.

The fact that paperback books paid a great deal of attention to lesbians and mainstream magazines offered numerous descriptions (along with a few pictures) of gay men in the late 1950s and early 1960s is at least partly attributable to the fact that publishers of books and magazines had found a new and vigorous competitor in the 1950s: television. Some of most interesting innovations in content, then, appear first and most fully in com-

munication media that are not the newest or technologically most innovative but that are in danger of losing audiences to newer media. The way in
which this will work out in the present communications revolution is not
entirely clear if in fact it is descriptive of what currently is happening at all.
But it is a distinct possibility that the explosion of programming about homosexuality on network and cable television is not only the result of the
competition between those two media but also due to the innovation of the
Internet and its ability to reach and thereafter create a larger and more specialized homosexual audience. Thus changes in communications technol-
ogy should be placed alongside political and cultural developments as we
struggle to account for transformations in the representation of sex and
sexuality.

Finally, as people learn about others they consider to be like themselves—with similar idiosyncrasies, preferences, fetishes, or behaviors—
a possibility exists that those traits might mutate into a shared identity.
And with a common identity, we can predict that the individuals might coalesce into a community. For gay men and lesbians, the innovations in sexual communication networks detailed in this book demonstrate how the
ways in which homosexuals discovered one another changed dramatically
between the 1940s and 1970s. Although I hoped to show that history did
not march in a predictable, progressive fashion toward wider visibility
and a greater ease to connect, I also demonstrate how the innovations in
networks increased the options available for connecting and established a
clearer set of guidelines instructing people how to connect and what engaging in that process might mean for one's sense of who they were and
what they might become. The influence of the Internet upon ideas about
identity and community—as well as the social and cultural history of
identity and community formation—is as of now unknowable, but if the
past is any indication, it will be major, profound, and long-lasting.[6]

A variety of scholars, for example, have begun to explore the influence
of the Internet on sexual identities, many under the rubric of studies of
globalization, of which the Internet is one of the most powerful engines.[7]
Looking back to the 1950s and 1960s, it is clear to me that representations
in the mass media influenced the ways in which people thought about sexual identity, but as the examples of *Life* magazine (with Hal Call's role in
establishing a masculine gay mis-en-scene) and Jess Stearn's *The Grapevine*
(with Del Martin's and Phyllis Lyon's roles in creating the new lesbian),
it also is evident that individuals affect the manner and content of representations. In other words, emergent groups can use both new and established media for their own purposes, purposes that may contradict or be
perfectly irrelevant to the gatekeepers of the media. I suspect something

similar is happening today with the Internet. While there exists a certain tendency within Internet-driven globalization to colonize and to foist Western identity categories on groups outside the West in order to continue the modernizing project of naming and knowing for administrative and commercial capitalist purposes, examples from *Contacts Desired* suggest that we also should look for countervailing tendencies at work today. Thus, I expect we will see a continued expansion in scholarship that looks beyond the ways in which non-Western peoples experience Western conceptions of sexuality (and "gay men's English" in particular) as a colonizing force, but rather focus on how the new modes of communication enable colonized / postcolonial peoples to influence sexuality in the West. In particular, we should begin to better understand how patterns of sexual behavior and languages associated with those behaviors in sending countries and cultures are being re-introduced to immigrant populations in receiving countries and cultures. In a manner similar to *Contacts Desired,* which attempted to move analysis of historic representations of homosexuality away from good / bad and production / reception models, future studies of Internet-driven globalization might also think about both the medium and its associated processes in more dynamic terms. Scholars may also temper their critiques of communicative globalization as a process. While retaining critiques of ways in which globalization works to dominate and define, scholars might find something to applaud in elements of exchange that at times can subvert reigning paradigms of experience and knowledge. The Internet, for example, may provide immigrants will another tool for resisting pressures of cultural evaporation while simultaneously providing a means through which resident populations might glean an understanding of differences within systems of sexual categorizing and thus resist "the modernist fantasy of convergence."[8]

And building upon McLuhan's insight that change in communication media "has heightened human awareness of responsibility to an intense degree," I think that we should not underestimate the role of communications revolutions in facilitating the struggle of peoples for the right of self-determination, especially following the 1948 United Nations' manifesto, "Universal Declaration on Human Rights."[9] Similar to the way in which activists within the broad homophile movement (including everyone from leaders of organizations to compilers of guidebooks) pursued a strategy that included establishing new networks of communication, individuals and groups seeking rights and justice for those who engage in non-normative sexual behavior and adopt non-normative gender identities today find that connecting to larger networks of support and knowledge is an essential element of their activism.[10] Like the struggle for gay male and lesbian equality and rights in the 1950s and 1960s, the fight for the rights of a variety of sexual and gender minorities around the globe will hinge upon the ability of groups to locate others they perceive to be like themselves and establish networks that erode the isolation and invisibility that make such peoples susceptible to erasure.

Everyone from scholars to politicians to political activists have speculated that change in the world around us might someday bring about the end of a separate homosexual identity—and, thus, of heterosexual identity, too. This idea was popular among gay liberation activists in the early 1970s—and clearly articulated by Dennis Altman in his 1971 book *Homosexual Oppression and Liberation*—who looked forward to an era in which sexual desire would not be a site of oppression and in which all sexual desires would be legitimate.[11] The disappearance of homosexual identity also was predicted by Marshall McLuhan, who expected the sexual revolution to usher in a golden age of guiltless heterosexual play and thus remove the necessity of lesser sexual outlets like homosexuality. Indeed, one wonders in the current context in which there appears to be a proliferation of queer-related sexual identities in the United States (e.g. leatherman, lipstick lesbian, DL, etc.) and abroad (*takatapui, tom-dee, kathoey, joto, bugarrón, bakla*, etc.) about the continued viability of a "gay" or even "lesbian" identity per se. The persistence of desiring, of seeking, of reaching out beyond the family or community into which one was born in hopes of finding sexual pleasure, companionship, and maybe even a new home may then actually spell the end of a gay male or lesbian or homosexual identity. However, in contrast to Altman's notion that homosexuality and heterosexuality will evaporate in the face of a universal polymorphous perversity, I think today's sexual identity structures might just morph into a multitude of specific sexual and gender identities that may or may not be thought to have any special relationship to homosexuality or even to queerness. The desire to connect, regardless, will continue to be influenced by larger social, cultural, and political forces and by innovations in communications, but that desire itself is a force of social change as it inspires people to speak in forums that previously had excluded their voices, to occupy places in which they had not been tolerated, and to name themselves a people in their own right.

Introduction

1. Desire, a central theme in this book, refers not only to the libidinous desire for sexual contact that motivates humans to look beyond their own bodies and seek fleeting and/or lasting partners but also to a desirous longing for companionship, for camaraderie, for solace, and for shielding from danger—in short, it refers to the human desire for fraternity and community. My thinking on the multiple meanings of desire was enriched greatly by Horacio Roque Ramirez, "Communities of Desire: Queer Latina/Latino History and Memory, San Francisco Bay Area, 1960s–1990s" (Ph.D. diss., University of California at Berkeley, 2001).

2. On the metaphor of reproduction within the gay world, see "Homosexual Procreation," *ONE,* 9, no. 3 (March 61): 6–8.

3. I do not mean to suggest that this process always happens in a predicable, linear fashion. There are simply too many examples of women and men who identify as homosexuals late in their lives and who already knew something of homosexual identities and communities, even to the point of participating in them to varying degrees.

4. While acknowledging the importance of recent studies that claim homosexuals in rural and isolated areas developed their own gay communities in decades past, this project complicates the story by demonstrating how knowledge of gay community and the process of community formation was distributed unevenly across the country: while some individuals in some rural areas found gay community in their immediate surroundings, many others did not. Moreover, the location of men and women "like that" in the history of rural America by historians should not obscure the fact that engaging in homosexual behavior is not the same thing as claiming a homosexual identity or participating in a large and diverse homosexual community. On gay life in rural areas, see John Howard, ed., *Carryin' On in the Lesbian and Gay South* (New York: New York University Press, 1997), and idem, *Men Like That: A Southern Queer*

History (Chicago: University of Chicago Press, 1999). On imagined communities, see Benedict Anderson, *Imagined Communities: Reflections on the Origin and Spread of Nationalism* (London: Verso, 1983); on imagined sexual communities, see Kath Weston, "Get Thee to a Big City: Sexual Imaginary and the Great Gay Migration," *GLQ: Gay/Lesbian Quarterly* 2 (1995): 253–277.

5. George Chauncey, *Gay New York: Gender, Urban Culture, and the Making of the Gay Male World, 1890–1940* (New York: BasicBooks, 1994), 1–29.

6. My account of Harry Hay's story comes from the careful and loving biography by Stuart Timmons, *The Trouble with Harry Hay: Founder of the Modern Gay Movement* (Boston: Alyson Publications, 1990), 35–37.

7. Timmons, *Trouble with Harry Hay,* 36.

8. Timmons, *Trouble with Harry Hay,* 36.

9. Timmons, *Trouble with Harry Hay,* 27.

10. Timmons, *Trouble with Harry Hay,* 42.

11. For more on subcultural networks, see the final section of this introduction, "The Gay Detective."

12. At this point it is worth commenting on the nature versus nurture issue in the question of sexuality origins. Ultimately, whether same-sex sexual attraction (homosexuality) or different-sex sexual attraction (heterosexuality) is inborn or developmental is irrelevant. The long sweep of human history has never been without either behavior—and hopefully never will be. I'm quite sure, however, that no one is born "gay" or "lesbian" or "straight." In American culture at the beginning of the twenty-first century, to be "gay" or to be "straight" are culturebound states of being that intersect with other such states like masculinity and femininity and whiteness and blackness. The literature on this issue is vast; for a useful overview, see Carole Vance's essay, "Social Construction Theory: Problems in the History of Sexuality," in *Homosexuality, Which Homosexuality?* ed. Dennis Altman, Carole Vance, Martha Vicinus, and Jeffrey Weeks (London: GMP Publishers, 1989), 13–34; also see Steven Seidman, *The Social Construction of Sexuality* (New York: Norton, 2003).

13. George Chauncey, "From Sexual Inversion to Homosexuality: Medicine and the Changing Conceptualization of Female Deviance," *Salmagundi* 58–59 (fall 1982–winter 1983): 114–46, idem, "Christian Brotherhood or Sexual Perversion? Homosexual Identities and the Construction of Sexual Boundaries in the World War One Era," *Journal of Social History* 19 (1985): 189–211, and idem, *Gay New York.*

14. Lois Banner, *Intertwined Lives: Margaret Mead, Ruth Benedict, and Their Circle* (New York: Knopf, 2003); Henry Minton, *Departing From Deviance: A History of Homosexual Rights and Emancipatory Science in America* (Chicago: University of Chicago Press, 2002); and Jennifer Terry, *An American Obsession: Science, Medicine, and Homosexuality in Modern Society* (Chicago: University of Chicago Press, 1999).

15. From reading volumes of correspondence, examining scores of memoirs, and conducting dozens of interviews, I would suggest that this is the most common path upon which individuals journey to gay male or lesbian identities. However, a certain amount of anecdotal evidence suggests that some individuals, perhaps more women than men, come to identity through what might be called an "experiential epiphany." One of the most eloquent descriptions of such an instance can be found in Samuel Delany's memoir, *The Motion of Light in Water: Sex and Science Fiction Writing in the East Village, 1957–1965* (New York: Arbor House, 1988). Yet, as Joan Scott makes clear in "The Evidence of Experience," in *The Lesbian and Gay Studies Reader,* ed. Henry Abelove et al. (New York: Routledge, 1993), 397–415, no matter how profound spontaneous experi-

ence is "felt" to be, it occurs within certain contexts that limit the range of one's interpretations of that experience.

16. Sociologist Duncan Watts and mathematician Steven Strogatz have found that the process by which people become connected with one another is far from random, that social structure, or networks, along with personal idiosyncrasies, play determining roles. But more than state the obvious, they developed a formula that suggests that social networks tend to behave according to a few set rules. In particular, they established that far from being a randomly disconnected society, human culture at the beginning of the twenty-first century is highly connected. It is so because people tend to build social networks and social networks tend to organize according to a standard model: individuals cluster together into groups and groups are linked to one another by a never-ending succession of relationships between individuals in different groups; this in turn creates a small world in which, according to the famous dictum, humanity is separated by fewer than six degrees of separation. The key elements in the degree of connectivity, in the shrinking of the world, are the robust links that bind one cluster to another. See Duncan Watts and Steven Strogatz, "Collective Dynamics of 'Small-World' Networks," *Nature* 393 (1998): 440–442; for accessible overviews of the fascinating science and sociology of networks, see Albert-László Barabási, *Linked: The New Science of Networks* (Cambridge: Perseus, 2002); and Duncan Watts, *Six Degrees: The Science of a Connected Age* (New York: W. W. Norton, 2003).

17. On how class structures homosexuality, see Alexandra Chasin, *Selling Out: The Gay and Lesbian Movement Goes to Market* (New York: Palgrave, 2000); and John D'Emilio, "Capitalism and Gay Identity," in *Powers of Desire: The Politics of Sexuality,* ed. Ann Snitow, Christine Stansell, and Sharon Thompson (New York: Monthly Review Press, 1983), 100–13. On race structuring homosexuality, see Miranda Joseph, *Against the Romance of Community* (Minneapolis: University of Minnesota Press, 2002); Siobahn Somerville, *Queering the Color Line: Race and the Invention of Homosexuality in American Culture* (Durham: Duke University Press, 2000); and several essays in Martha Hodes, ed., *Sex Love Race: Crossing Boundaries in North American History* (New York: New York University Press, 1999).

18. Undoubtedly many readers will be disappointed with what might seem to be a lack of attention to the critical issues of race and class in this book, issues that quite clearly deserve greater attention vis-à-vis the history of sexuality. Aside from the usual constraints of evidence available to the researcher and the number of words allowed by the publisher, I think it worth mentioning very briefly another: the continuing marginalization of the history of sexuality, and gay male and lesbian history in particular, in the academy. Recent surveys as well as anecdotal evidence suggests that not only do gay male and lesbian academics have a difficult time locating steady employment (and thus pursuing their research agendas) but that gay and lesbian scholars who research sexuality history are further stigmatized in the academy. As this situation continues — and as gay men and lesbians continue to be scapegoated by conservatives and liberals alike in the political sphere—I consider it a priority to conduct research that examines sexuality as the central factor and variable. For more on this, see Marc Stein, "Committee on Lesbian and Gay History Survey on LGBTQ History Careers," *Perspectives* 39, no. 5 (May 2001): 29–31; and George Chauncey, "The Queer History and Politics of Lesbian and Gay Studies," in *Queer Frontiers: Millennial Geographies, Genders, and Generations,* ed. Joseph Boone et al. (University of Wisconsin Press, 2000), 298–315. For a broader perspective, see Benedict Carey, "Long after Kinsey, Only the Brave Study Sex," *New York Times,* 9 November 2004, on-line edition.

19. On the drawing of queer maps, see Martin Meeker, "Sexual Orientations: Maps

Making and Critiquing Homosexual Community, 1960s–1990s," paper presented at the Print Cultures and the City conference, McGill University, Montreal, Canada, 27 March 2004.

20. This, of course, is not to say that race and racism are meaningless in the lives of white male and female homosexuals, as scholars of whiteness have so convincingly demonstrated. Fortunately, historians are beginning to explore the historical linkages and ruptures between homosexuality and race and among homosexuals of different racial and ethnic backgrounds. See, for example, Peter Boag, *Same-Sex Affairs: Constructing and Controlling Homosexuality in the Pacific Northwest* (Berkeley: University of California Press, 2003); John D'Emilio, *Lost Prophet: The Life and Times of Bayard Rustin* (New York: Free Press, 2003); Howard, *Men Like That*; Ramírez, "Communities of Desire"; Tim Retzloff, "Seer or Queer?: Postwar Fascination with Detroit's Prophet Jones," *GLQ* 8, no. 3 (2002): 271–96; Somerville, *Queering the Color Line*; Marc Stein, *City of Sisterly and Brotherly Loves: Lesbian and Gay Philadelphia, 1945–1972* (Chicago: University of Chicago Press, 2000); and Roey Thorpe, "The Changing Face of Lesbian Bars in Detroit, 1938–1965" in *Creating a Place for Ourselves: Lesbian, Gay, and Bisexual Community Histories*, ed. Brett Beemyn (New York: Routledge, 1997), 165–81.

21. Darnton asks this question at the beginning of *The Forbidden Best-Sellers of Pre-Revolutionary France* (New York: Norton, 1995); on communication networks more generally, see Robert Darnton, "An Early Information Society: News and the Media in Eighteenth-Century Paris," *American Historical Review* 105, no. 1 (February 2000): 1–35. The term "communication networks" comes from Darnton, *Forbidden Best-Sellers*, 181–97. For "communication" and "networks" in the social sciences, see Claude Fischer, *To Dwell Among Friends: Personal Networks in Town and City* (Chicago: University of Chicago Press, 1982). For recent studies that examine the role of communications in historical change, see Kenneth Banks, *Chasing Empire Across the Sea: Communications and the State in the French Atlantic, 1713–1763* (Montreal: McGill-Queen's University Press, 2002); and Daniel Headrick, *When Information Came of Age: Technologies of Knowledge in the Age of Reason and Revolution, 1700–1850* (New York: Oxford University Press, 2000).

22. See Marshall McLuhan, *The Gutenberg Galaxy: The Making of Typographic Man* (Toronto: University of Toronto Press, 1962), idem, *Understanding Media: The Extension of Man* (1964; Cambridge, MA: MIT Press, 1994), and idem, *The Medium Is the Massage*, with graphics by Quentin Fiore and Jerome Agel (1967; reprint, San Francisco: HardWired, 1996). On McLuhan's intellectual influences, see Graeme Patterson, *History and Communications: Harold Innis, Marshall McLuhan, and Interpretation of History* (Toronto: University of Toronto Press, 1990); and Tom Wolfe, "McLuhan's New World," *Wilson Quarterly* (spring 2004): 18–25.

23. Darnton, *Forbidden Best-Sellers*, 182.

24. See Jürgen Habermas, "The Public Sphere," *New German Critique* 1, no. 3 (1974): 49–55; idem, *The Structural Transformation of the Public Sphere: An Inquiry into a Category of Bourgeois Society*, trans. Thomas Burger (1962; reprint, Cambridge: MIT Press, 1989). Public sphere revisionist and media theorist Alexander Kluge described the public sphere as "the site where struggles are decided by means other than war"; see Oskar Negt and Alexander Kluge, *The Public Sphere and Experience: Toward an Analysis of the Bourgeois and Proletarian Public Sphere* (1972; reprint, Minneapolis: University of Minnesota Press, 1993). Also see the Black Public Sphere Collective, ed., *The Black Public Sphere* (Chicago: University of Chicago Press, 1995); Craig Calhoun, ed., *Habermas and the Public Sphere* (Cambridge: MIT Press, 1992); Johanna Meehan, ed., *Feminists*

Read Habermas: Gendering the Subject of Discourse (New York: Routledge, 1995); Bruce Robbins, ed., *The Phantom Public Sphere* (Minneapolis: University of Minnesota Press, 1993); and Michael Warner, "Publics and Counterpublics" *Public Culture* 14, no. 1 (2002): 49–90. On cultural production and reception, see Stuart Hall, "Encoding, Decoding," in Simon During, ed., *The Cultural Studies Reader* (New York: Routledge, 1993), 90–103.

25. Elizabeth Eisenstein, *The Printing Press as an Agent of Change: Communications and Cultural Transformations in Early-Modern Europe*, vols. 1–2 (Cambridge: Cambridge University Press, 1979).

26. See, for example, "AHA Forum: How Revolutionary Was the Print Revolution?" *American Historical Review* vol. 107, no. 1 (Feb. 2002): 84–128, especially the critique by Adrian Johns, "How to Acknowledge a Revolution," 106–25.

27. The notion that San Francisco's visible gay world of the 1960s and 1970s is primarily the result of the city's morally "wide-open" reputation of the nineteenth and early twentieth centuries has been a cherished but largely unproven thesis among many writers on San Francisco as well as their readers. While I agree that the long-present urban image has been influential, I argue that other factors (i.e., those discussed in this book) were ultimately more important and more directly responsible for making the city into a "gay mecca" by the 1970s. For various articulations of the "since the Gold Rush" thesis, see Howard Becker, ed., *Culture and Civility in San Francisco* (San Francisco: Transaction Books, 1971); Nan Alamilla Boyd, *Wide Open Town*, 2–5; Brian Godfrey, *Neighborhoods in Transition: The Making of San Francisco's Ethnic and Nonconformist Communities* (Berkeley: University of California Press, 1988); Randy Shilts, *The Mayor of Castro Street: The Life and Times of Harvey Milk* (New York: St. Martin's Press, 1982), 48–51; Deborah Goleman Wolf, *The Lesbian Community* (Berkeley and Los Angeles: University of California Press, 1980), 74–75; Les Wright, "San Francisco," in *Queer Sites: Gay Urban Histories since 1600,* ed. David Higgs (New York and London: Routledge, 1999), 164–89.

28. "Lou Rand" [Lou Rand Hogan], *The Gay Detective* (Fresno, CA: Saber Books, 1961), 40–41; in 1964, the book was republished in a slightly revised edition, Lou Rand, *Rough Trade* (Los Angeles: Argyle Books, 1964). Cleis Press of San Francisco reissued *The Gay Detective* in 2003 with a new introduction written by Susan Stryker and Martin Meeker.

29. On the *valet de place* in Paris, see Harvey Levenstein, *Seductive Journey: American Tourists in France from Jefferson to the Jazz Age* (Chicago: University of Chicago Press, 1998), 7, 8, 34, 72. On the role played by guidebooks more generally, see Catherine Cocks, *Doing the Town: The Rise of Urban Tourism in the United States, 1850–1915* (Berkeley: University of California Press, 2001); and Marguerite Shaffer, *See America First: Tourism and National Identity, 1880–1940* (Washington: Smithsonian Institution Press, 2001).

30. In these days of proliferating gay travel guidebooks and above-the-board queer nightlife, it is difficult to imagine a time when a person, let alone a resourceful one, would have had difficulty locating a city's queer sights. Though she did not admit to looking for the gay world, during her early 1950s visit to the United States, Simone de Beauvoir lamented that she was not able to locate San Francisco's late-night café society: "We wandered around Market Street, dropped into bars, newsreel movies and restaurants, or just drifted with the crowd; and I had the same sensation that I had often felt in Times Square: how to become one with the night? How to capture it? . . . There were certainly other places which might yield something of the city; but we felt sure we should not find them; other people knew them and could take us there, but we did not know them. We remained on the surface of the lights, noise and promises with

which a great city vibrates at night: we should never manage to penetrate deeper." *America Day by Day* (New York: Grove Press, 1953), 152.

31. On Comstock and the origins of "Comstockery," see Helen Lefkowitz Horowitz, *Rereading Sex: Battles over Sexual Knowledge and Suppression in Nineteen-Century America* (New York: Knopf, 2002).

32. See *Regina v. Hicklin* (1868), a decision, incidentally, from courts in England, not the United States; and *Roth v. United States* (1957).

33. Not only did the U.S. Post Office have an army of inspectors, it also solicited help from the public, asking them to report suspicious mail or neighbors.

34. Boyer notes that while "Massachusetts censorship came over on the Mayflower . . . it was not until the 1920s, however, that 'Banned in Boston' became a national joke." See Paul Boyer, *Purity in Print: The Vice-Society Movement and Book Censorship in America* (New York: Scribner, 1968), 167–206.

35. While the *Roth* (1957) decision was a landmark, it hardly succeeded in drawing a clear line between obscene and nonobscene materials; indeed, local, state, and federal courts continue to address the question today; see, for example, Herbert Foerstel, *Banned in the Media: A Reference Guide to Censorship in the Press, Motion Pictures, Broadcasting, and the Internet* (Westport, CT: Greenwood Press, 1998).

36. Although mannish women and effeminate men made guest appearances in the pages of the popular pulp magazines of the 1920s and 1930s, the representation of homosexuality was decidedly indirect and oblique, especially when compared to the explicit representations found in the paperback novels published in the 1950s and 1960s. On pulp magazines of the 1920s and 1930s, see Eric Smith, *Hard-Boiled: Working-Class Readers and Pulp Magazines* (Philadelphia: Temple University Press, 2000).

37. On the censorship of *The Fleet's In!* see Richard Meyer, *Outlaw Representation: Censorship and Homosexuality in Twentieth-Century American Art* (New York: Oxford University Press, 2002), 33–93.

38. Although the Production Code was instituted in 1930, it wasn't uniformly followed until the Catholic Legion of Decency placed considerable pressure on filmmakers in 1934; see Steven Vaughn, "Morality and Entertainment: The Origins of the Motion Picture Production Code," *Journal of American History* 77, no. 1 (June 1990): 39–65.

39. Jeffrey Moran, *Teaching Sex: The Shaping of Adolescence in the 20th Century* (Cambridge: Harvard University Press, 2000); and Julian Carter, "Birds, Bees, and Venereal Disease: Toward an Intellectual History of Sex Education," *Journal of the History of Sexuality* 10, no. 2 (2001): 213–49.

40. Carter, "Birds, Bees, and Venereal Disease," 214. Of course the sexually inquisitive, whether young or old, gained information and instruction in places other than classrooms, as Alfred Kinsey demonstrated in his two famous sex surveys; Kinsey and his colleagues found that American men and women learned about various facets of sexual behavior from as wide-ranging sources as from films, from observing animals, and from reading graffiti in bathroom stalls. See Alfred Kinsey et. al., *Sexual Behavior in the Human Male* (Philadelphia: W.B. Saunders, 1948); and idem, *Sexual Behavior in the Human Female* (Philadelphia: W.B. Saunders, 1953).

41. Meyer, *Outlaw Representation.* Meyer draws upon Michel Foucault's ideas about the tendency of censorship to produce "reverse discourses"; see Foucault's *The History of Sexuality: An Introduction,* vol. 1 (1978; New York: Vintage, 1990); also see Robert Post, ed., *Censorship and Silencing: Practices of Cultural Regulation* (Los Angeles: Getty Research Institute, 1998).

42. Three issues of *Shawger's Illiterary Digest* are held by the archives of the GLBTHS; they were donated by the Magazine, a San Francisco antiquarian periodicals and erotica store that acquired the apparently inconsequential mimeographed sheets in a collection with other publications. Historian Allan Bérubé uncovered a very similar newsletter called the *Myrtle Beach Bitch,* which suggests that as yet undocumented others existed as well; see Bérubé, *Coming Out under Fire: The History of Gay Men and Women in World War Two* (New York: Free Press, 1990), 105, 144, 216.

43. *Shawger's Illiterary Digest,* April 1945, [6].

44. Chauncey, *Gay New York,* 286.

45. Also see ibid., 40–41, 50–51, 56–57. This strategy, however, was not always successful; as Allan Berube details, the authors of the *Myrtle Beach Bitch* eventually were caught, court-martialed, and thrown in the brig; see Berube, *Coming Out Under Fire,* 144–45.

46. Queenie Cochran, "Cochran Cackles," *Shawger's Illiterary Digest,* March 1945, [2].

47. On the importance of travel to the formation of a gay identity, see John Howard, "Place and Movement in Gay American History" in *Creating a Place for Ourselves,* 211–26.

48. The periodical collection of the GLBTHS contains several issues of the *Hobby Directory* from 1946 to 1952. The *Hobby Directory* originally was part of the papers of Bois Burke, a gay man who lived in Berkeley from the 1940s through the 1950s; on Burke, see Jack Garnett, interviewed by Jim Duggins, 7 August 1994, Oral History Collection, GLBTHS.

49. *Hobby Directory,* June 1948, 6, GLBTHS.

50. Ibid.

51. Ibid., 8.

52. *Hobby Directory,* June 1950, 35.

53. George Chauncey notes that at least since the turn of the twentieth century men similarly "placed carefully coded classified ads in newspapers and magazines in order to contact other gay men," *Gay New York,* 288.

54. On the relationship between homosexuality and occupation, see Chauncey, *Gay New York,* 134–35, 274–76; Jeffrey Escoffier, "The Political Economy of the Closet: Toward an Economic History of Gay and Lesbian Life before Stonewall," in *American Homo: Community and Perversity* (Berkeley: University of California Press, 1998), 65–78; David Johnson, "The Kids of Fairytown: Gay Male Culture on Chicago's Near North Side in the 1930s," in *Creating a Place for Ourselves,* 97–118; and Elizabeth Lapovsky Kennedy and Madeline Davis, *Boots of Leather, Slippers of Gold: The History of a Lesbian Community* (New York: Routledge, 1993).

55. On the history of male physique photography, see F. Valentine Hooven, *Beefcake: The Muscle Magazines of America, 1950–1970* (Cologne: Benedikt Taschen, 1995); and Thomas Waugh, *Hard to Imagine: Gay Male Eroticism in Photography and Film from Their Beginnings to Stonewall* (New York: Columbia University Press, 1996).

56. *Hobby Directory,* June 1948, 6.

57. On the obscenity trials of *The Well of Loneliness,* see Edward de Grazia, *Girls Lean Back Everywhere: The Law of Obscenity and the Assault in Genius* (New York: Random House, 1992), 165–208; and, especially, Leslie Taylor, "'I Made Up My Mind to Get It': The American Trial of *The Well of Loneliness,* New York City, 1928–1929," *Journal of the History of Sexuality* 10, no. 2 (2001): 250–286; of the many excellent critical and historical studies of *The Well of Loneliness,* see, in particular, Laura Doan, *Fashioning Sapphism: The Origins of a Modern English Lesbian Culture* (New York: Columbia University Press,

2001); and Laura Doan and Jay Prosser, eds., *Palatable Passion: Critical Perspectives on "The Well of Loneliness"* (New York: Columbia University Press, 2001).

58. Lisa Duggan, *Sapphic Slashers: Sex, Violence, and American Modernity* (Durham: Duke University Press, 2000).

59. Laura Doan, *Fashioning Sapphism*, xiii; and Rebecca O'Rourke, *Reflecting on "The Well of Loneliness"* (London: Routledge, 1989), 114.

60. The 1986 survey was discussed by O'Rourke in *Reflecting on "The Well of Loneliness,"* 114–142.

61. Ibid., 119.

62. See Janice Radway, *Reading the Romance: Women, Patriarchy, and Popular Literature* (Chapel Hill: University of North Carolina Press, 1984); Tania Modleski, *Loving with a Vengeance: Mass Produced Fantasies for Women* (New York: Metheun, 1984); and for a brief, more personal perspective, see Anna Quindlen, *How Reading Changed My Life* (New York: Ballantine, 1998).

63. For more on this process, though in a slightly later context, see Monica Bachmann, "'Someone like Debby': (De)Constructing a Lesbian Community of Readers," *GLQ* 6, no. 3 (2000): 377–388.

64. Howard, *Men Like That*, 52.

65. Kennedy and Davis, *Boots of Leather, Slippers of Gold*, 152.

Introduction to Part 1

1. Marvin Cutler, ed., *Homosexuals Today: A Handbook of Organizations and Publications* (Los Angeles: Publications Division, One, Inc., 1956), iii.

2. The first historical work to consider the homophile movement was Jonathan Ned Katz, *Gay American History: Lesbians and Gay Men in the U.S.A.* (New York: Crowell, 1976). The first monograph on the homophile movement also was the first dissertation in gay history completed at a U.S. university; see Salvatore Licata, "Gay Power: A History of the American Gay Movement, 1908–1974" (Ph.D. diss., University of Southern California, 1978). Later books dealing in whole or part with the homophile movement include John D'Emilio, *Sexual Politics, Sexual Communities: The Making of a Homosexual Minority in the United States, 1940–1970* (Chicago: University of Chicago Press, 1983); Lillian Faderman, *Odd Girls and Twilight Lovers: A History of Lesbian Life in Twentieth-Century America* (New York: Columbia University Press, 1991); Nan Alamilla Boyd, *Wide Open Town: A History of Queer San Francisco to 1965* (Berkeley: University of California Press, 2003); Marc Stein, *City of Sisterly and Brotherly Loves: Lesbian and Gay Philadelphia, 1945–1972* (Chicago: University of Chicago Press, 2000); Rodger Streitmatter, *Unspeakable: The Rise of the Gay and Lesbian Press in America* (Boston: Faber and Faber, 1995); and Stuart Timmons, *The Trouble with Harry Hay: Founder of the Modern Gay Movement* (Boston: Alyson, 1990).

3. For a more concentrated critique of the prevailing historiography, see Martin Meeker, "Behind the Mask of Respectability: The Mattachine Society and Male Homophile Practice, 1950s–1960s," *Journal of the History of Sexuality* 10, no. 1 (April 2001): 78–116.

4. A similar point was raised first by George Chauncey in his book *Why Marriage? The History Shaping Today's Debate over Gay Equality* (New York: Basic Books, 2004), 121–122; for a historical overview of the concept, see Russell Kazal, "Revisiting Assimilation: The Rise, Fall, and Reappraisal of a Concept in American History," *American Historical Review* 100 (1995): 437–471.

5. For those already members, the organizations also published chapter newsletters, attempting to keep the rank and file abreast of the activities of the national group and of local chapters.

6. For an example of homosexuality as gossip—in this case, about auto heir Walter Chrysler, Jr.—see Brad Shortell, "How the Navy Ousted Its No. 1 'Gay' Gob," *Confidential*, January 1956, 10; also see "The Vanderbilt Heir's Lavender Hi-Jinks," *Confidential*, July 1956, 37; both publications are available in the Ephemera Collection, Gay, Lesbian, Bisexual, Transgender Historical Society of Northern California Archives, San Francisco, California (hereafter GLBTHS).

7. On the homosexual security risk, see David Johnson, *The Lavender Scare: The Cold War Persecution of Gays and Lesbians in the Federal Government* (Chicago: University of Chicago Press, 2004). On the representation of homosexuals during the mid-twentieth century, see Kate Adams, "Making the World Safe for the Missionary Position: Images of the Lesbian in Post–World War II America," in *Lesbian Texts and Contexts: Radical Revisions*, ed. Karla Jay and Joanne Glasgow (New York: New York University Press, 1990), 255–274; Edward Alwood, *Straight News: Gays, Lesbians, and the News Media* (New York: Columbia University Press, 1996); George Chauncey, "The Postwar Sex Crime Panic," in *True Stories from the American Past*, ed. William Graebner (New York: McGraw-Hill, 1993), 160–178; D'Emilio, *Sexual Politics, Sexual Communities*, 40–53; Estelle Freedman, "'Uncontrolled Desires': The Response to the Sexual Psychopath, 1920–1960," *Journal of American History* 74 (June 1987): 83–106; and Estelle Freedman, "The Prison Lesbian: Race, Class, and the Construction of the Aggressive Female Homosexual, 1915–1965," *Feminist Studies* 22, no. 2 (summer 1996): 397–423.

Chapter 1

1. Though the name "Mattachine Society" was used throughout the organization's life, I am following the distinction originally made by the leaders of the organization between the "Mattachine Foundation," as it was led by Harry Hay and others in Los Angeles (1951–1953), and the "Mattachine Society," as it was led by Hal Call, Don Lucas, and for a few years, Ken Burns (1953–1967). For more complete accounts of the Mattachine Society's founding, see John D'Emilio, *Sexual Politics, Sexual Communities: The Making of a Homosexual Minority in the United States, 1940–1970* (Chicago: University of Chicago Press, 1983), 57–62; John Loughery, *The Other Side of Silence: Men's Lives and Gay Identities; A Twentieth-Century History* (New York: Henry Holt, 1998); Eric Marcus, *Making History: The Struggle for Gay and Lesbian Equal Rights, 1945–1990* (New York: HarperCollins, 1992); Rodger Streitmatter, *Unspeakable: The Rise of the Gay and Lesbian Press in America* (Boston: Faber and Faber, 1995); and Stuart Timmons, *The Trouble with Harry Hay: Founder of the Modern Gay Movement* (Boston: Alyson, 1990). On the origin of the Mattachine name, see D'Emilio, *Sexual Politics, Sexual Communities*; and "Mattachine—What Does It Mean?" *Mattachine Review*, November–December 1955, 29. For more on the context of gay Los Angeles in the 1930s and 1940s, see Daniel Hurewitz, "Made in Edendale: Bohemian Los Angeles and the Politics of Sexual Identity, 1918–1953" (Ph.D. diss., UCLA, 2001).

2. D'Emilio, *Sexual Politics, Sexual Communities*, 64.

3. For the organizational history of the Mattachine Foundation, see Marvin Cutler, ed., *Homosexuals Today: A Handbook of Organizations and Publications* (Los Angeles: Publications Division, One, Inc., 1956); and D'Emilio, *Sexual Politics, Sexual Communities*, 57–74.

4. Historian David Johnson provides detailed evidence of FBI surveillance of ho-

mosexuals leading to arrests and firings in *The Lavender Scare: The Cold War Persecution of Gays and Lesbians in Federal Government* (Chicago: University of Chicago Press, 2004).

5. Pledge cited in its entirety in Timmons, *Trouble with Harry Hay*, 155.

6. Jim Kepner remembered that upon joining the Mattachine Society in the early 1950s, "The people who ran it had allowed rumors to circulate that some very influential people were behind it. The phrase, 'senators and generals,' was one of the first I heard," Kepner quoted in Marcus, *Making History*, 46–47.

7. An undated newspaper clipping (ca. mid-1950s) headlined "All Male Dance Raided" carries the information that "the affair was sponsored by the Mattachine Society, a national organization with headquarters here [San Francisco] dedicated to promoting better public understanding of homosexuality," FBI report, Lyon-Martin Papers, GLBTHS. Although none of the revelers were arrested, the party was disrupted when the amateur bartender was arrested for serving alcohol without a license, a form of harassment apparently not exercised against most other groups. Prior to the 1950 decision, *Stoumen v. Reilly,* a group of homosexuals gathered in public could be labeled disorderly and subject to regulations similar to those used against houses of prostitution; attending a meeting of the Mattachine thus conceivably put one in the same legal universe as if one were frequenting a brothel. See Sol M. Stoumen, Appellant, v. George R. Reilly, et. al., Respondents, 37 C.2d 713; 234 P.2d 969, 28 August 1951.

8. Paul Coates, "Well, Medium and RARE," *Los Angeles Mirror,* 12 March 1953, newspaper clipping, Don Lucas Papers (hereafter DLP), GLBTHS.

9. Publications Committee, "A Brief History of the Mattachine Movement," July 1953, DLP, GLBTHS.

10. Ibid.

11. Ken Burns, "Opening Speech – General Convention," 15 May 1954, DLP, GLBTHS.

12. Ibid. About the FBI visit, see Coordinating Council minutes, 5 June 1953, DLP, GLBTHS.

13. On Call's sexuality, see Marcus, *Making History*, 60. On his career interests, see Call, "résumé," 16 September 1957, DLP, GLBTHS. The résumé said, "From age 12 to the present, I have pursued all aspects of the printing craft or trade to one extent or another."

14. Call quoted in Marcus, *Making History*, 61.

15. Hal Call, interviewed by Chris Palumbo, 29 April 1998, San Francisco, CA; in possession of the author.

16. Ibid.

17. Hal Call quoted in Marcus, *Making History*, 63.

18. D'Emilio, *Sexual Politics, Sexual Communities,* 78–84.

19. Although Call added a disclaimer to the end of the document that "this is not an official publication of the Mattachine Society," it was clear he hoped that it would become that. San Francisco Publications Chapter [Hal Call], "Aims & Principles," ca. August 1953, DLP, GLBTHS.

20. Most of my information about Lucas's biography comes from the exhaustive series of videotaped interviews with Lucas conducted by Paul Gabriel, 1996 through 1999, San Francisco, CA, "Shedding a Straight Jacket," Oral History Collection, GLBTHS. On Lucas's childhood and adolescence, see tape 1, 30 December 1996, and 18 January 1997; tape 2, 18 January 1997; and tape 3, 27 March 1997.

21. Lucas, interview, tape 1, 30 December 1996.

22. Unpublished text for "The Illusion of Conformity: Sleight-of-Hand Activism in San Francisco, 1950s–1960s—The Papers of Donald S. Lucas," public exhibition, curated by Paul Gabriel and Martin Meeker, James C. Hormel Gay and Lesbian Center, San Francisco Main Public Library, 23 October 1999–20 January 2000. Also see coverage of the exhibit in David Lamble, "Magician Don Lucas's Reappearing Act," *San Francisco Frontiers*, 2 December 1999, 33–34. The homophiles were not the only activists in the 1950s and 1960s to use the illusion of conformity. For instance, Betty Friedan hid her activism behind the acceptable veneer of a middle-class housewife; see Daniel Horowitz, *Betty Friedan and the Making of "The Feminine Mystique": The American Left, the Cold War, and Modern America* (Amherst: University of Massachusetts Press, 1998). On the similar strategy of performing "respectability" but in a different context, see Evelyn Brooks Higginbotham, *Righteous Discontent: The Women's Movement in the Black Baptist Church, 1880–1920* (Cambridge, MA: Harvard University Press, 1993), 185–229.

23. "Vice Chairman, San Francisco Area" to Ken [Burns], 9 February 1954, DLP, GLBTHS.

24. Ken Burns, "Opening Speech – General Convention," 15 May 1954, DLP, GLBTHS

25. Call, interview. The need for self-representation was clear to the leaders of the San Francisco chapter as they assembled the first issue of the magazine; from the summer of 1954 through the end of the year, San Francisco law enforcement agencies and newspapers waged a war on the city's gay and lesbian bars. After the Mattachine Society defended one lesbian bar, the police sought to slander the infant Mattachine Society as well. Obviously, effective public relations by the society required not only distribution through established channels but a venue for the leaders to publish their own words. On the problems of 1954, see Nan Alamilla Boyd, *Wide Open Town: A History of Queer San Francisco to 1965* (Berkeley: University of California Press, 2003), 99–100.

26. Call presented preliminary plans for a magazine to the society's coordinating council in March 1954, then submitted an official proposal for approval at the May 1954 annual convention; see H. L. C. [Hal Call], "Report of the Publications Chairman to the Coordinating Council," 1 March 1954, DLP, GLBTHS.

27. Call, interview.

28. Ken Burns, "Opening Speech – General Convention" 15 May 1954, DLP, GLBTHS. Also see Harold Call, "Recommended Policy for Publications of the Mattachine Society on All Levels," 9 December 1953, DLP, GLBTHS.

29. Minutes, Mattachine Society convention, May 1954, DLP, GLBTHS.

30. Along with public relations and publications, the society also sought to create networks by setting up chapters around the country. In 1954 the Mattachine Society treasurer toured the United States, visiting Dayton, Cleveland, Detroit, and Chicago, where he attempted to organize new chapters, successfully in some cases; see "Treasurer's Report—'Extension Trip,'" DLP, GLBTHS.

31. [Hal Call], "Report of the Publications Chairman," Mattachine Society convention, 14–15 May 1955, DLP, GLBTHS.

32. It is unclear who the original seven members were, but Pan-Graphic was initially owned by five society members (Hal Call, Don Lucas, Jack Baker, Chal Cochran, and Tom Rolfsen); full ownership of the press was transferred to Call and Lucas in 1955.

33. The relationship between Pan-Graphic and the Mattachine Society raised eyebrows as then (as today) there were suspicions about the intertwining of activism and commerce and who should profit from activist work. On this question, see Alexandra

Chasin, *Selling Out: The Gay and Lesbian Movement Goes to Market* (New York: Palgrave, 2000).

34. [Hal Call], "Report of the Publications Chairman," Mattachine Society convention, 14–15 May 1955.

35. Ibid.

36. Ibid.

37. Ken Burns, "[To] All Members," 18 November 1954, DLP, GLBTHS.

38. Chal [Cochran] to Ken Burns, 14 November 1954, DLP, GLBTHS.

39. One of the critiques of the homophile organizations is that they remained invisible and thus unimportant to the majority of gay men and lesbians in the 1950s and 1960s. Lillian Faderman contributed to this opinion in *Odd Girls and Twilight Lovers: A History of Lesbian Life in Twentieth-Century America* (New York: Columbia University Press, 1991) when she wrote, "according to a mid-'60s study, only 2 percent of American homosexuals were even aware of the existence of homophile organizations" (192) and then cited Edwin Schur's *Crimes Without Victims: Deviant Behavior and Public Policy* (Englewood Cliffs, NJ: Prentice-Hall, 1965) as the source of her claim. However, Schur, a sociologist, did not produce his estimate from sound research but instead cited the work of Donald Webster Cory and John LeRoy as the source of his statistics. What ended up as a statement of fact in Faderman's book is nothing more than a tentative statement by Cory and LeRoy, the source of the estimate, who wrote, "Although no reliable figures are available, we would guess that not more than one or two percent of all the inverts in this country are even aware of the homosexual organizations and the significance of their work," *The Homosexual and His Society: A View from Within* (New York: Citadel Press, 1963), 247. Aside from the subjective nature of Cory's study, it is unclear whether the population to which Cory referred was the percentage among people with latent homosexual desire (a Kinsey-type figure) or the percentage of homosexuals already connected by some means to the gay world. Aside from the folly of making demographic claims about the gay world of the 1950s and 1960s in general, the source of this particular claim is highly dubious and should be treated with great skepticism.

40. [Cochran] to Burns.

41. See Hal Call to Ken Burns, 10 February 1955, DLP, GLBTHS.

42. See Harry Silver, "Vag Lewd: A Criticism of the California Statute," "Mattachine Newsreel," and "Inverts Are Not a Distinct Personality Type," all in *Mattachine Review,* January–February 1955.

43. Carl B. Harding [Elver Barker], "Whom Should We Tell?" *Mattachine Review,* August 1956, 8–14.

44. Mr. R. B., Australia, Readers Write, *Mattachine Review,* May 1959, 23–24; the article to which the man was referring was Harry Benjamin, "Self-Acceptance v. Rejection," *Mattachine Review,* March 1958.

45. J. M., New York, Readers Write, *Mattachine Review,* November–December 1955, 28.

46. For more on this, in the context of lesbianism, see Marianne Cutler, "Educating the 'Variant,' Educating the Public: Gender and the Rhetoric of Legitimation in *The Ladder* Magazine for Lesbians," *Qualitative Sociology* 26, no. 2 (summer 2003): 233–55; and Martin Meeker, "A Queer and Contested Medium: The Emergence of Representational Politics in the 'Golden Age' of Lesbian Paperbacks, 1955–1963," *Journal of Women's History* 17, no. 1 (spring 2005): 165–88.

47. Mattachine Review, board of directors meeting minutes, 4 September 1955, DLP, GLBTHS.

48. "Report to Subscribers," *Mattachine Review,* September–October 1955, 22A. As far as I have been able to tell, however, the large order from the New York distributor did not continue for very long; I suspect that because of legal problems encountered by *ONE* magazine, the New York distributor ceased to order homophile publications; for this reason and others that I will discuss, the distribution of the *Mattachine Review* declined over the next several years. On the *ONE* case and the decline of the *Mattachine Review,* see Streitmatter, *Unspeakable,* 17–81.

49. "Readership and Reaction," *San Francisco Bay Area Mattachine Society Newsletter,* December 1955.

50. Mattachine Review, board of directors meeting minutes, 4 September 1955, DLP, GLBTHS. The deal for newsstands was as follows: "Magazines are shipped on consignment, with 50% going to dealers or distributor, 50% to the *Review.* Shipments are billed when the following issue is sent from San Francisco. Full credit is made for unsold copies. Dealers can't lose"; letter to *Mattachine Review* subscribers, ca. November 1955, DLP, GLBTHS. For an insightful discussion of how newsstands dealt with homophile publications, see Craig Loftin, "Passionate Anxieties: McCarthyism and Sexual Identities in the United States, 1945–1965" (forthcoming diss.).

51. See Boyd, *Wide Open Town,* 99–100.

52. Lt. Eldon Bearden as told to Terry Hansen, "Don't Call Us 'Queer City,'" *Men,* ca. March 1955, 11–12, 60–63.

53. Ibid.

54. "S.F. Meeting Places Hit," *San Francisco Examiner,* 27 July 1954, 1; "New Military Squad Cracks Down on Bars," *San Francisco Examiner,* 29 July 1954, 1. For more on relations between the homosexual community and the police, see Boyd, *Wide Open Town;* and Chris Agee, "The Streets of San Francisco: Blacks, Beats, Queers and the San Francisco Police Department, 1950–1968" (forthcoming diss.).

55. Ernest Lenn, "Police Order Renews Drive on Sex Deviates," *San Francisco Examiner,* 26 May 1955, idem, "State Fights Bar Hangouts of Deviates," *San Francisco Examiner,* 25 May 1955, idem, "State Set to Accuse Four Deviate's Bars," *San Francisco Examiner,* 8 June 1955, and idem, "Five Bay Area Bars Accused by State in Morals Drive," *San Francisco Examiner,* 10 June 1955.

56. For more on the consequences that came with the formation of the ABC, see Boyd, *Wide Open Town,* chapters 2 and 3; and Agee, "The Streets of San Francisco."

57. See Sol M. Stoumen, Appellant, v. George R. Reilly, et. al., Respondents, 37 C.2d 713; 234 P.2d 969, 28 August 1951.

58. Dal McIntire [Jim Kepner], "Tangents," *ONE,* October–November 1956, 18.

59. Harry Graham, "What Makes Fairies Kill?" *SIR Magazine,* March, 1957, 19; on Fraden, also see "The Homosexual," *USA Inside Report,* December 1961, Ephemera Collection, GLBTHS. Lesbian paperback writer Vin Packer (Marijane Meaker) popularized the Fraden case in her novel, *Whisper His Sin* (New York: Fawcett Gold Medal, 1954).

60. On Leopold and Loeb, see Paula Fass, "Making and Remaking an Event: The Leopold and Loeb Case in American Culture," *Journal of American History* 80, no. 3 (1993): 919–951; on the Beekman Hill scandal, see Charles Kaiser, *The Gay Metropolis, 1940–1996* (New York: Houghton Mifflin, 1997), 19–26.

61. For a more detailed account of this particular feud, see Martin Meeker,

"Come Out West: Communication and the Gay and Lesbian Migration to San Francisco, 1940s–1960s" (Ph.D. diss., University of Southern California, 2000), 160–64.

62. "Recommendations of the San Francisco Area Council to the Third Annual Convention of the Mattachine Society, Inc." and "Constitution and By-Laws," revised May 1956, both in DLP, GLBTHS. Also see Don Lucas, interview by the author, 11 September 1999.

63. See, for example, the *San Francisco Mattachine Society Newsletter,* 15 August 1954.

64. *San Francisco Mattachine Society Newsletter,* 15 July 1954. The directory of publications was followed with this query: "Can you translate any of these languages? Because publications related to the sex variant problem are received by offices of the Mattachine Society, but lenders in many—if not all—instances are at a loss to translate them, because the publications are written in several different languages. Translators, therefore, are welcome and needed."

65. See: James Baldwin, *Giovanni's Room* (New York: Dial, 1956); and Robert Lindner, *Must You Conform?* (New York: Rinehard and Company, 1956), of particular interest to Dorian readers of *Must You Conform?* was chapter 2, "Homosexuality and the Contemporary Scene."

66. For a more thorough treatment of the Dorian Book Service and the *Dorian Book Service Quarterly,* see Meeker, "Behind the Mask of Respectability."

67. "Worth Looking Into?" *Dorian Book Service Quarterly,* first quarter 1960

68. "Report to Subscribers," *Dorian Book Service Quarterly,* fourth quarter 1960.

69. While Call and Lucas did not test obscenity laws within the context of the Mattachine Society, they commended those who did, like Barney Rosset of Grove Press; see Lucas's letter to Rosset quoted in David Allyn, *Make Love, Not War: The Sexual Revolution, An Unfettered History* (Boston: Little, Brown and Company, 2000), 63. Though the editors of the *Quarterly* changed regularly, the mainstays were Call, Lucas, Lewis Christie, Earl Holbrook, and Rolland Howard. Adding another layer of veneer to the mask, Call allowed Pan-Graphic Press to print but not publish under its name the short-lived magazine *Sex and Censorship* (1958–1959), which took a more aggressive anticensorship stance than even the *Quarterly;* see "The Magazine Folded, But Problem Lingers On," *Dorian Book Service Quarterly,* first quarter 1960, 16–20.

70. For background on obscenity and literature, see Edward de Grazia, *Girls Lean Back Everywhere: The Law of Obscenity and the Assault on Genius* (New York: Random House, 1992); and Rochelle Gurstein, *The Repeal of Reticence: A History of America's Cultural and Legal Struggles Over Free Speech, Obscenity, Sexual Liberation, and Modern Art* (New York: Hill and Wang, 1996). For a useful discussion of the relationship of sex to the First Amendment, see William Eskridge, Jr., *Gaylaw: Challenging the Apartheid of the Closet* (Cambridge, MA: Harvard University Press, 1999), 174–204.

71. H. L. C. [Hal Call], "Report of the Publications Chairman to the Coordinating Council," 1 March 1954, DLP, GLBTHS.

72. Thomas Waugh writes, "Statistics on the outreach of the magazines are easy to find but not as easily confirmed . . . One knowledgeable 1965 circulation estimate is 100,000 for the largest and most conservative of the small physique magazines, *Tomorrow's Man.* While one of the 'gayer' magazines, *Grecian Guild Pictorial,* estimated 75,000 total readers of physique magazines at the peak of the late fifties," *Hard to Imagine: Gay Male Eroticism in Photography and Film from Their Beginnings to Stonewall* (New York: Columbia University Press, 1996), 217.

73. Elver Barker to "Members of the Editorial Board, Mattachine Review," DLP, GLBTHS. A more complete study of pen pal clubs and other correspondence societies would make an excellent topic for further examination, including the way in which language was manipulated by club members and the fact that such clubs and societies have been a consistently important part of gay male culture throughout the twentieth century and, with added dimension of the Internet, into the twenty-first century.

74. Ibid.

75. Hal Call to Elver Barker, 26 December 1956, DLP. In the same letter Call added the following explanatory statement: "Same way with *Physique Pictorial:* In their new issue, they told their readers who might be interested in the homosexual problem to write to us and to *One,* and gave our addresses. This mention was made in connection with a short article in PP about 'Body Building and Homosexuality,' in which they said there was no particular connection to their knowledge, but supposed that homos appeared in body-building ranks about as frequently as in any other walk of life. We were glad he mentioned us, but, as Bob Mizer of PP requested, we 'won't return the favor,' because that WOULD put the kiss of death upon physique photos—see what I mean? Incidentally, we have got 12 replies from the mention in PP already." Also see letters from Bob Mizer to Hal Call, 22 October 1956 and January 1957, box 103-202, Hal Call Papers, One Institute; and "Homosexuality and Bodybuilding" *Physique Pictorial,* fall 1956, 17.

76. Call ended his letter by assuring Barker that, despite his misgivings about the society's involvement in such a club, it would not be a problem for Barker to participate on an individual basis. Hal Call to Elver [Barker], 26 December 1956, DLP, GLBTHS. For more on this issue, see Lyn Pedersen (Jim Kepner), "Why Not a Pen Pal Club?" *ONE,* September 1959, 5–9; William Lambert (Dorr Legg), "Sick Sick Sick," *ONE,* September 1959, 9–13; and "Readers on Writers," *ONE,* January 1960, 5–11.

77. For a critical perspective on the article, see John Arnold, "One More Phoney Expose," *ONE,* November 1958, 26–28.

78. *United States v. Zuideveld and Zuidevleld,* U.S. Court of Appeals, 7th Circuit, 316 F.2d 873 (1963). Both Zuidevelds were sentenced to one-year prison terms, but they were suspended to thirty days plus two years probation for Nirvana and five months plus two years probation for Jack. Of the three not convicted, two were found not guilty, and a third died before going to trial. I thank Bill Eskridge for this citation.

79. Ibid.; the Zuidevelds also owned Nirvack Publishing, which published *Vim* and *Gym,* the male physique magazines through which most men learned of the Adonis Male Club.

80. Again, for accounts that devote considerable attention to the Mattachine Society yet elide its anticensorship work or legislative reform, see, D'Emilio, *Sexual Politics, Sexual Communities;* and Streitmatter, *Unspeakable.*

81. And the Mattachine Society also helped other organizations deal with problems encountered when paving the paths of communication; for instance, in late 1958 the society held a daylong "Publications Workshop and Seminar" for all those involved in the West Coast homophile movement with the goal of strategizing methods for confronting obscenity laws that were beginning to strangle the distribution of their publications; see, Hal [Call] to Ron [Argall] and Bill [?], undated [ca. Late 1958], DLP, GLBTHS.

82. *The Homosexual in Our Society,* published transcript, KPFA-FM, Berkeley, CA, 24 November 1958 (San Francisco: Pan-Graphic Press, 1959); also see "2-Hour Broadcast on Homophile Problem," *Ladder,* January 1959, 7–14. On the history of KPFA, see

Matthew Lasar, *Pacifica Radio: The Rise of an Alternative Network* (Philadelphia: Temple University Press, 1999).

83. This and the following quotes from the broadcast are from *The Homosexual in Our Society.*

84. D. Stewart Lucas to KPFA, undated letter [ca. late 1958], DLP, GLBTHS.

85. Hal Call, "Challenge Ahead," *San Francisco Area Council Newsletter,* June 1958.

86. "James Fugate" [James Barr Fugate] to "Mr. Burns, and friends of the Mattachine," 9 May 1955, DLP, GLBTHS.

87. The *Chronicle* and the *Sun-Reporter* ads are part of the "Mattachine Foundation" FBI surveillance files, 100-37394-40 and 100-37394-42, Lyon-Martin Papers, GLBTHS. The first *Stanford Daily* ad appeared on the second page of the 14 May 1958 issue; the campus newspaper ran the ad six times but stopped running it by the end of 1958 when the "editorial policy" of the publication changed; see Readers Respond, *Mattachine Review,* December 1958, 12. I thank Gerard Koskovich for this citation.

88. See "Mattachine Salutes 'On the QT,'" *Mattachine Review,* April 1959, 2; Seymour Krim and David McReynolds, "Revolt of the Homosexual," *Village Voice,* reprinted in *Mattachine Review,* May 1959, 4–12.

89. See D'Emilio, *Sexual Politics, Sexual Communities,* 119–121; also Elver Barker, letter to the author, 21 September 1999.

90. Carl B. Harding [Elver Barker] to board of directors, Mattachine Society, Denver Area Council members, One, Inc., and the Daughters of Bilitis, Inc., 11 June 1959, DLP, GLBTHS.

91. Ibid.

92. Ibid.

93. "Dal McIntire" [Jim Kepner], "Tangents: News and Views," *ONE,* October 1959, 14–17; also see Dal McIntire [Jim Kepner], "The Campaign That Deviated," *ONE,* November 1959, 6–12; and "Mattachine Breaks Through the Conspiracy of Silence," *Ladder,* October 1959, 5–8.

94. "Sex Deviates Make S. F. Headquarters," *San Francisco Progress,* 7–8 October 1959, 1.

95. Russell Wolden, "The Truth about the Mayor's 'Clean' City—An Expose!" KNBC, 7 October 1959, 6:45 P.M., transcript, DLP, GLBTHS.

96. See "Wolden File, Article Registry," DLP, GLBTHS.

97. Hal Call to Dr. [Wardell] Pomeroy, 27 October 1959, DLP, GLBTHS.

98. Ibid.

99. "Christopher Victory Seen," *San Francisco Examiner,* 1 November 1959, 1; "GOP Elated by Victory," *San Francisco Examiner,* 5 November 1959, 1.

100. Back in Denver, however, the break in publicity that first seemed good quickly turned bad: the vice squad arrested one of the Denver Mattachine members on possession of pornography and instilled "a wave of fear" in the chapter's other members; see D'Emilio, *Sexual Politics, Sexual Communities,* 121.

101. See the editorial condemning Wolden's smear tactics, "Unforgivable Slur on San Francisco," *San Francisco Examiner,* 9 October 1959, 1; the *Ladder* reported that "the reaction of all three [San Francisco] papers following Wolden's 'expose' was almost unanimous. Although the *Chronicle* is an independent paper, the *Examiner* a Hearst paper and the *News-Call Bulletin* a combination of Hearst and Scripps Howard, all three called the Wolden blast 'smear.' And all three were eminently fair to the one or-

ganization primarily involved—the Mattachine Society," "The Role of the Press," *Ladder,* November 1959, 12.

102. Hal Call to Dr. [Wardell] Pomeroy, 27 October 1959, DLP, GLBTHS.

103. Wolden, "The Truth about the Mayor's 'Clean' City."

104. Hal Call to Dr. [Wardell] Pomeroy, 27 October 1959.

105. D'Emilio, *Sexual Politics, Sexual Communities,* 122.

106. Hal Call to Dr. [Wardell] Pomeroy, 27 October 1959; in this letter, Call also reported that in the twenty days since the story broke, the Mattachine Society gained ten new memberships while not losing any other members due to fear or panic. As the Mattachine Society basked in its prestige, however, the city's bars didn't fare so well. Following the campaign, reelected Mayor Christopher initiated a "clean-up" campaign against the bars to shore up his reputation; see D'Emilio, *Sexual Politics, Sexual Communities,* 182.

107. Marshall McLuhan, *Understanding Media: The Extensions of Man* (1964; Cambridge, MA: MIT Press, 1994), 349.

108. The scandal was briefly reported in the *New York Times,* and *Time* carried the following tidbit in its 16 November 1959 issue: "In his wild-swinging campaign, opponent Wolden accused Christopher's administration of permitting San Francisco to become national headquarters of 'organized sex deviates.' [Because of] the charge, which cosmopolitan San Francisco considered bad manners, . . . [he was] walloped by more than 50,000 votes."

109. Examples such as these suggest that the process by which "gay" and "lesbian" became globally salient identities began much earlier than the 1970s, 1980s, and 1990s, the decades upon which most scholarship has focused; see Dennis Altman, *Global Sex* (Chicago: University of Chicago Press, 2001).

110. Jess Stearn, *The Sixth Man* (New York: Doubleday, 1961); on the impact of Stearn's book and other popular sociological literature on individual gays and lesbians, see Jeffrey Escoffier, "Homosexuality and the Sociological Imagination: Hegemonic Discourses, the Circulation of Ideas, and the Process of Reading in the 1950s and 1960s," in *American Homo: Community and Perversity* (Berkeley: University of California Press, 1998), 79–98.

111. Stearn's account of a brutal gay bashing on Fire Island is a perfect example: as soon as the reader develops some sympathy for the gay victim, Stearn suggests that sympathy is unwarranted by adding a concluding remark, characteristically uttered by another gay man: "I suppose you'd call him a prostitute"; see Stearn, *The Sixth Man,* 75.

112. Stearn, *The Sixth Man,* 198–199.

113. Ibid., 200–205

114. Ibid., 205.

115. Ibid., 208

116. Ibid.

117. Escoffier, "Homosexuality and the Sociological Imagination," 92–93.

118. The March 1961 issue of the *Review* sold a total of 2,244 copies, with 1,515 sold at newsstands and with 73 distributed outside the United States; see "Statistics Review Mailings" and "Subscriptions by State," DLP, GLBTHS.

119. Lucas, interview by the author, 11 September 1999.

120. On some of the activities, see John Cavanagh, *Counseling the Invert* (Milwau-

kee: Bruce Publishing, 1966); and Guy Wright, "A Self-Help Organization for Men of the Third Sex," *San Francisco News-Call Bulletin,* 25 July 1961, 21.

121. See, for example, David Beito, *From Mutual Aid to the Welfare State: Fraternal Societies and Social Services, 1890–1967* (Chapel Hill: University of North Carolina Press, 2000).

122. ["Salomeo Aquino"] to "The President, The Mattachine Society," 11 September 1961, DLP, GLBTHS.

123. Ibid.

124. Ibid.

125. [Aquino] to "Mr. Lucas," 23 July 1962, DLP, GLBTHS.

126. On the patterns by which people connect to well-linked hubs in their search for information, see Albert-László Barabási, *Linked: The New Science of Networks* (Cambridge: Perseus, 2002), 57–58.

127. "Calling Shots," *Mattachine Review,* January 1959, 27–28.

128. Ibid.

129. F. K., "Office Traffic Increases," *San Francisco Area Council Mattachine Society Newsletter,* November 1958, 4.

130. "Standard Operating Procedures," board minutes, 13 September 1954, DLP, GLBTHS.

131. Ibid.

132. The assertion that the policy never changed comes after reading through all remaining Mattachine Society documents in the Don Lucas collection and a large portion of the Hal Call Papers, One Institute, Los Angeles, CA; the only change in procedure (though not policy) started occurring in the 1960s as the society itself began handling more cases on its own and, in some instances, psychologists and doctors began referring patients to counselors at the society.

133. "Coming out" in this passage refers both to coming out into the gay world as well as coming out as homosexual in the mainstream public sphere; this second sense of "coming out" was pioneered by the homophiles as a political strategy with the goal of challenging the twin problems suffered by homosexuals during the period: silence and stereotyping. See "Office Traffic Increases," *San Francisco Area Council Mattachine Society Newsletter,* November 1958, 4; also see "Social-Service Dept. 'Swamped,'" *San Francisco Area Council Mattachine Society Newsletter,* February 1959, 3, 7.

134. For more on the society's social service activities, see Meeker, "Behind the Mask of Respectability."

135. See Lucas, interview by Paul Gabriel, GLBTHS. Also see Nan Alamilla Boyd, "San Francisco Was a Wide-Open Town: Charting the Emergence of Gay and Lesbian Communities through the Mid-Twentieth Century" (Ph.D. diss., Brown University, 1995)," 123–132, for a mention of aid provided by the Mattachine Society to the victims of a raid on a lesbian bar.

136. Historians who have looked at gay life in rural areas argue that homosexuals were not as isolated as previously thought. The evidence I found, however, complicates this notion by demonstrating that isolation and connection are processes and that in many rural areas homosexuals remained isolated to one degree or another. On homoerotic life in the rural South, see John Howard, *Men Like That: A Southern Queer History* (Chicago: University of Chicago Press, 1999).

137. ["Thomas J. Forman"] to the Mattachine Society, 29 March 1962, DLP, GLBTHS.

138. Ibid.

139. Ibid.

140. [Thomas J. Forman] to the Mattachine Society, 16 April 1962, DLP, GLBTHS.

141. [Thomas J. Forman] to Don Lucas, 30 June 1962, DLP, GLBTHS.

142. Ibid.

143. Ibid.

144. Don Lucas to [Thomas J. Forman], 5 October 1962, DLP, GLBTHS. Only a small portion of the correspondence received by the society remains, and virtually no record of the thousands of telephone calls and office visits is preserved beyond documents indicating that they happened. That Forman's plea was not uncommon is obvious when reading the few hundred remaining letters and from the impressions I gained while interviewing Hal Call and Don Lucas.

145. Ibid.

146. See, "Comparative Statistics for a 12 Month Period—Mail Received," DLP, GLBTHS. Also see "Office Calls Statistics," "Telephone Calls Statistics," and "Record Mail Received," DLP, GLBTHS. Comparative statistics exist only for 1960–1961 and 1961–1962; for later statistics, see Call, "Breakthrough: When Will it Come?" *Mattachine Review*, April–September 1964, 5.

147. [Thomas J. Forman] to Don Lucas, 24 March 1963, DLP, GLBTHS.

148. Ibid.

149. Dr. Joel Fort often served as the liaison between the society and professionals working in mental institutions; see Dr. Joel Fort, interview by Paul Gabriel, 30 July 1997, GLBTHS.

150. Lucas, interview by Gabriel, tape 10, GLBTHS.

151. Ibid.

152. As far as I can tell, most of the Mattachine Society's "clients" were men; generally, when the organization received letters from women, whether lesbian or "questioning," the staff referred them to the Daughters of Bilitis, the organization in San Francisco run by and for lesbians.

Chapter 2

1. Del Martin and Phyllis Lyon, *Lesbian / Woman* (1972; Volcano, CA: Volcano Press, 1991), 219; also see John D'Emilio, *Sexual Politics, Sexual Communities: The Making of a Homosexual Minority in the United States* (Chicago: University of Chicago Press, 1983), 92–125.

2. Martin and Lyon, *Lesbian / Woman*, 219.

3. Nan Alamilla Boyd, *Wide Open Town: A History of Queer San Francisco to 1965* (Berkeley: University of California Press, 2003).

4. Martin and Lyon, *Lesbian / Woman*, 291–220.

5. Ibid., 221.

6. Ibid., 222.

7. Ibid., 221. My research has led me to think that the terms "middle-class" and "working-class" have become overly polarized in the writing of 1950s and 1960s lesbian history; specifically, I think that the term "middle-class" is problematic to use to describe women living lesbian lives in the 1950s considering the precarious status of jobs and living arrangements; for these women, I think it useful to add the word "striving" to account for their precarious class status. On the role of class in lesbian communities and in lesbian organizations, see Elizabeth Lapovsky Kennedy and Madeline

Davis, *Boots of Leather, Slippers of Gold: The History of a Lesbian Community* (New York and London: Routledge, 1993); and Katie Gilmartin, "'We Weren't Bar People': Middle-Class Lesbian Identities and Cultural Spaces," *GLQ: Gay Lesbian Quarterly* 3 (1996): 1–51.

8. Martin and Lyon, *Lesbian / Woman*, 11.

9. Ibid., 224.

10. For biographical information on Del Martin and Phyllis Lyon, see Martin and Lyon, *Lesbian / Woman*; D'Emilio, *Sexual Politics, Sexual Communities*; Kay Tobin and Randy Wicker, *The Gay Crusaders* (New York: Paperback Library, 1972); and Vern Bullough, ed., *Before Stonewall: Activists for Gay and Lesbian Rights in Historical Context* (Harrington Park Press, 2003). Also, Del Martin and Phyllis Lyon, interview by the author, 23 August 2000.

11. "Marvin Cutler" was a pen name used by longtime One, Inc., leader Dorr Legg.

12. Daughters of Bilitis, "Aims and Purposes," in *Homosexuals Today*, ed. Marvin Cutler (Los Angeles: ONE, 1956), 104. The statement of purpose was also published on the inside front cover of every issue of the *Ladder.*

13. Martin and Lyon, *Lesbian / Woman*, 224; the explanation continued: "Homosexuals today are not seeking tolerance; they are demanding total acceptance. But one must consider the times in which the DOB came into being. Just the month prior to the first publication, police had raided the Alamo Club . . . loading thirty-six patrons into their paddy wagons. DOB was also born on the heels of the United States State Department scandals of the early fifties, when hundreds of homosexual men and women had been summarily fired from their jobs with the federal government when their identity had been disclosed or even hinted at. Most Lesbians were completely downtrodden, having been brainwashed by a powerful heterosexual church and by the much-touted precepts of psychoanalysis. There was not the sense of community or solidarity that exists today. Lesbians were isolated and separated—and scared."

14. See, for example, *We Two Won't Last* (Greenwich, CT: Gold Medal Books, 1963), 46–48, in which author Ann Aldrich quotes a few lesbians who express this point of view. On the relationship between lesbians in and out of the DOB, see Boyd, *Wide Open Town;* and Kennedy and Davis, *Boots of Leather, Slippers of Gold.*

15. Historian Nan Alamilla Boyd makes a convincing argument that a number of women involved with lesbian bars in San Francisco were driving forces behind the move to establish lesbian rights to assembly; however, like the divide between homophile leaders and participants, leaders of the bar scene (whose livelihoods depended on the operation of bars) were likely to be far more politically committed than the casual bar patron who could simply look for another bar if one was shut; see Boyd, *Wide Open Town.*

16. On the 1954 U.S. Supreme Court decision, *Brown v. Board of Education of Topeka*, see Taylor Branch, *Parting the Waters: America in the King Years, 1954–63* (New York: Simon and Schuster, 1988). On questions of integration and conformity, see Barbara Stephens, "A Plea for Integration," *Ladder* May 1957, 17–18, and idem, "What Mental Health Is Not," *Ladder*, June 1957, 20–21, in which the author encourages readers to understand integration and conformity are not one and the same and asserts mental health "is not conformity. The mature person has the ability to stand apart from the crowd when conditions indicate."

17. Phyllis Lyon (?) to Mr. and Mrs. Larry Collins, 22 February 1958, Lyon-Martin Papers (hereafter LMP), GLBTHS.

18. D'Emilio, *Sexual Politics, Sexual Communities*, 103.

19. George Chauncey, *Gay New York: Gender, Urban Culture, and the Making of the Gay Male World, 1890–1940* (New York: HarperCollins, 1994), 179–205.

20. Martin and Lyon, *Lesbian / Woman*, 227.

21. DOB circular quoted in Sarah Elizabeth Boslaugh, "A History of the Lesbian Periodical *The Ladder,* 1956–1972" (M.A. thesis, University of Chicago, 1984), 45.

22. Kennedy and Davis, *Boots of Leather, Slippers of Gold,* 150.

23. Martin and Lyon, *Lesbian / Woman,* 223.

24. For a complete history of *The Ladder* see, Boslaugh, "A History of the Lesbian Periodical."

25. Lillian Faderman, *Odd Girls and Twilight Lovers: A History of Lesbian Life in Twentieth-Century America* (New York: Penguin, 1992), 130. On the image of the lesbian in postwar and 1950s America, see Kate Adams, "Making the World Safe for the Missionary Position: Images of the Lesbian in Post–World War II America," in *Lesbian Texts and Contexts: Radical Revisions,* ed. Karla Jay and Joanne Glasgow (New York: New York University Press, 1990), 255–274; Estelle Freedman, "'Uncontrolled Desires': The Response to the Sexual Psychopath, 1920–1960," *Journal of American History* 74 (June 1987): 83–106; Estelle Freedman, "The Prison Lesbian: Race, Class, and the Construction of the Aggressive Female Homosexual, 1915–1965," *Feminist Studies* 22, no. 2 (summer 1996): 397–423; and Donna Penn, "The Sexualized Woman: The Lesbian, the Prostitute, and the Containment of Female Sexuality in Postwar America," in *Not June Cleaver: Women and Gender in Postwar America,* ed. Joanne Meyerowitz (Philadelphia: Temple University Press, 1994), 358–381.

26. Edmund Bergler, *Homosexuality: Disease or Way of Life?* (New York: Hill and Wang, 1956), 246–247, quoted in Jennifer Terry, *An American Obsession: Science, Medicine, and Homosexuality in Modern Society* (Chicago: University of Chicago Press, 1999), 312.

27. On the Tommy's Place raid, see Nan Alamilla Boyd, "San Francisco Was a Wide-Open Town: Charting the Emergence of Gay and Lesbian Communities through the Mid-Twentieth Century" (Ph.D. diss., Brown University, 1995), 123–132.

28. Ibid., 123.

29. "Pulp" refers to a particular technique used in cheap book production in a historically specific era, roughly 1896–1953. On pulps, see Eric Smith, *Hard-Boiled: Working-Class Readers and Pulp Magazines* (Philadelphia: Temple University Press, 2000). On the history of the paperback, see Thomas Bonn, *UnderCover: An Illustrated History of American Mass Market Paperbacks* (New York: Penguin Books, 1982); and Kenneth Davis, *Two-Bit Culture: The Paperbacking of America* (Boston: Houghton Mifflin Company, 1984).

30. On the lesbian paperback, see Adams, "Making the World Safe for the Missionary Position"; Yvonne Keller, "Pulp Politics: Strategies of Vision in Pro-Lesbian Pulp Novels, 1955–1965," in *The Queer Sixties,* ed. Patricia Juliana Smith (New York: Routledge, 1999), 1–25; Chris Nealon, *Foundlings* (Durham: Duke University Press, 2001), 141–175; and Suzanna Danuta Walters, "And Her Hand Crept Slowly up Her Thigh: Ann Bannon and the Politics of Pulp," *Social Text* 23 (1989): 83–101.

31. See Tereska Torres, *Women's Barracks* (New York: Gold Medal Books, 1950).

32. Adams, "Making the World Safe for the Missionary Position," 258.

33. Ibid., 259, 258.

34. For example, there is no evidence that leaders of the DOB ever wished the magazine to be distributed in lesbian bars; whether bar owners would have allowed the DOB to distribute magazines in their saloons is another matter.

35. Martin and Lyon quoted in Boslaugh, "A History of the Lesbian Periodical," 58.

36. "Sherry Horn" to Del Martin, 31 October 1956, LMP, GLBTHS. Not everyone, of course, thought so much of the *Ladder*. In a number of cases, lesbians, having never seen anything like it, did not know what to make of it; one wrote to Del Martin, "As for knowing others who might be interested in 'The Ladder'—of all the people we do know, I can't think of anyone who would be. Of course, you're used to such discouragement . . . but I'll ask around and find out. I mean, I'll really plug it! . . . I think your publication is a great thing, but I do wonder about these meetings you hold. It seems that those attending and listening to a discussion are the very ones who would least benefit from hearing what is said. Other than the social aspect of a group, I don't yet see the purpose . . . We don't know too many girls down here, guess San Francisco has more to offer—everyone goes there—When we finish college, we may join the crowd, too." "Beth Ryan" to Del Martin, 9 October 1956, LMP, GLBTHS.

37. Sherry Horn to Del Martin, 31 October 1956, LMP, GLBTHS.

38. It is worthwhile to note that the DOB received discounted rates from the printers, one of whom was gay, the other not.

39. "Mary Beals" to Del [Martin], 1 November 1956, LMP, GLBTHS; [Mary Beals] to [Martin and Lyon], 30 April 1957, LMP, GLBTHS; [Mary Beals] to Del [Martin] and Phil [Lyon], 11 May 1957, LMP, GLBTHS.

40. For an elaboration of ideas about different categories of spatiality, including conceptual space, see David Harvey, *The Condition of Postmodernity: An Enquiry into the Origins of Social Change* (Cambridge: Blackwell Publishers, 1990); and Henri Lefebvre, *The Production of Space* (1974; Cambridge: Blackwell Publishers, 1991).

41. "Kay Ferris" to Del [Martin], 12 November 1956, LMP, GLBTHS.

42. Although the discourse of second-wave feminism that initiated thousands of consciousness-raising groups was not available to DOB members in the 1950s and early 1960s, it is clear that the parallels between DOB groups and later consciousness-raising groups went beyond the discussion format to include similar philosophical goals, the most obvious being the idealization a female-centered epistemology. On feminism and the practice of consciousness raising, see Alice Echols, *Daring to Be Bad: Radical Feminism in America, 1967–1975* (Minneapolis: University of Minnesota Press, 1989); and Ruth Rosen, *The World Split Open* (New York: Penguin, 2000). Other models for feminist discussion groups might be found in bohemian and literary salons, which were often hosted by women.

43. "Florence Ray" to [*Ladder*], 24 October 1958, LMP, GLBTHS.

44. "Jeani Gnapp" to Del Martin, [October 1956], LMP, GLBTHS.

45. Del Martin to Jeani Gnapp, 9 October 1956, LMP, GLBTHS.

46. She added that her brother, "Though not of the minority, has frequently more compassion and empathy than those of the minority have for each other"; Jeani [Gnapp] to Del Martin, 17 October 1956, LMP, GLBTHS.

47. [Gnapp] to Martin, 17 October 1956.

48. Gnapp added, "I, myself, would prefer this organization's creative activities and planned social events far more than time spent in a bar. Afterwhile, bar sitting becomes humdrum and boring regardless of the town's bigness and glamour"; [Gnapp] to Del Martin, 17 October 1956.

49. Ann Ferguson [Phyllis Lyon], "Your Name Is Safe!" *Ladder,* November 1956, 10–12.

50. Ibid.; the DOB's legal counsel was Ken Zwerin, a onetime Mattachine Society member who also served as counsel for that organization for a period of time.

51. Ibid.; although she based her conclusion in logic, it was a logic as yet untested in the courts; see *United States v. Rumely*, 345 U.S. 41 (1953).

52. Phyllis Lyon, "Ann Ferguson Is Dead!" *Ladder*, January 1957, 7.

53. Elizabeth Eisenstein, *The Printing Revolution in Early Modern Europe* (Cambridge: Cambridge University Press, 1983), 85.

54. Jeani [Gnapp] to Del Martin, 24 October 1956, LMP, GLBTHS.

55. [Del Martin] to Jeani [Gnapp], 25 October 1956, LMP, GLBTHS.

56. Ibid.

57. On the prohibition of homosexuals in the civil service, see David Johnson, *The Lavender Scare: The Cold War Persecution of Gays and Lesbians in Federal Government* (Chicago: University of Chicago Press, 2004); on the prohibition in the military, see Randy Shilts, *Conduct Unbecoming: Lesbians and Gays in the U.S. Military* (New York: St. Martin's Press, 1993).

58. Along with contributing to DOB's increasing inventory of people, Gnapp, as a teacher and librarian, provided the DOB with invaluable information about how to locate previously published books on homosexuality as well as advice on how to build and organize the DOB library; see Jeani [Gnapp] to Del [Martin], 6 December 1956, LMP, GLBTHS.

59. Jeani [Gnapp] to Del [Martin], 6 December 1956, LMP, GLBTHS. Del Martin replied to Gnapp a few days latter to "extend the invitation of two of the girls who said you would be welcome to stay with them. They have a couch in their front room which they claim is more comfortable than their own bed"; Del [Martin] to Jeani [Gnapp], 10 December 1956, LMP, GLBTHS.

60. [Gnapp] to Phyl and Del and Sandy, 8 January 195[7], LMP, GLBTHS.

61. Jeani [Gnapp] to "All," 30 March 1957, LMP, GLBTHS.

62. The exact date of Gnapp's move has not survived, but clear evidence of her move is provided by a subsequent change of address request postcard send to the DOB, noting her relocation from Fillmore Street to Shrader Street, both in San Francisco; see Jeani Gnapp, change of address postcard, 24 September 1957, LMP, GLBTHS.

63. See Rodger Streitmatter, *Unspeakable: The Rise of the Gay and Lesbian Press in America* (Boston: Faber and Faber, 1995), 28–29; also see Craig Loftin, "Passionate Anxieties: McCarthyism and Sexual Identities in the United States, 1945–1965" (forthcoming diss.).

64. H. S. [Helen Sanders?] to Del [Martin], LMP, GLBTHS.

65. The situation was somewhat different for more male-oriented homophile magazines which often were placed alongside male physique magazines on newsstands and, in the case of *ONE* magazine, included the word "homosexual" on the masthead (although the word "homosexual" often graced the cover of the *Mattachine Review*).

66. Kennedy and Davis, *Boots of Leather, Slippers of Gold*, 167.

67. H. S. [Helen Sanders?] to Del [Martin].

68. John Jensen to Del [Martin], 25 January 1960, LMP, GLBTHS. About six months earlier, Jensen warned Martin that "the censorship problem is at an all-time fever-pitch right now"; John Jensen to Del Martin, 18 July 1959, LMP, GLBTHS.

69. A number of the Supreme Court cases most often cited as evidence for the decline of censorship in the 1950s and 1960s (e.g., *Roth v. U.S., Ginzburg v. U.S.*) actually upheld the convictions of those arrested for producing and distributing obscene materials, thus leaving an ambiguous legacy. See Edward de Grazia, *Girls Lean Back Everywhere: The Law of Obscenity and the Assault on Genius* (New York: Random House, 1992).

70. For more on Gittings's tenure as editor, see Marc Stein, *City of Sisterly and Brotherly Loves: Lesbian and Gay Philadelphia, 1945–1972* (Chicago: University of Chicago Press, 2000), 220–243; and Streitmatter, *Unspeakable*, 54–78.

71. Barbara Gittings quoted in Streitmatter, *Unspeakable*, 55.

72. Del [Martin] to Mary S. Beals, 22 November 1956, LMP, GLBTHS.

73. Del Martin, "Why a Chapter in Your Area?" *Ladder*, February 1957, 7.

74. Phyllis Lyon to Maureen, DOB New York chapter president, 22 January 1962, LMP, GLBTHS.

75. Martin, "Why a Chapter in Your Area?"

76. D'Emilio, *Sexual Politics, Sexual Communities*, 115.

77. Helen Sanders to "Del and Phyl" [Del Martin and Phyllis Lyon], 3 February 1961, LMP, GLBTHS.

78. Phyllis Lyon and Del Martin, "Cleo Glenn (Bonner)" in *Before Stonewall*, 189–190; on African American women in the DOB, see Del Martin, "Pat Walker (1938–1999)" in *Before Stonewall*, 191–192, and "Interview with Ernestine," *Ladder*, June 1966, 4–11.

79. For more on race, class, and the definition of homosexuality, see Siobahn Somerville, *Queering the Color Line: Race and the Invention of Homosexuality in American Culture* (Durham: Duke University Press, 2000); Jennifer Terry, *An American Obsession: Science, Medicine, and Homosexuality in Modern Society* (Chicago: University of Chicago Press, 1999); and Lisa Walker, *Looking Like What You Are: Sexual Style, Race, and Lesbian Identity* (New York: New York University Press, 2001).

80. Phyllis Lyon to "Sue Marks," President, DOB Chicago chapter, 24 March 1962, LMP, GLBTHS; also see minutes, Chicago area provisional chapter, Daughters of Bilitis, 9 March 1962, LMP, GLBTHS.

81. Ibid.

82. Miranda Joseph offers a critique of the way in which community excludes as well as includes in *Against the Romance of Community* (Minneapolis: University of Minnesota Press, 2002).

83. "Jan Sheeler" to the *Ladder*, 21 July 1964, LMP, GLBTHS; emphasis in the original. Also see Reader's Respond, *Ladder*, June 1959, 24.

84. "Walli Polanski" to "Friends" [DOB], 14 October 1958, LMP, GLBTHS.

85. "Walli Polanski" to Del [Martin], 7 December 1958, LMP, GLBTHS.

86. Billie Tallmij to Walli [Polanski], 11 December 1958, LMP, GLBTHS.

87. And Gnapp was not alone in this regard. In 1959, only a few short months before the Wolden-Christopher scandal broke, Barbara Gittings of the New York chapter wrote to Del Martin, in an only somewhat sarcastic tone, informing Martin of the imminent departure of two members of the New York chapter. Gittings wrote, "Alas, they plan to move to San Francisco in October. Now Del, have pity on your thousands of sisters all across the country whose prophets and scholars desert them thus! You'll have no chapters if you encourage this exodus to your gayer social clime," Barb[ara Gittings] to Del [Martin], 9 August 1959, LMP, GLBTHS.

Introduction to Part 2

1. Marshall McLuhan, with graphics by Quentin Fiore and Jerome Agel, *The Medium Is the Massage* (1967; San Francisco: HardWired, 1996), 24.

2. R. E. L. Masters, *The Homosexual Revolution* (New York: Julian Press, 1962), xi.

3. At the heart of his book, Masters gave the future a time capsule, providing an eerily accurate answer to the question, "What do the homosexuals want?" His answer, by way of a nine-point litany, included the right to serve in the armed forces, recognition of same-sex marriages, an end to sodomy laws, fair representation in the mass media, and freedom to seek romantic relationships in public places like bars. All of the items yet to be achieved continue to be stated albeit controversial goals of the liberal organized gay and lesbian rights movement. See Masters, *The Homosexual Revolution*, 128–171.

4. Masters, *The Homosexual Revolution*, xvi.

5. Ibid., xiii.

6. See the first paperback edition: R. E. L. Masters, *The Homosexual Revolution* (New York: Belmont Productions, 1964).

7. Masters, *The Homosexual Revolution*, 71.

8. Ann Aldrich, *We Two Won't Last* (Greenwich, CT: Gold Medal Books, 1963), 133.

9. Ibid., 126.

10. See, for example, James Baughman, *The Republic of Mass Culture: Journalism, Filmmaking, and Broadcasting in America since 1941* (Baltimore: Johns Hopkins University Press, 1992) and Erika Doss, ed., *Looking at Life Magazine* (Washington: Smithsonian, 2001).

Chapter 3

1. Ann Aldrich [Marijane Meaker], *We Walk Alone* (Greenwich, CT: Gold Medal Books, 1955); idem, *We, Too, Must Love* (Greenwich, CT: Gold Medal Books, 1958); idem, ed., *Carol in a Thousand Cities* (Greenwich, CT: Gold Medal Books, 1960); idem, *We Two Won't Last* (Greenwich, CT: Gold Medal Books, 1963). Aldrich published one additional book in 1972, *Take a Lesbian to Lunch* ([New York]: MacFadden-Bartell, 1972); Jess Stearn, *The Grapevine* (Garden City, NY: Doubleday, 1964).

2. *One, Incorporated, v. Olesen, Postmaster of Los Angeles* (1958); the Court issued the decision without an opinion, but it did cite the Roth decision, which had redefined and generally shrunk the scope of what could be considered obscene, see *Roth v. United States* (1957).

3. On the fortunes of Hall's book, see Edward de Grazia, *Girls Lean Back Everywhere: The Law of Obscenity and the Assault on Genius* (New York: Random House, 1992), 165–208; and Leslie Taylor, "'I Made Up My Mind to Get It': The American Trial of *The Well of Loneliness*, New York City, 1928–1929," *Journal of the History of Sexuality* 10, no. 2 (2001): 250–286.

4. Bergler quoted in Aldrich, *We, Too, Must Love*, 170.

5. For an account of many of the articles as well as the CBS special, see Edward Alwood, *Straight News: Gays, Lesbians, and the News Media* (New York: Columbia University Press, 1996).

6. Tereska Torres, *Women's Barracks* (Greenwich, CT: Gold Medal Books, 1951); on *Women's Barracks*, see Yvonne Keller, "Pulp Politics: Strategies of Vision in Pro-Lesbian Pulp Novels, 1955–1965," in *The Queer Sixties*, ed. Patricia Juliana Smith (New York: Routledge, 1999), 1–25. Details from my account are drawn from a telephone interview I conducted with Ann Aldrich (Marijane Meaker) on 10 May 2004; Meaker worked as a "reader-secretary" for Gold Medal editor Dick Carroll shortly after the publication of *Women's Barracks*.

7. "Vin Packer," *Spring Fire* (Greenwich, CT: Gold Medal, 1952); see the 2004 edi-

tion of *Spring Fire* reissued by San Francisco's Cleis Press for a new introductory essay written by "Vin Packer."

8. Aldrich, interview.

9. Aldrich, *We Walk Alone*, vii.

10. W. E. B. DuBois, *The Souls of Black Folk* (1903; New York: Penguin Putnam, 1995); and James Weldon Johnson, *Autobiography of an Ex-Colored Man* (1912; New York: Vintage, 1989).

11. Elizabeth Francis, *The Secret Treachery of Words: Feminism and Modernism in America* (Minneapolis: University of Minnesota Press, 2002), 141. Aldrich, interview.

12. Aldrich, who frequented New York lesbian bars between about 1951 and 1958, remembered that in addition to the many mafia-run bars, a few enterprising lesbians took over the leases of legitimate bars whose owners were looking to get out of the business and then ran a lesbian bar for the few months or years remaining on the lease, largely out of sight of the police and the mafia. Aldrich, interview.

13. Aldrich, *We Walk Alone*, 57, 66, 57.

14. Aldrich, *We, Too, Must Love*, 71.

15. For discussions of readers of lesbian paperbacks see, Keller, "Pulp Politics"; Chris Nealon, *Foundlings* (Durham: Duke University Press, 2001), 141–175; and Suzanna Danuta Walters, "And Her Hand Crept Slowly Up Her Thigh: Ann Bannon and the Politics of Pulp," *Social Text* 23 (1989): 83–101.

16. Aldrich, *We, Too, Must Love*, 171.

17. On lesbian readership and the relationship of reading to identity formation, see Monica Bachmann, "'Someone like Debby': (De)Constructing a Lesbian Community of Readers," *GLQ* 6, no. 3 (2000): 377–388.

18. Lesbian author Ann Bannon similarly expressed frustration, writing, "The female readers wrote from little towns all over the country. Such was their isolation that many of them were grateful to me for reassuring them that they were not totally alone in the world . . . These women lived in a world where they thought themselves to be painfully unique . . . But these letters overwhelmed me. What to tell them? I was being appealed to for help as if I were a lesbian Ann Landers. Little did they know it was a case of the blind leading the blind. What could I, in my naiveté, possible say that would help them through their sexual exile, give them warmth and hope?" Ann Bannon, "Introduction: The Beebo Brinker Chronicles," in *Odd Girl Out* (San Francisco: Cleis Press, 2001), x–xi.

19. One of the main narrators describes just such a failed quest in the fantastic documentary, *Forbidden Love: The Unashamed Stories of Lesbian Lives*, written and directed by Aerlyn Weissman and Lynn Fernie (New York: Women Make Movies, 1992).

20. For a more lengthy examination of the Aldrich/DOB debates, see Martin Meeker, "A Queer and Contested Medium: The Emergence of Representational Politics in the 'Golden Age' of Lesbian Paperbacks, 1955–1963," *Journal of Women's History* 17, no. 1 (spring 2005): 165–88.

21. Del Martin, "An Open Letter to Ann Aldrich," *Ladder,* April 1958, 4–6.

22. Aldrich, *We Two Won't Last*, 119; see Damon's review of *We Two Won't Last*, in the *Ladder*, October 1963, 18–20.

23. Aldrich, *We Two Won't Last*, 16.

24. Aldrich's activities were confirmed in subsequent issues of the *Ladder* in which it was reported, "Aside from the mail you yourself [Aldrich] have received and graciously forwarded, letters and subscriptions have been pouring into the DOB office.

One letter addressed simply to 'Daughters of Bilitis, San Francisco, California' reached us," Readers Respond, *Ladder,* October 1960, 19.

25. Aldrich interview.

26. Stearn, *The Grapevine,* 5. Stearn's reference to "Sweet Thursday" is the only such reference I have uncovered in my extensive research into the history of homosexuality; whether he repeated a rumor, had the wool pulled over his eyes, or manufactured the idea himself remains a mystery.

27. Ibid., 5.

28. Ibid., 6.

29. See "The Lesbian in Mass Media," *Ladder,* August 1962, 16–19.

30. Ibid., 16.

31. Ibid., 17.

32. See John LeRoy, "The New Publicity Break: Where Do We Go From Here?" *Ladder,* December 1962, 16–17.

33. Del Martin to Marion Glass, 30 September 1962, Lyon-Martin Papers, GLBTHS.

34. Jess Stearn to Phyllis [Lyon] and Del [Martin], 23 December 1962, Lyon-Martin Papers (hereafter LMP), GLBTHS.

35. Jess Stearn to Phyllis [Lyon] and Del [Martin], 23 December 1962, LMP, GLBTHS.

36. Jess Stearn to Del [Martin] and Phyl [Phyllis Lyon], 8 March 1963, LMP, GLBTHS.

37. Ibid.

38. The influence upon Martin and Lyon (along with Don Lucas of the Mattachine Society) of what might be called New Age spirituality is as of yet unexplored, but it might just have been a meeting ground for Stearn (who later wrote about past lives and prophecy) and Lyon and Martin (who had been associated with the Prosperos School of Thane of Hawaii); see Properos files, LMP, GLBTHS.

39. [Del Martin] to Jess [Stearn], 30 April 1963, LMP, GLBTHS.

40. Del Martin to Daughters of Bilitis governing board and chapter presidents, 30 April 1963, LMP, GLBTHS.

41. Stearn, *The Grapevine,* 2.

42. Ibid., 14–15.

43. Ibid., 17–18, 93, 101.

44. Ibid., 248.

45. Ibid., 268.

46. Ibid., 281–282.

47. Ibid., 283.

48. Ibid. The ruling I assume to which he is referring is *One, Incorporated, v. Oleson* (1958).

49. Stearn, *The Grapevine,* 284, 295.

50. On mapping identity, see Joseph Boone, et al., ed., *Queer Frontiers: Millennial Geographies, Genders, and Generations* (Madison: University of Wisconsin Press, 2000); Gordon Brent Ingram et al., eds., *Queers in Space: Communities, Public Places, Sites of Resistance* (Seattle: Bay Press, 1997); and Patricia Yeager, ed., *The Geography of Identity* (Ann Arbor: University of Michigan Press, 1996).

51. Stearn, *The Grapevine*, 39–40, 204, 202.

52. Ibid., 115.

53. Ibid., 125.

54. Ibid., 163, 176, 184.

55. Ibid., 363.

56. Ibid., 348.

57. Lesbian paperbacks were generally reviewed only in the homophile press. Stearn's books were reviewed in local newspapers, national newsmagazines, and academic journals as well as in the homophile press. In addition to the review in *Library Journal* and those discussed below, blurbs from the 1970 paperback edition show that it also was reviewed in the San Bernardino *Sun Telegram,* Virginia Kirkus's *Bulletin, News-Sentinel* [Fort Wayne], *Publisher's Weekly, Star* [Chicago Heights], *Times* [St. Petersburg], *Independent* [San Francisco Bay Area], *News and Courier* [Charleston], and *Weekly* [Chapel Hill].

58. Eleanor Smith, "Review: *The Grapevine,*" *Library Journal,* 15 February 1964, 874–875.

59. Midge Decter, "Changing Tactics in the Battle of the Sexes," *Book Week,* 1 March 1964, 3.

60. Jess Stearn to Del [Martin] and Phyl [Phyllis Lyon], n.d., ca. early 1964, LMP, GLBTHS.

61. On the Long John Nebel show see unknown correspondent to "B" [Barbara Gittings] and "K" [Kay Lahusen], 1 March 1964, LMP, GLBTHS.

62. On Kennedy's *Contact,* see P. G., "Boston: Jess Stearn Makes CONTACT," *Ladder,* May 1964, 13–14. On the Vincent Tracy show, see Lee Nelson quoted in Barbara [Gittings] to Cleo [Glenn], ca. April 1964, LMP, GLBTHS.

63. V. P., "The Fourth Sex: The Lesbian; Review of *The Grapevine* by Jess Stearn," *Ladder,* January 1964, 4–5.

64. Ibid.

65. Gene Damon, "The Literary Scene," *Mattachine Review,* October 1964, 25.

66. Martin and Lyon, *Lesbian/Woman,* 55.

67. R. D., New York, "Readers Respond," *Ladder,* April 1964, 23.

68. Miss H. L. to "Madam" [DOB], 2 March 1964, LMP, GLBTHS.

69. Del Martin to H. L., 4 March 1964, LMP, GLBTHS.

70. See Donald Webster Cory, *The Homosexual in America: A Subjective Approach* (New York: Greenberg, 1951); Frank Caprio, *Female Homosexuality: A Psychodynamic Study of Lesbianism* (New York: Citadel, 1954); Alfred Kinsey, *Sexual Behavior in the Human Male* (Philadelphia: W.B. Saunders Co., 1948) and idem, *Sexual Behavior in the Human Female* (Philadelphia: W.B. Saunders Co., 1953).

71. Lee Dorian, *The Other Men* (North Hollywood, CA: Viceroy Books, 1966); Tor Erikson, *The Half-World of the American Homosexual* (North Hollywood, CA: Brandon House, 1966); Donald Gilmore, *Soixante Neuf: A Study of Oral-Genital Sex* (Torrance, CA: A Banner Book, Monogram Publications, 1968); also see Doris Hanson, *No Mans Land* (A Europa Original; New York: L.S. Publications, Corp., 1967), which uses "The Lesbian Grapevine" as a chapter title. These books were privately held by historian and antiquarian book dealer Gerard Koskovich at the time that I consulted them but they have since been acquired by Yale University library; I shall cite them here as the Koskovich Paperback Book Collection, or KPBC.

72. Miss X as told to Doris Hanson, *The Intimate Story of a Lesbian* (An Original Imperial Book; New York: L.S. Publications, 1965), 7–8, KPBC.

73. Lee Dorian, *The Young Homosexual* (New York: Imperial Books, L.S. Publications, 1965), 33, KPBC.

74. Ken Worthy, *The New Homosexual Revolution* (New York: Imperial, L.S. Publications, 1965), 87, 156, 174, 187, KPBC.

75. See Matt Bradley, *Faggots to Burn!* (Hollywood, CA: Intimate Books published by Art Enterprises, Inc., 1962); Roger Blake, *The Homosexual Explosion!* (North Hollywood, CA: Brandon House, 1966). Both books found in the KPBC.

76. The phrase "under the mattress library" came from Ann Aldrich; Aldrich, interview. Although university and public libraries did not collect paperback originals until very recently, the DOB kept a rather large library of such books and lesbian paperbacks also formed some of the initial collections of lesbian and gay community archives that were founded in the 1970s and 1980s. During one oral history interview, a narrator showed me her collection of paperbacks (including several Aldrich books) that she had proudly displayed in her living room, see Carol Seajay, interview by the author, San Francisco, CA, 28 March 1998 and 9 April 1998.

77. Copies of the first edition of *The Grapevine* can be found in 8 of the 9 University of California campus libraries. A total of two Aldrich books can be found in the UC library system, both of which are held at UC Davis.

78. Seajay, interview, 28 March 1998 and 9 April 1998.

79. Seajay qualified her statement: "Now what I learned as an adult and activist is it takes one lesbian to publish a magazine." Seajay was the publisher of—though not sole contributor to—*The Feminist Bookstore News*. Seajay, interview, 28 March 1998.

80. This issue of the *Ladder* to which Seajay was referring was May–June 1968.

Chapter 4

1. On the increasingly sexualized culture of the United States in the 1960s, see David Allyn, *Make Love Not War: The Sexual Revolution: An Unfettered History* (Boston: Little, Brown, and Company, 1999); Edward de Grazia, *Girls Lean Back Everywhere: The Law of Obscenity and the Assault on Genius* (New York: Random House, 1992); and John D'Emilio and Estelle Freedman, *Intimate Matters: A History of Sexuality in America* (New York: Harper & Row, 1988), 275–343.

2. The famous *Life* "essay" is actually two separately authored pieces: Paul Welch, with photographs by Bill Eppridge, "Homosexuality in America," *Life*, 26 June 1964, 66–74; and Ernest Havemann, "Scientists Search for the Answers to a Touchy and Puzzling Question: Why?" *Life*, 26 June 1964, 76–80. On *Life* magazine generally, see Erika Doss, ed., *Looking at Life Magazine* (Washington, D.C.: Smithsonian Institution, 2001); Wendy Kozol, *Life's America* (Philadelphia: Temple University Press, 1994); Curtis Prendergrast with Geoffrey Colvin, *The World of Time Inc.: The Intimate History of a Publishing Enterprise, 1941–1960* (New York: Antheneum, 1986); and Loudon Wainwright, *The Great American Magazine: An Inside History of Life* (New York: Alfred A. Knopf, 1986).

3. Mattachine Society president Hal Call claimed the issue sold out to "30 million readers"; "Paul Welsh [sic] Discusses Life Article Reaction," *Town Talk*, July 1964, 1. He later added that its circulation was "possibly surpassing the Kennedy assassination issue is some cities." "The Old Order Is Changing Whether We Like It Or Not," *Town Talk*, October 1964, 3. Former League for Civil Education president and San Francisco publisher Guy Strait claimed the 26 June issue sold 18 million copies and that "a day or

so after it was put on the newsstands there was not a copy to be found in most of the cities of the country." "Life," *Citizen's News*, 20 July 1964, 1–2. Call's and Strait's claims, though, each must be approached with some skepticism, as the recorded statistics reveal conflicting figures: The 26 June 1964 issue sold 7,288,348 copies (subscription and newsstand combined), which, according to Bill Hooper, Time, Inc., archivist, meant "the circulation of the June 26, 1964 issue of LIFE, was good, but not a record breaker . . . Several issues during that statement period had circulation figures that exceed 7.4 million." Hooper added, "According to the Audit Bureau of Circulations statement for the '6 Months Ending December 31, 1963,' LIFE definitely was a recipient of a pretty dramatic jump in sales as a result of Kennedy's assassination. Average circ[ulation] for that statement period was around 7.1 million—but jumped to—7.4–7.7 million for the three issues in November and December surrounding JFK's death. The final issue of 1963 (a special issue on 'The Movies') sold 7.9 million issues (a public desperate from some escapism after the previous month's news?)." Bill Hooper, e-mail to the author, 18 March 1999. Call and Strait were either misinformed or, perhaps, they exaggerated or invented figures for the purpose of political hyperbole in a willful act of image creation. Call's estimation that 30 million people read the issue was probably close to accurate considering that several people likely read each issue of *Life* in circulation.

4. Paul Welch, with photographs by Bill Eppridge, "Homosexuality in America," *Life International*, 27 July 1964, 44–52; and Ernest Havemann, "Why?" *Life International*, 27 July 1964, 53–58; Ernest Havemann, with photographs by Bill Eppridge, "El Drama del Homosexualidad," *Life en Español*, 26 October 1964. Although the editors provided a brief introduction and captions to the photographs, the text published in *Life en Español* was significantly different from the other published versions—the Welch text was omitted and replaced by a longer version of the Havemann essay, "Why?" that appeared in the U.S. and international editions.

5. Leo Richards, "Profusion: Confusion," *Drum*, May 1965, 23–24; this article also contained a bibliography listing twenty-two magazine articles about homosexuality published in 1964.

6. Examining the *Readers' Guide to Periodical Literature*, March 1963–February 1965 and March 1965–February 1966, Edward Alwood pointed out that more stories about homosexuality appeared in 1964 than in the previous three years combined; *Straight News: Gays, Lesbians, and the News Media* (New York: Columbia University Press, 1996), 50.

7. Observers at the time noted that two lengthy articles in *MacLean's*, Canada's newsmagazine, were important precedents; yet, because of its geographic distance and slight distribution in the United States, these articles will not be included in this study. See Sidney Katz, "The Homosexual Next Door," *MacLean's*, 22 February 1964, 10–30; and idem, "The Harsh Facts of Life in the 'Gay' World," *MacLean's*, 7 March 1964, 18–38. Marc Stein also has identified two important articles published in *Greater Philadelphia Magazine* in 1961 and 1962, see his *City of Sisterly and Brotherly Loves: Lesbian and Gay Philadelphia, 1940–1970* (Chicago: University of Chicago Press, 2000), 211–219.

8. William Helmer, "New York's Middle-Class Homosexuals," *Harper's*, March 1963, 85–92; Robert C. Doty, "Growth of Overt Homosexuality in City Provokes Wide Concern," *New York Times*, 17 December 1963, 1. Other important essays and newspaper articles published around the same time include Jean White's five-part series on homosexuality published in the *Washington Post*, 31 January–4 February 1965; and "The Homosexual in America," *Time*, 21 January 1966, 41.

9. Helmer, "New York's 'Middle-Class' Homosexuals." On one homophile's interpretation of this article, see G. Desmannes, "The Gay Bourgeoisie," *Ladder,* April 1963, 4–7.

10. On "deviance" and community, see Howard Becker, *Outsiders* (New York: The Free Press, 1963); Erving Goffman, *The Presentation of Self in Everyday Life* (New York: Doubleday, 1959); idem, *Encounters* (Indianapolis: Bobbs-Merrill, 1961); and idem, *Stigma: Notes on the Management of Identity* (New York: Prentice Hall, 1963).

11. Helmer, "New York's 'Middle-Class' Homosexuals," 88.

12. Doty, "Growth of Overt Homosexuality."

13. This approach builds upon so-called "balanced" or "objective" mode of discussing homosexuality first pursued by authors like Aldrich and Stearn. On the emergence of media objectivity in the coverage of homosexuality, see Larry Gross and James Woods, "Introduction: Being Gay in American Media and Society" in *The Columbia Reader on Lesbians and Gay Men in Media, Society, and Politics,* ed. Larry Gross and James Woods (New York: Columbia University Press, 1999), 3–22.

14. Alwood, *Straight News,* 50.

15. On Andy Warhol, see John Coplans, "Crazy Golden Slippers," *Life,* 21 January 1957, 12–13; on the Beats, see "Big Day for Bards at Bay," *Life,* 9 September 1957, 105.

16. Ralph Graves, telephone interview with the author, 14 September 1999.

17. On collective and personal memory, see Maurice Halbwachs, *The Collective Memory,* trans. Francis Ditter and Vida Yazdi Ditter (1950; New York: Harper & Row, 1980); David Paul Nord, Robert McGlone, and Jacquelyn Dowd Hall, "The Uses of Memory: A Round Table," *Journal of American History* 85, no. 2 (1998): 409–465; Alessandro Portelli, *The Death of Luigi Trastulli and Other Stories: Form and Meaning in Oral History* (Albany: State University of New York Press, 1991).

18. Kozol, Life's *America,* vii; see Mitchell Stephens, *The Rise of the Image, the Fall of the Word* (New York: Oxford University Press, 1999), 70–130.

19. I was able to pinpoint late February 1964 as the time when the *Life* journalists visited San Francisco because of a reference to the visit in a letter from Don Lucas on 7 March 1964, in which he stated, "It seems that we [Mattachine Society] are really arriving as far as being recognized as a reliable source of information on the whole aspect of homosexuality. We have just spent the last two weeks working with LIFE magazine on a story they are doing on the subject." Don Lucas to Harold Sylvester, 7 March 1964, Don Lucas Papers, GLBTHS.

20. Although the *Life* reporters spoke with the Daughters of Bilitis about lesbian life in San Francisco, there was only a passing mention of lesbians in the resulting article. Welch and Eppridge also visited Los Angeles and New York to collect material. According to Edward Alwood, "The day LIFE reporter Paul Welch and photographer Bill Eppridge walked into Don Slater's office at *One* [magazine] in Los Angeles, the volunteer staff practically dived under their desks in fear of being exposed in a national magazine. But Slater was far from apologetic about his homosexuality; in fact, he was the antithesis of sad and sordid. Not only did he allow LIFE to interview him for the article, but he agreed to allow the magazine to use his photograph. In addition, he served as a guide for the reporter and his photographer, showing them the gayest sections of Los Angeles." Alwood, *Straight News,* 51.

21. Hal Call quoted in Eric Marcus, *Making History: The Struggle for Gay and Lesbian Equal Rights, 1945–1990* (New York: HarperCollins, 1992), 65.

22. Ibid., 65, 63.

23. Call was arrested in Chicago in August 1952 on what he claimed were trumped-up charges of indecent behavior; see Marcus, *Making History*, 60–61.

24. On the making of queer icons in the 1960s, see Patricia Juliana Smith, "Introduction: Icons and Iconoclasts: Figments of Sixties Queer Culture," in *The Queer Sixties*, ed. Patricia Juliana Smith (New York: Routledge, 1999), xi–xxvi.

25. "Masculine and not feminine" does not mean "straight rather than gay" or "humorless instead of camp." In fact, sometime in the late 1950s or early 1960s, Call produced a campy, progay membership card to the fictitious organization "M.A.N."—Men Against Nellies—a faux-group of ostensibly masculine homosexuals; see "M.A.N.," Don Lucas papers, GLBTHS.

26. Because many of *Life*'s readers were subscribers, they unwittingly brought information about homosexuality into their homes—thus making the subscription magazine closer to the broadcast medium of television than the selective medium of a book.

27. In this context, the nascent movement for gay civil rights began pursuing its rather contradictory political program: asking for the right of homosexuals to be left alone through a vocal and visible demonstration that they were just like everyone else.

28. On the Tool Box, see Gayle Rubin, "The Valley of the Kings: Leathermen in San Francisco, 1960–1990" (Ph.D. diss., University of Michigan, 1994); also see her published essays: "Elegy for the Valley of the Kings: AIDS and the Leather Community in San Francisco, 1981–1996," in *In Changing Times: Gay Men and Lesbians Encounter HIV/ AIDS*, ed. Martin Levine, Peter Nardi, and John Gagnon (Chicago: University of Chicago Press, 1997), 101–144, and idem, "The Miracle Mile: South of Market and Gay Male Leather, 1962–1997," in *Reclaiming San Francisco: History, Politics, Culture*, ed. James Brook, Chris Carlsson, and Nancy Peters (San Francisco: City Lights Books, 1998), 247–272. Also see Jack Fritscher, "Artist Chuck Arnett: His Life/Our Times," in *Leatherfolk: Radical Sex, People, Politics, and Practice*, ed. Mark Thompson (Boston: Alyson, 1991), 106–118; and [Mike Caffee], "The Tool Box," unpublished essay [1999], in the author's possession.

29. San Francisco's first motorcycle / leather bar was the Why Not?, located at 518 Ellis Street in the Tenderloin; the short-lived bar was open from 1960 to 1962. Members of the motorcycle and leather scene point out that several bars in the old Embarcadero or waterfront of San Francisco were favorites of seamen, trade, and other rough types prior to the 1960s. South of Market was to become the "home" of the biker / leather / S-M sexual subculture in the 1960s and, especially, by the 1980s when there were at least twenty-five bars, clubs, and bathhouses—making it one of the most densely populated queer sites in the world. See Eric Garber and Willie Walker, "Queer Bars and Other Establishments in San Francisco" (San Francisco: GLBTHS, unpublished report, 1999).

30. On the genesis of the motorcycle clubs see Rubin, "Valley of the Kings," 128–133.

31. Mike Caffee, interview by the author, 26 July 1999, San Francisco, CA.

32. Ibid.

33. According to my sources, motorcycles with leather came first, leather as a fashion or lifestyle on its own followed shortly thereafter; Caffee, interview; Bill Reque, interview by the author, 8 September 1999, San Francisco, CA; and Bill Tellman, interview by the author, 18 May 1999, 8 June 1999, San Francisco, CA.

34. Reque, interview. Call later said, "We chose [to show the *Life* reporters the Tool Box] because it had a particular black-and-white mural of macho, leather cowboy types." Hal Call quoted in Marcus, *Making History*, 65.

35. Reque, interview; Caffee, interview. Call also was well acquainted with Tool Box employee, Mike Caffee, who worked for Call at Pan-Graphic Press and was listed on the masthead of the April–September 1964 issue of the *Mattachine Review* as "art director."

36. The following account of *Life's* examination of San Francisco's gay world comes from interviews with Call, Lucas, Reque (Tool Box manager), Caffee (Tool Box barback), and Tellman (Tool Box bartender).

37. In actuality, Reque was less than cavalier about the mass media exposing the gay world; he said, "I think frankly that at this point that had I been an owner of that bar or really involved with that bar and really cared about that bar that much, I would have probably said, 'No' [to *Life*]"; Reque, interview.

38. It is not clear, however, that the reporters from *Life* ever gained explicit permission from the bar's absentee owners in Los Angeles.

39. Hal Call quoted in Marcus, *Making History*, 65.

40. See also *Albert Vallerga and Mary Azar v. Department of Alcoholic Beverage Control and Russell S. Munro*, S.F. 20285, Petition for the Modification of Opinion Without Change in the Judgment and Petition for Rehearing, California Supreme Court. *Vallerga v. ABC* was the California Supreme Court decision that affirmed the right of homosexuals to gather in public places (i.e., bars). On the consequences of the decision, see Nan Alamilla Boyd, *Wide Open Town: A History of Queer San Francisco to 1965* (Berkeley: University of California Press, 2003), 181–184, 206–207; also see Call, interview; Larry Howell, interview by the author, San Francisco, 17 December 1998, 13 January 1999; and Bill Plath, interview by Paul Gabriel, 18 April 1997, Oral History Collection, GLBTHS.

41. Actually, the Black Cat Café lost its liquor license, forcing it to stop serving alcohol, which effectively ended its career as a bar. On the fascinating history of the Black Cat Café and the key role it played in San Francisco's gay community formation, see Boyd, *Wide Open Town*, 211–212. On the Tay-Bush Inn raid, see "A Gay Café Party—89 Men, 14 Women Held," *San Francisco Examiner*, 14 August 1961, 1.

42. D'Emilio, *Sexual Politics, Sexual Communities*, 184. The police harassment of San Francisco gay bars and gatherings continued virtually unabated until January 1965, when the police harassment of a gay benefit dance backfired and the city's newspapers and liberal churches came out in support of the gay community's right to be left alone.

43. On the crossing of cultural boundaries, see the abundant literature on sexuality and space: David Bell and Gill Valentine, eds., *Mapping Desire: Geographies of Sexualities* (London and New York: Routledge, 1995); Joseph Boone, "Queer Sites in Modernism: Harlem / The Left Bank/Greenwich Village," in *The Geography of Identity*, ed. Patricia Yeager (Ann Arbor: University of Michigan Press, 1996), 243–272; and Beatriz Colomina, ed., *Sexuality and Space* (New York: Princeton Architectural Press, 1992).

44. On Arnett, see Gayle Rubin, "Valley of the Kings"; Jack Fritscher, "Artist Chuck Arnett: His Life / Our Times"; Robert Opel, "Requim for a Toolbox," *Drummer*, August / September 1975, 28; Bill Tellman, interview by the author, 18 May 1999, 8 June 1999; and Caffee, interview.

45. Robert Ajemian, "Scranton on Uphill Trail," *Life*, 26 June 1964, 28–37. The 1964 Republican national convention was to be held in San Francisco shortly after *Life* localized homosexuality there.

46. On the appearance of similar identities in underground cinema, see Juan Antonio Suarez, *Bike Boys, Drag Queens and Superstars* (Bloomington: Indiana University Press, 1996).

47. Not to mention that his pants were so tight, as Tool Box bartender Bill Tellman remembered, "You could see what religion he is." Bill Tellman, interview by the author, 18 May 1999.

48. Welch, "Homosexuality in America."

49. Vito Russo, *The Celluloid Closet: Homosexuality in the Movies*, rev. ed. (New York: Harper & Row Publishers, 1987), 16; and George Chauncey, *Gay New York: Gender, Urban Culture, and the Making of the Gay Male World* (New York: BasicBooks, 1994), 328.

50. Kozol, Life's *America*, viii. On gender and representation in the 1960s, see Susan Douglas, *Where the Girls Are: Growing Up Female with the Mass Media* (New York: Times Books, 1994). On race and representation, see Ronald Jacobs, *Race, Media, and Civil Society: From Watts to Rodney King* (New York: Cambridge University Press, 2000).

51. See "Landmark II: Equal Rights," *Life* 26 June 1964, 4.

52. See Jane Howard, "Doom and Glory of Knowing Who You Are," *Life* 24 May 1963, 86B–90.

53. The misspelling of Reque's name in the article as "Ruquy" was done strategically to (thinly) disguise his identity. As far as I can tell, the description of Reque as "part owner of the bar" was simply a mistake.

54. Graves, interview.

55. Welch, "Homosexuality in America." Welch then pointed to the next article in the magazine, a related essay written by Ernest Havemann, a scholar from the Kinsey Institute, on the scientific issues surrounding homosexuality; Havemann concluded his article with resignation: "Many optimistic students of our society believe that we may some day eliminate poverty, slums and even the common cold—but the problem of homosexuality seems to be more akin to death and taxes. Even if every present-day American with the slightest trace of homosexuality could be deported tomorrow and forever banished . . . there would probably be just as many homosexual men in the U.S. a few generations hence as there are now." Havemann, "Why?" *Life,* 26 June 1964, 80.

56. Bill Hooper, e-mail communication to the author, 17 March 1999.

57. "Summary of Mail Received About *LIFE,* June 26, as of July 10, 1964," a *Life* magazine report quoted by Bill Hooper in an email from 17 March 1999. Unfortunately for the researcher, it is not the practice of magazines or newspapers to save all the letters to the editors that they receive; *Life,* however, does kept general statistics about the letters in addition to publishing a few excerpts in a "letters to the editors" column— from these two sources I have formed some general conclusions.

58. Arthur Demeritt, Brooklyn, New York, quoted in Letters to the Editors, *Life,* 17 July 1964, 28.

59. June Wucher, Austin, Texas, in ibid.

60. Tom Tendal, New York, New York, in ibid. The Los Angeles Police Department's entrapment scheme seems to have elicited a great deal of disgust from many presumably heterosexual readers who previously had been unaware of the intense, costly policing burdened on gay men; the San Francisco gay publication *Town Talk* reported on a meeting where the author of the *Life* article, Paul Welch, discussed writing the piece and the actions of the police in Los Angeles. The article reported, "Most impressive impact of the [*Life*] essay on average citizens unaware of the 'gay world' was the conversation of a police officer spending time (and tax dollars) trying to entice a 'solicitation' arrest . . . A man in Berkeley, father of a son and two daughters, seriously questioned this kind of emphasis in law enforcement as desirable." Hal Call, "Paul Welsh [*sic*] Discusses Life Article Reaction," *Town Talk,* July 1964, 1.

61. Patricia Spence, Peoria, Illinois, quoted in Letters to the Editors, *Life*, 17 July 1964.

62. "Summary of Mail Received about *LIFE*, June 26, as of July 10, 1964" a *Life* magazine report, quoted in Bill Hooper, e-mail communication to the author, 17 March 1999.

63. "Name Withheld," Pacific Grove, California, quoted in Letters to the Editors. *Life*, 17 July 1964.

64. "H. Patterson," Los Angeles, California, quoted in Letters to the Editors, in ibid.

65. Herb Caen, *San Francisco Chronicle*, 28 June 1964, 27. Walter Hart was a famous female impersonator who performed for several years at the North Beach cabaret, Finocchio's. Caen regularly mentioned in his column, with characteristic wit, the goings-on in San Francisco's gay world, including this missive published a week after *Life* magazine made the Tool Box famous: "As I noted a few days ago, some of the young fellers who hang out in the Tool Box at Fourth and Harrison wear an 'S' or an 'M' on their shirt pockets, to indicate 'Sadist' or 'Masochist.' Which prompted a relieved message from Harold [Hal] Call. 'I'm so glad you printed that,' he said. 'All this time I thought it meant 'Single' or 'Married.'" Caen, *San Francisco Chronicle*, 3 July 1964, 15.

66. Strait had long been a thorn in the side of the Mattachine Society and Hal Call. Yet, a much-needed study of interorganizational relations would reveal a story as complex as the Napoleonic personalities who founded the organizations; for example, despite writing scathing editorials against Hal Call, Strait nevertheless frequently announced Mattachine Society benefits, such as this ad that appeared next to the masthead of his *Citizen's News* in July 1964: "Benefits in the form of auctions will be held on Tuesday the 21st at D'Oak Room and on the 28th at the Jumpin Frog for the Mattachine Society. Bring junk and buy antiques and help a much needed organization." *Citizen's News*, 20 July 1964. Also see Guy Strait, interview by Olaf Olegard, 30 November 1986, Video History Collection, GLBTHS.

67. "Life," *Citizen's News*, 20 July 1964, 1–2.

68. Ibid. Strait also offered another critique by questioning *Life's* characterization of the Tool Box as a masculine bar that discriminates against queens wearing "fuzzy sweaters and sneakers"; Strait agreed more with the bar's owner, who called the Tool Box "the most genteel bar in town." The "true nature" of biker / leather / S-M bars is and has been a topic of contention over the years in part because of the inherently campy nature of the performance of masculinity in those spaces. Numerous "fuzzy sweater" queens I have interviewed over the years called the Tool Box's bluff, offering witticisms such as: "There would be 48 guys at the bar with leather jackets and helmets and one motorcycle outside." Perry Wood, interview by the author, 2 April 1998. Such lifestyle-based conflicts—and perceived conflicts—deserve further attention.

69. "Heterosexuality in America" marks the beginning of particularly popular brand of queer discourse in which the heterosexual gaze upon homosexuals is refracted in an attempt to demonstrate ludicrous assertions about homosexuality. For a discussion of the gay media's "queering"—or appropriation, resignification, and theatricalization—see David Halperin, *Saint Foucault: Towards a Gay Hagiography* (New York: Oxford University Press, 1995), 48–52.

70. [Guy Strait], "Heterosexuality in America," *Citizen's News*, 20 July 1964, 5–8. Another activist on the radical libertarian edge of the homophile movement was Philadelphia's Clark Polak, who published another satire of "Homosexuality in America"; see "P. Arody," "Heterosexuality in America," *Drum*, October 1964, 1–21. For more on Polak, see Marc Stein, "'Birthplace of the Nation': Imagining Lesbian and Gay Commu-

nities in Philadelphia, 1969–1970," in *Creating a Place for Ourselves,* ed. Brett Beemyn (New York: Routledge, 1997), 253–288.

71. "Heterosexuality in America," *Citizen's News,* 5. The photo of the KKK members was borrowed from the same issue of *Life* that contained "Homosexuality in America."

72. "Heterosexuality in America," *Citizen's News,* 6.

73. Merla Zellerbach, "Odd News about Heterosexuals," *San Francisco Chronicle,* 22 July 1964, 29.

74. Ibid.

75. Ibid.

76. Bill Tellman interview by the author, 18 May 1999.

77. Susan Sontag, "Notes on 'Camp,'" *Partisan Review* 31, no. 4 (fall 1964): 515–530. On camp, also see several essays in Fabio Cleto, ed., *Camp: Queer Aesthetics and the Performing Subject—A Reader* (Ann Arbor: The University of Michigan Press, 1999).

78. Sontag, "Notes on 'Camp.'"

79. Not all gay men responded to the article by being spurred to action. In fact, some gay men responded with a mix of recognition and alarm, such as one man who later wrote, "I'm age 52, from South Dakota . . . that issue [of *Life*] changed my life . . . from that article I understood what I was and that I could be arrested for being gay. It threw me into the closet so completely that I later married," e-mail communication to the author from [name withheld], 2 June 2004. Also see Sky Gilbert, "Age Before Beauty," *Eye* 7 September 2000 (www.eye.net/eye/issue/issue_09.07.00/columns/pink.html).

80. The Mattachine Society in San Francisco was not the only homophile organization to receive inquires as a result of the *Life* article; the archives of the ONE Institute in Los Angeles reveal that One, Inc., also was deluged with mail from homosexuals seeking help and looking to connect with others like themselves.

81. Reverend "Jerry Ross" to the Mattachine Society, 21 July 1964, Don Lucas Papers, GLBTHS. Other historians have reached similar conclusions about the impact of "Homosexuality in America"; for example, in *The Other Side of Silence,* John Loughery quotes a gay Texas man who was in his forties in 1964: "The first time I ever heard of *ONE* or Mattachine was in *Life*. It never would have dawned on me that anything like this was out there." Loughery added, "For hundreds of thousands of gay men, Henry Luce was generously, if unintentionally, instructive: yes, such things were out there; yes, such things were possible in America in the 1960s." Loughery, *The Other Side of Silence,* 258.

82. Reverend Jerry Ross to the Mattachine Society, 21 July 1964. Don Lucas Papers, GLBTHS.

83. Chauncey, *Gay New York,* 1–8.

84. Welch, "Homosexuality in America," *Life International;* Havemann, "El Drama del Homosexualidad," *Life en Español*. According to Bill Hooper, "*Life* moved into the 'global market-place' as a result of printing and distribution networks that were built during WWII. *Life* Overseas–Armed Forces Edition began in October of 1943—and evolved into *Life International* in July of 1946. The International edition then evolved into a separate Atlantic edition and Asia edition in July of 1966. Both of these editions ceased publication in December of 1970. Very briefly, *Life* experimented with an Australian edition, from February 1967 through September 1968. All of these editions were in English. *Life en Español,* began in January of 1953, and ceased publication in December of 1969." Bill Hooper, e-mail communication to the author, 12 April 1999.

85. "H. V. P. Nathan" to Hal Call, 18 December 1964, Don Lucas Papers, GLBTHS. Also see the letter of "Maurice Stein," writing from Istanbul, Turkey: "I owe the pleasure of having your address to the last issue of the 'LIFE INTERNATIONAL' . . . I take the liberty to write you being sure that you could assist me in getting in touch with some members of your Association and being 'decided gays.'" Stein to Hal Call, 28 July 1964, Don Lucas Papers, GLBTHS.

86. H. V. P. Nathan to Call.

87. Ibid.

88. On the globalization of Western sexualities, see Dennis Altman, *Global Sex* (Chicago: University of Chicago Press, 2001); and Elizabeth Povinelli and George Chauncey, eds., *Thinking Sexuality Transnationally* (Durham: Duke University Press, 1999).

89. McLuhan, *The Medium Is the Massage,* 67.

90. "Wes Kincaid" to Hal Call, 2 August 1964, Don Lucas Papers, GLBTHS.

91. Ibid. Though dramatic, Kincaid's letter was not hyperbole, especially when compared to another note addressed the Mattachine Society: "I am a male sexual deviate. I live in an anti-homosexual city [Annapolis, Maryland] and find it very difficult to remain here. I am on the verge of becoming psychoneurotic and I am taking tranquilizers at this time. I need help badly. I *must* get out of this town or, I'm afraid, I will try suicide. I can't find anyone to trust and tell my problem to. I am asking for your help . . . I would like to come to San Francisco." "Ronald Sutton" to the Mattachine Society, 17 December 1964, Don Lucas Papers, GLBTHS.

92. Kincaid to Call.

93. Walter Wedigo Watson, interview by the author, 17 May 1998.

94. Ibid.

95. Ibid. Watson remembered the photograph of the Jumpin' Frog bar as being particularly important: "I remember that picture of the guys in the bar watching the movie . . . I just thought it was cool. I love movies." Watson, interview.

96. Ibid.

97. Ibid.

98. Although the cover of *Life International* was different from its counterpart in the United States, the two articles on homosexuality within were precisely the same.

99. David Barnard, interview by the author, San Francisco, CA, 8 September 1999.

100. Cobbett Steinberg, *San Francisco Ballet: The First Fifty Years* (San Francisco: San Francisco Ballet Association, 1983), 99; also see Debra Hickenlooper-Sowel, *The Christensen Brothers: An American Dance Epic* (Amsterdam: Harwood Academic Press, 1998), 374–387.

101. "LIFE—A DO-It-Yourself Disaster," libretto by Herb Caen, music by Charles Ives, design by Cal Anderson, and choreography by Lew Christensen (San Francisco Ballet, 1965), San Francisco Performing Arts Library Archives.

102. Ibid.

103. David Barnard, interview by the author, 8 September 1999.

104. The motion was first made at the East Coast Homophile Organizations, 8 August 1964, meeting and then approved at their 19 September meeting; see the minutes of both meetings, Lyon-Martin papers, GLBTHS. A few months prior to this pronouncement, the minutes of ECHO reveal, "Inquiries concerning Mattachine have been received from all over as a result of the LIFE article. A trial free subscription will be sent to inquirers." See meeting minutes, 18 July 1964, Lyon-Martin Papers, GLBTHS.

105. "Kay Tobin" [Kay Lahusen], "Cross-Currents," *Ladder*, July 1964, 23.

106. Ibid.

107. Ibid.

108. See Hal Call, "Breakthrough: When Will it Come?" *Mattachine Review*, April–September 1964, 4–24

109. See Call, "Breakthrough: When Will it Come?"; also see Call, "Paul Welsh [*sic*] Discusses Life Article Reaction," *Town Talk*.

110. Call, "Breakthrough," 5.

111. Ibid., 4; Don Lucas, interview by the author, 11 September 1999.

112. On the Mattachine Society's six "working departments: publications, education, public relations, research, social service, and legal affairs" in the first half of the 1960s, see Mattachine Society, Inc., "Mattachine Society Today" (pamphlet, 1965), Lyon-Martin Papers, GLBTHS.

113. For more on the fate of the Mattachine Society after 1964, see Martin Meeker, "Behind the Mask of Respectability: The Mattachine Society and Male Homophile Practice, 1950s–1960s," *Journal of the History of Sexuality* 10, no. 1 (April 2001): 78–116. For a useful discussion of several of the organizations, see Boyd, *Wide Open Town*, 219–236.

114. Call, "Breakthrough," 5.

115. Ibid.

116. Ibid.

117. Ibid., 6.

118. Ibid.

119. Ibid.

120. Ibid.; Call added, "Four weeks after the LIFE article, we can say at Mattachine that not more than three paid memberships and as many subscriptions have come in as a result," 6–7.

121. Don Lucas, interview by the author, 11 September 1999.

122. On the role of imagination in the process of nation-building, see Benedict Anderson, *Imagined Communities: Reflections on the Origins and Spread of Nationalism* (London: Verso, 1983).

123. On homosexuality in the mass media between 1965 and 1970, see Alwood, *Straight News*, 37–98; and Steven Capsuto, *Alternate Channels: The Uncensored Story of Gay and Lesbian Images on Radio and Television, 1930s to Present* (New York: Ballantine Books, 2000), 46–58.

124. In 1964, Hal Call noted, "Authors of books and magazine articles, as well as reporters for the local and national press have made extensive interviews [at the Mattachine Society], some of which got into print (sometimes unfavorably), but most of which did not. TIME and Christian Science Monitor were two examples where material was submitted from the staff in the field which never saw the light [of] print. Call, "Breakthrough: When Will it Come?," 11; also see "A LOOK at Gay LIFE by Guess Who?" *New York Mattachine Review*, May 1964, 9–10.

125. Certainly more than three important articles appeared in mass circulation magazines between 1964 and 1970, but considering content and impact, these three are among the most important. Also see "The Homosexual in America," *Time*, 21 January 1966, 40–41; "Where the Boys Are," *Time*, 28 June 1968, 80; and "Homosexuality: Coming to Terms," *Time*, 24 October 1969, 82.

126. Jack Star, "The Sad 'Gay' Life," *Look*, 10 January 1967, 31–33.

127. *Time's* 1966 article, "The Homosexual in America," boldly stated, "San Francisco and Los Angeles are rivals for the distinction of being the capital of the gay world; the nod probably goes to San Francisco."

128. "The Homosexual: Newly Visible, Newly Understood," *Time*, 31 October 1969, 56–67.

129. An article on homosexuality in *Time* a month earlier featured another Eppridge photograph: the arrest of a homosexual by Los Angeles police. Considering that the article addressed the costly effects of overly stigmatizing homosexuals, the context of Los Angeles was especially revealing and again reinforced the perspective offered by *Life* in 1964; see "Homosexuality: Coming to Terms," *Time*. *Time* and *Life* had, since the latter's first appearance in 1935, been two separate publications of the same corporation.

130. "The Homosexual: Newly Visible, Newly Understood," *Time*, 31 October 1969, 56–67.

131. Tom Burke, "The New Homosexuality," *Esquire*, December 1969, 178 ff.

132. Ibid.

133. In late 1964, Guy Strait's *Citizen's News* (vol. 4, no. 3) carried this piece, "From the News-Call Bulltin of San Francisco, 'That South of Market bar featured with a two-page spread in Life Mag (June 27 issue), patronized by homosexuals who wear leather jackets, is about to close. Too few customers since that unwelcome notoriety.' Sad, sad, how the misinformation flies. Or perhaps it is not 'misinformation' but sheer bitchery. We keep telling the bartenders to take it easy with the nelly old aunties, they may well be columnists. Anyhow, we can report to Estabula, Ohio and Bugscuffle, Texas that the 'south of Market' bar is not suffering." Indeed, far from it. The Tool Box remained a very popular gay male bar until the early 1970s when it was forced to close because its building was slated for demolition as part of the Yerba Buena redevelopment project, as Rubin explains in "The Miracle Mile," 256–258.

134. Reque, interview; Caffee, interview.

Introduction to Part 3

1. See, for example, William Clements Library, *Do It Yourself!: Self Help Manuals of the Eighteen and Early Nineteenth Centuries* (Ann Arbor: University of Michigan, 1956).

2. Steven Gelber, "Do-It-Yourself: Constructing, Repairing and Maintaining Domestic Masculinity," *American Quarterly* 49, no. 1 (1997): 66–112.

3. On "little magazines," see Mark Morrisson, *The Public Face of Modernism: Little Magazines, Audiences, and Reception, 1905–1920* (Madison: University of Wisconsin Press, 2001); Jayne Marek, *Women Editing Modernism: Little Magazines and Literacy History* (Lexington: University Press of Kentucky, 1995); and Christine Stansell, *American Moderns: Bohemian New York and the Creation of a New Century* (New York: Henry Holt, 2001). For a discussion of the explosion in the number of such publications in the 1950s, see Alan Golding, "Little Magazines and Alternative Canons: The Example of *Origin*," *American Literary History* 2, no. 4 (winter 1990): 691–725.

4. Again, the leaders of the Mattachine Society and the leaders of the DOB were not in complete agreement on this matter, as was detailed in part 1 of this book.

5. On the alternative or underground press in the 1960s, see Lauren Kessler, *The Dissent Press: Alternative Journalism in American History* (Beverly Hills: Sage Publications, 1984); Abe Peck, *Uncovering the Sixties: The Life and Times of the Underground Press* (New York: Pantheon Books, 1985); and Ken Wachsberger, ed., *Voices from the Under-*

ground: Insider Histories of the Vietnam Era Underground Press (Tempe, AZ: Mica's Press, 1993).

6. On the gay and lesbian underground and alternative press of the late 1960s, see Marc Stein, *City of Sisterly and Brotherly Loves: Lesbian and Gay Philadelphia, 1945–1972* (Chicago: University of Chicago Press, 2000); and Rodger Streitmatter, *Unspeakable: The Rise of the Gay and Lesbian Press in America* (Boston: Faber and Faber, 1995).

Chapter 5

1. On nineteenth-century photographic erotica, see Thomas Waugh, *Hard to Imagine: Gay Male Eroticism in Photography and Film from Their Beginnings to Stonewall* (New York: Columbia University Press, 1996); on Tijuana Bibles (pornographic stories putatively printed in Tijuana, Mexico) and reprints of classic erotic novels, see Jay Gertzman, *Bookleggers and Smuthounds: The Trade in Erotica, 1920–1940* (Philadelphia: University of Pennsylvania, 1999); on photostatic reproductions of erotic art, see Thomas Waugh, ed., *Out/Lines: Gay Underground Erotic Graphics before Stonewall* (Vancouver, BC: Arsenal Pulp Press, 2002).

2. There is some debate about whether gay bars were more heavily policed before, during, or after Prohibition. George Chauncey makes the case that a general climate of lawlessness allowed queer bars to thrive in New York during the 1920s but with the creation of a State Liquor Authority in the 1930s, gay nightlife was suppressed. Nan Alamilla Boyd, however, argues that gay bars only became visible in San Francisco during the 1930s. See Chauncey, *Gay New York: Gender, Urban Culture, and the Making of the Gay Male World* (New York: Basic Books, 1994); and Nan Alamilla Boyd, *Wide Open Town: A History of Queer San Francisco to 1965* (Berkeley: University of California Press, 2003).

3. Examples of all three types of information are provided by Chauncey throughout *Gay New York*.

4. Edith Shelton and Elizabeth Field, *Let's Have Fun in San Francisco* (San Francisco: Edith Shelton, 1939), 79–80. Only a small portion of published listings and guidebooks during this period contained references to bars like Finocchio's and Mona's, each of which had cross-gender impersonator revues and which attracted a nominally mixed clientele. I have developed these ideas after reading through the entire "San Francisco Guides Collection" from 1921 through 1960, San Francisco History Center, San Francisco Main Public Library.

5. On bar raids in the 1950s and 1960s, see Chris Agee, "The Streets of San Francisco: Blacks, Beats, Queers and the San Francisco Police Department, 1950–1968" (forthcoming diss.); and Boyd, *Wide Open Town*. As I argued in part 1, the DOB maintained distance from lesbian bars for ideological and instrumental reasons, but the Mattachine Society established relationships with bar patrons and owners, especially in the 1960s.

6. Ann Aldrich [Marijane Meaker], *We Two Won't Last* (Greenwich, CT: Gold Medal Books, 1963); Jess Stearn, *The Grapevine* (Garden City, NY: Doubleday and Company, Inc., 1964); and Paul Welch, with photographs by Bill Eppridge, "Homosexuality in America," *Life*, 26 June 1964, 66–74.

7. Highlights from recent scholarship on tourism include Catherine Cocks, *Doing the Town: The Rise of Urban Tourism in the United States, 1850–1915* (Berkeley: University of California Press, 2001); Harvey Levenstein, *Seductive Journey: American Tourists in France from Jefferson to the Jazz Age* (Chicago: University of Chicago Press, 1998); Hal Rothman, *Devil's Bargains: Tourism in the Twentieth-Century American West* (Lawrence: University of Kansas Press, 1998); Marguerite Shaffer, *See America First: Tourism and National Identity, 1880–1940* (Washington: Smithsonian Institution Press, 2001); and Rich-

ard Starnes, ed., *Southern Journeys: Tourism, History, and Culture in the Modern South* (Tuscaloosa: University of Alabama Press, 2003).

8. On guidebooks, see Cocks, *Doing the Town*, 143–156; and Paul Groth, "Guidebooks as Community Service," *APCG Yearbook* 62 (2000): 122–136.

9. Shaffer, *See America First*, 6.

10. Publications listing sex sites in general predated gay-specific guidebooks by well over a century; see, for example, Elizabeth Campbell Denlinger, "The Garment and the Man: Masculine Desire in *Harris's List of Covent-Garden Ladies*, 1764–1793," *Journal of the History of Sexuality* 11, no. 3 (July 2002): 357–394; and Levenstein, *Seductive Journey*, 67–70.

11. Swassarnt Nerf et al., *Gay Girl's Guide to the U.S. and the Western World*, 3rd ed. (fall 1957), Pamphlets Collection, ONE Institute, Los Angeles; "Swassarnt Nerf" was almost certainly meant to evoke the French term, "swoisant noif," or "sixty-nine." Thanks to Craig Loftin for locating and copying the guidebook for me.

12. *Gay Girl's Guide*, 1.

13. Call quoted in Eric Marcus, *Making History: The Struggle for Gay and Lesbian Equal Rights, 1945–1990* (New York: HarperCollins, 1992), 68.

14. The earliest edition of *Le Guide Gris* I have been able to locate is from 1962, the third edition: *Le Guide Gris*, 3rd ed. (San Francisco, 1962), Don Lucas Papers, GLBTHS.

15. Bruce Baird, interview by the author, 12 August 2003, San Francisco, CA. Others described the process of locating gay sites in slightly different terms; for instance, in 1963 Ann Aldrich wrote, "One male homosexual told me, 'I have it down almost to a science. First locate the YMCA in the city. Then look for the nearest bar to that "Y." Of course, you really don't ever have to [go to] the "Y," but I like to have a few drinks first . . . If there isn't a bar near the "Y," then a bar near the bus station or city park will probably have homosexuals in it,'" *We Two Won't Last*, 57.

16. Baird, interview.

17. The first few editions of the guidebooks were published without the author's name. In subsequent editions the author was listed as "Brice Bard" or "Bryce Bard." Explaining his use of pseudonyms, Baird said that the 1960s were a "shy time." Baird, interview.

18. For a critical take on the creation of a gay niche market, see Alexandra Chasin, *Selling Out: The Gay and Lesbian Movement Goes to Market* (New York: Palgrave, 2000).

19. Late 1960s and early 1970s editions of *Le Guide Gris* also were advertised in *Vector, California Scene*, and the *Los Angeles Advocate*.

20. Baird, interview.

21. While I welcome Alexandra Chasin's critique in *Selling Out* of the way in which corporations have capitalized on the gay male and lesbian market niche, I take a critical view of her attempt to characterize the fledgling institutions and publications of the gay world as somehow perpetuating a system of social hierarchies from which they were excluded in the first place. See, for example, her assertion that 1950s physique magazines "rhetorically supported U.S. national interests." *Selling Out*, 89.

22. *The Lavender Baedeker*, 1st ed. (San Francisco: Guy Strait, 1963); for biographical information on Elmer Guy Strait, I have drawn from one published source, Clifford Linedecker, *Children in Chains* (New: Everest House, 1981), 227–242; and a few unpublished sources: Guy Strait, interview by Olaf Olegard, 30 November 1986, Video History Collection, GLBTHS; Strait's original Social Security Administration application;

and Guy Strait Files, Federal Bureau of Investigation, U.S. Department of Justice, Freedom of Information Act Request No. 945853.

23. On Sarria's role in San Francisco's bar scene see, Boyd, *Wide Open Town*, 20–24, 57–62; on the *U.S. News and World Report* lawsuit, see Rodger Streitmatter, *Unspeakable: The Rise of the Gay and Lesbian Press in America* (Boston: Faber and Faber, 1995), 73–83.

24. Boyd, *Wide Open Town*, 200–236.

25. Strait first indicated his intention to publish a guidebook in the 24 June 1963 issue of *LCE News* with following item: "The News is preparing to publish a new travel guide to the United States. Such a guide, skillfully prepared could be of invaluable assistance to the motorists as well as to the travelling public. Our files are relatively up to date but there are always changes being made. It is with this in mind that we appeal to our readers to send us the name of any bar, hotel, motel, Men's Shop, etc that would welcome a visit from our readers. Never before has this been successfully done and it presents a big job of compilation. All persons contributing to the Guide will be sent a copy without any charge."

26. Gerson Goodkind, interview by the author, 6 September 2003, in Oakland, CA.

27. Goodkind, interview.

28. In 1941, Gerson Legman offered this explanation of the term "lavender": "A term implying homosexuality in most contexts; a chapter in Gene Fowler's 'The Great Mouthpeice' (1931), for instance, concerning the imputed homosexuality of a prominent penologist, is called 'An Allegation in Lavender,'" see "Appendix VII: The Language of Homosexuality: An American Glossary," in George Henry, *Sex Variants: A Study of Homosexual Patterns* (New York: Paul Hoeber, 1941), 2: 1170. Baird remembers employing a similar technique with *Le Guide Gris*: "Because this was another age, I would refer to toilets [t-rooms] as 'interesting places' . . . the point is, your Aunt Maude could pick this up and say, 'Oh it's a travel guide isn't that interesting'" and she wouldn't notice its gay content; Baird, interview.

29. *The Lavender Baedeker* (1st ed.), 1. Claims to accuracy were one of the prime selling points of the various guidebooks, but due to a variety of factors (e.g., bar closures, imprecise information, 'padded' listings) the guidebooks rarely provided the quality of information that they promised.

30. *The Lavender Baedeker* (1st ed.), 1; a few months after Strait published the guidebook, he refused to explicitly label a bar gay in a publication; he offered the following rationale: "Our readers will have to bear with us when we do not disclose the name of the rest of the bars because Big Brother up in Sacramento would like to have documentary evidence that such and such is a gay bar," *Citizen's News*, vol. 4, no. 5 (ca. December 1964), 6.

31. While Call and other homophile activists believed that same-sex-desiring individuals in rural areas were isolated during the period, their actual (and likely varying) degrees of isolation and connection were not the subject of sustained discussion; for a recent account that claims isolation did not define the lives of men who had sex with men (although perhaps not including self-identified homosexuals), see Howard, *Men Like That*.

32. San Franciscans were not alone in exploring this connection. Clark Polak, from Philadelphia, also combined the two pursuits; on Polak, see Marc Stein, *City of Sisterly and Brotherly Loves: Lesbian and Gay Philadelphia, 1945–1972* (Chicago: University of Chicago Press, 2000). On commerce and sexuality, see Chasin, *Selling Out*, and, for a latter period, Katherine Sender, "Gay Readers, Consumers, and a Dominant Gay Habitus: Twenty-Five Years of the 'Advocate' Magazine," *Journal of Communication* 51 (2001): 73–

99, and idem, "Sex Sells: Sex, Class, and Taste in Commercial Gay and Lesbian Media" *GLQ* 9, no. 3 (2003): 331–365.

33. Guy Strait, "The Fight for the Gay Dollar: A Market Survey" *Citizen's News* vol. 3, no. 22 (ca. September 1964).

34. Bob Ross, interview by the author, 9 January 2002, San Francisco, CA.

35. *The Lavender Baedeker* (1st ed).

36. Benedict Anderson's work on "imagined communities" and the relationship of print culture to the formation of nationalities has been employed by historians of homosexuality to good effect; see, for example, Kath Weston, "Get Thee to a Big City: Sexual Imaginary and the Great Gay Migration," *GLQ* 2 (1995): 253–277; on the relationship of maps to the formation of imaginative communities and nations, see Benedict Anderson, *Imagined Communities: Reflections on the Origin and Spread of Nationalism* (London: Verso, 1983); Thongchai Winichakul, *Siam Mapped: A History of the Geo-Body of a Nation* (Honolulu: University of Hawaii Press, 1994); and Martin Meeker, "Sexual Orientations: Maps Making and Critiquing Homosexual Community, 1960s–1990s," paper presented at the Print Cultures and the City conference, McGill University, Montreal, Canada, 27 March 2004.

37. H. Lynn Womack's Guild Book Service (Washington, D.C.) and Directory Services, Inc. (Minneapolis, MN), two other publishers that compiled and distributed gay bar guidebooks in the mid-1960s, were not based out of San Francisco but were closely aligned with the communicative activism of the homophile movement as publishers of male physique magazines and as vocal advocates on behalf of First Amendment freedoms. On Womack see, Jackie Hatton, "The Pornography Empire of H. Lynn Womack" *Thresholds* vol. 7 (spring 1993): 9–32.

38. See, for example, Howard, *Men Like That,* 97–98.

39. In an interview, Bruce Baird recalled being surprised when an innkeeper in Rome demanded to be removed from his list because it had given her accommodations either unwanted attention from the police or, more likely, too much attention from gay travelers; Baird, interview; on this issue, also see, Ross, interview. Chauncey suggests that the contemporary gay bar as defined here existed in New York City at least as early as if not before it did in San Francisco, e-mail communication, 8 November 2004.

40. Goodkind, interview.

41. Guy Strait, "What Is a Gay Bar?" *Citizen's News,* vol. 4, no. 5 (ca. December 1964), 6; also see Wayne Sage, "Inside the Colossal Closet," *Human Behavior* 4, no. 8 (1975): 16–23.

42. Strait concludes, "A gay bar is nothing more or less than a place where any person of any sexual persuasion can go and enjoy themselves so long as they do not attempt to convert the homosexuals away from their way of life. Gay bars are not the best pickup spots but they are the safest," Guy Strait, "What Is a Gay Bar?" Strait, however, had mixed feelings about this shift; in the 26 April 1965 issue of *Citizen's News* he wrote, "The 'gay' bar of old has taken its place in the history of the United States . . . they have gone [i.e., become] elegant or raunchy, leather or lace, staid or pill-roller"—in other words, the polymorphously perverse spaces had become increasingly specialized, catering not to queer people in general but to people with very particular tastes in their own and their partner's clothing, class, and sexual preferences.

43. For a fascinating series of essays that explore the dissonance between non-gay–identified same-sex sexual encounters and gay identified ones, see Toto le Grand [Lou Rand Hogan], "The Golden Age of Queens, Part I," *Bay Area Reporter,* 4 September 1974, 6, 8.

44. For examples of works of gay literature in which travel is used as a motif, see several excerpts reprinted in Michael Bronski, ed., *Pulp Friction: Uncovering the Golden Age of Gay Male Pulps* (New York: St. Martin's Press, 2003); on gay travel and tourism, see Boyd, *Wide Open Town*, 237–242; Stephen Clift et al., eds., *Gay Tourism: Culture, Identity and Sex* (London: Continuum, 2002); and Howard, *Men Like That*, 78–124.

45. On the nominally gay-centered lives of homosexuals in nonurban areas, see Will Fellows, *Farm Boys: Lives of Gay Men From the Rural Midwest* (Madison: University of Wisconsin Press, 1996); Howard, *Men Like That*; and James Smith and Ronald Mancoske, eds., *Rural Gays and Lesbians: Building on the Strengths of Communities* (New York: Haworth Press, 1997).

46. Chauncey, *Gay New York*, 271–299.

47. On the defining importance of scale and specificity in the context of the distribution of information, see Elizabeth Eisenstein, *The Printing Revolution in Early Modern Europe* (Cambridge: Cambridge University Press, 1983); Marshall McLuhan, *The Gutenberg Galaxy: The Making of Typographic Man* (Toronto: University of Toronto Press, 1962), and idem, *Understanding Media: The Extension of Man* (1964; Cambridge, MA: MIT Press, 1994).

48. *Citizen's News*, vol. 3, no. 8 (27 Jan. 1964).

49. See *Mattachine Review*, July 1966; *Town Talk*, 15 August 1965, 9; and Dorian Book Service flyer, Lucas Papers, GLBTHS.

50. The 1968 edition was the last published by Pan-Graphic and the last on which Hal Call worked as editor; Damron's Calafran Enterprises (later Bob Damron Publishing) began distributing and publishing *The Address Book* with the 1969 edition. Mail order forms were to be found in a variety of Calafran erotica publications, including: *Golden Boys, Springtime Youth, Nude Reflections, Mr. Groovie,* and *Black Male.*

51. See Chasin, *Selling Out.*

52. For overviews of change within the gay male world in the 1960s, see David Allyn, *Make Love, Not War: The Sexual Revolution, an Unfettered History* (Boston: Little, Brown and Company, 2000); John D'Emilio, *Sexual Politics, Sexual Communities* (Chicago: University of Chicago Press, 1983); Charles Kaiser, *The Gay Metropolis, 1940–1996* (New York: Houghton Mifflin, 1997); John Loughery, *The Other Side Silence: Men's Lives and Gay Identities* (New York: Henry Holt, 1998); and Stein, *City of Sisterly and Brotherly Loves.*

53. The Oscar Wilde Memorial Bookstore in New York's Greenwich Village is commonly called the nation's first, but it did not open until late November 1967; on the Oscar Wilde Bookstore, see Martin Duberman, *Stonewall* (New York: Plume, 1993), 163–166.

54. On these individuals and their activism, see Bill Plath, interview by Paul Gabriel, Oral History Collection, 97–24; and Bill Beardemphl and John DeLeon, interview by Paul Gabriel, Oral History Collection, 97–30, GLBTHS.

55. For instance, while Hal Call was friendly with bar owners like Bob Damron, onetime SIR president Bill Plath was the owner of one of the most popular gay bars in 1960s San Francisco, the D'Oak Room. While the links between mainstream gay activists and gay bar owners remained strong in San Francisco through the 1960s and 1970s, the situation was quite different in places like New York City, where gay bars were the object of critique and protest by activists of the liberation era; on the New York perspective, see Duberman, *Stonewall*; and Karla Jay, *Tales of the Lavender Menace: A Memoir of Liberation* (New York: BasicBooks, 1999).

56. Hatton, "The Pornography Empire of H. Lynn Womack"; the Ephemera Collection of the GLBTHS contains a good sampling of Womack's guidebooks.

57. Ephemera Collection / Guidebooks, GLBTHS.

58. See, for example, *Directory 43* (Minneapolis: Directory Services, 1965); *Gunnison's Guide to Gay Pride* (Hartford, CT, 1973); *Gay Directions: A Guide to Toronto* (Toronto: Community Homophile Association of Toronto, 1973); and *Guide for the Naïve Homosexual* (Vancouver: Roedy Green, 1971); all guidebooks found in the "Our Own Voices: Lesbian and Gay Periodicals" Collection, Canadian Lesbian and Gay Archives, Toronto, Canada.

59. *The Address Book*, 2nd ed. (San Francisco: Pan Graphic Press, 1965), 2.

60. Ross, interview.

61. Interestingly, the West Coast publications, like *The Address Book,* lagged behind East Coast publications, like the *International Guild Guide* (from Washington, D.C.) in recognizing racial characteristics of gay bars. Whether this was attributable to integration or racism in the west, visible and established black gay bars in the east, or neither is worthy of greater exploration.

62. Like "heterosexual bars," gay male and lesbian bars also would have followed local and regional social codes and not admitted patrons on the basis of race, ethnicity, or gender.

63. *The Lavender Baedeker* (1st ed.), 16; on the Cellar, see Howard, *Men Like That,* 95.

64. *The Address Book* (2nd ed.), 2; the other codes included: "*" for "very popular"; "C" for "coffee" (which might have meant that it was an after-hours establishment); "D" for "dancing"; "H" for "hotel"; "M" for "mixed and / or tourists"; "P" for "private ("make inquiries locally as to admission policies"); and "R" for "restaurant."

65. Gina Gatta, private communication, 18 July 2001.

66. See *The Address Book* (1964–1967); *Bob Damron's Address Book* (1968–1985); *The International Guild Guide* preceded *The Address Book* in this regard, naming such sites "lesbian" bars by the middle 1960s.

67. Ross, interview.

68. Carol Seajay, interview the author, San Francisco, CA, 28 March 1998 and 9 April 1998; and Gina Covina, interview by the author, 21 September 2003.

69. *Bob Damron's Address Book* (San Francisco: Calafran Enterprises, 1970). Not until the 1980s did the guidebooks acknowledge that racial difference was more complex than black-white, although a few guidebooks appeared that specialized in revealing queer sites in Latin America, such as *Douglas Dean's Gay Mexico* (San Francisco: Barbary Coast Publications, 1973).

70. On race (specially blackness and whiteness) and homosexuality, see Keith Boykin, *One More River to Cross: Black and Gay in America* (New York: Anchor Books, 1996); Robert Reid-Pharr, *Black Gay Men: Essays* (New York: New York University Press, 2001); Siobhan Somerville, *Queering the Color Line: Race and the Invention of Homosexuality in American Culture* (Durham: Duke University Press, 2000); also see Martin Manalansan IV, *Global Divas: Filipino Gay Men in Diaspora* (Durham: Duke University Press, 2003).

71. Ross, interview.

72. Eisenstein, *The Printing Revolution,* 55–56.

Chapter 6

1. One of the ironies of lesbian historical research is that more seems to be known about lesbian bars of the 1940s and 1950s than those of the 1960s and early 1970s; for

more on the lesbian bar in this understudied period, see memoirs (and memoirlike novels) such as Leslie Feinberg, *Stone Butch Blues: A Novel* (Ithaca: Firebrand Books, 1993); Karla Jay, *Tales of the Lavender Menace: A Memoir of Liberation* (New York: Basic Books, 1999); Audre Lorde, *Zami: A New Spelling of My Name* (Watertown, MA: Persephone Press, 1982); Joan Nestle, *A Restricted Country* (1987; San Francisco: Cleis Press, 2003); also see Lillian Faderman, *Odd Girls and Twilight Lovers: A History of Lesbian Life in Twentieth-Century America* (New York: Columbia University Press, 1991); Rochella Thorpe, "'A House Where Queers Go': African-American Lesbian Nightlife in Detroit, 1940–1975," in *Inventing Lesbian Cultures in America,* ed. Ellen Lewin (Boston: Beacon Press, 1996), 40–61; and the documentary film *Last Call at Maud's,* directed by Paris Poirier, 1993.

2. For a lively account of these years, see Ruth Rosen, *The World Split Open: How the Modern Women's Movement Changed America* (New York: Penguin, 2001), 63–93.

3. Friedan quoted in Rosen, *The World Split Open,* 74. On the predecessors of second-wave Feminism, see Leila Rupp and Verta Taylor, *Survival in the Doldrums: The American Women's Rights Movement, 1945 to the 1960s* (New York: Oxford University Press, 1987).

4. For overviews of feminist organizing and publishing, see Alice Echols, *Daring to Be Bad: Radical Feminism in America, 1967–1975* (Minneapolis: University of Minnesota Press, 1989); Rosen, *The World Split Open;* Rodger Streitmatter, *Unspeakable: The Rise of the Gay and Lesbian Press in America* (Boston: Faber and Faber, 1995); and Mary Thom, *Inside Ms.: 25 Years of the Magazine and the Feminist Movement* (New York: Henry Holt, 1997).

5. A rough estimate of the number of such books published is rather difficult to come up with, considering that many were published by small and fleeting printers, that many were collections of previously published essays and articles, and that library searches also retrieve books about feminism that are not written from a feminist point of view. Based on searches for "feminism" and "women's rights" for books published between 1966 and 1976 entered into two library catalogs, the Library of Congress and MELVYL, the catalog for the combined libraries of the University of California, I located 496 items in the Library of Congress and 929 items in the University of California system.

6. A search in the Library of Congress catalog retrieved 219 "feminist" periodicals published in English in the United States between 1966 and 1976; a search in Catalog Q (a database of periodicals stored in six California collections of GLBT materials) retrieved 794 "feminist" periodicals largely from the 1970s and 1980s. For a more narrow time period, 1968–1973, Anne Mather found some 560 feminist periodicals, "A History of Feminist Periodicals, Part I," *Journalism History* 1, no. 3 (fall 1974): 82; also see Mather, "A History of Feminist Periodicals, Part III," *Journalism History* 2, no. 1 (spring 1975): 19–23.

7. Arguably the first "lesbian-feminist" periodical was called the *Furies,* which was produced by the Furies Collective in Washington, D.C., beginning in January 1972. However, this periodical was preceded by the *Ladder,* which became increasingly feminist in its orientation in the early 1970s; and many publications produced by radical (though not necessarily lesbian) feminists and the counterculture included articles about lesbian-feminism; see, for example, *Rat, Village Voice* (especially Jill Johnston's column), *oob,* and *It Ain't Me, Babe;* on these publications, see Echols, *Daring to Be Bad.*

8. For more on NACHO, see John D'Emilio, *Sexual Politics, Sexual Communities: The Making of a Homosexual Minority in the United States, 1940–1970* (Chicago: University of Chicago Press, 1983), 196–204.

9. "A Recap of Ten Days in August," *Citizen's News,* October 1966, 8.

10. For instance, Willie Brown and John Burton each played important parts in the

battle to strike down California's sodomy statutes, which they succeeded in doing by 1974 after a long legislative battle. On sodomy laws in California, see William Eskridge, *Gaylaw: Challenging the Apartheid of the Closet* (Cambridge, MA: Harvard University Press, 1999), 104–108.

11. While members of the DOB began to push for lesbian issues such as rights for lesbian mothers, to a certain extent they were complicit with male homophiles in emphasizing issues generally considered to be of more concern to gay men, such as police entrapment, censorship, and venereal disease; see, for example, "San Francisco on the Spot: Issues and Questions," *Ladder* July 1966, 4–7, and "Issues and Answers," *Ladder* July 1966, 8–9.

12. For a clear articulation of the emerging lesbian point of view, see a 1966 speech by Shirley Willer, reprinted as "What Concrete Steps Can Be Taken to Further the Homophile Movement?" *Ladder* November 1966, 17–20.

13. On "second-wave" feminism, see Echols, *Daring to Be Bad*; and Rosen, *The World Split Open*; also see the classic collection of essays and documents related to the women's liberation movement, *Sisterhood Is Powerful*, ed. Robin Morgan (New York: Vintage, 1970).

14. Sarah Elizabeth Boslaugh, "A History of the Lesbian Periodical *The Ladder*, 1956–1972" (M.A. thesis, University of Chicago, 1984), 78–79. At the same time, Boslaugh notes that the *Ladder* became less explicitly political and instead focused on literature. For works that pioneered the discussion of intersectionality of identity (race, class, gender, ethnicity, sexuality, etc.) in a feminist context, see Toni Cade Bambara, ed., *The Black Woman: An Anthology* (New York: Penguin, 1970); Beverly Guy-Sheftall, ed., *Words of Fire: An Anthology of African-American Feminist Thought* (New York: New Press, 1995); and Barbara Smith, ed., *Home Girls: A Black Feminist Anthology* (New York: Kitchen Table, 1983).

15. Del Martin, "The Lesbian's Other Identity," *Ladder* December 1968–January 1969, 16–17; Martin further noted that individual memberships were $7.50 and $10 for couples, "One lesbian couple has already been accepted under the couple rate."

16. On the removal of the *Ladder* to Reno and away from the DOB, see Martin and Lyon, *Lesbian / Woman* (1972; Volcano, CA: Volcano Press, 1991), 252–253; and Boslaugh, "A History of the Lesbian Periodical *The Ladder*," 83–98.

17. Mary Thom, *Inside Ms.*, 1; for a first-person account of the sit-in, see Jay, *Tales of the Lavender Menace*, 107–122.

18. Rosen, *The World Split Open*, 211.

19. On the "Lavender Menace" action, see Echols, *Daring to Be Bad*, 201–215; Jay, *Tales of the Lavender Menace*, 137–146. Critiques were similarly raised by working-class women and women of color who experienced both liberal and radical feminism as exclusionary, see Echols, *Daring to Be Bad*, 204–210; Rosen, *The World Split Open*, 276–291; and several essays in Guy-Sheftall, ed., *Words of Fire*.

20. Echols defines "zap" as a political act "designed to shock and offend," *Daring to Be Bad*, 76. Along with shattering preconceptions, however, this zap also was designed to educate.

21. Karla Jay identifies March Hoffman, Lois Hart, Rita Mae Brown, Ellen Shumsky, Cynthia Funk, "and a few others" as the authors of the manifesto; Jay, *Tales of the Lavender Menace*, 140. "Woman-Identified-Woman" has been reprinted in dozens of publications; I read the version reprinted in Karla Jay and Allen Young, eds., *Out of the Closets: Voices of Gay Liberation*, 20th anniversary edition (New York: New York University Press, 1992), 172–177.

22. The manifesto elaborated a few paragraphs later: "Our energies must flow toward our sisters, not backward toward our oppressors. As long as women's liberation tried to free women without facing the basic heterosexual structure that binds us in one-to-one relationships with our oppressors, tremendous energies will continue to flow into trying to straighten up each particular relationship with a man, into finding how to get better sex, how to turn his head around—into trying to make the 'new man' out of him, in the delusion that this will allow us to be the 'new woman.'"

23. Echols, *Daring to Be Bad*, 243–286. For an insightful reevaluation of cultural feminism, its relation to lesbianism, and its historical legacy, see Verta Taylor and Leila Rupp, "Women's Culture and Lesbian Feminist Activism: A Reconsideration of Cultural Feminism," *Signs* 19, no. 1 (fall 1993): 32–61.

24. Jill Johnston, *Lesbian Nation: The Feminist Solution* (New York: Simon and Schuster, 1973).

25. On lesbian-feminism and reproduction, see Laurel [Galana], "Radical Reproduction: Women without Men," *Amazon Quarterly*, March 1974, 4–19; and Greta Rensenbrink, "Reshaping Body Politics: Lesbian Feminism and the Cultural Politics of the Body, 1968–1983" (Ph.D. diss., University of Chicago, 2003).

26. On countercultural communes in 1960s United States, see Timothy Miller, "The Sixties Era Communes" in Paul Braunstein and Michael William Doyle, eds., *Imagine Nation: The American Counterculture of the 1960s and 1970s* (New York: Routledge, 2001), 327–352.

27. Publications are found in "Catalog Q," the online catalog of five California-based collections of LGBT periodicals.

28. Phyllis Birkby, "Amazon Architecture," *Cowrie: Lesbian / Feminist*, April 1974, 13–14; on "Amazon" as a popular euphemism for a lesbian, particularly the gender non-normative lesbian, see Katie Gilmartin, "The Very House of Difference: Intersection of Identities in the Life Histories of Colorado Lesbians, 1940–1965" (Ph.D. diss., Yale University, 1995), 71–72.

29. Like many feminist women of the era, both Galana and Covina rejected their patrilineal last names and adopted ones of their own choosing. Laurel began life with the last name of her father, Holliday, changed it to Ackers when she was married in college, changed it again to Galana (a modification of her middle name, Gail) in the context of lesbian-feminism, and then changed it back to Holliday by the early 1980s; see Laurel [Galana] Holliday, telephone interview by the author, 28 April 2004.

30. Holliday, telephone interview; the event is mentioned by Diane Roberts in "Free Speech Shouldn't Be Limited," *St. Petersburg Times*, 5 April 2002, on-line edition.

31. On the free speech movement of fall 1964, see Robert Cohen and Reginald Zelnick, eds., *The Free Speech Movement: Reflections on Berkeley in the 1960s* (Berkeley: University of California Press, 2002); and Malcolm Rohrbaugh, *Berkeley at War: The 1960s* (New York: Oxford University Press, 1990).

32. Gina Covina, interview by the author, 21 September 2003, Laytonville, California.

33. Ibid.

34. Ibid.

35. Gina Covina, "AQ The First Year: Changes," *Amazon Quarterly*, October 1973, 50.

36. Ibid.

37. While Covina remembers connecting with this group, Galana could not recall such a connection in specific terms.

38. On the influence of Anderson upon Covina and Galana, see Covina, interview; Laurel [Galana], "Margaret Anderson, Part I," *Amazon Quarterly*, fall 1972, 55–60, idem, "Part II," *Amazon Quarterly*, February 1973, 50–54, and idem, "Part III," *Amazon Quarterly*, May 1973, 30–33.

39. See Covina, "AQ The First Year: Changes"; Holliday, telephone interview.

40. Ibid. Although 400 prepublication subscriptions were a great many for a do-it-yourself lesbian-feminist publication, *Ms.* magazine, which had a professional staff and industry backing, received about 26,000 orders following its preview issue; see Thom, *Inside Ms.,* 24.

41. Covina, interview.

42. Ibid.; the first classified ad for *Amazon Quarterly* in *Ms.* appeared in the March 1973 issue.

43. Covina, interview.

44. *Amazon Quarterly*, fall 1972, 5.

45. Laurel Galana, "Conversation," *Amazon Quarterly*, fall 1972, 7. Galana remembered idealizing the long conversations had by Margaret Anderson and Jane Heap and she remembered striving to establish a sort of 1930s Parisian salon, only not in Paris and not in a single locale like a salon; Holliday, telephone interview.

46. Galana, "Conversation"; in the same issue, another article exploring similar ideas but also taking them into new territory, arguing that in order to have good conversation, "deviants" must continue to develop their own languages independent of "public languages"; these "private languages" would allow lesbians to communicate amongst themselves as well as explore "the social-economic public male realm" while avoiding the "rigid and conservative" world of mass communications; in my reading, this is precisely what do-it-yourself publications like *Amazon Quarterly* were attempting to accomplish; see Peggy Allegro, "The Strange and the Familiar: The Evolutionary Potential of Lesbianism," *Amazon Quarterly*, fall 1972, 37–39.

47. *Amazon Quarterly*, December 1973, 4.

48. "What's What?" *Amazon Quarterly*, May 1973, 4–5.

49. Ibid.

50. Laurel Galana and Gina Covina, eds., *The New Lesbians: Interviews with Women across the U.S. and Canada* (Berkeley: Moon Books, 1977), 10.

51. Covina, interview.

52. Galana and Covina, *The New Lesbians*, 11.

53. Deborah Wolf, "Noitan Naibsel: A Statistical Analysis," *Amazon Quarterly*, October 1973–January 1974, 30–34. Covina and Galana conducted fifty-two interviews, Wolf based her analysis on the twenty-one interviews that had been transcribed by that point; twenty interviews eventually were published in *The New Lesbians*. The rest, apparently, are lost.

54. Data on the racial composition of the sample were not included in the article, if it was collected at all.

55. "Resource Directory," *Amazon Quarterly*, October 1973–January 1974, 60–72. Galana remembered that she had a healthy disrespect for copyright laws and wouldn't have thought that such information in fact could be owned, Holliday, telephone interview.

56. Although a few organizations listed referred to their nonwhite ethnoracial focus (e.g., the Chicana Center in Los Angeles), most were self-identified solely as institutions for women and / or lesbians. Thus, while the directory provided a space for the

recognition of ethnic and racial differences among women, the names of the organizations themselves favored an expression of universality based on gender.

57. Covina, "AQ The First Year: Changes," 51.

58. See, for instance, Allegro, "The Strange and the Familiar."

59. Laurel Galana, "How to Make a Magazine, Part I," *Amazon Quarterly*, May 1974, 66–70; Galana, "How to Make a Magazine, Part II," *Amazon Quarterly*, July 1974, 63–68; and Galana, "How to Make a Magazine, Part III," *Amazon Quarterly*, November 1974, 71–72.

60. Galana, "How to Make a Magazine, Part III," 72.

61. *Amazon Quarterly*, July 1974, 2; also see Covina, interview.

62. Galana and Covina, *The New Lesbians*, 41–42.

63. Echols, *Daring to Be Bad*.

64. Ibid., 244.

65. There are notable exceptions to this general trend, including what Echols called "one of the most puzzling parts of the [Washington, D.C.–based] Furies story . . . : the transformation of the anti-imperialist women from reluctant feminists to die-hard lesbian separatists," Echols, *Daring to Be Bad*, 231. In "Women's Culture and Lesbian Feminist Activism," Taylor and Rupp also note that a changing historical context necessitated a change in feminist strategy.

66. Echols added, "Cultural feminism modified lesbian-feminism so that male values rather than men were vilified and female bonding rather than lesbianism was valorized, thus making it acceptable to heterosexual feminists," Echols, *Daring to Be Bad*, 244.

67. On lesbian-feminists, gay men, and the movement toward cultural formations, see Elizabeth Armstrong, *Forging Gay Identities: Organizing Sexuality in San Francisco, 1950–1994* (Chicago: University of Chicago Press, 2002), 56–110.

68. On the social function of women's cafés and bookstores, see Anne Enke, "Smuggling Sex through the Gates: Race, Sexuality, and the Politics of Space in Second Wave Feminism" *American Quarterly* 5, no. 4 (Dec. 2003): 635–667.

69. Covina, interview.

70. For more on feminist institution building and commercial pursuits, see Echols, *Daring to Be Bad*, 269–281; and Faderman, *Odd Girls and Twilight Lovers*, 218–226.

71. See, for example, Elizabeth Barnhart, "Friends and Lovers in a Lesbian Counterculture Community" in *Old Family / New Family: Interpersonal Relationships*, ed. Non Glazer-Malbin (New York: D. Van Nostrand, 1975), 90–115; Denyse Lockard, "The Lesbian Community: An Anthropological Approach," in *The Many Faces of Homosexuality: Anthropological Approaches to Homosexual Behavior*, ed. Evelyn Blackwood (New York: Harrington Park Press, 1986), 83–95; Jean Weber, "Lesbian Networks" *Christopher Street*, April 1979, 51–54; and Deborah Goleman Wolf, *The Lesbian Community* (Berkeley: University of California Press, 1979).

72. See listings in *Echo of Sappho*, August–September 1972, 3; "Groups, Bars, Etc.," *Portcullis East / West*, 1, no. 2 (1972): 23–24; and "CLL Survey, Chicago Bars," *Lavender Woman*, January 1973, 13. For a fascinating first-person account of a lesbian-feminist who felt great ambivalence toward, but did not completely reject, lesbian bars, see Karla Jay, *Tales of the Lavender Menace: A Memoir of Liberation* (New York: Basic Books, 1999); also see Deborah Goleman Wolf, *The Lesbian Community* (Berkeley: University of California Press, 1979), 42–47.

73. "CLL Survey, Chicago Bars," *Lavender Woman* January 1973, 13.

74. *The Gay Girl's Guide 1974: Your Own Guide to Gay Living International* (London and San Francisco, 1974); and *Gaia's Guide,* 3rd ed. (San Francisco, CA, 1976), Ephemera/Guidebooks Collection, GLBTHS.

75. *The Gay Girl's Guide 1974* [n.p.]; Although this guidebook included listings of feminist organizations, bookstores, and groups offering social services, their use of the word "Ladies" suggests that their feminism was incipient rather than highly articulated.

76. Ibid.

Epilogue

1. For a general overview that places the Internet in a broad historical context, see Asa Briggs and Peter Burke, *A Social History of the Media: From Gutenberg to the Internet* (Malden, MA: Blackwell, 2002); a few of the many books studying the impact of the Internet on society and culture include, for example, Manuel Castells, *The Rise of Network Society,* 2nd ed. (Oxford, UK: Blackwell, 2000); Pamela Donovan, *No Way of Knowing: Crime, Urban Legends, and the Internet* (New York: Routledge, 2004); Philip Howard and Steve Jones, eds., *Society Online: The Internet in Context* (Thousand Oaks, CA: Sage, 2000); Robert Klotz, *The Politics of Internet Communication* (Lanham, MD: Rowman and Littlefield, 2004); and James Slevin, *The Internet and Society* (Cambridge, UK: Polity Press, 2000).

2. See Albert-László Barabási, *Linked: The New Science of Networks* (Cambridge: Perseus, 2002); and Duncan Watts, *Six Degrees: The Science of a Connected Age* (New York: W. W. Norton, 2003).

3. Marshall McLuhan, *Understanding Media: The Extension of Man* (1964; Cambridge, MA: MIT Press, 1994), 5.

4. San Francisco, along with New York, Boston, Washington, Chicago, St. Louis, Milwaukee, New Orleans, and Philadelphia were listed as "homosexual capitals" in Xavier Mayne, *The Intersexes: A History of Simisexualism as a Problem in Social Life* (1908; New York: Arno Press, 1975), 640.

5. On sexuality identity and the Internet, see, for example, John Edward Campbell, *Getting It On Online: Cyberspace, Gay Male Sexuality, and Embodied Identity* (New York: Harrington Park Press, 2004); and J. Dallas Dishman, "Ecologies of Cyberspace: Gay Communities in the Internet," in *From Chicago to L.A.: Making Sense of Urban Theory,* ed. Michael Dear (Thousand Oaks, CA: Sage Publications, 2002), 297–316. Thanks go to Mary Gray of Indiana University for helping for me sort out the surprisingly meager literature on this subject.

6. Perhaps even more interesting is the matter of how people adopting these identities may also be influencing the structure of the Internet itself in the process in a way that better suits their needs associated with identity acquisition and community building. Again, thanks to Mary Gray for helping my thinking along these lines.

7. See, for example, Dennis Altman, *Global Sex* (Chicago: University of Chicago Press, 2001); Chris Berry, et al., eds., *Mobile Cultures: New Media in Queer Asia* (Durham: Duke University Press, 2003); William Leap and Tom Boellstorff, eds., *Speaking in Queer Tongues: Globalization and Gay Languages* (Urbana and Chicago: University of Illinois Press, 2004); and Martin Manalansan IV, *Global Divas: Filipino Gay Men in Diaspora* (Durham: Duke University Press, 2003).

8. William Leap and Tom Boellstorff, introduction, *Speaking in Queer Tongues,* 7.

9. See Micheline Ishay, *The History of Human Rights: From Ancient Times to the Globalization Era* (Berkeley: University of California Press, 2004).

10. See Kenneth Cmiel, "Human Rights, Freedom of Information, and the Origins of Third-World Solidarity," in *Truth Claims: Representation and Human Rights*, ed. Mark Philip Bradley and Patrice Petro (New Brunswick: Rutgers University Press).

11. Dennis Altman, *Homosexual Oppression and Liberation* (1971; New York: New York University Press, 1993).

Berlin, Germany, 205
Bérubé, Allan, 265n42
Black Cat Café (bar), 209, 291n41
Black Woman (Bambara), 230
Board of Equalization (California), 51
Bonner, Cleo Glenn. *See* Glenn, Cleo
books. *See* communications media;
    individual book titles
Book Week, 140–141
Boslaugh, Sarah, 229, 305n14
Bowman, Dr. Karl, 59
Boyd, Nan Alamilla, 85, 87, 209, 269n25,
    278n15, 291n40, 298n2
Brandhove, William, 64–65
Brando, Marlon, 158
Brownmiller, Susan, 231
Brown v. Board of Education, Topeka, 83,
    278n16
Brown, Willie, 228
Burke, Bois, 265n48
Burke, Tom, 192–194
Burns, Ken, 40, 46, 52–53
Burton, John, 228

Caen, Herb, 175, 183–184, 293n65
Caffee, Mike, 158–161, 162f, 291n35
Cahill, Thomas, 63
California College of Arts and Crafts, 236
Call, Hal (Harold), 40–42, 166f, 219,
    268n13; on contact clubs, 56–59; on
    gossip, 55–56; guidebooks and, 204–
    205, 212; featured in *Life*, 164, 166f,
    171; work with *Life*, 156–161; critique
    of Mattachine Foundation, 41; on the
    Mattachine Review, 45; move to San
    Francisco, 40–41; relationship with
    Strait, 293n66. *See also* Lucas, Don;
    Mattachine Review; Mattachine
    Society
camp culture. *See* language, coded
Caprio, Frank, 86, 117
Carol in a Thousand Cities (Aldrich), 125–
    126
Carpenter, Edward (*The Intermediate Sex*),
    7–8
Cebu City, Philippines, 69–70
censorship, 19–22, 26–27, 54–56, 98, 117,
    201–202, 264n31–41, 272n69, 281n69.
    See also law
Chanson de Bilitis, Les (poems), 78

Chasin, Alexandra, 269n33, 299n21
Chauncey, George, 5, 7, 10, 22, 84, 165,
    179, 216–217, 266n4, 298n2
Chicago Daily News (newspaper), 118
Chicago, Illinois, 102–103, 248–249
Christopher, George, 63–66, 67
Citizen's News (newspaper), 175–177, 207,
    209, 218f, 297n133
class, 10, 11–12, 56, 79, 101–102, 198–199,
    227, 240, 261n18, 277n7
Coates, Paul, 136–137
Cochran, Chal, 46,
Columbus, Ohio, 182–184
"coming out," 2, 48, 49f, 71, 92–93, 236,
    246, 276n133
commercialism, 207, 299n21; activism re-
    lated to, 52, 57, 207, 209, 212–213,
    243–245, 269n33
communication media: books, 7–8, 16–
    17, 26–27, 31, 54, 66–70, 82–83, 87–
    88, 109–112, 115–150, 120f, 129f, 202–
    224, 206f, 208f, 227; films, 20, 164, 192;
    Internet, 251–258; magazines, 23–26,
    25f, 34, 43–50, 49f, 51, 54–59, 72, 73f,
    86, 88–99, 97f, 112, 149f, 151–158,
    161–195, 162f, 166f, 167f, 191f, 192f,
    193f, 198–199, 219, 227–230, 232–249,
    233f, 241f; maps, 12, 64f, 207, 232–234,
    233f; newsletters, 22–23, 43, 53; news-
    papers, 62–66, 153–155, 175–177,
    218f, 248–249; radio, 59–60, 112, 117,
    141; television, 112, 117, 118, 136–137,
    189, 255–256. *See also* censorship;
    contact clubs; "do-it-yourself";
    guidebooks; language; paperbacks
communication networks, concept of,
    13–16, 95, 262n21. *See also* networks,
    sociological theory of
community. *See* homosexual community
Comstock, Anthony, 19–20; "Comstock
    Act," 19–20, 26
consciousness-raising groups, 90, 226–
    227, 280n42
contact clubs, 23–26, 56–59, 104–105,
    244–245, 273n73
Cory Book Service, 54
Cory, Donald Webster (Edward Sagarin),
    93, 109, 119, 270n39
Council on Religion and the Homosexual,
    187

Harper's (magazine), 153–155
Harry's Bar, 205
Hart, Walter, 175
Havemann, Ernest, 287n2, 292n55
Haver, Martin, 57
Hay, Harry, 5–8, 32
"Hays Code." *See* Motion Picture Producers and Distributors Association
Helmer, William, 153–155
Henry, George, 117
heterosexuality, 21, 24, 58, 66–67, 78, 83–84, 110, 113, 116, 119, 128–133, 138, 146, 165–169, 166f, 167f, 173–174, 175–178, 176f, 184, 185f, 194, 227, 230–231, 234–235
"Heterosexuality in America" (article), 176–178, 176f
"Hicklin Test," 19. See also *Regina v. Hicklin*
Hitchcock, Alfred, 52
Hobby Directory, 23–26, 25f
Hogan, Lou Rand. *See* Rand, Lou
Holiday (magazine), 118
Holliday, Laurel. *See* Galana, Laurel
Hollywood. *See* Los Angeles
homophile movement, 31–35, 106–108, 110–112, 202–203, 219, 228–229, 266n1; assimilation and, 33; critiques of, 33, 270n39; outside the United States, 48, 54, 69–70, 179–180; representational politics of, 50, 130–131, 156–157; respectability and, 33; second wave of, 187, 208–209, 219. *See also* Daughters of Bilitis; *Ladder;* Mattachine Society; *Mattachine Review; ONE;* One Inc.; social movements
homosexual community: connecting to, 2–3, 5, 6–9, 16–29, 67–68, 72–76, 79–80, 95, 111, 114–115, 121, 124–125, 127, 143–144, 178–184, 197–198, 204–211, 230, 238–240, 242–243, 246–249, 254, 256–258, 260n15; formation of, 11–12, 203; geography of, 4–5, 12–13, 64f, 111, 113, 133–134, 137–140, 144, 154, 178–179, 210, 214; globalization of, 256–258; historiography of, 4–5; isolation from, 2–3, 5, 69–76, 79–80, 114, 123–124, 143, 179–184, 212, 236, 246, 276n136; pluralism within, 223; representation of, 34–35, 153–155,

165, 170–171. *See also* gay male identity; lesbian identity
homosexual identity. *See* gay male identity; lesbian identity
Homosexual Explosion (Blake), 146
Homosexual in America (Cory), 47, 119
Homosexual in Our Society (radio program), 59–61, 273n82
"Homosexuality in America" (article), 151–153, 155–195, 252–253; circulation of, 152, 287n3; gender and, 169; Greenwich Village in, 165–168, 167f; legacy of, 178–195, 185f, 191f, 192f, 193f; Los Angeles in, 168–169, 172; precedents to, 153–155; race and, 169; response to, 172–195, 176f, 292n60, 294n79, 294n81; San Francisco in, 163–165, 162f, 166f, 170–172. See also *Life*
Homosexual Oppression and Liberation (Altman), 258
"Homosexual: Newly Visible, Newly Understood" (article), 191–192, 192f
Homosexual Revolution (Masters), 109–112
Homosexuals Today (Cutler), 31–32, 35, 82–84, 99–100
Hooker, Evelyn, 47, 228
Hooper, Bill, 287n3, 294n84
House Committee on Current Pornographic Materials, 87
Howard, John, 27–28, 259n4, 276n136, 300n31
"How to Make a Magazine" (article), 243–244
Hurewitz, Daniel, 267n1

Imperial Court, 187
International Congress for Sexual Equality, 32
Internet. *See* communications media
Intersexes (Mayne), 309n4
It Ain't Me Babe (newspaper), 235–236

Jensen, John, 98
Johnson, David, 267n4
Johnson, James Weldon, 119
Jones, T. C., 126
Joseph, Miranda, 282n82
Jumpin' Frog (bar), 159, 164, 166f, 170, 192, 192f, 295n95

Look (magazine), 61, 190–191, 191f
Los Angeles: gay men and, 168–169,
166f, 167f, 172; as a gay capital, 216,
297n127; homophiles and, 32, 37–39,
82; lesbians and, 138–139; Silverlake
district, 37. *See also* Pershing Square
Los Angeles Police Department, 168, 172,
173–174
Loughery, John, 294n81
Louys, Pierre, 78
Lucas, Don (Donald), 42–43, 68–76, 94,
219, 269n22; elected Mattachine
president, 53; on *Mattachine Review,*
68; learning of Mattachine Society,
42; on media coverage, 60; social
services and, 68–76; spirituality of,
285n38; upbringing of, 42. *See also*
Call, Hal; *Mattachine Review;* Mattachine Society
Lucien Press, 98
Lyon, Phyllis, 77–82, 278n10; as Ann Ferguson, 92–93; meeting Del Martin,
81; DOB philosophy of, 83–84; joining NOW, 229; on public forums, 100;
spirituality of, 285n38. *See also* Daughters of Bilitis; *Ladder;* Martin, Del

MacLean's (magazine from Canada), 118,
288n7
Macon, Georgia, 179
magazines. *See* communications media;
individual magazine and article titles
Man's Magazine, 57–58
Marietta, South Carolina, 180–181
Martin, Del (Dorothy), 77–82, 278n10;
critique of Aldrich, 125–126; meeting
Lyon, 81; joining NOW, 229; on public forums, 100–101; spirituality of,
285n38; on Stearn, 131–133. *See also*
Daughters of Bilitis; *Ladder;* Lyon,
Phyllis
mass media. *See* communication media
Masters, R. E. L., 109–112, 126, 283n3
Mather, Ann, 304n6
Mattachine Foundation, 37–39, 267n1; cell
structure and, 37–38; communism
and, 37, 39; conventions, 39, 41; dis-
cussion groups, 41; pledge of, 38. *See
also* Mattachine Society; *Mattachine
Review*

Mattachine Review, 34, 43–50, 49f, 68, 73f,
199; circulation of, 44–47, 50, 68,
271n48, 271n50; content of, 47–50;
decline of, 68, 187–189; funding of,
45–46; *Grapevine* review, 142; idea
for, 43–44; *Mattachine Review Extra,*
44–45; reading, 47–50; response to,
48–50, 70. *See also* Mattachine Society, Pan-Graphic Press
Mattachines (traveling performers), 37
Mattachine Society, 32, 39–76, 94, 107–
108, 178–182, 186–189, 267n1; 1959
election scandal, 61–66, 64f, 67,
274n101, 274n108; area councils and
chapters, 40, 53, 269n30; "Brief History of the Mattachine Movement"
(1953), 39–40; conventions, 40, 42, 44,
53, 61–65; dance raided, 268n7; DOB,
compared to, 78, 105, 106–108; decline of, 186–189; Denver chapter,
61–66, 274n100; guidebook produced
by, 204–205; "Homosexuality in
America" and, 171, 178–182, 186–
189; membership, 42–43, 188–189,
275n106; newsletters, 53; publications
chapter, 41–47; public relations of,
61–63; referrals by, 70–71, 74–75;
representational politics of, 50, 156–
157, 269n25; representation of, 57,
59–68, 171, 269n25, 296n124; San
Francisco headquarters, 44, 52–53,
65, 71; in *The Sixth Man,* 66–68; social
services and, 68–76, 187–188; structure of, 39. *See also* Burns, Ken; Call,
Hal; Dorian Book Service; *Dorian
Book Service Quarterly;* homophile
movement; Lucas, Don; Mattachine
Foundation; *Mattachine Review;* Pan-
Graphic Press
McIlvenna, Ted, 228
McLuhan, Marshall, 14, 65–66, 109, 111,
180, 243, 252–253, 257–258, 262n23
Meaker, Marijane. *See* Aldrich, Ann;
Packer, Vin
media. *See* communication media
Medium Is the Massage, The (McLuhan),
109
Mendenhall, George, 219
Meyer, Richard, 21–22
Minton, Henry, 10

Mizer, Bob, 273n75
Modleski, Tania, 27
Morgan, Robin, 237
Motion Picture Producers and Distributors Association, 20; production code ("Hays Code"), 20, 264n38
motorcycle clubs, 158, 290n29
Ms. (magazine), 227, 230, 238, 307n40
Mueller, Janis, 94–95
mutual aid societies, 69

Napa (California) State Hospital, 75–76
National Association for Sex Research, 32
National Organization for Women (NOW), 226–227
Nebel, Long John, 141
networks, sociological theory of, 11–12, 70, 261n16. *See also* communication networks
New Homosexual Revolution (Worthy), 145
"New Homosexuality" (article), 192–194, 193f
New Lesbians (Covina and Galana), 245–247
newspapers. *See* communications media; *individual newspaper and article titles*
newsstands, 47, 50, 95–98, 271n50, 281n65
Newsweek (magazine), 118, 128
New York (magazine), 230
New York City, 50; gay men in, 153–155; in *Life,* 165–168. *See also* Greenwich Village; Washington Square Park
New York Times, 66, 153–155
"New York's Middle-Class Homosexuals" (article), 153–155
"Nightmare World of the Gay Man" (article), 57–58
North American Conference of Homophile Organizations (NACHO), 228–229
"Notes on 'Camp'" (article), 177–178. *See* language

Oakland, California, 227, 236
obscenity law. *See* censorship; law
Odd Girl Out (Bannon), 116
Oedipus (motorcycle club), 158
Ohio State University, 183
Old Wives' Tales (bookstore), 150

ONE (magazine), 32, 34, 47, 50, 51, 62–63, 271n48, 281n65
One, Inc., 32, 294n80; Midwinter Institute (1956), 32–33, 82
One, Inc. v. Olesen, 98, 117, 137, 283n2
On the QT (magazine), 61
O'Rourke, Rebecca, 26–27
Oscar Wilde Memorial Bookstore, 301n53
Other Men (Dorian), 145
Owensboro, Kentucky, 72–75

Pacifica Radio Network, 60
Packer, Vin (Marijane Meaker), 118–119. *See also* Aldrich, Ann
Pan-Graphic Press, 44, 52, 54–57, 89, 160, 207, 213, 269n32, 272n69. *See also* Call, Hal; Dorian Book Service; Lucas, Don; *Mattachine Review;* Mattachine Society
paperback books (pulps), 87–88, 96, 113–128, 120f, 144–150, 225, 255, 286n57, 287n76; as erotic literature, 87, 116, 118, 123; as resource books, 123–125, 148. *See also* Aldrich, Ann; communication media
Paramount Placement Agency, 74
pen-pal clubs. *See* contact clubs
Periodical Distributors of Greater New York, 50
Pershing Square (Los Angeles), 7–8, 167f, 168. *See also* Los Angeles
personal ads. *See* contact clubs
Philadelphia Magazine, 118
physique photography and magazines, 24, 58, 272n72, 273n75, 273n80, 281n65, 299n21. *See also* communication media; pornography
Plath, Bill, 219, 302n55
Polak, Clark, 293n70
Polanski, Walli, 104–105
police. *See* specific police departments
pornography, 26, 57, 201. *See also* physique photography and magazines
Portcullis East / West (newspaper), 248
Postal Service. *See* U.S. Postal Service
Presidential Report on American Women, 226
Presidio (San Francisco) Military Hospital, 75

production code. *See* Motion Picture Producers and Distributors Association
pseudonyms, 38, 62, 92–93, 118, 122–123, 170, 292n53, 299n17, 306n29. *See also* language
P-Town Landing (bar), 123
public sphere, 14, 151, 173–175, 262n24. *See also* communications media; space
pulps. *See* paperback books

race, 11–12, 56, 61, 101–102, 146, 169, 176–177, 222–223, 227, 235, 261n18, 262n20, 303n61, 303n69, 307n56
Radicalesbians, 231–232
radio. *See* communications media
Radway, Janice, 27
Rand, Lou, 16, 301n43. See also *Gay Detective*
Ray, Florence, 90–91
Read, Jerry (Jerry Reed), 162f, 190, 191f
Regina v. Hicklin, 264n32. *See also* "Hicklin Test"
Reid, Ann Carll, 82
Reque, Bill, 159, 170, 291n37, 292n53
Rich, Adrienne, 238
Rope (film), 52
Roque Ramirez, Horacio, 259n1
Rosen, Ruth, 230
Ross, Bob, 220, 222
Rosset, Barney, 272n69
Roth v. United States, 19, 264n35, 283n2
Rubin, Gayle, 290n28, 297n133
Ruquy, Bill. *See* Reque, Bill
Russo, Vito, 165

"Sad 'Gay' Life" (article), 190–191, 191f
Sagarin, Edward. *See* Cory, Donald Webster
Salt Lake City, Utah, 91–95
Sanders, Helen. *See* Sandoz, Helen
Sandoz, Helen (Helen Sanders), 89, 101, 229
San Francisco: bar raids in, 51, 159, 214, 275n106, 278n13; as "Bay City," 17–18; as DOB headquarters, 90, 99, 115, 136, 139, 146; dot.com boom and bust in, 251–252; as a euphemism, 15–16; as a gay capital, 16, 111, 152, 170, 175, 181, 189–195, 216, 297n127; as a gay

mecca, 4, 15–16, 40, 253–254, 263n27; lesbians in, 87, 139–140, 146, 148–150; in *Life*, 162–165, 162f, 166f, 170–171; as Mattachine Society headquarters, 44, 52–53, 63–65, 67; migration to, 40, 42, 72–76, 90–95, 178–185, 235, 280n36, 282n87; as a "Queen City," 175; South of Market neighborhood, 158, 194–195, 290n29
San Francisco Ballet, 183–184, 185f
San Francisco Chronicle (newspaper), 61, 177
San Francisco Examiner (newspaper), 51, 65, 87
San Francisco Police Department, 51, 63–65, 94, 159, 214, 291n42
San Francisco Progress (newspaper), 63–65
Sarria, José, 171, 209
Satyrs (motorcycle club), 158
scandals, 51–52, 58–59, 63–65, 64f, 87, Scranton, Bill, 161
Seajay, Carol, 147–150, 287n79
Seattle, Washington, 81
Second Congress to Unite Women, 231
second-wave feminism. *See* feminism
Sesso e Liberta (magazine from Italy), 54
Seven Steps Down (bar), 123
Sex and Censorship (magazine), 55, 272n69
Sex and the College Girl (Greene), 140–141
sex education, 21
sexuality studies. *See* gay and lesbian history
Sexual Politics (Millet), 230
Scott, Joan, 260n15
Shaffer, Marguerite, 203
Shawger's Illiterary Digest, 22–23, 265n42
SIR (magazine), 52
Sisterhood Is Powerful (Morgan), 230, 237
Sixth Man, The (Stearn), 66–68, 69, 110, 128, 140. See also *Grapevine;* Stearn, Jess
Slater, Don, 32, 168–169, 166f, 289n20
social movements, 13, 31–35, 106–108, 110–112, 190, 199–200, 202–203, 226–250. *See also* Daughters of Bilitis; homophile movement; Mattachine Society
Society for Individual Rights (SIR), 187, 219

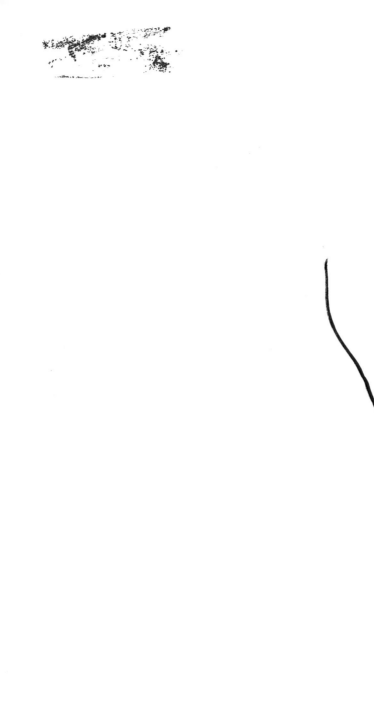